Where Were You?

America Remembers the JFK Assassination

Compiled and edited by
Gus Russo and Harry Moses

Foreword by Tom Brokaw

LYONS PRESS
Guilford, Connecticut
An imprint of Globe Pequot Press

Dedicated to the generation of Americans who were alive on November 22, 1963

Copyright © 2013 by Gus Russo and Harry Moses

Lyons Press is an imprint of Globe Pequot Press.

Title page photo courtesy of the Library of Congress. All archival photos courtesy of interviewees, except Mike Barnicle: Boston University; Harry Belafonte and JFK: JFK Library; Joseph Califano: Columbia University; Robert Caro: *Newsday*; Jimmy Carter: Carter Center; John Glenn 1962: NASA; Richard Goodwin: JFK Library; Doris Kearns: Colby College; John Kerry: Seth Poppel Yearbook Library; Peter, Paul, and Mary: JFK Library; Clay Shaw: Tulane University; Andrew Young: AP Photo Images. All interview stills courtesy of NBC News.

Library of Congress Cataloging-in-Publication Data

Russo, Gus.
  Where were you? : America remembers the JFK assassination / compiled and edited by Gus Russo and Harry Moses ; foreword by Tom Brokaw.
    pages cm
  Includes index.
  ISBN 978-0-7627-9456-0
  1. Kennedy, John F. (John Fitzgerald), 1917-1963—Assassination. I. Moses, Harry. II. Title. III. Title: America remembers the JFK assassination.
  E842.9.R877 2013
  973.922092—dc23

2013030984

Printed in the United States of America

10 9 8 7 6 5 4 3 2

Interviews with the contributors who appear in this book often lasted an hour or longer. In many cases, what appears in the *Where Were You?* television special distills those sessions to just a few minutes. What follows in this book are selections from those interviews that have been edited to conform to prevailing standards of accuracy, grammar, style, and usage.

PART ONE
DALLAS

Historians and JFK admirers reveal what we didn't know about the secret side of his personal life, about his legacy and, always, the what-ifs. What if he had lived? Would he have expanded the Vietnam War? Could he have gotten the Civil Rights Bill through Congress, or did it take his death and his successor, Lyndon Johnson, to accomplish that historic achievement? Did the very manner of his death and its subsequent investigation change us?

The intersection of those key questions—Where were you? How did it impact your life and America's psyche? What if?—offers a meeting place for Americans to ponder half a century after those shots were fired into a presidential limousine on a Dallas street. They form a fixed part of history and myth, a provocative examination of who we were then and what we became after.

John Fitzgerald Kennedy, wealthy young aristocrat, war hero, and ladies' man, remains ageless in our memories and in the official and informal photographs from his presidency. He was already preparing to run for a second term and beginning to muse on what he might do after eight years in the White House. We'll never know, of course, but his life and then his sudden, violent death remain an indelible part of our history.

We invite you to join the conversation that provoked this project. Where were you?

—Tom Brokaw

to deal with, notably: Would the University of Nebraska play its biggest rival, the University of Oklahoma, in Lincoln the following day? The game went on, as did others across the country, and as a reporter in the stadium, I remember that the cheering Nebraska fans offered a raucous contrast to the solemnity everywhere else.

We were suddenly a different people, and, as you will read in the following pages, for those who lived through the news from Dallas and the mourning that followed, we were bound first by the common experience of sharing our grief and the rituals of transferring power as it all played out on network television. Half a century later, future presidents, astronauts, students, doctors who received the president's shattered body, journalists, historians, and even Russian spies remember exactly where they were and what they thought when they heard the news. Don't we all?

Marie Tippit, wife of the Dallas cop murdered by Lee Harvey Oswald after the president was shot, treasures a painfully poignant letter she received from Jackie Kennedy the following week. John Brewer's life is still measured by that day when he saw Oswald duck into a movie theater and followed him inside. Buell Frazier's life became a living hell when word got around that he drove Oswald to work that day, a favor that has shadowed him ever since. Andrew Young, the civil rights leader, breaks down even now remembering how poor country church parishioners wailed in their grief when they heard the news. Mort Sahl, the president's friend and joke writer, will never believe it was just Oswald. Pentagon Counsel Joe Califano helped Bobby Kennedy select the president's gravesite and then went to work for the new president, who, Joe says, believed Castro somehow played a part.

I was in an Omaha newsroom, having finished my chores as morning news editor for an NBC affiliate. I was twenty-three, married just a year, and hoping one day to become a Washington reporter. Kennedy was my kind of president: young, stylish, witty, with a glamorous wife and celebrity friends who included both astronauts and movie stars. Like many of my generation, I saw him as a welcome change from the grandfatherly figures of Eisenhower and Truman. He sailed

and played touch football, shunned fedoras and double-breasted suits.

When I read those first alarming bulletins, running to get them on the air, I was roiled by conflicting emotions: *My God, who would do this? Shooting a president? In America?* As I raced out to the nearby headquarters of the Strategic Air Command, a Cold War nerve center, to check its status, extra heavy security turned me away at the gate. I remember thinking, *What now? This is going to be a different country.* The innocence of my '50s, Midwest upbringing shattered.

The Midwestern governors were meeting in Omaha, and I interviewed the best known of them, George Romney of Michigan, a man with his own presidential aspirations, but that day he was another grieving citizen. I later described to his son Mitt how his father comforted my cameraman. In Nebraska, a conservative state, there were other issues

> *As I raced out to the nearby headquarters of the Strategic Air Command, a Cold War nerve center, to check its status, extra heavy security turned me away at the gate.*

FOREWORD

November 22, 1963—a day that began with John Fitzgerald Kennedy making a short flight from Fort Worth to Dallas for a motorcade designed to take the young president through the streets and into the hearts of Texas voters. It was a momentous event for Lone Star State politics, but for most Americans it was just another late autumn day.

The wife of a doomed policeman was fetching a sick child from school. A young shoe store manager had no idea what lay in wait for him later that day. A future president was tending to his peanut farm. One of his successors had just finished a high school class. A future vice president was standing on the steps of his college library. A big-city preacher was meeting with folks in a country church. A Georgetown student was looking forward to playing the piano for the president when he returned to Washington, DC, that evening. A future movie star was attending his second-grade art class.

An ordinary day—until suddenly first radio and then television broadcast a staccato message from Merriman Smith, the legendary UPI wire service correspondent covering the president's trip:

THREE SHOTS WERE FIRED AT PRESIDENT
KENNEDY'S MOTORCADE IN DOWNTOWN DALLAS . . .

FLASH
FLASH

KENNEDY SERIOUSLY WOUNDED
PERHAPS SERIOUSLY
PERHAPS FATALLY BY ASSASSINS BULLET.

The three years that Jacqueline Kennedy later called Camelot came to a terrible, shocking end that sent the country into a spiral of grief and bewilderment, a national mourning at once majestic and haunting in its reminder of our crushing loss.

Dan Rather

In November 1963 Dan Rather—now a preeminent TV newsman and winner of numerous Peabody and Emmy awards—was the thirty-two-year-old CBS bureau chief in New Orleans. The network had sent the native Texan to Dallas to coordinate its coverage of JFK's campaign fundraising swing through the state. As fate had it, Rather found himself at a film drop-off site just steps from the infamous grassy knoll when the shots rang out.

I was just past the railroad overpass. You have the School Book Depository here, and the street runs under a railroad overpass, and I was just past that overpass. I was there to take a film drop. Remember: It wasn't videotape at the time. We were shooting—everybody was shooting—in film by and large. It was to be a place where the White House film crew was to throw off some film, and we had these positions all along the motorcade route. It was the last place. The official motorcade through the city was to end when it went under the underpass. Then they were going out to Trade Mart, where the president was going to speak. So I had positioned myself there to take the last throw of film off the photo truck, which was part of the motorcade, and take it back and have it processed and feed it to New York. I didn't hear a shot. I had no idea that a shot or shots had been fired. I was frankly sort of relaxed because it was a routine day. When I thought I saw the motorcade flash by, I wasn't even sure. I could hear the crowd, but I said to myself, *Was that the president's limousine? Was that the first lady I saw in that car or not?* My first impression— we talk about nanoseconds here—was *Maybe not,* because the rest of the motorcade didn't come behind it. But then very quickly after that, when the rest of the motorcade didn't come, I said, "Well, something must have

happened, because the rest of the motorcade isn't coming through here, and was that the president's limousine or not? Was that the first lady?"

I thought they were going to the Trade Mart. They seemed to me to take another turn. Now I was supposed to be in charge of our coverage—the whole coverage. I wasn't the lead correspondent. Our White House correspondent, and a great one, the late Bob Pierpoint, was to beat his piece that day. I was there to facilitate the coverage, so I was out of position. I said to myself, *Wow, if anything has happened, I've got to get back to KRLD,* which was our local station that we were using as a feed point; it was only about four blocks away. I'm out of position here, so I took off. There's a rise—what is now the infamous grassy knoll. As soon as I topped that, a scene of almost unbelievable chaos, even panic: There were men falling on top of their children and wives, people screaming. At that second I said, "Not only has something happened, but something really big has happened." What was in my head was, *I'm way out of position here. I shouldn't have been over there.* So I took off, just hightailed it. Yes, you can make a case that I should have stopped and got my notebook out.

4

I should have stayed there. But my job, remember, was to facilitate our coverage and be the key person in getting the material to New York.

I ran back to the station. I had no idea that shots had been fired. I had no idea that the pres-

I got back and practically blew the hinges off the door getting into the station.

ident was hurt in any way at that time. All I knew was something had happened, something really big and important, and, well, if not important, certainly the crowd thought there was.

So I got back and practically blew the hinges off the door getting into the station. This is KRLD, where we were doing our feed point. I just said, "Get the police radios up. Something has happened." Tumultuous things happened immediately, and Merriman Smith, the late UPI reporter, had the now-famous bulletin from Dallas.

I knew Parkland Hospital, where they took him, and so I immediately got on the telephone, knowing that if he had been taken there, it wouldn't be long until all the lines would be busy. I got through to Parkland Hospital, and a switchboard operator—which tells you how long ago this was—put me through first to a doctor, then to a priest. I said, "Has the president been shot?" They said, "Yes, the president's shot, and the president's dead."

"The president's dead"—what a hammer to the heart and the psyche.

All that was known, and it wasn't widely known immediately, was that shots had been fired at the president and he had been taken to Parkland Hospital. CBS News had a team operation. We concluded he was dead before the official announcement. On radio we made the announcement that the president was dead. The decision was made by the television part of the CBS News operation, "We're just going to wait for the official announcement." The official announcement came shortly after 1:00 p.m.

The CBS people there, including me, with Eddie Barker's operation, found the Zapruder film by making a lot of telephone calls. When something happens—never mind something this big—the first thing you look for are pictures. Remember, this is not a time when everybody has a camera, phone or otherwise. Phone cameras didn't even exist then. Not everybody has a motion picture camera. But what we wanted to do, as every other journalist enterprise wanted to do, was find the pictures. The president's been shot. The president of the United States is dead in front of thousands of people. There have to be pictures. Motion pictures—what we called in the film days pictures that wiggle, motion-picture pictures—would be preferable, but any kind of photographs. So we started making phone calls.

When I say we, probably twelve or fifteen people started asking questions, making phone calls. Within hours, maybe less than that, a policeman told somebody on the KRLD staff, "There was a guy with a movie camera."

"Was he an official? Was he government?"

"No, no. I think he was just a citizen."

Keep in mind there weren't that many movie cameras around. Who might he be? Somebody thought he might recognize him, and we tracked down phone numbers. Finally, almost miraculously, we got Mr. Zapruder on the phone. He confirmed that, yes, he had filmed the whole thing. Of course the film needed to be developed. We helped make the contact with Kodak to process it overnight. In those days, if you had a home movie camera, it'd take three days, maybe a week, to get it processed. But under these circumstances, you got it processed overnight.

By the next morning, Mr. Zapruder quite wisely had a lawyer. He realized what he had was going to be quite valuable. We had told him, "We'd like to get the film." He said, "I don't quite know how that works."

We wound up in Mr. Zapruder's lawyer's office. I thought that CBS News had the only access to Mr. Zapruder, but when I got to the lawyer's office, which was in downtown Dallas, my heart sank because Dick Stolley—a great reporter at *Life* magazine at that time and later the creator of *People* magazine—was there. Stolley, whom I knew, and knew to be a tough reporter, was working for an outfit with deep pockets—I

> *A policeman told somebody on the KRLD staff, "There was a guy with a movie camera."*

6

hated to see him there. But the lawyer said, "Here's the situation: We're going to show you this film. We're going to show you it one time. Then, in effect, we'll put it up for bids."

It wasn't a screening room. They just put it up on the wall. They showed it one time. I'll never forget being in that room. My head was back, my eyes were wide, my mouth was agape because, as everyone now knows, it was all laid out there.

The only thing in my mind was: *This is news.* Even I, dumb as a fence-post about a lot of things, knew this was news. I went out of the room—well, flew out of the room. I said to the lawyer: "I'm going to report this on television, what I've seen. I'll be back. Do I have your promise that nothing will happen before I get back?" Now he has another version of this, I think, but I thought I had a promise. Our studio was a short distance away. I ran all the way over, sat down and, from memory, with no notes, recounted what I had seen. They asked me to redo it once because, frankly, they hadn't liked how I described what I'd seen of Mrs. Kennedy trying to get out of the car—and rightly so. They knew this was a very sensitive point, so they asked me to redo it.

Then I went running back over to the lawyer's office. When I got there, they asked, "What do you think it's worth?" I said, "This is way beyond my pay grade. I have no idea." So I went back to CBS. They said, "Start with ten thousand dollars, and we'll give you maybe thirty-five thousand/fifty thousand dollars top." It was a quick conversation with news people, not with the business people. I went back to the lawyer's office, and Dick Stolley was smiling like a deacon with four aces.

I said to the lawyer, "I want to talk about maybe making—"

"It's been sold," he said. "*Life* magazine has bought it." Naturally I wasn't happy about that and said, "How could you do this? That was supposed to be—"

"They made a preemptive bid," he said.

Life magazine didn't allow the film to be seen by the public. The public didn't see the film for, I think, something like twelve years. But even during that period, when I'd seen it only the one time, it played—and still plays to a degree, like a looped videotape—in the back of my head. Sometimes in off moments, when I'm thinking about something else, it'll just play. Fair to say, as I get older and my steps grow slower, I think of it less in recent years. But when we have a year like the anniversary year, that videotape plays from time to time, you bet.

Dallas is seen, for better and for worse, in the state as a whole—this was certainly true in my youth and I think to a degree is true now—as the only place in Texas that looked north and east for approval. Most Texans say, "Frankly I don't give a damn what you think. I'm a Texan," and such things as "Listen, if it's true, it ain't lyin', you know." But the rest of the state's always said, "We don't care what people in the North think." But Dallas, partly because it was a commercial center, a banking center, was the only place in the state that looked northeast for approval. To say that Dallas was psychologically devastated wouldn't be too strong a word. There were people who said, "Texas killed Kennedy," or "Dallas killed Kennedy." The city was in a state of shock like the rest of the country, but their shock was exacerbated by the sense of shame—I wouldn't say guilt—about what had happened there. It took some years to overcome that. There was some pride that Lyndon Johnson had become president, but the Dallas of 1963 is light years away from the Dallas of today.

Lyndon Johnson was not an overwhelmingly popular person when he was a senator or vice president, but it was a sense of "OK, the country has to go through this period. Good that a Texan's in charge." With that was a sense of "We Texans hate the idea that this happened here. We hate the idea that it happened at all." There were other folds underneath this. Texas was and is a gun culture, and the whole business of "How in the world could a president of the United States be assassinated and then the assassin be assassinated. . . . What kind of state do you have down there? What kind of city do you have down there?" It took a while, particularly for Dallas, to outgrow that.

It changed me. I think the experience changed every American. But perhaps because I was there, it changed me in several senses. First of all, it made me a more skeptical reporter. You never want to descend into cynicism. But skepticism in a reporter—a fairly strong sense of skepticism—is important. So it developed that in me. It also developed in me a stronger sense of life, every day for what there is, because life is fragile. What you most expect frequently doesn't happen. What you least expect too often happens. It also gave me a renewed respect for those in public service. You can say, as some people were fond of saying when he was alive, "John Kennedy was born with a silver spoon in his mouth. His father has all the money in the world. He has all the money in the world. He had the benefit of education, one thing, another." But he gave himself to public service and believed deeply in it, and so many people around him did too—not just White House staff people, the Secret Service people. It gave me a renewed sense of patriotism and a renewed sense of love of country, a new respect for public service, those people who dedicate their lives to public service. It also brought me closer to my family.

Robert Grossman

Now the chair of the Department of Neurosurgery at Methodist Hospital in Houston, Texas, in 1963 Robert Grossman was a thirty-year-old neurosurgery resident at Parkland Hospital in Dallas when President Kennedy was brought there immediately after being shot.

I was sitting in my laboratory at South Western Medical School, talking with Kemp Clark. Kemp and I were the two neurosurgeons at Parkland. Kemp was the chairman. He was thirty-eight; I was thirty. That was my first job after finishing my training in neurosurgery. I'd been at Parkland for about five months at that time. I was on the faculty; I had finished my training. We were talking about the president's visit and that it was controversial. There was some feeling that the president was not welcomed by certain groups in the community; I think that was a very small aspect of the community. There were huge crowds greeting him, very enthusiastic, and I think he and Jackie were actually much-loved figures. Kemp and I were sitting and talking about the trip. The phone rang, and someone said to me, "Come to the emergency room. President's been shot." I told Kemp. We thought it was a prank. Then we looked at each other and said, "We had better go and see."

We started walking to the elevator and took the elevator down. The medical school building was across the parking lot from the hospital. When we got downstairs, we could see limos, police cars, and an ambulance at the entrance to the emergency room, so we started running. We ran into the entrance to Parkland, down the hall to Trauma Room One. We had no idea of how serious it was at the time.

There was the president of the United States lying motionless, surrounded by physicians—it was a tremendous emotional shock. It was very

clearly the president. He was a very striking, very handsome figure, even in that extreme situation. There was no sense of panic or of fear in the room. I think Parkland physicians were used to taking care of very serious injuries, and I think everyone was doing their job, was very contained. It was really quite businesslike.

The president had been seen first by Jim Carrico and Malcolm Perry. Jim was chief resident. Malcolm was on the faculty; he was a vascular surgeon. They had done an intubation and a tracheotomy because they had seen a wound in his throat. They thought at the time that it was an entrance wound. They started intravenous fluids. It was clear that he had a severe head wound. There was a great deal of bleeding from his head, but at that point no one had examined his head carefully.

Kemp and I went to the head of the gurney and stood behind the president. The assistant, if you have a right-handed surgeon, stands at the right hand of the surgeon. So Kemp was on the left, I was on the right, and we both picked his head up to examine the wound. The scalp had been shattered, and the skull had been shattered and lifted up like a plate of bone. You could see that the president's brain tissue—which was badly disrupted in an area about the size of your hand, over what's called the parietal boss—had been blown out where this was an exit wound. Lifting his head up, I could see an entrance wound with brain extruding

We both picked his head up to examine the wound.

Mrs. Kennedy was standing in one corner of the room.

from it. It was immediately clear to me that he had been shot from behind, the bullet coming out through the parietal area and blasting the tissue outward.

It was clear that this was a fatal injury, and what was going through my mind was: How long would he live? Would he be in a coma for days, even weeks? People can be kept alive on respirators with life support. I was wondering whether he would be in that situation, with the whole country held in suspense, the whole world around us watching.

Everyone at Parkland, from the highest to the most unfortunate, is treated the same way. I don't think it would've made any difference if it was somebody else. There was a tremendous effort to see if his heart could be started. An EKG was taken. There was no organized electrical activity in his heart, so I think people's attention was really focused on whether he could be resuscitated. But after cardiac massage and artificial respiration, it was clear that his heart couldn't be started. Dr. Clark Kemp, who was the most senior person in attendance, said we should stop resuscitation efforts.

Mrs. Kennedy was standing in one corner of the room. She had blood and brain on her dress; she was wearing that iconic pink outfit. I think there were some tears on her face. But she wasn't out of control in any way. She was standing there quietly. The Secret Service agents must have been in the room, but they didn't interfere or interrupt the medical care.

Dr. Clark made the call, I think, because the clear cause of death was the head wound. I think it devolved upon him to make that judgment.

Texas law was that a person who has been shot or murdered should have an autopsy in the county in which the murder occurred. Earl Rose, who was the coroner, stood in front of the Secret Service as they were wheeling the body out and tried to stop them. But the Secret Service wouldn't have any of that. They pushed him out of the way and continued to take the president back to Washington.

It's difficult to say whether an official autopsy would have made a difference in terms of findings. The autopsy records aren't as detailed as one would wish, and the physicians in Bethesda who did the autopsy were under a great deal of time pressure to complete it. The X-rays that were taken were not as complete, not as thorough as could've been done. The drawings that were made were rather crude. But whether it would've been done better in Dallas, no one can say.

Seeing the president dying in front of you—the feeling is one of awe. Everyone was concerned. There wasn't much discussion in the room obviously. Everyone was concentrating on the medical aspect. But I think everyone was concerned: *What does this mean for the country? Was this the start of World War III?* I think that was the first thought everyone must've had. Was this a deliberate attack? What better way to destabilize the country than to kill the president. Was this a deliberate attempt by Russia? We were at the height of the Cold War. We'd just had the Cuban Missile Crisis. Was it the Cubans? Was it the Russians? We had fought the Chinese and North Koreans. Was China or North Korea behind this? Was it a right-wing hate group, a left-wing group? All those thoughts were going through our minds.

I got home later that afternoon—I don't remember the exact time. I told Ellen, my wife, about what had happened. We had two young daughters: Amy, who was about three, and Kate, who was one. They were too young to remember of course. But I told Ellen and waited to go in the next day. As you know, Oswald was captured and then shot, and I was asked by the surgical service to examine him. He was in deep shock. The question was whether the bullet had penetrated his spine or the shock was simply due to abdominal bleeding. I examined him. As best as I could determine, the bullet had not entered his spine.

I don't think Oswald could have been saved, even if he'd gotten better treatment en route to the hospital. He had lost a great deal of blood and, even if re-infused, if the person has been in shock too long, the nervous system will not recover. I don't think he would've recovered.

Later that Sunday, we were very much focused on what the president's death meant for the country rather than on any personal change or effect

I don't think Oswald could have been saved.

on us. It made me proud to be an American because unlike in many countries in the world, where an assassination might result in a military takeover, nothing like that happened. Everything was orderly. Our Constitution was respected. Everyone knew what he or she should do and followed through properly.

There are some unanswered questions, and I think that probably the most controversial aspect of the Warren Commission report is the question of the order of the shots: whether there was one shot that hit both the president and Governor Connally or whether there were separate shots. I think no one can give a definitive answer to that.

At the time this was thought to be an entry wound, but actually it was an exit wound. We should've undressed the president and examined his entire body, but we didn't do that out of respect for him. There would be an autopsy in Washington, and the thought was that they would do whatever was necessary. I think if we had examined him, we would've seen the entry wound, which was in his upper back.

That bullet had come out through his throat, so he clearly was shot twice. I guess the question is whether there was a separate shot that hit Connally. But I think that's the most controversial aspect. Out of respect for the president, nobody wanted to undress him and examine him completely. I think everyone was in such a state of shock that the notes made by the physicians weren't detailed. Nowadays, with everyone having a smart phone with a camera, we would've photographed the body. We would've photographed the wounds.

I always drew the pathology of the operations that I did—I learned that from my residency chairman, Jay Lawrence Poole, at Columbia. He was a wonderful medical artist, and he would draw the anatomy of the tumors, the aneurysm we operated on. I should've made a drawing of what I saw, but it just never crossed my mind. I suppose I was in shock from the events. I don't think there ever has been a protocol for reporting what you have seen, except to dictate it. Even the dictated notes were not very detailed, because it was really like being in the center of a hurricane and more wondering about the implications of what had happened.

I went back into the hospital the next day and made rounds. I don't remember really watching television that much afterward. The atmosphere in the hospital was actually fairly calm; I think people were keeping their concerns to themselves. There wasn't an atmosphere of panic or chaos in any way. It was very professional.

I can still visualize picking the president's head up. He had very thick hair, but even with that you could see the blasted out area of his skull and his brain. It seems like yesterday.

I have a photograph of President Kennedy that has never been published. It was taken by a friend when Kennedy came to talk at Rice University a year before, when he talked about putting a man on the moon. My friend was the photographer for the *Rice Thresher*, the university newspaper, and took a wonderful photograph of the president in the car, which I have at home. That's the way I'll remember him, not as he was on the gurney but as a vital human being. Robert Dalleck's book *An Unfinished Life*—that is the sad part, because we don't know what he might have accomplished had he lived. He really did have an unfinished life.

Robert Caro

In 1963 Lyndon Baines Johnson biographer Robert Caro was a twenty-eight-year-old reporter for _Newsday._ In 1974 he wrote _The Power Broker,_ a biography of New York City urban planner Robert Moses, which the Modern Library chose as one of the hundred greatest nonfiction books of the twentieth century. To date he has written four of five planned volumes of _The Years of Lyndon Johnson_ (1982, 1990, 2002, 2012), a landmark biography of the former president. He has won two Pulitzer Prizes and numerous other literary awards.

When he comes to Congress in 1947—the summer after the first session—he has been sick all his life with the same symptoms: constant nausea, inability to gain weight. He's so skinny that you can see the ribs, count the ribs on him. He has a constant pain in his stomach, which he defines as "like it's a hard knot inside me," and he has this yellowish tint. He's been diagnosed with everything, including leukemia and hepatitis. None of the diagnoses was correct, so none of the treatment was correct. In 1947, after his first year in Congress, he goes to England to visit his sister and falls terribly ill. And for the first time they have the right diagnosis: Addison's disease.

In 1947 Addison's disease is often fatal, and the physician who treats him in London tells Pamela Churchill, whose house he was staying at, "You know that young friend of yours from America? He hasn't got a year to live." He's brought back to America in the sick bay of the _Queen Elizabeth_ on a stretcher. He's so sick that when he gets to New York, a priest comes on board to administer the last rites. He's flown into Boston, where he does gradually recover. In 1949 cortisone is starting to be used, and it's a miracle drug to treat Addison's disease, which really had no cure before.

Kennedy starts to change, to fill out. His face starts to fill out. But just about that time, his back, which has always been terribly bad, becomes so bad that he's walking on crutches. When he campaigns for the first time for the Senate against Henry Cabot Lodge, he's often on crutches. He's ashamed of them. He tries to hide them. When he's in

the Senate, there's a committee hearing; he tries to get there a little early to put the crutches under the table so nobody will see them. Sometimes there's no room under the table, so you see the crutches standing against the wall behind him.

Doctors don't want to operate because Addison's disease has such terrible effects on the immune system. He decides to have the operation, and the surgeons at the Lahey Clinic in Boston refuse to operate because it's too risky. His father says to him, "Don't have the operation. Roosevelt was on crutches. You can still have a full life." Jack Kennedy says to his mother, "I would rather die in the operation than live the rest of my life hobbling around on crutches with pain all the time."

In '54 he has an operation on his back despite these terrible risks. They only give him a 50/50 chance of surviving the operation. The operation doesn't work, and four months later, in February '55, he has a second operation. The incision doesn't close. It's eight inches long, so he basically has a hole in his back. At that time he goes to see a doctor named Janet Travell.

I was a reporter on *Newsday*, and for a brief time I covered Bobby Kennedy's run against Kenneth Keating in '64. Bobby always used to say about Dr. Travell, "Without her, my brother would never have been president." She was Kennedy's White House physician, and then she was Johnson's White House physician. She told me this story, which she later recounted in her own memoir:

Jack Kennedy doesn't want anyone to know he was sick, so when he comes back from the second operation, he first goes down to Palm Beach to get a tan. He comes back. He leaves the crutches on the plane; the photographers take pictures of him walking off the plane with this big grin. The *Herald Tribune* writes, "Tanned and fit, Jack Kennedy comes back to the Senate." Dr. Travell has read all this and isn't quite sure why he's coming to see her. Her window faces the steps; she sees Jack Kennedy get out of his taxicab, and she sees this crippled man. He's on crutches. It's hard for him even to get down the three steps. When he's talking to her, she says, he can't turn. He can't turn his head to talk to her unless he turns his entire body. When she asks him to describe his medical history, the symptoms, he does it in such a discouraged, tired voice, as if he has told this story too many times before. But she starts to do the things that need to be done: She treats him with injections, and she puts him in a rocking chair so that the muscles of his back are constantly in motion. This treatment is so outside normal medical procedures. She injects procaine and Novocain into the back spasm—and almost immediately starts to get him better.

But she sees his ambition. As soon as her treatments start to work, he starts to run for president, crisscrossing the country, seeing political leaders in all the states. Then his father calls Dr. Travell and says, "You know, he's in terrible pain still. Can you come down to Palm Beach?" She comes down to Palm Beach and sees laid out on a table a big map of the United States, all the places he's going to travel to, and she sees there are no days off, no time for rest, and he's in pain. She says, "You must take time off for rest," and he basically tells her, "I won't take the time off." His back gradually starts to get better. He stays in the rocking chair. He continues to be treated by her, and he crisscrosses the United States over and over again, learning the new forces in politics.

Johnson said for the record, "What was Jack Kennedy? Jack Kennedy was a sickly man, malaria ridden." (He thought Kennedy had malaria.) "Yellow in cast," he said, "sickly, weak, not a man's man." That was Lyndon Johnson's estimation of Jack Kennedy. It couldn't have been more wrong, but he was judging Kennedy on the fact that he didn't really work or do very much in Congress or the Senate. That's how Johnson looked at people. Everybody had the same view of Kennedy. Speaker of the House Sam

Rayburn said of Kennedy, "A nice boy, but he doesn't like the grunt work. He doesn't like to really work at congressional work." No one understood that the real reason for this wasn't a lack of willingness to work, wasn't a lack of ambition. It was this terrible illness, and later his back, that drained his energy.

In 1958 Lyndon Johnson is going to be the next Democratic nominee. He is the mighty Senate majority leader; he runs the Senate. Someone wrote about him, "He stands there with his arm upraised, directing the votes to go faster and slower. He makes a gesture. Two more men run out of the cloakroom. He makes another gesture, another man comes out. My God, running the world. Power enveloped him."

So Johnson thinks he's going be the presidential nominee. In the beginning of 1958, he is going to be the presidential nominee. But Jack Kennedy is going around the country, and he's learning that there's a new force in politics. Johnson thinks it's the senators, the old bulls, who are running things back in their states. But there's a new generation of politicians, men who were veterans of the Second World War, like Jack Kennedy. Now they're rising up. They identify with Kennedy. A new organization is starting up, and Johnson will not campaign. He thinks Kennedy will never get the required 761 votes on the first ballot—or any ballot. There's no way Kennedy is going to get a majority. If Kennedy doesn't get that majority, it's going to go into the back room. What does the back room mean? They're old-time politicians, and Johnson says, "They talk my language. They don't talk Jack Kennedy's language. If I can get it into the back rooms, I will be the nominee." He doesn't realize what's happening. Jack Kennedy is taking the nomination away from him.

Kennedy had a great understanding of the world. He had traveled. He had been in England. He wrote *Why England Slept,* which analyzed what led up to the Second World War. He was a reader of history. During the Cuban Missile Crisis, he kept referring to a book, Barbara Tuchman's *The Guns of August,* about how the First World War came about because of miscalculations and follies. People rushed to do things, made the wrong decision. Throughout the Cuban Missile Crisis he was saying, "Let's take time. Let's not take this step because it'll lead to other steps." He kept pulling back the hawks, standing in their way. He said, "If we can just give peace another day, maybe I can negotiate with Khrushchev. Maybe he'll come around."

—◦—

It's amazing. The newspapers and magazines have lists of vice presidents, and Lyndon Johnson's name is on none of them. He has all this power as a majority leader. Why would he give up that power to be vice president, which is a powerless post? No one thinks there's a chance of that, and Kennedy hasn't even hinted at it. The labor leaders and liberal leaders are scared that Lyndon Johnson might become the vice presidential candidate. Kenny O'Donnell says he had given assurances, with Kennedy's approval, to labor and liberal leaders that it wouldn't be Lyndon Johnson. Kennedy is nominated one night. The next morning at eight o'clock, the telephone rings in Lyndon Johnson's bedroom where he's sleeping with Ladybird. It's Jack Kennedy.

He says, "I want to come down and speak to you." They make an appointment for ten o'clock, and someone says to Johnson, "What did he call about?" Johnson says, "He's going to offer me the vice presidency." At about the same time, Jack Kennedy is calling his brother Bobby. In the Biltmore Hotel in Los Angeles, Kennedy has the corner suite on the ninth floor; 9333 is the number. Johnson is two floors down: 7333. Bobby Kennedy is in the middle, on the eighth floor. Jack Kennedy calls Bobby early in the morning and says, "Count up all the votes we'd get if I hold the big states in the North that I know I'm going to hold, and add Texas." Bobby Kennedy calls in two of his aides, Kenny O'Donnell and Pierre Salinger, and tells them to count up those votes.

> "Count up all the votes we'd get if I hold the big states in the North that I know I'm going to hold, and add Texas."

Salinger says, "You're not thinking of nominating Lyndon Johnson, are you? You're not going to do that?" And Bobby says, "Yes, we are."

That is startling and also brilliant. Jack Kennedy always sees the big picture. Maybe no one else had bothered to add that up. They were all focused on the nomination. No one had bothered to add up what Jack Kennedy was going to win once he got the nomination. Was he going be president of the United States or just a defeated nominee for president? He was going to have a tough race against Richard Nixon. Had Jack Kennedy been thinking about this all along? We will never know. But as soon as he's nominated, the very next morning he's offering the vice presidency to Lyndon Johnson.

Suddenly Johnson finds he has no power at all. During the three years of Kennedy's presidency, Johnson spends very little time with the president. Evelyn Lincoln, Kennedy's secretary, put together from the presidential log just how little time Johnson was alone with Kennedy, although he wanted to be alone with him a lot. The first year, 1961, he's alone with Kennedy ten hours and nineteen minutes. Second year, I don't remember the number, but it's less. The third year, in the whole year of 1963, the vice president is alone with the president only an hour and some minutes. Johnson is cut out of power completely.

Johnson was the great legislative magician. He passed bills no one else could pass. In fact, in 1957 he passed the first civil rights bill that had been passed since Reconstruction. But under the Kennedys he isn't allowed to participate in the legislative process at all. Part of it is simply that they're afraid of Lyndon Johnson. They had seen him in his days of power, how he was the most powerful man in Washington. They want to keep Lyndon Johnson on a very short leash because if they let him off the leash, who knows what he's going to do? Second, Johnson is always interested in publicity for himself. They're afraid that if they let him run the legislative program, it will become Lyndon Johnson's program and not Jack Kennedy's program. Third is simply the hatred between Johnson and Robert Kennedy.

The Kennedys do everything during that presidency to humiliate Johnson. He's not allowed to have a plane to go to an event unless Robert Kennedy personally approves it. Every speech, even a minor speech, has to be approved by the Kennedys. They leave him with no power at all. Of all the things that bothered Johnson, nothing bothered him as much as not being allowed to ride on Air Force One with the president. At one point Kennedy says to Evelyn Lincoln, "You don't mean he's asking to ride on Air Force One again? I've told him that for reasons of security, the vice president and the president should never travel on the same plane."

When they get off the plane [in Dallas], the second car of the motorcade is a Secret Service car. They call it the *Queen Mary* because it's so heavily armored and jammed with Secret Service men with their automatic rifles hidden on the floor and four agents on the running boards. In the first car are Kennedy and Connally, with his leonine head, and Nellie Connally, the former sweetheart of the University of Texas. Then there's a seventy-five-foot gap. The Secret Service insists there be a seventy-five-foot gap between the president's cars. Then there's the Johnson car, which is an open convertible with Johnson sitting on the right in the backseat, Ladybird in the center, and Senator Yarborough on the left; in the front is Secret Service agent Rufus Youngblood.

Suddenly there's a crack—a sharp, cracking sound. People think it's a backfire from a motorcycle, or they think it's a balloon popping. But Connally told me, "I was a hunter. I knew the moment I heard it that it was the crack of a hunting rifle."

Rufus Youngblood in Johnson's car hears the noise, doesn't know what it is, but he says, "I suddenly saw not normal"—those are his words—"not normal movements in the president's car. The president seemed to be tilting to the left." At the same moment he sees in the *Queen Mary*, the Secret Service car, an agent jump to his feet with a rifle in his hands; he's looking around, trying to find out what's going on. Then the other shots crack out. It's only eight seconds between the first and the last shot. Everyone knows what they are now.

Youngblood whirls around in his seat. He grabs Johnson by the right shoulder and says, "Get down. Get down." Youngblood shouts in a voice that Ladybird says she had never heard him use before. He pulls Johnson to the floor and sort of falls over the back of the front seat and lies on top of Johnson, shielding him from bullets. As they're lying there, Youngblood has a radio strapped to his shoulder. The radio is basically in Johnson's ear, and he hears the words, "He's hit. He's hit," and he hears the words, "Hospital, hospital." Not only has the president been wounded but the governor's been shot. Who knows if Johnson was the next target or not?

Youngblood tells him to keep down, and he realizes his best chance of protection is to put his car as close to that Secret Service car in front of him as he can. So he tells the driver, a Texas highway patrolman named Hershel Jacks. A typical Texas patrolman—laconic, cool—Jacks puts the car just a few feet from the bumper of the Secret Service car. The three cars—Kennedy's, the Secret Service's, and Johnson's—roar up a ramp onto the expressway, roar down the expressway, and squeal off the expressway and into the emergency bay at Parkland Hospital.

Youngblood says to Johnson, "When we get to that hospital, don't stop for anything. Don't look around. We're taking you to find you a secure place." So they yank him out of the car. His car is right next to Kennedy's. He never has a moment to look to the left to see what's in Kennedy's car. What's in Kennedy's car is the president's body. They haven't taken it out yet, with the blood pooling from his head on Jackie's lap as she's sitting there. But he doesn't know this. He doesn't know what's happened to the president. They run Johnson—four agents with the agent behind them carrying a rifle in his hand—looking for a secure place.

The Secret Service agents sort of lift Johnson out of the car and run him down one corridor, down another one, and finally they get to what they call the medical section. They find a cubicle that's been divided into three sections. Johnson is put against a back wall. They close the blinds on the windows. For forty-five minutes, Johnson stands there. They bring in a chair, and Ladybird sits beside him. But Lyndon Johnson is standing there. Then Ken O'Donnell suddenly walks through the door. Ladybird was to write in her diary: "Seeing the stricken face of Kenny O'Donnell, who

> *The radio is basically in Johnson's ear, and he hears the words, "He's hit. He's hit," and he hears the words, "Hospital, hospital."*

Another Kennedy aide, Mac Kilduff, runs into the room and runs over to Johnson and says, "Mr. President." It's the first time he knows he's president.

loved him, we knew." A moment later, another Kennedy aide, Mac Kilduff, runs into the room and runs over to Johnson and says, "Mr. President." It's the first time he knows he's president. This is one of the pivotal moments in American history.

❧

I was a reporter for *Newsday,* a Long Island newspaper. I was in the middle of Arizona. Actually I was in the middle of the Mojave Desert. I was doing a series on elderly retirees who were trying to live on retirement homesites in the middle of the Mojave Desert, and we found out they were basically being gypped by their companies. The Senate had sent an investigator out with me. I had found that the elderly women who were trying to live there didn't have water or anything and had to drive to get water. We were trying to get the names and addresses of these women so that the Senate could bring them to Washington. We were there all of November 22. We had been staying in Las Vegas and driving down to the Mojave Desert. You couldn't get reception on our car radio. There was so much static early in the day that we turned off the radio. In the evening we were driving back to the main highway. I think it was Route 66. It went up to Las Vegas. As we got to the intersection and turned on the radio, the first words we heard were, "Doctors are operating on Governor Connally at this moment," something like that.

What is this about? and then there was static. All of a sudden we came up to Route 66, and there was a big truck—as I remember, a big trailer truck—with a driver sitting in the window. He was crying and said something like "Have you heard?" and told us the news. This was already evening or close to evening of that day, hours after the assassination. I didn't hear about it until then.

Johnson is transformed. The Kennedys had almost broken his spirit; he had changed in appearance from the mighty majority leader to this guy with a hangdog look. Suddenly he's back in charge. The moment he's addressed as Mr. President, he is giving orders. The Secret Service runs into him, and Youngblood says, "We have to get you back to Washington. The place we can keep you secure is the White House."

Remember, we're only thirteen months from the Cuban Missile Crisis. Was Russia behind this? Was Cuba behind this? Who was behind this?

They say, "We have to get you back to the White House."

Johnson says, "No. I'm not leaving the hospital without Mrs. Kennedy."

They say, "Mrs. Kennedy won't leave the hospital without her husband's body."

Johnson says decisively, "We will go back to Air Force One, and I'll wait there for her to come with the body." He directs them: "Get cars. Let's go to the airport by a different route than the one they expect us to go. No sirens in the car." They speed to the airport, and Johnson literally runs up the steps with the Secret Service onto Air Force One to wait for Kennedy's body.

Talk about scenes in American history. Johnson goes into President Kennedy's bedroom [on the plane], and he takes off his jacket. According to different accounts, he either lies down on the bed, sprawls on the bed, or sits on it and calls Robert Kennedy. Robert Kennedy and Lyndon Johnson hate each other. Hatred is not too strong a word to describe the feeling between Robert Kennedy and Lyndon Johnson. For three years Robert Kennedy has done everything he can to humiliate Johnson, and in a moment, in the crack of a rifle shot, the tables are completely turned. Now Johnson has the power. He calls Robert Kennedy and asks him, "Should I be sworn in here in Dallas before I get back to Washington?" and "What's the wording of the oath?"

Robert Kennedy is having lunch that day with his wife, Ethel, and Robert Morgenthau, the district attorney for the southern district in New York, at History Hill, the Kennedy house. It's this old white frame colonial house in McLean, Virginia, with a long lawn that slopes down to the swimming pool. The house is being painted. Suddenly two things happen at once. Morgenthau sees one of the painters clap a transistor radio to his ear with a look of shock and horror on his face and start running down the lawn toward the swimming pool as fast as he can. The same moment, the telephone rings on a table on the other side of the swimming pool. Ethel Kennedy goes to answer it, and it's J. Edgar Hoover. He has Robert Kennedy come over to the phone and tells him that his brother has been shot and perhaps killed.

A few minutes later, the phone rings again. It's Lyndon Johnson, whom Robert Kennedy hates, fifteen minutes or so after he learns his brother is dead, asking him for the wording of the oath of office and the exact procedure for taking over the presidency. Two people heard that call. Kennedy's deputy, Nicholas Katzenbach, is patched into it. He's the number-two man, the deputy attorney general of the United States.

I asked Katzenbach. He said, "Johnson could've asked any one of a hundred officials for the wording of the oath. He could've asked me; we worked together a lot. It's appalling that Johnson called Robert Kennedy. He shouldn't have done it."

Marie Fehmer is Johnson's secretary. She is in John Kennedy's bedroom [on Air Force One] with Johnson, and she hears Johnson's end of the call. Johnson says to her, "Get on an extension, and take down the exact wording of the oath."

I asked her, "What were the voices like on the phone?" She said, "Katzenbach's voice was like steel. Bobby Kennedy's wasn't. I kept thinking, *You shouldn't be doing this.* But the call is made."

Another thing happens that increases the tension. While this is all going on, Jacqueline Kennedy is coming onboard with a heavy bronze coffin containing her husband's body. They put the coffin in the compartment next to the president's stateroom, and Jacqueline Kennedy wants to go into the stateroom—basically her and the president's bedroom. She opens the door, and there's Lyndon Johnson in his shirtsleeves. Depending on whose account it was, he is either sprawled on the bed or sitting on it. But Marie Fehmer says, "It was a horrible moment, and we rushed out of the stateroom."

So you have this plane carrying two presidents, one alive and one dead. It's flying across the United States. In the rear compartment is the president's coffin. Sitting next to it is Jacqueline Kennedy. Her skirt is covered with blood. She has taken off the white gloves she was wearing. They're caked with blood.

The Kennedy loyalists—Godfrey McHugh, O'Brien, O'Donnell—are standing with her sort of next to the president's body. In the next room, the president's stateroom and office, Lyndon Johnson is giving orders. The orders are taken up to the cockpit and radioed to Washington. In the front of the plane is where all the press and the passengers sit. One of the reporters was asked, "What was it like there?" He said, "You've heard of strong men weeping. Well, we had it there that day." Kennedy's secretaries are crying too.

At this point, no one knows if it's a conspiracy. We are shortly going to be reading headlines: "Oswald visited the Cuban embassy." "Oswald visited Soviet embassy in Mexico City." No one knows, but the Cuban Missile Crisis is very fresh in everybody's mind. During the flight, which is something like two hours and six minutes long, on every air base along the route, fighter planes are actually on the runways. The pilots are in the cockpits, strapped in; the engines are running. In the radar shacks at the bases, men are huddled over the radar screens. "Is any blip approaching Air Force One?"

That's the atmosphere, and as the plane flies across the country, church bells are starting to ring in a thousand towns and cities. Flags are being lowered to half-mast as the body of Jack Kennedy is flown back to Washington. It's one of the pivotal moments in American history; it's also a moment that for sheer poignancy is almost unequaled in our history.

———

Johnson evokes Kennedy's memory. He says, "Let us continue." He says, "The first priority is to pass the bill the president fought for all this long year, the Civil Rights Bill."

At the time President Kennedy is killed, that Civil Rights Bill is going nowhere. The Senate was always the great barrier to civil rights with its use of the filibuster. But the bill's not even in the Senate. It's not even on the House floor. The House Judiciary Committee has passed it, but they sent it to the Rules Committee, which is presided over by Judge Howard W. Smith

of Virginia, the archest of segregationists. He won't even tell
anybody when he will start
a hearing. At approximately
the same time as the Kennedy
motorcade is going through
Dallas, John McCormick, the
Speaker of the House, is asking Judge Smith, "What's the
schedule? When are you going
to start hearings?" Smith is saying, "I don't know."

The *Washington Post* interviews Smith and asks, "What
are your plans for the Civil Rights Bill?" He says, "No plans." That bill is
not getting out of the Rules Committee; it's completely stuck.

Three nights after Kennedy's assassination, Johnson's going to give
his first speech to the joint houses of Congress. Johnson's not even in
the Oval Office yet; he's still living at home. In the dining room, around
his kitchen table, his advisors are drafting the speech. Johnson comes in,
and they tell him, "Don't emphasize civil rights. Don't make that a priority. You're going to alienate the Southern Democrats. It's a lost cause,
anyway. It's a noble cause, but it's a lost cause. Don't waste your prestige
immediately on it." And Johnson says, "What the hell's the presidency for,
then?" He makes civil rights a centerpiece of his speech. He puts it in the
context of Kennedy's memory. "This is what he fought for. This is what he
wanted." Sympathy for Kennedy is not the whole story, but it's a big part
of the story of why that Civil Rights Bill gets passed.

Jack Kennedy had this great gift for appealing to the better side, "the
better impulses in America's nature." He said, "Ask not what your country ..."
He stirred everybody.

One minute it was the Eisenhower era, where people were interested in materialism and making money. Then Jack Kennedy made these
speeches at the beginning of his presidency, and all of a sudden, everyone
wanted to go to Harvard Business School. The next minute, everyone

wanted to enroll in the Peace Corps or work for Bobby Kennedy's Justice Department. He appealed to America's ideals, and he did so in words of genius. The words of his speeches are the words of a man who knew what ideals America should be striving for and knew what words to put them into. He's unforgettable in that.

In foreign policy, when you listen to the tapes of the Cuban Missile Crisis, you hear over and over again moments you can hardly believe. The Russians shoot down the airplane, and you hear the voices of George Bundy, McNamara, and the others saying, "Now we promised we'd retaliate. We have to attack now. We have to bomb now." Kennedy basically says, "Gentlemen, let's take a little break. Let's be calm. Let's come back in a few minutes and talk about so-and-so." Over and over again, he pulls the hawks back from war. If he hadn't been president, would we have had a nuclear war over the Cuban Missile Crisis?

In those respects, Kennedy was among our greatest presidents. You also have to say that in domestic affairs, Kennedy was not effective. His legislative program and the ideals he articulated for Medicare, for tax reform, for civil rights weren't going anywhere. Would they ever have gone anywhere? If he had a second term, would they have gotten passed? Perhaps, but there's no sign of that. Both of his two big bills, the tax cut bill and the Civil Rights Bill, were absolutely stalled in Congress.

When you look at the Kennedy assassination and Lyndon Johnson's ascension to power, you say, "This is one of the pivotal moments of the twentieth century." It's a watershed moment, and what do I mean by "watershed"? I use it in the exact meaning of the term. A watershed is the top of a mountain divide. On one side, the waters run one way; on the other side, the waters run another way. On November 21, 1963, America was not the same country as it would be five years later—five years after Jack Kennedy's death—when Lyndon Johnson's presidency ended. America changed. When you look at the whole landscape of America in the twentieth century, John F. Kennedy's presidency was a pivotal moment when everything started to change. There are many reasons for that. Part of it is the unique place Jack Kennedy holds in American political history—because of the unique, unforgettable way he made America remember what ideals it stood for.

Buell Frazier

Nineteen years old at the time, Buell Frazier worked at the Texas School Book Depository and lived a few blocks from Lee Harvey Oswald's wife, Marina, in Irving. He considered Oswald a friend and drove him to work on that fateful day.

The first day I met Lee Harvey Oswald was his first day at work. Mr. Shelley, my supervisor, called me over to his office. I met Lee Oswald outside of his office. He explained to me that Lee was a new hire and that he wanted me to teach him how to fill orders there at the Texas School Book Depository. I got to know Lee through working with him. I was teaching him how to pull orders for different publishers. "Sometimes," I said, "you will have to read the line all the way across, because it will tell you which textbook you want."

We filled orders for five states out of there. We did New Mexico, Texas, Oklahoma, Louisiana, and Arkansas; the public schools in Arkansas might use one version of an algebra book, and maybe Texas would use another. Even though the covers looked the same, you had to know where to look on the case or look inside the book to know which textbook to send. Lee was very smart. He learned very quickly.

One time, when we were riding home, Lee asked me, "Do you follow politics?" and I said, "No, not really." I explained to him that I just didn't have much faith in politicians. He didn't tell me a lot about living in Russia. I did find out later, however, that he did live in Russia. But as far as what type of work he did there or anything like that, it was never talked about. I've since learned a lot about Lee, where he was, and things he did before he met me. They're just things I found out on my own through reading or watching programs and so forth.

At work, he didn't really fit in. He tried, but he just didn't fit in. He wasn't a slacker; he was a good worker. I told him many times after he'd worked there for several days, "Now, you're coming along pretty good." When you're teaching somebody, you feed something to them as fast as they can absorb and retain it, and Lee was remarkable in that. He learned so quickly. He was very dedicated in what he was doing. He was a no-nonsense person when he was working.

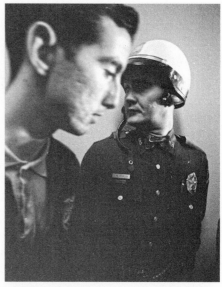

Frazier in police custody (PHOTOGRAPH BY LAWRENCE SCHILLER)

Lee rode out to Irving, where he spent the weekends with his wife at Miss Ruth Paine's house. He rode out every weekend except one.

November 22 was on a Friday. I was running a bit late that morning. I don't know what I was doing, or I overslept a little bit. I got to the breakfast table there in the den area at my sister's home, where I was living, and I was eating my breakfast.

My sister was over to my left at the kitchen sink, washing some dishes, and she observed Lee carrying a package. He put the package in the backseat of my car, and then he came around and looked in the window. My mother was there, and she looks up and says, "Who's that man looking in the window?" I said, "Oh, that's just Lee."

Then I looked at my watch and said, "Oh, I'm running late," so I went to the door. Lee came to the carport, and I told him, "I'm just finishing up breakfast; I'll be out in just a minute." I went back, finished whatever I was eating, and went and brushed my teeth. Then I went out to meet him. Lee was outside there on the carport. We walked around and got in the car.

As I was sitting down, I glanced over, looking at him, and I saw a package in the backseat. I said, "What's the package?" and he said, "You remember I told you yesterday I was going home to get some curtain rods?" I said, "Oh, okay." That's the last I thought about it. But much later, I was asked a lot of questions about the package.

We got in the car and went on to work. The weather was overcast and cloudy, and it was misting rain—real fine, little specks, much like a straight pin, about that size, real small. While we were going to work, I said, "I wish this rain would stop," but we didn't talk a lot about a lot of things that morning. The rain didn't seem to bother him. He just observed what I said and said, "Okay," or something like that. Then we got to work, and a few minutes before work I sat there and charged the engine on my car a little bit because I'd been having trouble sometimes with it starting. While I was doing that, he got outside the car, and he got the package and stood there for a minute. Then he decided to go on, and he walked on ahead of me.

The area where I parked was down in the employees' parking lot, which was a good two hundred yards or more from the building where we worked. We had to walk through a rail yard, where they switched and put a lot of trains together. I was always fascinated with trains, even when I was a little boy, so I'd watch the guys doing that. When Lee first started out, he was probably fifty feet ahead of me, and as we walked along, he got a little further and a little further ahead. When I was getting close to the building, I noticed something: He was going up the steps on the dock, and he went inside. I didn't see him for some time, so what he did once he got inside, I don't know.

I did see Lee that day. I could go to any floor we had. We had seven floors and a basement. The first floor is where we put a lot of the orders together and shipped them out, by parcel post or freight. The basement had certain publishers in it. A man by the name of Jack Dougherty mainly

> *I said, "What's the package?" and he said, "You remember I told you yesterday I was going home to get some curtain rods?"*

worked the basement floor. Jack was a great guy, and sometimes I would go down and help him. We got along wonderfully. It was nice and cool down there, even in the summertime.

Jack didn't talk about President Kennedy coming by that day, and Lee didn't say anything about it. But one of the workers there, a man by the name of Junior Jarman, always bought a paper every morning before he'd come to work. He was looking at me and said, "Look at this! The presidential parade's going to come right by, out in front of the building." He said, "Do you think we'll get to go out there and watch that?"

I said, "I don't know." I had a good rapport with the supervisor. So when one of the workers looked at me, I said, "You all have been talking about that for a couple hours. Why don't we just find out?"

They said, "Well, who's going to go find out?"

I said, "I'll go find out," so I went and asked Mr. Shelley, and he said, "Let me check with Mr. Truly," which was his boss, Mr. Roy Truly. He checked, and then he went up and talked to a man by the name of Mr. Casin, and they realized what a great opportunity that was. When you stop and think about it, how many times do you get a chance to see the president of the United States in a motorcade in your lifetime? Unless you're in a business where you travel with him and do a filming, that doesn't happen very often—or at least it didn't back in that time.

That's something I think somebody should understand, because the country back in 1963 was a lot different than it is today. We didn't have the technology we have today. There's just a lot of things we didn't have. But we did fine.

When the presidential motorcade came by the Texas School Book Depository, I was standing on the top step, on the first floor when you go out the front of the building. I think there were seven steps there. I was standing on the top step, but I was in the shadows. If you were out taking a picture, you wouldn't have seen me because there were people down in front of me. While we were out watching the parade, I didn't see Lee.

I was just thinking to myself as they were coming down Houston Street and getting ready to turn, and as they turned, I said to a lady, "Look how realistic, how normal they look!" I said it because at that time we had *Life* magazine, and the photography in the *Life* magazines were just really something special. I remember seeing pictures of the Kennedys in different places throughout the world, and I remarked on how beautiful Jackie was and how real. I just couldn't believe that I was that close to the first lady and the president of the United States.

It was exciting. Here was a little country boy from a rural town in East Texas, and I had a chance to come to the big city. I was excited about that, and I was working. When I was a child, I thought everybody was my friend. I know different now; that's not true.

When the motorcade was turning the corner, they were being led by a group of motorcycle policemen, and they were cutting the motorcycles on and off, making them backfire. At the first shot, I thought it was someone still doing the backfiring. But when the second and third shots came, I realized it was no longer backfire, and the acoustics down in the Dealey Plaza—how sounds bounce off one building onto another—has given the impression to some people there were more shots than three.

A lady came running up the sidewalk to right where Elm goes down to the underpass. She was coming right up by where we were standing, at the steps, and she said, "Somebody has shot the president." It was real bad. People were running and hollering and falling down. No one knew what was really going on. I just couldn't believe it, because back in that time, and even today, that's such a tragedy. I hope it never happens in this country again. It was just hard to believe that somebody would do that. I never thought of anybody doing that, in the wildest imaginations that you could come up with. I never thought anybody would do that.

I stayed right there in the step area. Billy and Mr. Shelley said they were going down to see if they could learn more about what had just happened. The whole time when we were watching the parade and everything, I never thought about anybody except just being so close and being able to witness that live. I look back on that now—that really meant a lot to me, and I didn't realize that at the time.

I stayed there outside, the steps there for a while with some people. After some time, we decided to go back into the building. I'd gone back in with some other people, and then, I know this may be strange, but I was hungry. I always kept my lunch down in the basement, where it was nice and cool, so I told somebody, "If Mr. Shelley or Mr. Truly's looking for me, I'm going down to the basement to eat my lunch."

I'd gone down, and I was sitting there, eating my lunch, and I heard a door open. I looked up, and there was a policeman; he asked me, "You been down here very long?"

I said, "Not too long."

He noticed I was eating my lunch and said, "Have you seen anybody walking around down here?"

I said, "No, sir." He asked me several questions. When he got through, I said, "Anything else?"

He said, "No, you've told me everything I need to know."

So I finished eating my lunch, and then I went back upstairs. Then we had a roll call, and everybody was there but Lee. I remember them calling out his name and Lee not responding. Lee hadn't taken his lunch that day. I asked him that on the way to work. I noticed he didn't have his lunch, and I said, "You didn't bring your lunch today?" He said, "No, I'm going to buy my lunch today." We had a catering truck, which used to come at break time around ten o'clock, and some of the guys would buy their lunch off the catering truck. There were also places that you could go sit down, like a lunch counter. I thought, *Maybe Lee might've wandered off to one of those places where you could get a sandwich and he just hadn't gotten back.*

Mr. Truly announced that because of what had occurred, the School Book Depository was closing early that day, and that we would resume our normal work schedule on Monday morning. So I walked down to my car.

Lee had told me the night before that he wouldn't be going home with me on Friday. That morning, I checked: "Now, you told me that you didn't want to be going home with me this afternoon."

He said, "That's correct; I won't be going with you."

So I asked him, "You got something planned?"

He said, "Yes," something about a driving test or something like that.

> *Then we had a roll call, and everybody was there but Lee.*

35

I used to listen to the radio. One of my favorite stations was KBLX 1480; it would tell you about traffic, where the accidents were, so I was listening to that, and then they broke into the normal radio station. They said that the president had been severely injured, that he'd been taken to Parkland Hospital, and that he had been pronounced dead. I said, "Oh, my gosh." I just couldn't believe all this happened—things happened so fast—and I just couldn't believe anything like it would happen, but it did.

Before I got off to Irving, the radio said they had captured a man outside of the Texas Theatre in Oak Cliff, and the more they talked about what went on, I put things together and realized they were talking about Lee. I said, "My gosh. I can't believe what I'm hearing." Since I'd gotten off early, my mother and my stepfather were up visiting one of my sisters and her husband and three children. He had had a heart attack, so he was in the hospital at Irving Boulevard and Pioneer. I thought, *I can stop by and check on him*, so that's what I did. I was in his room, and then a nurse came to the door and said, "I have a phone call for you at the desk."

I said, "Just patch it through here to the room."

She said, "I'm new; I don't really know how to do that."

I said, "OK, I'll be there in just a minute." Well, I opened the door to go to the nurses' station, and two guys grabbed me and threw me up against the wall; I was totally shocked. I said to them, "What is going on here? Why are you doing this to me?"

They said, "We're arresting you."

I said, "For what? I haven't done anything."

That was Detective Rose and Detective Stovall. They took me to their car, and we stopped at the Irving Police Station. They talked with someone there, and then they took me on to downtown Dallas. They asked about everything you could think of. It was just repetitious—over and over and over for hours. Detective Rose and Stovall started off; then they took a break, and two more detectives come in and quizzed me with the same questions, over and over. They just asked me things about Lee and my work and stuff like that. Things I knew I could tell them. They asked about the package Lee had with him. I said, "He did bring a package with him this morning." They asked me about the length of the package, and I told them, "It was roughly two feet, give or take an inch or two either way."

Every answer I gave them was the answer I knew. One time, Captain Will Fritz, who was head of the Homicide Department, brought in a typed statement, and he wanted me to sign it. Now, Captain Fritz, I'm sure, did a lot of good things for the Dallas Police Department, but over the years, I've asked myself: *Somewhere along the line did he become like the people he hunted?*

When he put the paper down in front of me, I started to read it. He wanted me to sign a paper that I was confessing to being part of the assassination and that I knew of it—that I had knowledge of it and that it was going happen. I told him I wasn't signing that. I told him it wasn't the truth. Well, Captain Will Fritz was quite hot-tempered. When I told him I wasn't signing it, he drew back his hand to hit me, and I took my arm up to block. I was sitting there at the table, and all during the questioning, I just had to look straight into a wall. I couldn't look sideways or anything, and when I told him I wasn't going to sign it, I think he really could have struck me. But I told him, "Outside that door are some policemen, and before they get in here, we're going to have one hell of a fight. I'm going to get some punches in." He walked out, and I never did see the man again. I don't want to come across as though I hated the man. I just was so unhappy with the way he treated me.

On Saturday morning I was cleared to go home. They cleared me one time, and we were on the way out to Irving when they got a call and turned around and brought me back. That's when they did the fingerprints and a mug shot. I couldn't believe what was going on. This was kind of like a nightmare to me. We went back, and after more questioning and so forth, they finally let me go. I didn't know anything about Lee shooting the policeman, J. D. Tippit. When I'd tell them something, they'd come back and say, "That's not true." But I knew it was. I knew what I was telling them was the truth, and I didn't deviate from that.

On Sunday morning I was in the kitchen there at the house. I'd just got through eating breakfast.

> *"Outside that door are some policemen, and before they get in here, we're going to have one hell of a fight."*

Someone turned the TV on, and there it was, live. They were going be transporting Lee from the jail on Horowitz Street down to another jail. They were in Dallas, and then they were in the basement. They said where they were. There was a transfer, and everything was going to happen. As we were watching, Jack Ruby stepped out of the crowd and stepped right in to Lee and fired the shot.

———

It wasn't easy. I just sat down and asked myself, *What have you gotten yourself into?* All I'd wanted to do was come to work in Dallas, save money, go to college. I wanted to go to college right out of high school, but I didn't have the money.

Since that weekend, it's been kind of like a roller coaster. My life has been valleys and peaks, and most of it's been living in valleys far more than peaks. Hasn't been good. I've had some good times, but I've also had some rough times, trying to figure out: How do you adjust this. How do you go on with this? I was just a young boy, nineteen years old, from a rural town. I wasn't worldly; I wasn't ready for anything like this. It was just very hard. There were jobs I lost because they found out I was a friend of Lee Harvey Oswald at one point. I have a hard time understanding why someone would take something out on you when you had nothing to do with it. Now, we know people read things, and the fact is: Everything you read about the John F. Kennedy assassination is not true.

There's so many books that have been written about this subject, and some of the authors give their readers the impression that they know me personally and they've talked to me. I wouldn't know them if I passed them on the street. I've never talked with them. A lot of them just take something out of somebody else's book and put it in their book. The truth is the only thing that matters. So many people have not done that.

I know that right after this happened, the language I used to converse in was very bad. I'm really ashamed of that, but that's the way I talked. That's who I was at that time. A person can use bad grammar, but that doesn't mean you're a bad person. If I had been investigating this and I was questioning a young boy, me, what I would be most interested in was the truth. Whether he used the correct grammar or not, that wouldn't even be considered by me. I've made a lot of improvements in my grammar, but I still make a few errors now and then. It's just hard to realize that this thing happened, even though it's been nearly fifty years.

I've asked myself many times, *How could you be involved in it? How'd you get involved in that? Why'd that hap-*

pen to you? I'm not angry with anybody. It's just a bad thing that happened, and I just happened to be there. So I tell myself every morning when I get up and shave, I look at myself and say, "Who is Buell Frazier?" I know—but a lot of people don't have a clue because they try to judge me from my past.

I try to stay out of the limelight. I do things sometimes with the Sixth Floor Museum, but I don't go out looking for publicity. That's just not me. I think about it every year, but I just have some way I just deal with it, because I know I can't change anything. If I could go back and change things, it would never have happened—not to me, not to anyone. But it did, and so you have to regroup and move on, and hopefully you learn from things. Hopefully this country's learned a few things.

I firmly believe, if you go back and look at where America was in 1963, with the assassination of John F. Kennedy, that's when America began to fall from God's grace. The man I know as Lee Oswald, I didn't think he was capable of the assassination. I'll tell you why. My sister's three little girls used to go down the street about half a block to Ruth Paine's house. Lee and Marina had two children. They had two girls. One was just an infant when this happened, and the other one was several years old. Lee used to play with the neighborhood children around that large oak tree that still stands there today, and sometimes I would hear them laughing.

They said, "That man that rides to work with you; he's a nice man." You stop and think about a child. A child can see a lot of things in a person that adults can't see. So, two Lee Harvey Oswalds? Possible. I think they had the body exhumed, and they measured it and so forth. Or did he have split personalities? I've asked myself that many times over the past years. I've asked myself, *Did I really know the true Lee Oswald?*

I don't come to Dallas very often, because it has a lot of bad memories for me.

Marie Tippit

In 1963 Marie Tippit was living in the Dallas suburb of Oak Cliff, not far from Lee Oswald's apartment. She was thirty-five, married for eighteen years to thirty-nine-year-old Dallas policeman J. D. Tippit. The couple had three children—two boys, ages thirteen and five, and a girl, age ten— and lived paycheck to paycheck on J. D.'s $490-per-month income. Officer Tippit was cited for bravery twice. On the morning of November 22, 1963, Marie got a call that their son, Allan, was sick and needed to be picked up from school. He was there when his father came home for a quick lunch. About an hour later, a relative called with the news: J. D. had been shot to death by the man suspected of assassinating the president.

It started out as an ordinary day: Got the kids off to school; J. D. went to work. He was working day hours. He had the rotating shift, so everything was going as usual. Allan, the oldest, got sick at school, so I went to school and picked him up and brought him home. Then J. D. called and said could I make him a sandwich; he wanted to stop by and have a bite to eat. They were real busy; the president was coming to town, so he could just run by and get a sandwich. I was really fast in those days. I'd fry some potatoes and have the sandwich ready by the time he drove there. This was really something for him to come home for lunch. J. D. never got to come home for lunch.

He ate lunch and of course left. Allan was watching the television, waiting for the president to come on so that he could see what they were doing. He had the radio on as well because they had announced that the president was shot. I said, "OK, Allan, you're going have to turn one of those off. How about just turn the radio on in your room?" I think that's how we missed hearing J. D.'s name mentioned on the television.

His district was in Oak Cliff, so I thought he would probably be safe, just busy, you know, working on things that happened in that area. Little did I know that he would encounter the killer of the president.

From what I was later told, J. D. noticed Oswald walking down the street toward the squad car, and when Oswald saw that it was a squad car, he turned around and started going the other direction. That was when J. D. became suspicious.

J. D.'s sister, Chris, called and asked, "Have you heard from J. D.?"

J. D. and Marie Tippit

I said, "Well, he came home for lunch."

She said Wayne, their brother who lived in Lubbock, had just called and said he had heard—on the radio or television. I don't remember which—that J. D. had been killed. She said, "You need to go check and find out for sure."

I didn't really want to believe that. So I called the station and told them who I was and asked them, would they check on Officer J. D. Tippit—that I needed to know if he was all right. They told me that, no, he was not. J. D. had been killed. This was a day that everything was turned upside down.

I called very quickly. I didn't give them a chance to visit me—they probably would have later, but I didn't give them a chance. I had called already. Patsy Anglin, the wife of another policeman, lived three doors down and was my best friend. I called her and told her that she needed to come down quickly. I needed her. At that point, Allan and I were both crying. It was just unreal. He was so upset, and so was I. He came down and stayed with me, and one of the neighbors went to the school and brought Brenda home.

People start showing up at our door at that point, police officers and news media people as well. I was so upset that I just—it was so unbelievably horrifying that I appreciated their company and their concern and their love for me, that they came and showed they cared. I never got bitter and angry. That's not a Christian's attitude. You just go to the Lord, and you pray about it, so that's what I did. I asked the Lord for his guidance and strength to see it through. Without that, I don't think I would have made it then or now, so I'm really thankful looking back that I didn't get bitter. That wouldn't have brought J. D. back, and that's all I wanted.

It was so hard because when you're married, you grow closer together. We'd grown so close together that he was the other part of me that was missing, and I didn't know what to do about it. I didn't know how I was going to carry on.

I got mail from all over the world, and there were a thousand cranes that Japanese students made and sent to me that signified that you had a million years of happiness on Earth and in Heaven. I kept them hanging in my house as a reminder to the children that people care about others all over the world. You don't have to be next door to care about them. We got some financial support as well. The financial support certainly helped take care of the children, and it showed them all the love that the people felt and the concern they had, realizing the situation we were in. We were so grateful and appreciative.

Robert Kennedy called me and told me that he was so sorry that J. D. had been killed and that if Jack hadn't come to town he would probably still be alive. I said, "Yes, that's true, but both of them were doing their job. J. D. as the patrolman out there, and him as the president of the United States. They just happened to be at the wrong place at the wrong time." He was such a nice fellow. It was just so nice

I didn't know how I was going to carry on.

43

to talk to him because he had genuine concern, and I felt that he could understand. We were comforting each other.

Lyndon Johnson called me as well, and I spoke with him. I appreciated that. I did correspond with Jacqueline Kennedy. She sent me a letter, and I appreciated it so much because she said in the letter if she could ever do anything for me just to let her know. She said that she had lit a flame for Jack and it would burn forever, and she would consider that it burned for my husband too.

Dear Mrs. Tippit,

What can I say to you? My husband's death is responsible for you losing your husband. Wasn't one life enough to take on that day? You must be so bitter. I don't blame you if you are. Please know that I think of you all the time, not that that can help in any way. It doesn't seem fair to me that, because my husband was more famous than yours, that more attention is turned toward my bereavement than to yours.

If there is anything I can ever do for you for the rest of my life, it would make me so happy if I knew you would ask me. You know, I lit a flame for Jack at Arlington that will burn forever. I consider that it burns for your husband, and so will everyone who ever sees it.

With my inexpressible sympathy,
Jacqueline Kennedy

That tells you what a wonderful lady she was. She was so considerate and thoughtful of other people, and this was someone who could understand how I felt; we really shared a bond. That's the thing you always want: somebody just to understand how you feel—and she did. She had children she had to raise by herself. Even though she was first lady of the United States,

"I lit a flame for Jack at Arlington that will burn forever. I consider that it burns for your husband, and so will everyone who ever sees it."

she recognized that I was suffering too. Isn't that wonderful, that we had a first lady that was so caring of everyone?

Afterward, life became very much a struggle because I had to deal with three kids who loved their daddy so much and were so close to him. Curtis would sit at the window and watch for him when it was time for him to come home. That's pretty emotional. Brenda was getting stomachaches every day. Curtis was getting stomachaches. You have to deal with all that, along with your own grief. How can you have the strength, as Mrs. Kennedy said, to keep going?

Now there is a plaque where J. D. fell. I'm so proud we have that now. When I'm there, I just tell him how much I loved him, how much I miss him, that someday I'll be able to see him again in Heaven. I wished for that many times—that I could have another conversation with J. D., that I could just see him again. I think that's normal, isn't it? Probably everybody does that. I'd tell him how much we miss him, how much we need him and love him. I'd tell him his name lives on forever, not only in my heart and the children's hearts, but many others' I know as well.

People began to be more concerned about others. I know there were a number of good things that happened for others as a direct result of J. D.'s death. The police department had no insurance for their police officers, and because of J. D. they went ahead and got insurance for them. The state didn't pay any money for widows to help them, and now they do. J. D. caused that. I'm thankful for that. When there's such a tragedy, there's always something good comes of it, and that was good.

I've thought about that day every day for fifty years. J. D. had a wonderful sense of humor. He was caring about everybody else. He was such a loving person, and he made friends easily, and he was a Christian man. He wanted to do things that were right, and that really attracted me as well. As long as he was around, I knew I was loved. There'll never be another man for me.

John Brewer and Ray Hawkins

About ninety steps from the movie theater where Oswald sought refuge after killing both President Kennedy and Officer J. D. Tippit, twenty-two-year-old John Brewer was managing Hardy's Shoe Store. Listening to reports about the assassination, he learned about Tippit's murder just blocks away. After Oswald walked down Jefferson Boulevard and ducked into the theater, Brewer alerted police, who quickly came and arrested the assassin. On the day Kennedy came to Dallas, thirty-one-year-old Ray Hawkins, a married father of two, was one of the few patrolmen not assigned to the presidential visit. Instead he was working as a traffic accident investigator when he heard over the police radio that an officer had been shot in the Oak Cliff suburb. Each man played a key role in locating and arresting the assassin, and this is the first time the two have sat down together to recall the events of the day.

JOHN BREWER: I had noticed this guy as he walked into the window area of our storefront, and I thought it was pretty strange that somebody would be shopping for shoes with all the commotion going on and the police cars going by. Then I said, "I know this guy from somewhere. I recognize him." But mainly it was his actions and his trying to avoid any part of what was going on out here that caught my attention. I was listening to the radio, knowing a policeman had been shot; they'd give a description, but instantly, when he walked into the recessed area, it was like, *I've seen him somewhere before.* I couldn't place where.

What led me to pursue him wasn't so much that I'd seen him before but the way he was acting—hiding himself from all the police cars that were converging at the Tenth and Patton area. So those two things: One, I'd seen him, and the way he acted.

(PHOTOGRAPH BY LAWRENCE SCHILLER)

It took a while, but I realized that he had been a customer weeks before. I had sold him a pair of shoes, $4.70. (Our highest-price shoes, the deluxe shoes, were $7.70.) It was at night, and stores were only open one night a week, on Thursday. This was a Thursday night and, as near as I can figure, maybe six weeks before. He was a very fastidious customer, very hard to make up his mind. I just let him be and stepped away from him. In sales, the last person who speaks wins . . . or loses—so I let him try them on, and finally he said, "I'll take them."

On this day, when the police cars went by, I was standing just inside the door observing him, and he was looking at me—he looked me square in the eye too. He was looking through the door, and I know there was recognition because he'd seen me. When the police cars all got by and the sound was more in the distance, he turned around, looked over his shoulder, and walked out and proceeded up the street.

I just had a feeling that something was wrong with this picture—that he was suspicious—and yet

> *I was standing just inside the door observing him, and he was looking at me.*

he wasn't panicky; he wasn't running. I've heard he was running—he wasn't—he was just walking at a nice pace. But it was just a gut feeling that something was up. Why do you pretend to be shopping for shoes when all this commotion is going on?

I didn't connect him to the assassination, which I had heard about. I was also aware that Officer Tippit had been shot and killed just a few blocks from here, and that probably—with a description from the radio station I was listening to—led to more wonderment and *What the heck is going on here?* While I was walking, he had already entered the Texas Theatre—you could see him go in. I stood there for a second and thought, *What am I fixin' to get into?*

Exterior of the Texas Theatre, where Oswald was apprehended
(PHOTOGRAPH BY LAWRENCE SCHILLER)

Interior of the Texas Theatre (PHOTOGRAPH BY LAWRENCE SCHILLER)

Why am I doing this? But I just kept walking.

The story got out that Oswald was busted for not buying a ticket. Totally wrong. I asked Julie Postal, the cashier, if

I didn't know the guy had a .38 in his pocket.

she had sold a ticket to a man matching his description. I only wanted confirmation that somebody else saw what I saw. I could have cared less if he was buying a ticket, so he wasn't busted for that. She said, no, she hadn't sold a ticket to anybody that matched that description; she had been out on the sidewalk watching all the commotion as well. I said, "The fella I saw went into the theater; I'm going inside." Once I got inside, I saw Butch Burrows, who was the concessionaire. I asked him the same question. "Did you see this fella"—matching the description I gave him— "come in?" He said, no, that he'd been busy stocking his concessions. I said, "Well, he came in here, and there's something funny about him. Let's go look."

Butch went with me. We went up to the balcony, didn't see anything, and then went back down to the theater's lower level; didn't see him. I went behind the curtain that leads out to the fire escape, out into the alley, and I said, "Butch, I'm going to stand here. You go up to the front, and if anybody matching this description starts to leave, stop him." I didn't know the guy had a .38 in his pocket.

I came back out and reported to Julie Postal that the guy was still there. She hadn't seen him. I said, "Call the police," so Julie made the phone call. That's when I went back in. Butch was up front, and I was in the back; I still hadn't seen him.

The house lights in the theater came on, and that was the first time I really spotted him inside the theater. He stood up for a second like he was going to leave and then just turned around and sat right back down within one seat or so of where he had been sitting. That was the first time I saw him in the theater, but I thought, *Gotcha!*

I still had no idea what he had done, no clue. But, son, you did something. You did something. When he pulled that gun out on Officer McDonald, I *knew* he had done something.

RAY HAWKINS: John Brewer and I first met at the back door of this theater. All we had was the description that John had given whenever he talked on the phone. He said that a suspicious man dressed like the suspect had come in here. We were over at the library at that time. We first had a report that someone fitting his description had gone into the library. We found out that wasn't true. Then they said John had called in, that there was a man in the theater who hadn't paid to go  in, so that's about what we knew then. I knew that J. D. had been killed, so it was a very dangerous situation. I was an accident investigator at the time, and of course I was in uniform, but no bulletproof vest.

When I first came through the door, I thought John was the suspect.

BREWER: I remember opening a door and being immediately grabbed—I don't know how many were out there, but there had to be at least half a dozen to ten or so. I had to explain quickly that there was a person in here that I was suspicious of and, basically, "I'm on your side. I'm not the bad guy." Officer McDonald asked if he should go out here, and, just before he knocked on the door, the house lights came on. That was actually the first time I saw Oswald, even though I was sure he was in the theater. There was a curtain back by the exit, and I was looking through the curtain when the house lights came on. The movie continued to play. Oswald stood up as if he was going to leave and moved maybe one seat over but basically sat back down in the same position on the same row. Officer McDonald, myself, and another officer—I don't know his name—walked out on the stage. I pointed to Oswald, and Oswald was just sitting there, calm as he could be.

I pointed him out from the stage, but I probably wouldn't have been there if I'd been aware that he was armed. I had no idea—didn't even enter my mind. He just kind of stared, glared back. I jumped off the stage, and Officer McDonald came up the left side, as you face the audience. Another officer and I walked up the right side. Officer McDonald was tapping people on the shoulder, telling them to get up, to move, but all the while he was keeping his eye on Oswald. Just as Officer McDonald walked into the aisle, tapping him to get up, Oswald got up. He threw a hard left cross and knocked Officer McDonald back into the seat.

I'm standing maybe ten or twelve feet away. Almost in the same motion, he reaches under his shirt, which was not tucked in, and pulls out a pistol—I think it was a revolver—and puts it right in Officer McDonald's face. Officer McDonald had recovered basically; he got back up, wrestled the gun away from him, and I'm sure I saw Oswald pull the trigger. But Officer McDonald has said that the hammer hit the fleshy part between his thumb and forefinger, preventing the gun from firing. Immediately the gun was taken away from Oswald, and then cops were coming over the backs of the chairs. They weren't getting cheap shots in, but they were going to arrest this guy.

HAWKINS: I came up the aisle and heard Nick McDonald say, "I've got him." Then at I saw that they were locked up in a fight, and I went up and got Oswald's left hand into the handcuffs; it seemed like two or three minutes, but it wasn't that long. It was a lot of chaos. It rained police. One of the officers even jumped down off the balcony to assist in the arrest, but we had enough police there at that time. The only thing I heard Oswald say was "I haven't done nothing." That's exactly what he said. Other than that, I didn't hear anything. There were so many police then and so much confusion, it was kind of hard to hear who was saying what.

BREWER: As they were leading him out toward the side I was standing on, he looked me straight in the face, and I heard him say, "I'm not resisting arrest." That was kind of hard to swallow, that he wasn't resisting after having tried to kill a policeman. At the time, I really wasn't thinking he might've been the assassin of President Kennedy because of the distance from downtown to here. I felt that maybe he did have something to do with Officer Tippit's murder, but it didn't really dawn on me until I got home that evening,

It rained police.

turned on the television, and there was Oswald, down at the police station with Captain Will Fritz. I said, "Damn."

HAWKINS: When I came in here, I was also looking for somebody who had shot Officer Tippit. I hadn't yet made the connection to President Kennedy. When I heard that he was the chief suspect in the assassination of the president—oh, my—I thought we were lucky to be here, just living through that. But I don't even know what I thought when we were coming up the aisle in the theater before we found out he could be connected with the assassination. It was just really a weird night, a weird day and a weird night, really. We were lucky that nobody else was shot. I don't know why Oswald let us walk all the way up in the theater and didn't shoot one of us. I thought of that afterward; I didn't think of it then. I thought we were lucky just to lose one officer.

BREWER: When Oswald pulled the pistol, it kind of brought me back into focus, and still I'm wondering, *Why am I doing this? What have I just got myself into? What am I doing here?* Pretty soon, it kind of all came together that it was probably a pretty good thing. It happened so fast, and yet it kind of plays back in slow motion a lot of times. But I really didn't have time to think about what was going on, what danger there might be, or anything—it was just fast.

HAWKINS: They had a car out front that we put him in after we got him handcuffed and everything. There was quite a crowd out there too. They wanted to do their own justice. They were angry.

BREWER: I didn't see that because I was detained here, getting information. By the time I got outside, it'd already cleared out and was just like a ghost town. Shops were closing up.

HAWKINS: When I saw his face, he looked like just another citizen. He had a little mark across his face or two after we arrested him. But he just looked like an ordinary citizen, someone you would see walking down the street, which he had been doing. Nothing outstanding in one way or another that I could see.

BREWER: I got home and turned on the TV. My wife at that time worked for Blue Cross Blue Shield downtown. They had closed down, as everybody else had. I've got the TV on, and my wife says, "That happened pretty close to where you—" I said, "Yeah, that happened pretty close."

Then my mom called from Lockhart, Texas, and said, "I just saw that Oswald was arrested by your shop. I just pray you weren't anywhere near that."

I said, "Mom, I got a story to tell you." It still didn't dawn me, really. But then the news came in more and more. They're showing Oswald; they're showing the rifle there at the police station, showing Captain Will Fritz. And then you hear Oswald saying he didn't do anything—he was seeking representation, I believe. It really started sinking in that he actually was the main and only suspect for the Kennedy assassination, and it was pretty much a given that he had murdered Officer Tippit.

I came to work the next morning, and of course there were sound trucks and all sorts of media trucks out. I thought, *I'm not used to that,* and it was just pretty much rapid fire, speaking with reporters, media. In fact, it got pretty annoying after a while, and it went on for quite a while, maybe a couple of months. Then I was transferred to the downtown store on Main Street, and it kind of started quieting down. We didn't have that mass or instant media like they've got now. It still didn't dawn on me just how big an operation that was, but it did dawn on me that, like Ray said, a lot of people could have got hurt.

HAWKINS: The next day at headquarters, we were still doing reports and getting it all together, and it was really busy. There were four or five of us who had come in the theater first, and we were all writing up reports and letters to the chief on what had happened. But what had happened finally sank in that day. It didn't seem that night like any of this stuff had happened earlier, or it wasn't anything. Then it did sink in—the next day, really—that any number of us could have been killed. I could have been shot; any of us could have been shot.

On Sunday I was watching TV at home. I saw Jack Ruby shoot Oswald. I knew Jack, had been to his club a few times. He wanted to be noticed and known; he really liked the police. He just wanted everybody to like him, I would say, especially the police. Several of them went to his club, kind of a police hangout, because he was friendly with police. You could go after hours and have a beer.

I didn't realize who it was at first. Then I heard them, or I saw when they pulled him back who it was, and I thought, *Oh, no.* I just couldn't believe it was Jack who did it. Then a lot of people said he was connected with the Mafia here and in Chicago and all this, but I never did get that impression of him. He was just somebody who liked the police and was good to the police and wanted a little attention. He liked it. He liked us to recognize him, and if we took someone down to his club, he was always friendly. But it was a surprise.

BREWER: I was out in the parking lot when Ruby shot Oswald, washing this brand-new Ford Galaxy XL that I'd taken delivery on the night before the assassination. I wasn't even supposed to be on duty at the store the next day. My assistant called in, his young child was ill, so I went to fill in. I had every intention just to cruise around in that car, which had a police interceptor engine in it, so I didn't see the Ruby shooting at all. My wife came out and said, "Come in; you're not going to believe this." It was just—damn, when is this going to stop?

I thought before and after that it wasn't Dallas's fault. A lot of people took it upon themselves to make Dallas the whipping child. Dallas, to me, didn't change. I enjoyed Dallas, I enjoyed going to the Cotton Bowl, where we would watch Tom Landry and Roger Staubach.

HAWKINS: I agree with you, John. The city itself got a bad name, but there was really no way of stopping what occurred. It seemed that after this happened, the citizens banded together; they even seemed to take more interest in the police department. I think it hurt a lot of people. I know I didn't appreciate the things that were said about Dallas, but I was born and raised in Dallas. I felt it was a bad story that they put on the city, but there's not a whole lot you can do about that.

BREWER: When I got out of the service in 1969, I had the option of staying in Dallas, retaining my job. I'd already grown tired of the assassination, so I moved to Austin. To this day—it's kicked off a little bit the past couple of years—there are people who have known me for the longest time, who I work with, who have no idea I was involved, unless they came into the house and might have seen something framed. There was a letter from President Johnson, and they'll ask, "What's this?" But I play it really low key. Many people don't have a clue. I have recently been recognized by the Dallas Police Department, got its Good Citizen Award—but I was just in the right place at the right time, however dangerous it was.

Brewer (left) and Hawkins

HAWKINS: And you handled it right, didn't get shot at the back door or anything.

BREWER: I appreciate that. The assassination brought the country together. It was scary times when we listened to the Cuban Missile Crisis live broadcast of the Russian ships turning around, so there was a lot of Cold War tension. The assassination kind of centralized Dallas, and afterward I don't know if it was a coming together or just a realizing that, hey, we've all grown up here pretty quick.

HAWKINS: I think it did bring the country together. The United States, a lot of people, myself being one of them, didn't really pay much attention to the election. We voted, but I don't think we really put that much into it. I think this got everybody more interested in government, exactly what was going on, and things our government was doing. I felt like it did that much for us. It changed me. I, one of those who didn't pay a lot of attention to politics, now tried to stay up on things that were happening in the country more than I had before.

BREWER: A couple of weeks later I had a customer on a late afternoon and saw a taxi pull up out front. This lady got out, and I recognized her from TV. It was Marguerite Oswald. She walked in just like *Here I am* and said, "Mr. Brewer." I said, "Yes, Mrs. Oswald?" My customer kind

It was Marguerite Oswald. She walked in just like Here I am *and said, "Mr. Brewer."*

of looked up. She only wanted to say that she felt Lee was innocent, and she wanted to hear from me what had happened. Not taking any sides, I said, "Mrs. Oswald, I don't know for sure that he did kill the president, but I'm pretty sure he killed a policeman. I'm pretty sure he was involved, but, as a mother, you're standing up for your son." She said nothing, she just twirled around, hopped in the cab, and away she went.

I still see that scene in my mind fifty years later, every day just about. Something just real brief, but I think about it quite a bit. I don't dwell on it, but it was a part of my life and continues to be. Not a bad part at all, but I'm not just a one-trick pony. I've done other things to define my life. But it'll be part of the legacy, I guess. Not a bad one, not a bad one at all. I acted on instinct, not knowing where it was going or how big it was—a little instinct and some stupidity probably, not knowing what could happen.

Ruth Hyde Paine

Raised in Columbus, Ohio, Ruth Hyde Paine, a Quaker convert, moved to the Dallas suburb of Irving with her husband after he got a job with Bell Helicopter in Fort Worth. By 1963 they had separated amicably, and she was a thirty-one-year-old single mother and part-time Russian language teacher. That same year, through her interest in Russian, she met and befriended the Oswalds.

I was in Irving, which is a suburb of Dallas. A friend of mine knew that I was studying Russian and knew this couple was coming to a party he was having, so he invited me, thinking I might enjoy meeting them. Marina was a young mother who didn't speak English and didn't understand the English at the party, so I talked with her in a bedroom where she was changing June's—her baby's—diaper. We just talked about mother things; we both had very young children.

She was glad to have someone to talk to. I had studied enough Russian that I could converse with her a little bit, and I could understand what she said, which helped a lot. Her husband, Lee, was enjoying the attention of telling about going to Russia, then deciding that wasn't a good place, then coming back. He was talking to the group in the living room or kitchen, wherever it was, about that. But I wasn't really listening; I was mostly spending my time with Marina in a separate room.

I realized she was feeling very lonely, so I got their address—they didn't have a telephone—and wrote to her. I asked if I could come by sometime to visit, and we worked that out. I visited at least once, and another time we invited both of them to my house to have dinner with me and my husband. Although we were separated at this point, he did come for dinner occasionally; we all had dinner together.

Ruth Hyde Paine visits the Dallas Police Department (PHOTOGRAPH BY LAWRENCE SCHILLER)

Lee didn't talk very much. He didn't want to talk English with me, but he would talk with my husband, Michael. I overheard some of the conversation. I felt like Lee would take offense if you disagreed with him, that it was easy to have him dismiss you as somebody who didn't understand things. I wasn't willing or able, for that matter, to talk politics with him, so I avoided talking with him.

Marina really did care about him. He was kind of exotic in Russia, somebody very different and interesting, and apparently he paid attention to her and so on. But she did find herself in a country where she didn't speak the language, and he didn't want her to learn it, which really bothered me. She just didn't have very many friends. I learned later that they did have some friends in the Russian community but at that point were not seeing them, and they had very little money. He lost his job in Dallas at a photographic shop. I went to visit one time when they were living in Oak Cliff, and he said he was going to look for work in New Orleans and had bought a bus ticket for Marina to go to New Orleans with her little baby and all the paraphernalia that goes with that. I was kind of appalled. He was going to send a letter when he had a place for her to come to, and I said, "Why doesn't she just come and stay with me for a couple weeks or whatever it takes while you look for a place? Then you can call me and say when you're ready to have her come down."

He did, and after about two weeks I drove Marina and the baby, along with my two kids, to New Orleans. They were there over the summer, and when I visited them in New Orleans, I discovered that Marina, eight months pregnant, had never seen a doctor. I was worried about that.

> *I wasn't willing or able, for that matter, to talk politics with him, so I avoided talking with him.*

Then Lee was saying he was going to look for work somewhere else. He'd lost his job again, and I said, "You haven't been able to get medical care here because you haven't lived in Orleans Parish long enough to get help with that. But you've lived in Dallas County long enough. Come back, and she can stay with me. I can get her to a doctor's care, and to the hospital if necessary, and could translate to do that. So how about if she just stayed with me for a little while?" He was really quite glad of that. He seemed grateful, helped us pack up the car and everything.

He looked quite sad when she was leaving. There really was caring between them. It was a troubled relationship, and Marina did wonder whether she could stay with him and whether it would be all right. She said, "He has fantasies," and she was worried about his doing things in order to think of himself as a great man. I could see how she was worried about him.

We got back to Irving, and she was at my house from the end of September really until the day after the assassination. Lee showed up early in October to say he was in town and ask if he could come out. He actually asked if I could come and get him in Dallas, and Marina, who talked with him on the phone, said I couldn't because I had just given blood at Parkland Hospital, anticipating that she would be there. They wanted a blood donation as the only way we could pay for entering there if the baby came.

Anyway, he hitchhiked out and spent the weekend, and he spent almost every weekend from then until Thanksgiving. They were definitely friendly. Probably being separated was actually good for the relationship; they then enjoyed each other, and he was relieved of some anxiety about their care. They sat on the sofa, watched a movie or something together; he patted his lap, and she sat on his lap—there was definite affection there.

My neighbor said her brother was working at the School Book Depository, and he thought they might be still hiring.

One day I was next door at a neighbor's, discussing the fact that it'd been well over a week, maybe two, and he wasn't having any luck finding a job, and his unemployment payments were coming to an end. Here was a young man who didn't drive. He went right into the Marine Corps at age seventeen, lied to get in, and the kinds of jobs he could get were pretty limited. My neighbor said her brother was working at the School Book Depository, and he thought they might be still hiring; it was early fall.

They were delivering books, so I translated to Marina what the conversation had been about. She asked me to tell Lee that when he called, which he usually did in the evening to talk to her. I told him; I guess he showed up at the School Book Depository, and they hired him.

⌐ ⌐

There was a lot of fear about President Kennedy coming to Dallas. Just a few weeks before, Adlai Stevenson had been poorly received there. A lady banged him on the head with a placard, and there was a lot of hostility. People were worried. It was definitely in the air.

Marina thanked me for turning on the TV that morning, and we watched the motorcade as it came into Dallas. It was such an enthusiastic crowd, and the feelings were so good in the reception. I heard over the television that shots had been fired and that the president's head had been hit. I was afraid it might be fatal.

Marina said, "Oh, this is so sad for Mrs. Kennedy and for the two children." She was feeling as a parent how that would be. I lit a candle, and she said, "Is that a way of praying?" I said, "Yes, it's just my way." Then we sat watching television until we heard that he was, in fact, dead.

It was really not too long after that there was a knock at the door, and several police officers said they had Lee Oswald in custody for shooting an officer. They wondered if they could come in, and I asked, "You have a warrant?" They didn't, but I didn't see any problem with their coming in. One of them asked, "Did Lee have a gun?" I said, "No," and translated to Marina. She said, "Yes, he did," and led them into the garage, where there was a blanket roll. She thought the gun was in there; she had seen it there.

The police officer picked up the blanket roll and it folded over his arm. I realized that there had been a gun and that it was gone, that he probably had come out that night, as he never had on a weeknight before, and got the gun. It was at that point, when I saw the blanket roll was empty and discovered that he'd had a gun, that I thought it could've been Lee. I felt like, whatever these policemen need, I'll help them find what they need. But it was the loss of Kennedy that was the most powerful feeling for me right then. That it might've been Lee who shot him was added distress. But I really was like the rest of the country, feeling that loss.

It's very hard to go back through the pain of that time.

The police wanted us all to come down to the police station, to make statements and so on. Marina really didn't say anything. She was very worried and distressed, but we all were. They wanted her to come, but they wouldn't let her go into the bathroom to change her clothes; they didn't want her to disappear from their view. I had to get a babysitter to stay with my son, who was asleep. The police had no idea who we were or what kind of people we were, so they were very nervous. At the police station, we were separated, put in different rooms, and I was grateful to hear that they'd arranged for a translator to be with Marina. They interviewed me and had me look over a statement, which I signed after I corrected the grammar. My mind was reeling at that point—you go into a kind of stupor almost, not really able to take it all in.

We went back to my house after the police station. We came back, and Lee's mother was there as well. She didn't know about the new baby—the second daughter was born in October, and Lee didn't want his mother to know about it. He didn't want any contact with his mother. Marina felt that was wrong, so when she saw Marguerite Oswald, there was a reunion; Marina showed her the baby and so on. They all came back to my house. Marguerite hinted that it would be very hard for her to get back to Fort Worth, so I said, "If you can sleep on the sofa, you can stay at my house."

Marguerite and Marina were together in the evening, and I was putting my kids to bed; it was late. We knew it was going be a hard day the next day; we'd better get sleep if we could. I don't really know what Marina did at that point with her mother-in-law. The next morning some people Marguerite had invited from *Life* magazine came with a translator; they were going with Marina and Marguerite to try to see Lee at the jail. They left that morning with Marina's two little girls. I didn't see Marina again until after she testified in Washington. She left on the 23rd, that next morning, and it was well into March of the next year before I saw her. I think she was getting advice, probably from Oswald's brother, not to talk to me.

General Walker—that's a very important story, and it's often overlooked, especially by the people who want the assassination to be a plot. I learned all this after the assassination, as did the rest of the world. Nobody knew about it until after the assassination, except Marina. Lee had written her a note, and he left, not saying where he was going; he had a whole plan diagrammed. He'd taken photographs of the home where Edwin Walker lived. This was in April, less than a month after he got his mail-order rifle.

He actually thought he had hit Walker—he broke the glass, but Walker had moved just at that point. Lee apparently hid the rifle and either walked home or took a bus or something. Then he made fun of the people who said they saw cars speeding away. He said, "Everybody in America thinks you have to have a car." But Marina was very distressed, didn't know what to do. She was very dependent on her husband, so she hid the note he'd written: "Here's the key to the post office. If I am arrested, this is where the jail is. Don't keep my clothes, but keep my papers. You can get help from the embassy"—a variety of things that said he didn't expect to come home or that he might not. She hid the note in a book, telling him that if he ever showed crazy ideas like this, she'd tell the police or something.

I didn't know the note was in the book, but I was sending things to Marina those days after she left, things for the babies that she called and asked for or letters that came for her, money—people were very generous to help this woman who was a stranger in our land. One of the things I sent was this book. When Oswald was shot on Sunday, an Irving police officer arrived at the front of my house in a car. He came into the house and wanted to close all the curtains and peer out, not knowing what else might be going on. I convinced him that he didn't have to close the curtains. I was afraid he'd scare my kids. But I was sending things through the Irving police. I'd take things to their police officer out in front of my house and say, "Can you get this to Marina?" and I'm sure they did.

The book was one of the things that went to Marina. This was almost two weeks after the assassination. Two Secret Service guys showed up at my house and showed me the note that was in the book; it was in Russian. Whoever wrote it didn't know the word for "key," because he transliterated it. The Russian speaker, who apparently was trying to see what language I knew, did all the talking.

He said, "Mrs. Paine, you sent this note."

I said, "No, I've never seen this note."

"Do you recognize the handwriting?"

"No, I don't recognize the handwriting."

He was back and forth. I was saying, "I don't know a thing about this," and he was saying, "You did this." So I finally got polite and talked to the English speaker and said, "He's telling me that I sent this note, and I'm telling you I didn't."

The other guy said, "Well, it was in a book."

I said, "I sent a book."

We might never have found out about that attempt except for the accidental discovery through the book. Because the Oswalds' things were

When Oswald was shot on Sunday, an Irving police officer arrived at the front of my house in a car. He came into the house and wanted to close all the curtains and peer out, not knowing what else might be going on.

in my garage, they could've come and gone after the assassination, the book included, and that note would never have come to light. I'm distressed that it doesn't get more attention, that people don't recognize the importance of Lee's having tried to kill General Walker.

I was watching television and saw Lee shot. It was around noon, and there was quite a while when I couldn't manage lunch. I did feel some relief in a sense, like a closure. It was only later that I realized we'd lost a lot of information—what he could've told us about why, or what he thought.

He was already a fragile personality, and he might've come apart while in prison. He had done an odd thing, like telling us how to call him if the second baby came while he was in Dallas but not telling us the name to ask for. He was using an assumed name. So I had only just the week before seen that he wasn't really glued together very well. There were gaps, and I think he would've deteriorated in custody.

Some time later, Marina invited me to meet her at a friend's house in Dallas, and I went over. She wanted to reassure me that the interview with the old men at the Warren Commission would be all right and that they were nice people. She was just being careful, friendly, to tell me that. She'd been through a great deal of course.

She's never tried to reach out to me again. I was following the lives of Marina and the children for a while through Priscilla Johnson McMillan, who interviewed Marina at length and was close to her. But recently I don't know the story of their lives. I knew at one point that she was persuaded by the plot people to think that it could've not been Lee. I suppose, in her place, one would prefer it not to be Lee.

I think he did it, and I think he acted alone. The
Walker incident really illustrates how he could plan
something and carry it out and that he was willing
to try to kill somebody.

It comes up very little today. Very few people know unless I tell them. It will come up because I had to say where I was going today. I feel very lucky that most of the people who are sure there was a plot don't even look me up. I'm spared that for the most part. I don't think there was plot. I think he did it, and I think he acted alone. The Walker incident really illustrates how he could plan something and carry it out and that he was willing to try to kill somebody.

Why he did it? That's the hardest thing of all. I don't understand it all. I think he had no particular anger at Kennedy. I feel like he was shooting at the office, not at the man, that he wanted to do something big, which he did. In the meantime, he cared something about his wife and family, but what could he have done that was worse for them?

History has been poorly served by all the plot stories that came out. A book was written, within a month or shortly after the assassination, by Mark Lane, who made quite a living talking to people about what he thought. But he wouldn't talk to the Warren Commission. All these people seem unwilling to think a single disgruntled person could do this. The Secret Service has learned what kind of personality to watch. There was a program about that, and, boy, they nailed it. They said: a person who could do planning, was reasonably intelligent, but was angry, dissociated from other folks, and had the opportunity—and that was Lee.

The emotions really don't fade. It's like any form of grief. It's always there. You go on; you do other things. I've lived a couple of lives since then; that's the way it feels to me. I went back to school, became a school psychologist, taught, and so on. But the pain doesn't go away. I don't think my faith was changed, really. My belief in trying to help other people and to do what I can to make the world better just goes right on.

Lawrence Schiller

In November 1963, twenty-six-year-old Los Angeles photojournalist Lawrence Schiller was on assignment for the *Saturday Evening Post*, arriving in Dallas on the press flight in time to photograph Lee Harvey Oswald after his arrest. He later landed Jack Ruby's final interview. He became close with the Rubenstein family, as well as the family of Lee Oswald. Marina and her children vacationed with him in California a number of times. He later produced *The Trial of Lee Harvey Oswald* and other feature films. For many years Schiller was Norman Mailer's research associate, and he persuaded the KGB to release its voluminous Oswald file to the duo for their book *Oswald's Tale*.

Growing up as I did on the West Coast, I didn't have a sense of Eastern politics. The first time that I really got into politics was when, as a photographer, I was asked to photograph Eisenhower as president. Then I became really aware of the political system. Of course when I read Norman Mailer's piece, "Superman Comes to the Supermarket," I became aware of John F. Kennedy.

I was very young, in my twenties, when John F. Kennedy was elected president. I'm a kid coming out from the surf of La Jolla, California. I remember the first images I saw of him with these crowds and his hands out. Then reading that he was Catholic, I said, "He's the pope who came off the wall and got in the gutter with the rest of the sinners." He was so lovable, he was so likable. I couldn't find a flaw in him, looking or hearing him or even feeling him. He was young. He was almost like an athlete in some ways. I didn't know he had back problems and things like that, but he seemed almost like a gazelle in the wild. He didn't look like Eisenhower. As years went on, I photographed many of the Kennedys. They understood grassroots like nobody else did. They understood that they had to communicate with the people.

I was taking a shower in my home in California when my wife ran in and said, "It's on the radio that they think somebody's shot John F. Kennedy." I jumped out of the shower, took the third drawer of the dresser, flipped it over into the suitcase, and grabbed my cameras—I was one of five staff photographers for the *Saturday Evening Post* at that time. I didn't even say a word to Judy. I got in the car and drove directly to LAX airport. I didn't even call the magazine or anything. I arrived at the airport, and of course it was just inundated by the media. I didn't realize at the time that Los Angeles was the closest media center to Dallas. Chicago was farther away, and there was nothing in Atlanta in those days. I remember the rush to get on an American Airlines flight. Only when we were in the air did the pilot inform everybody that John F. Kennedy had died.

I was thinking as a journalist and understanding the magnitude. I can't say that Lincoln's assassination came into my mind, but I remember seeing an incredible image out of Japan of a politician being assassinated, stabbed in the back, just months before. Another event in my life a month before went through me. It was chills, because I had flown to Rome with Madame Nhu and hid out with her and her husband, Ngo Dinh Nhu. His brother had been assassinated. Many people thought the CIA was involved in that assassination in Vietnam, and the first thought that went through my mind was: *Is the death of Kennedy linked to the assassination one month before?*

The first thing you do when you go into a strange city is try to find somebody who knows that city inside out. The first thing I do when I go

I jumped out of the shower, took the third drawer of the dresser, flipped it over into the suitcase, and grabbed my cameras.

into a small town is I hire a taxicab driver 24/7. I went immediately to the Dallas police station and asked, "Where do the cops hang out?" They told me the third floor. I went up to the third floor and said, "Is there anybody off-duty here who wants to be hired?" Believe it or not, I was able to hire an off-duty police officer who worked for me for three days.

Marina Oswald's first contact with the media—I believe after she was interrogated by the police and Secret Service—was with Richard Stolley at *Life* magazine, a very fine editor. But as time went on, the *Saturday Evening Post* was looking to buy rights. At the same time, I was deeply involved in looking into Jack Ruby, the man who killed Lee Harvey Oswald. Through Earl Ruby, his brother, and Eva Grant, his sister, I started to get to know everybody. One day, quite honestly, I just called Marina Oswald up and said, "I'm Larry Schiller from the *Saturday Evening Post*; I'd like to come out and see you. I want to introduce myself to you."

Years later, she came to California and vacationed with me and my second wife. She even wrote very personal letters about whether she should get a divorce from Mr. Porter and remarry. As time went on, Norman Mailer and I decided to do a book, *Oswald's Tale,* about the years Lee Harvey Oswald spent in the Soviet Union. It was very important that Marina introduce us to certain people, which she did. Mailer and I spent five days interviewing her in Dallas at an Embassy Suites hotel. She had, like a pendulum, been moving back and forth. At first she was thoroughly convinced that her husband had done it, but as time went on she moved in the opposite direction, that he was part of a conspiracy. Where her head is at today, I don't know.

Marina screamed and hollered at me, telling me I was worse than the Secret Service, that my interrogation of her in Dallas for those five days was horrible; I should be ashamed of myself. I said, "The difference is, I know more about you now, thirty years later, than they knew eighteen hours after." She was very upset that we knew that much about every aspect of her life. Mailer and I had spent an entire year and interviewed 114 people in the Soviet Union. We had followed people who emigrated all over the world—into Argentina, into Chicago. The people who lived above Marina and Lee moved to Chicago, and we went and saw them. She was furious that we knew so much about her life in Leningrad and how she had been sent into internal exile in Belarus.

What Norman and I discovered after a year working in Minsk, Belarus, was that there was no connection between Oswald and the KGB. They didn't try to turn him. They thought, as a defector, he was a new channel into the Soviet Union. When he came back, he did get involved with some White Russians.

I'll say one thing: If Lee Harvey Oswald had succeeded in killing General Walker, which he attempted prior to shooting Kennedy, I think John F. Kennedy would be alive today. Oswald was looking for acknowledgment, a certain gratification, a certain sense of accomplishment, which he didn't seem to have in his life. This is evident from the investigation Mailer and I did for over a year in the Soviet Union and the access we had to the KGB files. When Oswald came back to the United States, that's what was driving him. He needed to be accepted. He needed a sense of accomplishment.

I don't know specifically what might have motivated him to take a shot at General Walker, but Walker was very right wing, completely on the opposite side of where John F. Kennedy was. Marina Oswald described to me in a detailed interview how her husband sat on the porch of their house at that time, on the second floor, with the gun, the same Mannlicher-Carcano, propped up in the corner, listening to the radio for news that Walker had been killed or Walker had been shot. He became more and more depressed when there was nothing on the news. They kept it very quiet. In fact, the bullet missed Walker by something like six inches. He missed Walker, and he went into a tremendous depression. Sad to say, if Walker's life had been taken, John F. Kennedy, in my opinion, would still be alive.

Oswald was a lone assassin. The psychological profile that Mailer and I developed during our year in the Soviet Union told us that. Mailer went to the Soviet Union thoroughly convinced that Oswald was part of a conspiracy, and Mailer came back saying that he had done it alone. We wrote *Oswald's Tale* because we were looking for a pattern in the Soviet Union with his relationship with Marina, his wife, and other people. What were the triggers that got him upset? What were the triggers in the Soviet Union? Could you take that pattern, that grid, and place it in Dallas at the time of Kennedy? Could you find the same triggers? One of the triggers that would get him upset in Minsk was his wife saying, "Get your dirty feet off the pillow"; he'd get furious. We know he went crazy over things like that because all of that was bugged by the KGB; we had access to those transcripts.

But we couldn't find anything that was outside of a sense of accomplishment. One of the biggest mysteries was that Marina had had relationships with other men before marrying Lee Harvey Oswald, but when he walked into the radio factory he brought in a piece of sheet with blood on it in—a Russian tradition—and walked around, showing that his wife was a virgin. We were looking at all of those events to see what was inside this man's head. In the end result, he just wanted to be accepted, and he wanted to accomplish something that nobody else had accomplished.

In the United States, Marina was a fish out of water. She didn't know what to do. The interrogations by government sources were beyond her comprehension. I just think she was afraid to move. She had two children. She was a woman without any resources. She had left the Soviet Union and had no connections here. Her Aunt Valya, who was still living in Minsk at that time, eventually came to the United States to live with her for a short period of time. The friends she did make weren't going to give her enough security to walk away from Lee Harvey Oswald.

There are many questions that have no answers, but that doesn't mean somebody's withholding an answer. We have to accept that fact. Any two people can come up with different things that I'd like to know. Yes, there are things that I would like to know about Lee Harvey Oswald. The night before the assassination, really, his leaving the wedding ring when he leaves the house that morning? Marina still can't explain that. There are things about Oswald we'll never know. But the effect of what he did will never leave us.

Mark Lane and Edward J. Epstein, in their own ways, had a certain amount of credibility because they made us think about the subject in a certain manner; the general public wasn't being pointed in that direction. The Warren Report, whether it was under the influence of Lyndon Johnson, certainly was pointing America in a certain direction. Mark Lane, whether you agree or disagree with his tactics, was very important. He made us reevaluate it. Edward J. Epstein, who was just a graduate student, wrote a book called *Inquest* that made us look at the details as we hadn't before. Those two men and people like Penn Jones, Sylvia Meagher, and others who were critics of the Warren Report all had their place. The dialogue was very good for America. We should be forced to question and look at things and not accept the status quo. Whether in time one of these people or more than one of them will prove to be more correct than we think they are now, I don't know. But I still believe that Oswald pulled the trigger alone.

I was on the second floor of the Dallas police station. I have a lot of pictures, including historic pictures of that gun. Oswald enjoyed being run up and down the hall. Oswald looked at that 16mm movie camera; he looked at that television camera at the end of the hall and smiled. He enjoyed those moments. I remember arriving at the police station, and my contact sheets show that he was run up and down the hall at least four times while I was there. Then you have Jack Ruby, who we later found out was all around there. He's even in the corner of one of my pictures in the basement. The access was quite different than what we have today.

Jack Ruby was a nebbish. Many things say to me that he was not part of a conspiracy: his waiting in line at the Western Union station and not knowing how long the people in front of him are going to take to send a money-gram, nobody knowing

> *Oswald enjoyed being run up and down the hall.*

exactly when Oswald's being brought down. They take his belt off, or they put his belt on. There were things that delayed his transfer. The meeting of these two men was, I think, just fate. Ruby at that moment wanted to be a star. He's always wanted to be a star.

I knew Jim Garrison. I photographed him in Las Vegas with his Mafia connection and so forth. Clay Shaw wasn't involved. I know exactly where Clay Shaw was. He was in San Francisco on a cruise boat. I was deeply involved in all the facts. Garrison, I think, was a little too much off base. Oliver Stone is a great filmmaker. He's a friend of mine. He was at a benefit I had last year and gave a wonderful speech. He makes us think about things we should. I'm not saying we have to accept them, but I think he's a great filmmaker.

John F. Kennedy and Bobby Kennedy—I didn't know the other brother [Teddy] at all—were two men who really related to everybody, and emotionally they were great men. At age seventy-six, I look back at those two men, both lives taken by people who had no idea of the effect of what they were going to do. Their acts were selfish. We were deprived, maybe not of a great president, but of an experience with John F. Kennedy, and America was deprived of an experience with Robert Kennedy. I had no comprehension at all of the magnitude of how it would affect me emotionally in years to come, and how it would change the course of American history.

Two hundred years from now, will we still be talking about this in the same way? Probably not. We talk about Lincoln so many years later because Lincoln changed the course of American history. I don't think

John F. Kennedy's presidency changed the course of American history. I don't think we'll be talking about it in the same way, but I think it's good that we address the issues while we still have memories of it.

I don't think about it every day, but it never leaves me. I always see an image, I always see something that reflects back into those years of the Kennedys. They were exciting years for young people. They gave us a view of what could be achieved and what should be achieved. And they gave us a view that anybody can obtain it.

Oleg Kalugin

In 1963 twenty-nine-year-old Oleg Kalugin was operating undercover in New York as chief of KGB operations in the United States. He was later assigned to Washington, DC, with a cover as deputy press officer for the Soviet Embassy, where he became one of the KGB's top officers, playing a major role in the John Walker spy ring. As a result, he was promoted to general in 1974, the youngest in the institution's history. He returned to KGB headquarters to head the foreign counterintelligence of the First Chief Directorate. He was also an elected member of the Soviet parliament during Gorbachev's administration and was one of the first reformers of the KGB. Gorbachev signed a decree in 1990 stripping Kalugin of his rank, decorations, and pension, and he went into exile in the United States. In 1995 he accepted a teaching position at the Catholic University of America and has remained in America ever since, becoming a naturalized citizen in 2003 and writing a book about Cold War espionage that was published in 2008. He now works for the Centre for Counterintelligence and Security Studies and sits on the advisory board for the International Spy Museum.

The largest number of Soviet sources inside any Western country was in the United States. I will give you some statistics, which are not classified anymore but not known generally. In 1953 the Soviets supervised nearly three hundred assets in the United States. The US intelligence services did not have a single one in the USSR, so the score was three hundred to zero until, I believe, May of '53, when a Russian lieutenant colonel from military intelligence who was stationed in Austria was acquired by the United States. In 1960, when John F. Kennedy ran for president, then 1961, the Soviets had about thirty-five Americans working for them. Kennedy had every right at that time to be suspicious—the Soviets were trying to spread this gospel of Communism across the world. We succeeded more or less in parts of Europe, but only because of the Soviet military.

Castro came to power without Soviet support. That was a self-made revolution. Putting the missiles in Cuba was part of Soviet solidarity with pro-Communist reformers who would inevitably at some point be allies of the USSR. Once Fidel revealed that he was also leaning toward Communist ways of thinking and solutions, the Soviets immediately took advantage and brought intermediate-range missiles to Cuba. That was one of the first Soviet gestures of trust to Cuban leadership. Second, it was a reminder to the United States that they better not try again, or the Bay of Pigs would be just a tale of humor. You will meet a serious challenge, and our missiles are just a matter of fact you have to face.

I lived in and worked in the United States at the time, and as it [the Cuban Missile Crisis] played out, I thought that common sense would prevail on both sides. I knew the Kennedy administration, as I saw it from my Russian standpoint, as reasonable enough, and though I knew Khrushchev was a very emotional guy, he would also stop at some point, somewhere. That's exactly what happened.

It would be a nuclear war, and both sides understood that a nuclear war would mean no victory for anyone. It would be the end of humanity perhaps. I had been watching all these developments from an early age, and now fortunately the United States and Russia have found a way to live together despite differences, and there is no threat of war between the two countries. But the fear has moved to the Middle East—Iran, Israel—that complex world. It is truly something we have to be fearful about and try whatever we can to stop a confrontation.

Actually I think I'm worried now more than in the old days because I was a representative of a great nation that suffered so much from war. We lost, according to the latest statement made by President Putin, twenty-six million people. I knew other figures, but that's the latest: twenty-six million people. That was in World War II, and a nuclear war would be total destruction of the world. The stress internationally and militarily have moved down south. If that confrontation takes place, it will truly be not the end of humanity but something terrible. In my own way, as much as I can, I'm trying to state that we have to find ways to get rid of that threat to the world.

— —

When Kennedy was elected, I was stationed in the United States as a Radio Moscow correspondent at the United Nations as my KGB cover. I was even elected vice president of the Correspondents Association at the United Nations. That was a great honor. I was young man and in New York City, and then I appeared in the *New York Times* when I was a Fulbright scholar in '59.

I thought highly of Kennedy. I thought he was a likable personality, a shrewd man, attractive. The Bay of Pigs, his unsuccessful attempt to overthrow Castro, in many ways ruined his reputation. I was involved in the post–Bay of Pigs events as a Radio Moscow correspondent, undercover. I traveled to Florida with my colleague from the KGB. He worked for TASS News Agency as his cover. We both traveled to the Miami area and came to the headquarters of the Cuban émigré anti-Castro organization. We introduced ourselves as members of NATO countries. I said I was from Norway, and my colleague, Armenian by birth, said he was from Turkey. We said to the Cuban senior émigré that we officials in NATO and in Europe were disgusted with the lack of action against the Castro regime.

What happened? They were a little shocked by our honest statements, but one of them, the leader of that Cuban émigré organization, said,

"Listen, we would do it at any moment. We are ready, but those guys in the White House would not let us do it." For us it was crucial information, which we reported back to Moscow immediately. The Cuban émigrés are willing. They're ready, anxious to, but the White House, the government of the United States, would not support them in another military venture against Cuba. That was our report to Moscow. That's when I thought of Kennedy much better, because he understood that another invasion might lead to a major confrontation with the Soviet Union.

My superiors in Moscow, they liked Kennedy, as a matter of fact. He was a personable man, an individual who was liked by many people, and he was a smart man, unlike some of his predecessors. He would play the rules of the Cold War in a gentler way. That's why he was viewed as a guy we could make a deal with. Khrushchev was very tough on him, and Kennedy was the first to admit that. Khrushchev by nature was that kind of a man. He was rough and tough and rude to many people in power, and that was what eventually led to his early political demise. He was practically thrown out of power in '64 because he insulted so many people. He just didn't deal correctly with the military or with the security services. In fact, Khrushchev made a historic speech at the Communist Party Twentieth Congress, his secret speech denouncing Stalin's crimes. In my view—and I'm sure the view maintained by millions of people around the world and in Russia—that was the end of the illusion about Communism. I was an ardent, dedicated Communist, but after Khrushchev's speech I realized that you cannot build the future of humanity on the corpses of millions of people. That was what Khrushchev revealed in his anti-Stalinist speech, talking about the crimes committed by Stalin.

The Russians would not abandon Cuba. It was a matter of Russian ideology, national pride, and military strategic interest. The US government had its own agenda, also understandable, regarding a Communist state just ninety miles away from the United States. That was also difficult to swallow. During the Cold War, the Soviet expansion westward, with the occupation of part of Europe after World War II, was a constant reminder that the Soviet expansion may go further, and Cuba was a specific example. The Soviets tried to take advantage of events in Argentina and Chile, but they failed in the long run. The Soviets were sort of internationalist in the sense of spreading their ideals of Communism, not in theory but in practice, and supporting all sorts of revolutionary moments that in one way or another were in line with the Soviet foreign and ideological policies.

— ⌣ —

I was in New York at that time representing Radio Moscow; that was my KGB cover. When I heard that Kennedy had been assassinated, I was terrified. My immediate reaction was that there would definitely be a public linkage of Lee Harvey Oswald to Russia, and Russia would be figured as a country that may have been involved. I had learned very quickly— because Moscow headquarters was very quick in providing us with the information—that Lee Harvey Oswald indeed had been in Russia. As an American, Oswald was viewed as a potential recruit for the Russian Security and Intelligence, and they planted a lady who would work with him, trying eventually to make him a resource for Soviet intelligence and counterintelligence. At some point the Russians understood that he was a misfit. He was not a guy who would be useful. Our view was, in fact, better get rid of him. When Oswald left with his Russian wife, the Russians were happy to get rid of him. That's how it happened.

Marina was planted just to find information. The Russians always suspect that every foreigner, particularly Americans coming on diplomatic missions or otherwise, does some work for the CIA or whatever. Everyone was a suspect. Later the KGB made a deal with her that if she came here to the United States—she was recruited; let's put it that way. But she didn't perform the mission. She was actually thrown out of the Russian network of sources—totally useless.

The Russian version is that the right-wing forces of the United States were behind the assassination. That's it. But Oswald was kind of a misfit. It reminds me of the more recent case in Boston, the two Chechens, the Tsarnaevs.

On that same day in 1963, we received a cable from KGB headquarters: "Meet as many Americans as you

She was recruited; let's put it that way.

78

can, official, unofficial, whomever. Tell them we are very sorry. Russia liked Kennedy. We do not stand behind anything. We are with the American people and give condolences." We tried to impress the Americans because there were some stories. In fact, there was a story made up in Russia

by our special Active Measures Department that behind the assassination was the right-wing circles of the United States—those who hated Kennedy for his progressive, forward-looking, democratic way of solving things. These are the guys, the neo-fascists; they killed him. That's when the Soviet propaganda centered on right-wing society, whatever they were called at that time. Some of the guys from federal agencies like the CIA and DIA were also unhappy with President Kennedy, so that was a part of the Soviet propaganda campaign to convince the world that the American right-wing forces were behind the murder of President Kennedy.

I knew that, and I understood at that time that Oswald acted on his own. It was not a Soviet move, not at all. He was just a psychiatric case, someone who reminds me of the Boston tragedy with the Tsarnaev brothers from Dagestan. The Soviets would do their best to dissociate themselves from Oswald and just call him what they thought he was. When he was killed, I think the Soviets even felt relieved that they didn't have to now prove anything

As an American, Oswald was viewed as a potential recruit for the Russian Security and Intelligence.

> ## *Oswald acted on his own. It was not a Soviet move.*

because the guy was no longer in this world. That was a solution, sort of.

The Soviets were somewhat concerned, because Kennedy was known to be a reasonable guy, an intelligent guy. But Johnson was an unknown, and the Russians were somewhat fearful. Who knew what would come next? Maybe there would be another attempt, another Bay of Pigs, only more successful.

Any new president in the United States was viewed with fear, suspicion, and distrust in old Soviet Russia. Thank God, things changed since then. The Cold War is over, and the current Russian regime looks at what has been going on in the United States in a more realistic way, not tainted by ideology. It's Russian national pride, Russian national interest, economics; that's okay. But that mentality of spreading Communism around the world is no more. It's all over.

Darwin Payne

A newspaper reporter for the *Fort Worth Press* and the *Dallas Times Herald,* Darwin Payne, then age twenty-six, also reported and did commentary for *Newsroom,* the groundbreaking public television news show on KERA-TV. He taught journalism at Southern Methodist University for thirty years and is recognized as one of the foremost scholars of Dallas history. Payne was at the *Fort Worth Press* city desk rewriting a story on Jackie Kennedy when word of the shots came.

The political climate in Dallas was very toxic; it was very tense. The extreme right-wing elements had been very active before, and there was a lot of work on preparing for the Kennedy visit because most people thought something might happen. They were very concerned about that. There was a terrific publicity campaign to ensure that he had a good visit and that the people received him with cordiality and support.

No one anticipated someone taking a shot at Kennedy, but they did anticipate a disturbance of some kind. In fact, the City Council the week before had passed an ordinance making it illegal to disturb a public meeting, because that had been done during the Adlai Stevenson visit just a month before. A terrific struggle had taken place between the right-wing elements and the supporters of Stevenson and the United Nations. It happened when LBJ came in 1960 campaigning as vice president under Kennedy. He was mobbed at the Adolphus Hotel, and we were really concerned about what might happen.

Fort Worth didn't have the toxic climate Dallas had at the time, and we

Most people thought something might happen.

knew that Kennedy's reception in Fort Worth was just a very brief appearance after spending the night at the Texas Hotel. The main visit was in Dallas. There were rifts in the Texas Democratic Party at that time. Senator Yarborough was a liberal Democrat; Lyndon Johnson was identified as a conservative Democrat, and Yarborough was very angry with Johnson. Yarborough refused to ride in the car with Johnson, and Kennedy ordered him to take part in the parade motorcade.

My assignment that day was to be on the rewrite desk. I was to take story notes from a reporter on the scene at Love Field and a reporter at the Trade Mart. They were going to talk about Jackie Kennedy and how she looked, the crowd's reaction, all of her reactions as well. I was to piece together that story for our afternoon paper, and we were past deadline. Deadline for an afternoon paper was 11:30—and he arrived of course at about 12:30—so we were holding up the paper, and there was a lot of pressure to get a lot of material in that late edition story.

I was at a typewriter in the city room in the *Times Herald* office, which was about five blocks from the School Book Depository. We had a police reporter who was monitoring the police radio, and that was being relayed to our city editor. We were all sitting around our desks, doing whatever we were supposed to do at the time, and the city editor suddenly said, "He's been hit! They're sending code three—homicide detectives to School Book Depository."

"He's been hit with what?" I asked. I was thinking he might have been hit with a sign, as Adlai Stevenson had been hit with a sign the month before, but they didn't know for sure. The city editor asked me and another reporter to run down to the School Book Depository to see what was happening there, so the other reporter, Pyle Rosenfield, and I took off. I saw bedlam there. There were police officers with rifles, a fire truck, spectators who were in shock. I started interviewing people, trying to determine what had happened and trying to find eyewitnesses to it.

I was operating on one track, as a journalist. Luckily I was a journalist—because if I hadn't been, I would have been totally devastated. I would have been unable to do anything. But I sincerely felt a duty to get to the truth of the story, so I worked very hard. I was thinking of it, as everyone was, as a historic moment, that we really had to do a good job on getting information.

I thought the right-wing elements that had been so dominant in the city for so long had been guilty of the assassination. I anticipated that they were holed up in the School Book Depository and that I and the rest of us would ultimately see a shootout or something like that. I thought they would be up on that sixth floor and soon surrounded by police. That of course didn't happen.

None of the eyewitnesses had seen the assassin, Oswald, and they generally had the same description: Most of them thought the shots came from the School Book Depository. Some were uncertain. They weren't positive about how many shots were fired, but a number of them said three, and I thought their stories were quite reasonable. They didn't mention an individual firing shots from the "grassy knoll," but there were some who thought that the shots might have come from that area.

I found out about Zapruder by interviewing eyewitnesses. He was a garment manufacturer who had the building next door to the School Book Depository, and they said, "Our boss has pictures of it. He was taking moving pictures." In his office, Zapruder had the television going. It was giving all the news accounts about the shots being fired at the president. It was being said that Kennedy was wounded, perhaps fatally. He was very much upset over what he had seen. He was in tears much of the time, very distraught. Zapruder said, "No, no, he's dead. I know. I was watching through my viewfinder, and I saw his head explode like a firecracker." So

Zapruder said, "No, no, he's dead. I know. I was watching through my viewfinder, and I saw his head explode like a firecracker."

I assumed that Kennedy was dead at that moment. Shortly thereafter, the news came that he was dead.

Zapruder's film was on top of a filing cabinet in his office, and I saw the camera there. I was trying to get him to take the film and the camera to the *Times Herald,* assuring him that we would have it developed to see if it was as good as he thought it was. The random thought occurred of course that, *Heck, I could grab that camera and take off.* Obviously, I wasn't going to do that, but I did call the publisher of the *Times Herald*—I'd never met him—and told him what I had and suggested that he send a car down to the School Book Depository with the words DALLAS TIMES HERALD on the side to assure Zapruder that we would take care of him and the film. But Zapruder didn't want to do that. He wanted to turn it over to the FBI and/or Secret Service, which ultimately he did.

While I was there, they came in. They had with them Harry McCormick, the legendary police reporter for the *Dallas Morning News,* and they all went into an office with Zapruder. I started following them in because I wanted to be there myself, and they said, "No, no, who are you?" I told them. They said, "You can't be here," and I said, "Here is Harry McCormick of the opposition. If he's there, I have to be there." So they kicked McCormick out and then took off with the film to have it developed.

I saved the notebook that I had when I went to the School Book Depository on November 22 and used to take notes while interviewing eyewitnesses and Abraham Zapruder. I've treasured it since that time. It's the only notebook I saved from all my reporting days. It's in pencil. These are notes I took when I went up to Zapruder's office afterward. They were quite sketchy. I'm not terribly proud of them, but they're original.

"I got film," he said. "I saw it hit him in the head. They were going so fast. He slumped over with the first shot. With the first shot, he bent

84

over and grabbed his neck as he sort of did. The second burst hit him in the head. It opened up. Couldn't be alive.

"Jackie was beside him. After the last shot, she crawled over the back of the car."

Then I got his name, "Zapruder, Abraham, president."
This is from another eyewitness.

"We saw the president making it under the triple underpass. We heard something that sounded like a truck backfired or a firecracker. Saw the president slump forward. And we thought he was ducking. A lot of people hit the dirt. The president's car hesitated for a moment, then lurched forward. A lot of people hit the ground. Then, a lot of confusion. I didn't know what happened. Couldn't pick up anything on the radio. When we heard the president was hit on the radio, the police arrived."

I went back after that to the School Book Depository. I was able to go up on the sixth floor and look out the window, see the sniper's lair where the boxes were arranged. Then I went back to the office. It was getting late in the afternoon, and the city editor told me, "Here's an address, 1025 North Beckley. This is where Oswald lived. Go there, and see what you can find." It wasn't far away, just over the viaduct in Oak Cliff.

I didn't hear Oswald's name at the School Book Depository; I heard it when I got to the office. It had been revealed that he had shot the police officer, Tippit, and that he'd been a defector to the Soviet Union before. So we knew quite a bit about him by the middle of the afternoon. When the officer was shot, there were other reporters there from the *Times Herald*. We had a little confab because an officer had been shot over in Oak Cliff. Maybe some of us should go. I didn't want to go over to Oak Cliff because I thought the assassin or assassins were still in the School Book Depository building. I wanted to stay and see what happened there. Others thought the shooting had a connection to the assassination. They took off for the Texas Theatre and saw Oswald captured, but I missed that opportunity because I was intent on seeing what happened at the School Book Depository.

—⁓—

Saturday night I was at the police station on my normal beat as the Saturday night police reporter; I stayed up very late there. Sunday morning I slept late but got up in time to see Ruby shoot Oswald. I went to the newspaper again, did some work there, and then went to Ruby's apartment in Oak Cliff and interviewed people there. I'd never heard Ruby's name, but many other reporters did know of him. The other reporters thought that Jack Ruby was sort of a tough character, owning those night clubs. He was a police buff. The things we generally now know about him, they confirmed right at that moment. They understood him for what he was: somebody who liked to hang around the police department, give passes to his Carousel Club, and try to ingratiate himself with the police.

The police had guards set outside the driveway into the police basement who supposedly weren't going to let anybody in. But the crowd that Sunday consisted mainly of plainclothes detectives, police officers, and some reporters. The Warren Commission report later said that a mob of reporters had permitted Ruby to conceal himself, but he was standing next to police officers who knew who he was.

—⁓—

Dallas was very protective of itself on Monday morning. We were receiving an awful lot of criticism from around the world and throughout the nation, and that seemed to be acceptable because, after all, it was a horrible thing. But when you had people from Dallas saying that perhaps the climate we had here had something to do with it—the awful political climate, the extremist demonstrations and assaults they'd made on people like Stevenson and Johnson—those people came under serious immediate attack from the leaders of Dallas. They portrayed them as traitors to Dallas when they should have been defending the city.

That was the first reaction. A little bit later, the city leaders moderated. The Birch Society and the extreme right wing did nothing, and a sense of moderation took over. People like Stanley Marcus ran an advertisement in the *Dallas Morning News* called "What's Right with Dallas," which really was an ad saying what had been wrong with Dallas. He was clever in giving it that title. He talked about some of the positive things in Dallas, but he also pointed out what we needed to do to have a tolerance for other viewpoints, to be more mindful of minorities and that sort of thing. That helped turn the tide; we started realizing that we needed to start accepting all viewpoints.

The mayor of Dallas was Earl Cabell. He resigned that office to run against the Republican congressman, Bruce Alger, who had been a leader of the right-wing forces in Dallas, and defeated Alger by a huge majority. Of our delegation in Austin for the Texas legislature, eight out of nine of those members were right-wing Republicans. Democrats swept the field against them that fall, and all the Republicans were defeated. You had that sort of political change happening in Dallas.

The relationship between Dallas and Fort Worth changed, which was a very important thing. The new mayor we had was Eric Johnson, who'd been one of the founders of Texas Instruments. Dallas and Fort Worth were under a directive to find an airport—midway between us—or they would find it for the two cities. Johnson, the new mayor, said, "We've fought it long enough." He was alone in this among the Dallas leaders at the time. He was strong enough, though, and he persuaded them, "We've got to cooperate now." That's how he led the move to get Dallas and Fort Worth to agree on a mid-cities airport, and he became chairman of the airport board for the next eight years. Through the force of his personality, he was able to persuade all the people who were working on the project to build an extra-large airport. They were thinking of an airport of maybe six thousand acres or so; he went up to eighteen thousand acres. That was a terrific economic engine for the Dallas–Fort Worth area.

The city got a new federal building, which Bruce Alger had opposed. The establishment very much wanted a federal building here, and they got it. They got a new city hall designed by I. M. Pei, which was a spectacular building. All of that came about because Eric Johnson was mayor.

By and large, I believe that the city today has forgotten about the assassination. But as the fiftieth anniversary approaches, city leaders have become very mindful of it and have made very careful plans to have some sort of observance that's respectful and proper.

The Dallas Cowboys were an important factor in making the nation and the world forget about the assassination when they thought of Dallas. They started thinking about the Cowboys, who were on TV all the time in the late '60s with some great success. Another program started about that time, the TV show *Dallas*. [Note: *Dallas* began airing in 1978.]

Those took some negative attention away from Dallas. Perhaps more important in taking away the city's opprobrium was the fact that two other cities experienced assassinations in 1968—Los Angeles with Robert Kennedy, and Memphis with the assassination of Martin Luther King Jr. Were we going to blame those cities for what happened there? Could we forgive Dallas now? I think that attitude prevailed.

The assassination ushered in this great period of uneasiness, of upheaval, including the disturbances of the '60s and the civil rights movement. It made the youth disparage the establishment. What could they believe in if our president could be assassinated by an individual like that? It was a period of disillusionment. It shaped the '60s and the '70s. Indirectly it led to positive things. There was a change in the nation's tenor, the sense that we've got to do better. Idealism arose among the youth, who started protesting and demanding certain things.

The civil rights movement picked up. LBJ became president with the goal of realizing the ideals of John Fitzgerald Kennedy, which hadn't gone very far, but LBJ carried them nearly to completion. Those sorts of things happened as a result of the assassination. LBJ did a wonderful job as president. He got a lot of legislation passed. The 1964 Civil Rights Act and the 1965 Voting Act really liberated the African-American population to be able to participate in the American system.

I had always approved of Kennedy, as he was the first president I voted for. I thought the world of him. I thought he was a terrific president, and I was very distraught at the time of the assassination. I remember being in Zapruder's office, looking out the window, seeing the School Book Depository, the crowds out there, and thinking, *It's a good thing I'm working as a reporter; otherwise, I don't know how I could go on.* It was really very distressing, but I did have things to do, and that kept me occupied that day. I was lucky to have that.

PART TWO
SOLEMNITIES

Joseph Califano

A thirty-two-year-old New York attorney in 1963, Joseph Califano was working as Pentagon general counsel. He went on to become special assistant to President Johnson and secretary of health, education, and welfare under President Carter before founding the National Center on Addiction and Substance Abuse at Columbia University.

I was in the bottom of a dam in West Virginia. I was general counsel to the Army and was also responsible for all the civil works of the Army, and that's where I was. Somebody from the Army shouted down, literally shouted down, so I came up out of the dam, and he said, "The president's dead."

I said, "Take me back to the Pentagon."

When I got to the Pentagon, I first went right to Cy Vance, who was secretary of the Army, and said to him, "I'm going to leave and go back to New York. This is the best of my generation, and that's why I came down here."

Vance said, "No, stay here. You don't know Lyndon Johnson. Things are really going to move. This is a different kind of person." Vance had been Johnson's counsel during the Missile Gap hearings that he held as senator. "In any case, I have something for you to do."

I asked, "What?"

He said, "Jacqueline Kennedy wants the president buried in Arlington Cemetery."

This is the same day, this is November 22. Jacqueline Kennedy wants the president buried in Arlington Cemetery. "I want you to go over tomorrow morning, meet Robert Kennedy over there, and pick the place." I was responsible for Arlington Cemetery because I wore another hat for the Army.

I knew Bobby from the years I had been in the Pentagon, and I'd worked with him. He was going to pick out the burial site, but we were going to do it together. I just was overwhelmed. I went home. I had two young kids, and my wife—I was just in shock. I guess I was like the rest of the country, but I knew I had things to do.

The next morning I met Robert Kennedy at Arlington Cemetery. It was pouring rain, pouring rain, and we walked around that plot, above the Lincoln Memorial Bridge. I had a little map of Arlington Cemetery, and I marked out the 3.2 acres, what turned out to be 3.2 acres, with him. He was shattered. I'll never forget the way . . . he was hollow eyed. He looked like a truck had run over him and so different from the Bobby Kennedy I had seen dealing with the problems in the South and segregation. Then, almost in a whisper, he said, "This is where the president will be buried." Then he left, and I went back to the Pentagon.

When I was back in my office, I got a call from Secretary [Robert] McNamara. He said, "I hear you picked the land," so I assumed Bobby had talked to him. "I want to make sure we own that land. I want you to have a title search."

I told Bob, "This is Arlington Cemetery."

I was responsible for Arlington Cemetery.

He said, "I want to make damn sure this land is locked up and we own it. Get a title search, and write an opinion."

So I sent one of my lawyers and Ramsey Clark, who was then the

94

assistant attorney general for the Lands Division. They went over to the Alexandria courthouse on Sunday. We had to get the courthouse open because that's where the records were. They did a title search. I came back to my office, worked Sunday and Sunday night, and we wrote an opinion. I prepared an order for the secretary of the Army to sign, setting aside that land forever. I brought it to Cy Vance, and he okayed it.

Then McNamara called again and said, "Jacqueline Kennedy wants to have a torch, a light, that will be eternal. I want you to go over there and make sure we set that up."

I said, "OK." He and I went over there with an Army general, and we plotted out roughly where the eternal light would be. We talked about getting copper tubing to put the wires in, making sure it was deep enough so that spiked heels didn't break it. I said this can never go out because McNamara had told me, "Jacqueline never wants this to go out."

McNamara said he wanted to sign the order. He had no authority over Arlington or the Army at that point, so we came up with an approve line for him. I went over later—either later Sunday afternoon or early Monday morning, I can't remember which—and McNamara was in a car parked at that side of the Lincoln Memorial Bridge. He had gone over to make sure that the 3.2 acres, and where the grave would be set in there, was going to be exactly in the center of the bridge as you came across. I handed them the order, and he signed it.

He was, I think, shaken. But he was an efficient machine in many respects. He actually said to me: "I want you to make damn sure that a wire is low enough so that some woman doesn't break it with her heels."

I said, "Already done that."

He said, "That's a great job," and then he said, "You stay around. We're going to need people like you."

I was home that day [of the funeral]. I was like every other American; I was watching every single thing that happened.

To see the burial site for the first time on television . . . We were really frozen in time, and this was sort of the greatest president—the only president I'd ever known anything about in an intimate way. I'd read about

Roosevelt and Eisenhower like any other kid growing up, but it was just fantastic. It was in a sense one of the greatest things I'd ever been part of. The Army was terrific with stuff like this. They got it right—and remember: All the stone and all that stuff wasn't all set at that point in time. I went back there when Robert Kennedy was killed.

I was working for President Johnson, and we went over to the burial site at night when he came down from New York on the train. That's probably the next time I saw it. At that point, I just never wanted to go over there. I've seen it several times since then. You drive across that bridge, and it's fantastic. It's great for the country. It's not just great for President Kennedy and his family and Jackie, but it's great for the country.

They were obsessed with getting rid of Castro. About a year after the Bay of Pigs invasion failed, Robert Kennedy ransomed the Cuban brigade. I was then still general counsel to the Army working for Vance, and the Army was given responsibility for assimilating the Cuban brigade into American life. We brought them into the Army, the Navy, and the Air Force. We wouldn't let them fly planes because we didn't want a plane going over Cuba.

President Kennedy created the Interdepartmental Coordinating Committee for Cuban Affairs. It was nominally chaired by a State Department fellow named Sterling Cottrell, but it was in fact chaired by Robert Kennedy. He ran that committee—and the object of that committee was to overthrow the Castro regime. Vance was the committee's Defense Department member. He made me his alternate, and we planned, tried, to do all kinds of things: putting sugar in the gasoline, putting bad bacteria in petroleum, sabotage, everything.

Robert Kennedy was constantly saying, "This is the most important thing we've got to get done; we have to get rid of Castro." Now, "get rid of" in that committee meant to overthrow the Castro regime. But at some point there was a discussion in the committee of assassinating Castro. A Justice Department lawyer named Joe Dolan, who was the Justice Department alternate, and I argued against that. Throughout this discussion, the CIA was totally silent.

I began to say, "There's something else going on besides what we're actually doing in this committee." Vance was very disturbed about what he thought was an effort to assassinate Castro and almost resigned on that issue.

We had a meeting before President Kennedy at one point. It was the only time I was ever in a meeting with President Kennedy, Cy Vance, and a Marine general named Brute Krulak, who was the tough counterinsurgency, dirty-tricks guy, and some State Department people, because we disagreed.

We wanted to do much tougher things. We wanted to sabotage boats. We wanted to blow up bridges. We wanted to send people in who were trained by the CIA in sabotage. The State Department wanted a much meeker program of Latin American press and stuff like that. Vance laid out our arguments. The State Department laid out theirs. President Kennedy read a paper we had given him and just got up and left. He said nothing [except], "I'll be back." Kenny O'Donnell came in about fifteen minutes later and said, "The meeting's over—these kinds of disputes should be solved by White House staffers, not by presidents." Eventually we got approval for most of the things we wanted to do in the Pentagon. We got approval to send Cubans in to sabotage, to mess up the oil and the petroleum.

They were crazy things. I mean, this was Keystone Kops. I'll give you one example, which I'll never forget. At one point the chief of Naval Operations said, "One possibility is to fly over Cuba and drop an enormous number of bats on Cuba with incendiary devices tied to them. The bats will go down. They won't want to be out in the daytime. They'll go into buildings all over. We'll have the incendiary devices timed so that they'll go off that night, and we'll have fires all over Cuba." Rejected—not because it was a crazy idea but because the planes would have to fly so low; we were afraid Castro would knock one of them down and find out it was an American plane. The pressure was enormous to just do something, do something.

Then the CIA representative Dick Helms and Desmond Fitzgerald, who was their operations guy, said to me, "We would like you to identify a number of Cuban generals, if you can from talking to your brigade people, who are still there around Castro so that we can get a better sense of what's going on."

But, as we now know and as we suspected, what they really were looking for were generals who might kill Castro. Indeed, in a briefing they gave the Joint Chiefs of Staff, Helms said, "We're looking at the possibility of doing this, and we're studying what Hitler's generals did to Hitler, to see if there are any lessons there that we could use." As we now know, they had given people a poison pen. They had given them a sniper's rifle and everything in order to try and kill Castro. There's no question in my mind that that was the objective.

Reflecting over the years, I think the paroxysms, the overwhelming grief, that Bobby Kennedy felt, that paralyzing grief . . . a large part of that was due to the fact that he suspected or worried—"worried" is probably the better word—that maybe the efforts to assassinate Castro had resulted in his brother getting killed, that there was a Cuban connection.

Lyndon Johnson said to me and to other people, "Kennedy tried to get Castro, but Castro got Kennedy first." Remember, shortly before Kennedy was assassinated, or within a few months, the president had approved the coup in South Vietnam, which ended up in the killing of [Ngo Dinh] Diem, the head of South Vietnam.

Castro told the Associated Press, I think in September of 1963, "If the Americans think they can try and kill our leaders, their leaders aren't safe." So we'll never know. I think we still don't know the answer to that. The Warren Commission never interviewed me, never interviewed Cy Vance, as far as I know, never interviewed anybody who was involved in the Cuban coordinating committee. Why, I don't know.

The Warren Commission never interviewed me, never interviewed Cy Vance, as far as I know, never interviewed anybody who was involved in the Cuban coordinating committee.

Johnson said he accepted the findings of the Warren Commission at the time. There's no question about that. But he did say when I was on the staff, and I think he may have told Walter Cronkite—he told somebody at one point in an off-camera part of an interview—the same thing: that Castro was involved. I remember something else. Shortly after Johnson became president, I was still in the Pentagon. Johnson disbanded the committee and ordered a stop to all this activity. I was sent around the country to meet with various Cuban brigade units to tell them that it was over. There would be no more sabotage, there'd be nothing else; there would never be another invasion of Cuba. Their hope hadn't really died yet, so that was quite a moving and difficult experience. But Johnson stopped it all. By February of '64, all that activity was totally turned off.

I am persuaded that Oswald was working in concert with Castro's people. I really am. I'm persuaded of that when I just put those pieces together. We know Oswald went to Mexico, to the Cuban embassy there. He said he was all for the Cubans. We know he'd been to the Soviet Union. When you just think about those events, and if you were Castro and you saw Diem knocked off, you *had* to know we were trying to kill you. I mean, there were too many crazy attempts to do that—and Castro's little statement in September 1963 that "they're trying to kill me or our leaders; their leaders are vulnerable too."

I think someday there will be a final connection, but we may never know until the Castros are out of power or until we have access to all their files the way we have access to so many of the Soviet files. We learned so much about what was going on between Soviet spies and the KGB and the United States.

When I started doing my memoir, *Inside: A Public and Private Life,* I went in to get as many documents as I could. I knew there had been a meeting among Dick Helms, Fitzgerald, and the Joint Chiefs of Staff. It was a meeting they wouldn't let me go to, even though I was Vance's alternate. It was a meeting at which Vance was not present. I used the Freedom of Information Act to get the memorandum of that meeting. That confirmed my suspicion, because that memorandum literally states that the CIA people were looking at what Hitler's generals had done to Hitler to see if they could learn something from that vis-à-vis Castro. At that point in time, I was having people interview Cuban military exiles to see if they could identify Castro generals or top Castro military people who might have access to him. It was clear to me, at least at that point, that one of the things they were trying to do was maybe get the generals to knock off Castro.

The day Kennedy was assassinated, the CIA had a guy in Paris meeting with a man I think was nicknamed AM/LASH who was asking for a sniper's rifle. The CIA was giving him a pen with lethal poison in it. So there's no question what we were trying to do. The other thing I don't know the answer to is: Why didn't the Warren Commission ever talk to anybody who was involved in that?

I asked Jerry Ford that once, and he said none of that ever came to their attention. Jerry Ford deeply believed that Oswald acted alone. There was also a great sense of putting this to rest. If you go back and listen to the Johnson tapes, you hear his conversation with Dick Russell, with senior senators saying, "You've got to go on this," and getting Earl Warren to become chairman and getting Jerry Ford, the House minority leader, to go on. You listen to Johnson on the phone saying, "We've got to do this; we've got to put this to rest. We've got to deal with this for the American people." And they did put it to rest.

I also think you have to remember that Johnson really did turn this whole Cuban operation off. Kennedy's assassinated on November 22. Within days or weeks after Johnson becomes president, before the end of the year, all the Cuban coordinating committee activities are turned off. In early 1964, in early February, I'm sent out to go around the country and tell all these people it's over. For whatever reason, Johnson didn't want any part of that; he didn't want that going on.

One of the things they were trying to do was maybe get the generals to knock off Castro.

There's no doubt in my mind that President Kennedy approved of what the CIA was trying to do with Castro. The documents show higher authority [but] never mentioned the president knew this. I do know the president pretty much approved all of the sabotage things that we wanted to do eventually, and believe me, I know Dick Helms. I know the CIA. They wouldn't have done what they were doing—in Paris giving AM/LASH a poison pen to kill Castro—if President Kennedy and Robert Kennedy hadn't okayed the idea. There's no question. That committee was driven by Robert Kennedy. Have no illusions; he was at most of the meetings. When he wasn't at the meetings, somebody from the Justice Department was telling us what they wanted to do, and it was constant: "You've got to find other ways. You've got to do something. We've got to get rid of this." He called it, at one point, one of the most important things we were doing in the government.

I think—and I use this in the best sense of the word—Johnson was enormously opportunistic in terms of dealing with the assassination and getting all the good he could out of it. You think about him saying, "There's no greater tribute we could pay to John F. Kennedy than the 1964 Civil Rights Act." Then you think of him saying, "There's no greater tribute we could pay than getting the tax bill." With many of the programs Johnson proposed, which we know were in his head during his years in Congress and the Senate, he constantly invoked President Kennedy: "Let's do this for President Kennedy."

Little Washington, DC, was a cultural desert. For years there had been attempts to have a cultural center in Washington, DC. Nobody had been able to get it passed, but Johnson said, "We have to have the Kennedy Center." He got the Kennedy Center. In that sense, the assassination had a significant impact. It was one of the key factors in Johnson's ability to revolutionize the country in those four years. It also started to shake up the country in the sense that followed, in April of '68, Martin Luther King's assassination and then, in June of '68, Robert Kennedy's assassination. What an incredible group of years.

Camelot, we know, was a myth. There's no question about that. I think Kennedy did the best he could. I think you have to look at it in the context of the Cold War. Remember, Eisenhower had put in motion something to get Castro thrown out. Eisenhower puts in motion the Bay of Pigs invasion. Kennedy runs against Richard Nixon in 1960, and the campaign is, "I can be tougher than you can be on Castro." Both of them are saying, "I'll be tougher; I'll do this; I'll do that." Even after the Bay of Pigs invasion failed, Kennedy goes down to Miami, to the stadium down there, and says, "This flag will fly in a free Havana. We'll take it there."

Robert Kennedy never could quite tell the Cuban brigade, as we had in the Army and elsewhere, that we weren't going back to Cuba. He felt, I think, so guilty. Remember, one hundred Cubans lost their lives at the Bay of Pigs. We tend to forget that. Every time I put some restriction on them, they'd go to him. They had total access to the attorney general, and Bobby would reverse it; tell me, "No, don't do it."

We know that Camelot is a myth. But it's not only John Kennedy. Robert Kennedy also is portrayed as a saint. We have two saints there. Saints aren't perfect. And we know Robert Kennedy could be pretty tough in a whole variety of ways. I think he changed when he started running for office. He changed not only on the war. When there was pressure in the Kennedy administration about civil rights and "Do something about the '64 Civil Rights Act, open up public accommodations, end discrimination in employment," the whole focus of the Kennedy brothers was on politics: "What are the politics of this?"

And there's the meeting in the cabinet room where Johnson says, "This is not a political issue. This is a moral issue. We should do this." In his book, Taylor Branch writes that Martin Luther King said, "Johnson was a breath of fresh air because, every time President Kennedy talked to me or Bobby, the first thing they'd say is, 'You've got to get rid of

Communists that may be advising. You've got to get rid of them. That could be a real problem.'" Johnson never mentioned that. It was always, "How do we get the Civil Rights Bill passed? How do we get the Voting Rights Bill passed?"

Those were the times, and they were part of a post–World War II culture in which the CIA believed: "We can do it," and it's fine to assassinate people if that would be a good thing for America.

Joe English

Native Philadelphian Joseph English, MD, was thirty years old at the time of JFK's death. After Dr. English had served as a research fellow at the National Institute of Mental Health, Sargent Shriver made him the first chief of psychiatry for the Peace Corps. When President Johnson appointed Shriver head of the War on Poverty, Shriver asked Dr. English to become its director of Health Affairs. He played a major role in the development of the Community Health Centers Program and other initiatives of the War on Poverty. Wilbur Cohen, President Johnson's secretary of health, education, and welfare, asked him to become head of the largest health agency in Washington. In early 1970 New York mayor John Lindsay tapped him to head the New York City Health and Hospitals Corporation, where he stayed until 1973, when he became chair of the Department of Psychiatry at St. Vincent's Catholic Medical Centers of New York. He now serves as Sidney Frank chairman of the Department of Psychiatry and Behavioral Sciences of the New York Medical College.

I'm not so sure that President Kennedy wasn't a little skeptical about the Peace Corps, as most of the people in the Foreign Service community were, because of the idea of having young students running around in various countries causing international incidents. I think when he began to see its potential is when he gave that speech at the University of Wisconsin at three o'clock in the morning.

The reaction he got from young people when he started describing something like the Peace Corps was the beginning of it. But when you saw him seeing off the Peace Corps volunteers, the very first who went abroad, from the White House, as he often did, then you knew that he

John Landgraf (center left), Joe English, and Sargent Shriver flanked by guides in North Borneo

understood they were not only going to grow but they were going to come back with an understanding of the developing world that we didn't have in this country. He was already beginning to sense that there was poverty in this country to rival anything we could find in the outside world, and these young people would come back and be able to help with that from the experience they'd gained abroad.

So many things developed as a result of the Peace Corps and not just from the volunteers—for example, Kennedy's commitment to helping the volunteers stay well. He said, "I don't want our volunteers to become a burden on the host country." That's why we were permitted to put a young doctor in every country the Peace Corps volunteers went to. The doctor's task was to keep them well. They got so good that these young doctors began to find themselves advising the health minister in the country on how to improve health generally. Those doctors came back, and many of them didn't go into private practice. They continued in public service with that spirit of the Peace Corps and became some of the leaders of great innovations in health care around the country in the years following.

I had just been at the White House because I was being asked to become a special assistant for Health. Stafford Warren had been in that position and was going back to Stanford, and they wanted me to take it. That was of course a great honor. I was essentially a college psychiatrist, and the thought of leaving the Peace Corps was unthinkable. It was also considered unthinkable by Dr. Warren that someone wouldn't accept this. I had just turned it down and gotten back to the Peace Corps office on Friday morning.

I was up in my office, thinking I had just made the greatest mistake of my life, when the medical director of the Peace Corps came in with tears streaming down his eyes and said, "We just heard the president was shot; they want you down in his office," in Sargent Shriver's office. Mr. Shriver and Eunice were off for an obstetrician appointment, then having lunch. I waited in the office until they returned, and the three of us awaited the news.

The first report was that it was a head shot, and then I thought, *Oh . . . here I am, a psychiatrist. I should know what to do because the next news is going to be worse.* It wasn't long until the cable came in and I told them. I've never felt so helpless in my life. It was something I thought I ought to be able to help with—but I was helpless. Sarge said, "Eunice, I think we should kneel down around my desk and say the rosary for Jack." Eunice, a strong woman as she always was, knelt down, as Mr. Shriver and I did, and we did that. That gave me a chance to collect my thoughts.

She was shaken, as we all were. I went to her. I knew she was pregnant, and I said to her, "Eunice, you have two people to worry about here; I'm not so sure this is where you ought to be. I think we ought to get over to the White House and see if perhaps you shouldn't go to Hyannis to be with your mother."

We got into a car and went over to the White House. Young Teddy came down, and he had apparently had the same thought. He took Eunice up to Hyannis to stay with her mother. Sarge was asked to organize the funeral once the body of the president got back to Washington. Bobby Kennedy took care of things until then. Sarge asked Dick Goodwin and me to stay in to help with the funeral.

At the White House, people were totally in disbelief, crying. We got into Ralph Dungan's office, which is one of the larger offices in that wing. You had Supreme Court justices, members of the staff, a few people from the Secret Service, and people at first couldn't believe it. It was almost Greek tragedy. In the midst of all of that, Bill Moyers became the man who was going to help the president. The new president really felt that the way the country was going to grieve would have a lot to do with how they felt about what had happened, so he asked Bill to ensure that, as the funeral was planned, anything the family, and particularly Mrs. Kennedy, wanted would occur. It was in the wake of that that Mr. Shriver started trying to organize the funeral, but I've never seen such a sight of tremendous sadness and grief.

There were many issues. One was whether the casket should be open. Some on the new president's staff felt that it should be so people could see that it was really him and that there was no conspiracy here. No one really knew what had happened. There was a question of whether he had been kidnapped and all kinds of things going around. In addition, we were going on the highest military alert I think we ever had because all of this was going on together.

So the question was whether the casket should be open. Mr. Shriver came down. He had been talking with her [Mrs. Kennedy] about that, and she had asked if Robert McNamara and I would view the remains and give some advice. They cleared the East Room and closed it off; the two of us climbed a little ladder, and they opened the casket. I must say, it was really tough. It was clear that it *could* have been open, but that wouldn't have been the way the American people would want to remember their president. That was our advice to Mrs. Kennedy. Secretary McNamara and I agreed. It would have been possible if it had been desirable. The president's head was turned to the side because of what had happened to the back of his head, and there was makeup and the sort of things embalmers do. It wasn't the president that we'd seen and known.

The two of us climbed a little ladder, and they opened the casket.

Mr. Shriver, who was really thinking of everything, realized we should have a Mass card, which is pretty standard at a Catholic funeral. Heads of state were arriving from all over the world, and he wanted to have something to give them. Even more meaningful to me personally, he asked me if I would develop the Mass card. The first thing was to find a picture for the card. There was a wonderful man in the White House at the time, Sandy, and he was the lithographer. Sandy was a very important person in the Kennedy White House; he was the one who had the pictures, and I went to see him. With the tears coming down, he said, "Let me show you this picture. This was President Kennedy's favorite picture; he didn't want it used except for a special occasion," and Sandy said, "I think this is the occasion."

We chose that picture to show to Mrs. Kennedy, and I got the traditional prayers that go on the back of a Catholic funeral card. Sarge said, "You better go up and show the picture and the prayers to Mrs. Kennedy." So I went up to where she was sitting in the bedroom and showed her the picture. You can imagine what the reaction was. Then I showed her the prayers; she looked at them.

The presence she maintained, despite all of this, was quite remarkable. She said, "No. I want the prayers to be ones that Jack wrote himself. Go over there and get that book," which had his inaugural address in it. Then she circled in the inaugural address what she considered to be his prayer. That's what's on the back of the Mass card.

<hr />

There are heads of state coming in without notice, landing at the airports, and now this is the day that we're marching down to St. Matthew's for the funeral Mass itself. Various rooms on the first floor of the White House had the Supreme Court in one, the cabinet in another, the family in a third, the former presidents in another. In the East Room was assembled the greatest gathering of heads of state, they tell me, in the history of the world. Angie Duke was very concerned because we were late, and he thought somebody ought to apologize to them. At the same time, he was trying to figure out how to line them up for the march, because there had been a decision that there was going be a march to St. Matthew's.

He asked, "Who's willing to go in there and tell them how they should line up?" I said, "We have something called a peer rating." He said, "That's a fine idea."

I was the box carrier for the Mass cards. We

> *In the East Room was assembled the greatest gathering of heads of state, they tell me, in the history of the world.*

walked in and wondered who in the world would be first in line. As you may know, it was Haile Selassie; standing behind him was Charles de Gaulle, and then Prince Philip.

We knew the emperor well because we had three hundred volunteers in Ethiopia. Mr. Shriver went up to him and said, "Your Majesty, we apologize we're a little late, but we wanted you to have a memorial of President Kennedy," and presented him with a card. [Emperor] Haile Selassie, with tears streaming down his face, said, "Mr. Shriver, we need no memorial beyond the three hundred of Kennedy's children who serve the people of my country." It was a very difficult time to keep things together, but Mr. Shriver was able to do that. De Gaulle said similarly wonderful things, and as we went around the room, almost everyone linked Kennedy and the Peace Corps. Of course they knew that Sargent Shriver had developed it for him—an extraordinary experience.

Angie and Mrs. Duke said, "My God, the two former presidents are about to arrive; they're in that room, and there's nobody to meet them." He said, "I have to go up, do something."

They asked me, "Would you stand here and make sure they get to the right room?"

I said, "Of course I will," and the first one to arrive was President Truman, who was my father's hero in Philadelphia. I escorted President Truman in and had a steward bring him some coffee. He was standing there with his back to the door, looking out the window, when I saw a car drive up, and there was Ike: General Eisenhower, President Eisenhower.

He got out and took my arm. As we approached the room, he tensed a little bit because he saw President Truman in there. I remembered hearing that they weren't on the best of terms. I thought I'd excuse myself to get him some coffee, but he said, "You stick right with me, son." It's very difficult to turn down a five-star general, let alone a former president of the United States.

President Truman was aware that somebody had come in. He turned around and was a bit surprised to see President Eisenhower, who then said to him, and I'll never forget it, "Harry, what are us two sons of whatever standing here alive with that young man down the hall dead? You and I have seen too many young men die." Then they hugged.

Needless to say, I made my exit. I don't know whether they had had any prior encounters, but that was an extraordinary one. You could see how the death of this president, which produced so many things, brought them together.

I was trying to get a ride to the funeral Mass when Mr. Shriver said, "Get into your mourning coat."

I said, "What do you mean?"

He said, "We've got a mourning coat there for you. We want you to march in the procession."

I asked, "Sarge, why would I do that?"

He explained, "We're not sure the emperor's going to make it. It's kind of a long walk, so we want you to walk behind the emperor and help him out if anything happens." I got into the mourning coat and did walk behind him. He started to fade back, but he did finally make it.

The walk was a little bit scary. There were rumors that there was an assassin out for de Gaulle. We heard rumors that they took someone off the roof of one of the buildings during the march. Obviously there were great security concerns. But Mrs. Kennedy decided she was going to march with those children. The minute President Johnson heard that, that

> *Eisenhower said to Truman, "Harry, what are us two sons of whatever standing here alive with that young man down the hall dead? You and I have seen too many young men die."*

settled everything; the president was going to march with her, and therefore everybody followed.

—⁓—

President Johnson was extraordinarily sensitive, and I think here he had a lot of help from Bill Moyers. The president felt that, not only in this country but around the world, the perception of this whole event would in some ways be determined by the funeral. Which is why he made it perfectly clear to Bill—and Bill really made it clear to me that I was to be down there while Sarge was trying to organize things—to be sure the family got anything they wanted, that the funeral could be as they wished, and it would be moving.

Because of President Kennedy's military background, Mr. Shriver was asking that there be troops along the road. I think the commanding general of the District at that time thought that Mr. Shriver's rank was sergeant because he didn't seem to be too accommodating and mentioned that it would take more troops than they had available. I thought that was my cue, so I bolted out of the room and went down. The cabinet meeting was going on. I knocked on the door; when Bill came out I said, "Bill, we've got a problem. You know, troops."

Bill said, "I get it."

Next thing I knew, Mr. McNamara came out, put his arm around me, and said, "I understand Sarge is having a problem." I said, "Yes, as a matter of fact, a number of them." He said, "Come on; let's go down."

Down he went. He sat on the arm of the chair, put his arm around Sarge, and said, "Sarge, I understand we have some problems here."

Sarge said, "I'd like to have an honor guard, but it seems we don't have enough troops."

It was very clear that the general knew who the secretary of defense was, and he stood like a rod. McNamara said to him, "General, if it takes five hundred troops, they shall be there. If it takes five thousand, they shall be there. If it takes fifty thousand and you have to mobilize the reserves, do it immediately." The guy was just—needless to say, he got the message.

Then he turned to Sarge and asked, "Is there anything else?"

McNamara came out, put his arm around me, and said, "I understand Sarge is having a problem."

Sarge said, "I think the president would have liked the Air Force to have a chance to participate as well. But they say there can't be a flyover because it will scare the horses; they're very concerned about that."

This time, McNamara's gaze went to the Air Force aide. He said, "General, I want on my desk by the end of the afternoon the exact altitude at which a flyover can occur without scaring horses," and it was done.

That's the kind of thing that went on. I think when you put it all together, there was an extraordinary attention to detail. The troops were there; the flyover was perfect. So many things, and a lot of that was because the new president was so sensitive. I think he was aided a lot by Bill Moyers in this regard, to recognize the fact that the world would grieve.

Another question came up that demonstrated this to me. The new president, in the course of his first cabinet meeting, was raising questions about the Peace Corps: Would the volunteers return from all over the world as a result of this? The last thing he wanted was for it to appear that the wonderful things Kennedy started were over. So he wanted to know if they would come home. I was the Peace Corps psychiatrist and supposedly should know something about that. Bill came out and asked me, and I said, "Oh, they're not going to come home."

He said, "I'd like you to come in here and tell the president that in front of the cabinet."

Sometimes you have to know when to say no. I said, "Bill, I can't do that." I couldn't imagine going in there in that circumstance.

He said, "You've got to think of something, because it's on the president's mind."

I found out the power of a White House phone. A great professor at Harvard by the name of Gerald Caplan had helped us develop the mental health program of the Peace Corps and had seen almost as many Peace Corps volunteers as I had around the world. I told the White House operator, "I need to talk to Gerald Caplan at Harvard." Within ten minutes, she had him on the phone.

The sense I got then was that the whole world was watching that White House for the first time. Not only in this country but all over, people were watching. To get a call from the White House during that time was extraordinary.

I asked Dr. Caplan, "Will the volunteers come home?"

He said, "Absolutely not."

I asked, "How do we convince the president of this?"

He said, "That I can't tell you."

I asked, "Would you be willing to go to Bogotá, Colombia, tonight?" —where the first group of volunteers in Latin America had landed—"and talk to them?" He was gotten down to Colombia *that evening*. I don't know how it happened, but they arranged transportation for him.

He met with the Colombia volunteers and was able to cable us back that not only were they not coming home but they were going to be rededicated. But they had a problem: Out in the boondocks where they were working there was no television. They wouldn't be able to grieve the way the rest of the world and the rest of the country would. If we could figure out some way to help that happen, that would be the best thing we could do.

Mr. Shriver—and I'm not sure whether he asked the president to do this or whether he did it himself—got in touch with Punch Sulzberger and asked if the four-page coverage the *New York Times* was going to have of the event could be made into a special edition. He said, "Of course."

That four-page edition went to every Peace Corps volunteer in the world within a week after the funeral. It was one of the few things Peace Corps Washington did that those volunteers were grateful for. That was the way they grieved, reading those editions together.

———

I keep thinking of the tremendous things that lived long after Kennedy was buried there in Arlington. For example, we had one hundred young doctors taking care of the Peace Corps volunteers. If anything, I think their spirit and dedication were increased by the world's reaction to what they were doing and the association with President Kennedy.

They came back; one of them became the first medical director of the Job Corps. Another one, Lee Macht at Harvard, developed the mental health program of the Peace Corps. Another developed the Alaskan Health Care Federations. They became the leaders of the health centers that developed under President Johnson's administration as a part of the War on Poverty. There were so many good things. These were people who, as a result of that experience, were so imbued with [a sense of] public service that instead of doing what they would normally do after their tour of duty—going back into private practice, whatever—they did great things. Thinking about this documentary stirred up a lot of things. For example, look at the effect that period had on the mentally ill in this country and the mentally retarded. President Kennedy was interested in helping the retarded, as was his sister.

He made two ten-year commitments. One was that we would be on the moon; he kept that one. The other one is less well known: that the state hospitals, which were not the best places to be—and the mental retardation centers even worse—would be diminished by half within ten years, which was something nobody ever thought was possible. It was done. It wasn't done as perfectly as Kennedy would have wanted it, but it started the process. The Community Mental Health Center program, the Community Mental Retardation program—all those things came out of that period. President Johnson continued them, and they go on today. That's an example of the way President Kennedy's legacy continues.

Richard Goodwin and
Doris Kearns Goodwin

In 1963 Richard Goodwin was a thirty-two-year-old advisor and speech-writer for President Kennedy, having joined his staff in 1959 when the commander in chief was a senator. Goodwin became Kennedy's deputy assistant secretary of state for Inter-American Affairs and helped develop the Alliance for Progress, which aimed to bind the US and Latin America closer together. He later served as secretary-general of the Peace Corps, remained in the Johnson White House as an advisor, and coined the phrase "the Great Society" for Johnson's reform program. Since leaving politics, Goodwin has authored numerous books, plays, and articles. Future Pulitzer Prize–winner Doris Kearns was a twenty-year-old student at Colby College in Maine, soon to graduate magna cum laude. She also worked in the Johnson administration and then taught at Harvard before writing several widely acclaimed books on American presidents. She appears regularly on *Meet the Press.*

RICHARD: Kennedy had been in World War II. He'd been wounded badly, and he had suffered, and all that suffering and pain really made him much more aware of people who didn't have those privileges. During his campaign for the presidency, he was probably most moved by going into the coal mines of West Virginia and seeing real poverty. He had taught himself that a lot of people were suffering, and he might be able to do something for them.

DORIS: Adversity is a great teacher. Just as FDR wouldn't have been the same empathetic president had it not been for his polio; he shared a fate of hurt with lots of other people. The war was a huge binder of people—a common mission, with people from different parts of the country, different economic backgrounds—that a lot of our politicians don't have today, that shared background of having been in war together. He had pain, it was said by Bobby, almost every day in his life, so he knew how to get through difficulties and could project that

onto other people to whom fate had also dealt an unkind hand, whether it was poverty, discrimination, or racial problems.

RICHARD: We knew he was often in pain; you could see that by the way he moved. He was taking medication of various kinds, but I don't think any of us—not me, anyway—knew the extent to which he was suffering most of the time from medical problems. His adrenal gland insufficiency almost killed him. He had been through a lot of pain and suffering. That tempered him a lot, changed his outlook on the world—if you think you're about to die, as he did many times on his way up the ladder.

DORIS: There was a sense, just while growing up in the 1960s, that there'd been a big divide between then and the '50s, which was my high school years, when there was Eisenhower, when there was a sense of lack of forward movement on domestic progress. I was part of the civil rights movement. I'd gone down South. I'd been at Martin Luther King's "I Have a Dream" speech. There was now a sense of this decade promising real change.

There also was a sense, for me, having been at that "I Have a Dream" speech, of wishing that JFK would come there and feeling disappointed that he hadn't. There was a sense that the civil rights movement was ahead of JFK at that time. It's not as if I looked upon him as a great hero, but I did feel that time was an exciting time to be alive, to be in college, to be

one of those young people, to be a part of the civil rights movement. It was a sense of knowing that you're in an era that's going to change the country and feeling proud to be young at that time.

The presidents who have made a mark on our country's history have understood the technology of their time and what the moment of communication was. Lincoln understood that speeches would be printed in pamphlets and read in their entirety, so he worked on those speeches endlessly. Teddy Roosevelt understood that it was time for mass media, so you had to have shorthand phrases like "Carry a big stick, speak softly" that would make headlines in the country. FDR understood the power of radio. JFK understood the power of television, the power of photography, and the power of the moving picture. Those have kept him alive ever since.

RICHARD: The private Kennedy had a lot more humor. He could joke about what was happening. He also said he was "going to go get" guys who opposed him on something. He was vindictive that way, but he was always cool about it. Really, the modern phrase "cool" probably applies to him better than anyone else who's ever occupied the White House. Tough. Cool, but tough. He could swear. He'd swear a lot. We all did. He was leading a very active social life while he was in the White House, as we all know now. We had a pretty good idea about it, but I never knew the dimensions of it. But that something that was going on, yes. We saw every beautiful woman hanging around. We were all young ourselves too, and we had that terrible reaction you do to sexual beings.

DORIS: No guilt seemed to transfer from one part to the other. That's an extraordinary thing, to be able to know that you're risking—or maybe he doesn't know that he's risking—the country's image of him by the girls he's bringing into the White House. The reporters weren't covering it in those days, so you weren't taking the same risks. They didn't write about it. Everybody was doing the same thing.

RICHARD: The reporters and the White House staff, all of us knew. What you couldn't do today, we did. Now there's too much of a spotlight on it, but that really seemed trivial at the time, and we all partook.

Kennedy had had successes for his entire life, and then he ran into the Bay of Pigs, which was a disastrous failure and which caused him, I think, to cry in his bedroom that night after a brigade had been defeated. But I think the job did enlarge him. He got more tolerant of other people and other views. Failure's a great teacher, and he was a man who was capable of learning. At the time he was killed, he had expanded himself and was much more tolerant of other people.

I was home, at my house in Virginia. I had talked to Kennedy the night before, when he was down in Texas, and I knew he was going to appoint me to another job in his administration. I called him and told him the news had leaked and that the *New York Times* had it, and he said, "We better announce it right away."

I was at home writing that announcement for myself, having been partying with Teddy the night before with a group of Latin American people. We were up pretty late, and I was probably a little hung over. I had to check on something, and I called Kenny O'Donnell to clear some of the names with him. His secretary answered; I asked for Kenny, and she just said he wasn't there. He was in Texas of course. Then she said, "Haven't you heard, Mr. Goodwin? The president's been shot, and he's dead." I hadn't been listening to anything because I'd been writing. It was a terrific shock to me because, I think, like everyone else who worked for him, I loved the guy.

I got in my car; I didn't know what to do about it, so I drove down to the White House. I figured there, at least, I could find out what was going on. The streets were all silent. I was silent. I walked into the White House, and the mourners were sitting there. Arthur Schlesinger was there. Kay Graham was there, Ken Galbraith. They'd all heard the word that Kennedy had been killed. We just sat down and talked and grieved together.

But then we had to prepare for the return of the body from Texas, and we had some very explicit instructions on how to do that from Jackie. She wanted the East Room made up as it had been when Lincoln was shot. I didn't have any idea where that was, so I just scrambled around. I called the Library of Congress and got a description of the East Room as when they had Lincoln's body there. We instructed the people who were working with us that they should set

> *She wanted the East Room made up as it had been when Lincoln was shot.*

it up exactly the same way. That's what they tried to do and what I tried to do as much as we could. We were just racing about frantically trying to be true, literally true, to what Jackie said she wanted.

My initial reaction was just grief—wailing, "How could they do this to him?"—and disbelief. Then we all kept busy arranging for the funeral that was going to happen in the next day or two. That's the best thing when you're experiencing a grief reaction, if you keep yourself busy doing things. We brought in a catafalque for the body, and Jackie had said something about getting an eternal flame. Of course I had no idea what that was. She said it was like the flame at the Arc de Triomphe. That task was delegated to me. I thought the only people who might know about it would be the military. I called the Pentagon and told the general in charge, and he said, "We don't have an eternal flame."

I blew up. I said, "You guys can blow up the world, but you can't find a little eternal flame for the president's body?" They got something, using piped-in gas. Then we just worked through the night on details of the funeral and what the White House would look like. They put an honor guard in front of the White House, waiting for the body to come. I don't know if it was surreal. Actually it was too real.

I don't think I had much thought about Johnson, whom I had known a little, but I could feel the loss of Kennedy. Kennedy's great contribution to the country was that he made us all feel a little better about ourselves and that there was movement on things. He had a youth, and he had humor. He had become much better at directing things since the Cuban Missile Crisis, and that was now gone. I knew nothing much about Johnson except that the Kennedys didn't like him. [To them] he was just a

"You guys can blow up the world, but you can't find a little eternal flame for the president's body?"

hanger-on basically, even though he was vice president. Kennedy always made sure Johnson had something to do, sending him on foreign trips and that kind of thing. Kennedy never joined any talk about Lyndon being crude. We had a sense that we were going through a big transition, but that wasn't the concern on that night. We just knew Kennedy was gone, and he had been the center of our lives.

DORIS: Dick has an amazing story from having written a campaign speech for JFK. He and [Ted] Sorensen were in the plane together for the whole time of the 1960 election, and Dick had written a line for JFK talking about his programs and what might be accomplished. The line had read, "All this will not be accomplished in one hundred days." Kennedy slashed it out. "I don't want to be measured by one hundred days, the New Deal." He changed it to a thousand days, which turned out to be the number of days of his life as president.

⁓

I was a college student, and I was on my way from Colby College in Maine to New Haven to go with a boyfriend to the Yale-Harvard game. In a certain sense, the bus trip was a microcosm of what happened in the country because at first, when we found out about it [the assassination] by stopping at a gas station, everybody looked to one another for comfort and solace.

There was a real sense of camaraderie on the bus. Midway through, we found out he had actually died, and later that the Harvard-Yale game was going to be canceled. Then some of the feisty sporting guys on the bus got really angry: "Why are they canceling it just for this?" It was that whole mixture of emotions—from sadness, reaching out to one another, to where, by the end of the bus ride, I felt like I was just all by myself, all alone, experiencing this. I couldn't wait to get back to college with my friends, where I would go right after I got to Yale, and then go back home again so that I could be with them to deal with this whole thing.

—⚬—

RICHARD: I think what they [Kennedy's cabinet] were trying to do to Castro was very foolish, and they obviously didn't succeed in doing it. Castro outlived all of them and is still there; he's still alive. There were attempts to assassinate him, and they didn't work. Bobby did want to pursue the Cuban Communist government, and he was clearly involved in that. I was traveling with Bobby in Latin America, and Communist groups were demonstrating against him. He said to me, "God, I saved that guy's life." What he meant by that was somehow he had prevented Castro from being killed. I don't know if that's true of course, but that was Bobby's reaction to the people demonstrating against him.

DORIS: Dick once met with Che Guevara, who gave him a box of cigars to bring back to Kennedy. Dick didn't know that one of the ways they had considered for killing Castro was with an exploding cigar. He gave the box to Kennedy, who asked, "Are they good?" and he said, "Mr. President, they're the best." Kennedy took it, cut it off, and lit it. Then he turned to Dick and said, "You should've smoked the first one." Only later did he come to realize what that meant.

RICHARD: I had no idea at the time. I was involved in it only at the very beginning, when we were beginning to set up a counter-Castro operation. After that I was involved with Latin America as a whole and had very little to do with the anti-Castro operations, which were looking silly then as they did now.

After Kennedy was killed, I thought there was a possible conspiracy there. There was a lot of hatred running around the country at the time, especially given his sympathy for blacks and civil rights, but in all the years that followed we've never come up with anything. Bobby Kennedy thought there might be something else there, and I think he said he would pursue it if he got to be president. I've read all the books and heard all the arguments. We're unwilling to believe that a lone, crazed individual could have done this to our country, but the evidence is that that's what it was. I'll have to go with that.

Bobby never wanted to talk about it, but he suddenly turned to Dick when they were in New York socially together and said, "If it was anybody, I think it was the Mafia, not the Cubans."

DORIS: Bobby never wanted to talk about it, but he suddenly turned to Dick when they were in New York socially together and said, "If it was anybody, I think it was the Mafia, not the Cubans."

RICHARD: "If anybody else was involved." But it's that "if." Bobby had made deep enemies among some of the Mafia chiefdoms. They obviously hated him. But nobody was ever able to link it. And God knows enough people have studied it.

DORIS: Johnson would talk about JFK and rather with warmth toward him. Johnson hated being vice president, and he wasn't happy at all in that role. But instead of blaming JFK, he much preferred blaming Robert Kennedy. Johnson hated Bobby, hated him with a passion. I think he projected all of his anger about being vice president and being impotent onto Bobby.

Johnson said, "JFK liked listening to my stories." Every now and then he said, "You know, he was a young whippersnapper when I was the majority leader." Kennedy had that yellow, jaundiced face when he was in the Senate. When he was swimming in the pool, telling those stories, you could tell Johnson loved the idea that at one point he'd been on top of JFK. I'll never forget when Chappaquiddick happened; I was with Johnson at the time. At first he felt sad. How could this happen once again to the Kennedy family? It just seemed like fate was unkind. Then he turned around and said, "If I were in a car with a girl and a bumblebee stung the girl, I'd be in Sing Sing. This guy's going to be a hero." He didn't turn out to be a hero for it, however.

Passing the Civil Rights Bill took both Kennedy's death and Lyndon Johnson's leadership of the Senate. It was an extraordinary thing LBJ did in that very first speech to the joint session of Congress: "No memorial could speak more eloquently to JFK's death than the passage of this civil rights bill at the earliest possible moment." He made it the test of his first year in the presidency, and that was a risky thing to do. Had he not succeeded in that between November 1963 and his own election in 1964, he would have been a failure. The chances of getting that filibuster broken were very slight in anybody's mind. It had never been broken on the Civil Rights Bill.

But LBJ was at home on Capitol Hill. This is what he was made for. It was what he was born for. It became a deeper passion for him than I think it was for JFK. Johnson called senators in the middle of the night. He had them over for breakfast, for lunch, for dinner. He loved it. I don't think JFK loved putting his arm around these guys and doing the false things that you have to do. JFK was rational; he thought it was time for the civil rights movement. He would've done what he needed to, but I don't think he would have put his whole soul and person, capacities, or talents into it. So that's a huge thing that happened. The civil rights movement itself started it. JFK gave words to it, and that's where JFK could summon the country in a way that LBJ wasn't as easily able to do. But then LBJ got it done, and Johnson also did it pretty well with the Voting Rights Act.

RICHARD: Johnson was much more skillful dealing with Congress than Kennedy ever could've been. Johnson knew all these people. He lived among them on the Hill; he knew how to deal with them, and he was shameless when he did that.

When Johnson was president, I left the White House to go into opposition on the Vietnam War. Would Kennedy have continued it? I don't think so, because John Kennedy was a profoundly rational human being. Bobby was much more guided by his emotions, but John Kennedy was guided by his reasoning and thought. The Vietnam War turned out to be trying to do something that was impossible. It became totally irrational and very costly for the United States, and I think Kennedy would've stopped at that point. But nobody can know what he would've done if he was confronted with the reality of losing in Vietnam, which was going to come. I like to think he would have gotten out and stopped.

The only way to end the war was to get out, and it destroyed Johnson's presidency because he didn't get out. I prefer to believe that Kennedy would've realized that. I think he would've tried to get out of it, but I don't know. That decision is lost to history. He also had the strength of the five advisors. He would've turned them around. When they saw what he wanted to do, they would move in that direction.

DORIS: The promise is big because it sets forth for people what might have been, not just for Kennedy but for the country, had that movement of caring about social justice and economic opportunity not been cut by the war. Three years isn't a very long time to become a great president. Most of our great presidents have had two terms, not one—much less just three years.

I remember Dick telling me he had a discussion with Bobby Kennedy at one point. Bobby was lamenting that it wasn't fair that his brother had only had three years, and how could he be a great president with only three years? Dick, trying to console him, said, "Julius Caesar only had three years." Bobby looked at him and said, "Yeah, but it helps to have Shakespeare write about you."

Among popular opinion, Kennedy still ranks up there among high presidents, which just shows the power of the memory and the power

---

Dick, trying to console him, said, "Julius Caesar only had three years." Bobby looked at him and said, "Yeah, but it helps to have Shakespeare write about you."

of the pictures. Among historians, I would guess he's probably an average president. I haven't seen a recent poll, but I think the Cuban Missile Crisis will always be considered a huge turning point. The fact that he turned away from that and then gave the American University speech shortly thereafter will be a big thing. The fact that he was there when the civil rights movement was being pushed forward will help. But there just wasn't time for his promise to be fulfilled, to allow him to become a Washington, a Lincoln, an FDR.

When you think about the eras of progressive change that America went through in the twentieth century, you had one at the turn of the twentieth century with the Progressive Era. You had the New Deal, and you had the 1960s. Those are eras when the country was moving toward its own ideals and trying to realize them: social justice, economic opportunity.

When you look back on those times, you feel proud of what your country was doing and what it was working toward. Kennedy was there at the conjunction of a lot of different movements. You've got the civil rights movement; you've got the women's movement. Those things are moving forward and fundamentally changing people's lives, and the fact that he was there, even if he didn't start those movements—he fostered them perhaps, and his being there helped to engender them—it reminds you of what the country can be like. That's really special. The other thing I think has lasted for him forever is photography and moving pictures.

Had he lived in the time of Lincoln, where we only would've seen him without a smile on his face, with his back stiff in front of a camera, in two dimensions, I'm not sure the hold would have been there. But we have that ever-present young person shot down in the prime of his life— so handsome, so vital, so full of life. Everybody looks back and remembers a time when he or she was young as a result of that.

On top of that you have the family. Had he not had Teddy and Bobby and all the people who have come since, you wonder whether the story might have had an earlier ending, but the family kept going on in public life. Then with the family having the deaths they had; when Bobby dies, you go back and watch JFK's assassination, and you think about him. It just kept that memory alive for a much longer period of time. Modern technology and the photography, when he was president historically and what the country was going through, and the fact that there was a family so that the chapter didn't end with his death, I think, makes a difference.

PART THREE
POLITICS

Mike Barnicle

Veteran journalist and commentator Mike Barnicle began his career as a speech writer and aid to prominent political figures, including former California senator John Tunney, vice presidential hopeful Edmund Muskie, and Robert F. Kennedy. Moving into journalism, he wrote for the *Boston Herald, New York Daily News,* and *Boston Globe.* Barnicle's regular column in the *Globe* ran from 1974 to 1998, and his mid-1970s coverage of school desegregation in Boston helped earn the paper a Pulitzer Prize for Public Service. He has won numerous awards and recognition for his work over the years—including honors from the Associated Press, United Press International, and DuPont Columbia— and has appeared frequently on MSNBC's *Morning Joe, Hardball with Chris Matthews,* and NBC's *Today Show.* In 1963 he was a twenty-year-old student at Boston University.

I was in a second-floor apartment that I was sharing with two other guys. We were going to Boston University at 834 Beacon Street in Boston, Massachusetts, right outside Kenmore Square. Like most Americans my age, I can shut my eyes and see everything as if it's a Moviola replaying itself. I can remember the bulletin on the radio: Three shots had been fired at the presidential motorcade in Dallas, Texas. I remember the bulletin a few minutes later that the president had been taken to Parkland Hospital and then reports that the president had died. I can remember going to the window of the apartment; there was a liquor store beneath. The owner of the liquor store came out into the street with her hands up in the air shrieking, shrieking, "*Someone shot the president!*" Passersby not knowing—there was no instantaneous communication news in those days as there is now—passersby stunned and shocked.

John F. Kennedy was shot on a Friday, and I took the train from Boston to Fitchburg, where my mother lived, that Friday afternoon. It was a train of grief—completely silent. By noontime the next day, Saturday, my mother insisted that someone had to represent the family at the funeral in Washington, DC. I didn't have a car. I barely had a license. A couple of friends of mine, older friends, were going to drive to Washington to the funeral. We didn't know anything from anything. We drove to Washington. We stood outside the Capitol for nearly a day, when the casket bearing the president was brought to the rotunda. We felt then that we had attended the wake of the president of the United States, and then we drove ten hours back to Massachusetts. So my mother was happy. She was satisfied that the family had been represented at the funeral. It was an Irish Catholic pilgrimage.

We weren't alone, my two friends and I. People had come in buses and trains. I likened it to reading about Lincoln's funeral and Roosevelt's funeral, where the train came north from Georgia, because to look around the Capitol Mall and outside the Capitol from in front of the Capitol all the way to the Supreme Court: hundreds of thousands of people. They weren't rich people. They weren't famous people. They were ordinary people with calluses on their hands who had felt compelled and been drawn to Washington to bury their president.

———

The Kennedy compound is literally a bookend of so much of our history—the lawn we see here, the house itself, which is a museum to a family that has made a stamp on American history. Senator Ted Kennedy sat on this porch on summer nights, sometimes with me, and talked in a nostalgic and wistful way about the helicopter coming from Otis Air Force Base to land on this lawn carrying the president of the United States, his brother, John F. Kennedy. The children who were around at that time, the Kennedy children, competed with one another on the weekend to see which one was best in order to take the helicopter ride back to Otis with the president on Sunday night.

All of this was started by Joseph P. Kennedy, who came here as a second-generation Irish American, a Catholic, who prospered and knew what he wanted for his family from a very early time. Only in later years did people like Ted and Robert Kennedy realize the hold, the grip, Ambassador Kennedy had on the family. The love they had for him and the influence he had on them, I think, only became apparent really as they proceeded to the presidency, in the case of John F. Kennedy, and to the Senate in the case of Robert and Edward Kennedy. The impact he had on the family, it's here today. They were given a path, and they didn't have to worry about what the rest of us have to worry about. But they worried about other things, they'll tell you. They had the license and the liberty, freed from having to make money to feed their families that most people have to do. They had the license and the liberty to carve out their own lives, and that's what Ambassador Kennedy really intended for them to do.

In talking to Ted Kennedy several times about that, part of John F. Kennedy's appeal, part of his wry, ironic humor, his approach to life itself, was because he knew innately that he was number two in the ambassador's mind in terms of who would be president, who could be president among his children. Joe Kennedy Jr. died over the English Channel toward the conclusion of World War II, and the mantle passed to Jack Kennedy, and he certainly was carrying the mantle. But he always knew, according to Teddy, that he was number two.

I became aware of them quite early in my life. I was a little kid. My uncle had been killed at Midway, and he received the Distinguished Service Cross, which was the second-highest award granted to those who die in a war. My grandmother thus was a gold star mother. When he was running for reelection to the United States Senate from Massachusetts in 1958, John F. Kennedy visited my grandmother at our home. I can remember then being dazzled by the sight of the United States senator—one, by an Irish Catholic United States senator, and two, by a United States senator and Irish Catholic who had almost attained the nomination for vice president of the United States in 1956.

They came to Hyannis on weekends. Politics was always the meal that was served here, I think, three, four, five times a day with everyone around the table. It was all politics. Fun— but it was always competition with the fun, the touch football games they did out here. There was always a fierce sense of competition that they handed down to everyone amazingly.

John F. Kennedy Jr. had a touch football team here. He gathered neighborhood kids, but he selected which kids in the neighborhood he thought were better than the other kids so that his team could win, so he could beat Robert Kennedy Jr. The competition gene in that family is incredible. As a family, they were all for one and one for all, but within the family the competition could be pretty brutal in terms of how they would go after each other. I don't mean physically. But no one was spared the cutting humor, the joke, or, if they overstepped their bounds, getting called on.

I don't think the succeeding generations can sustain the legacy. We think writing now is 140 characters in a tweet. Everybody has a blog. We beep at drive-through windows. We're such an impatient culture. I don't think the memory of that family, the legacy of the family, of the presidency, can sustain itself.

So that was the pane of glass I was looking through, and I still think I'm looking through it in a sense when I think of him, when I see him. I still see him in terms of either 1958, coming to visit my grandmother, or in 1962, the presidential motorcade going up Commonwealth Avenue in Boston as he was en route to a Democrat state fundraising committee dinner on behalf of his brother, Ted, who was running for the Senate in 1962. I still see those things.

One night several years ago, the fog just coming in over Hyannis Port Harbor, Senator Ted Kennedy was sitting on the porch, smoking cigars, having some after-dinner refreshments. I asked him, "Do you ever sit here and look out at the ocean, and when you shut your eyes do you see your brothers?"

He said almost instantaneously, "All the time, all the time. When I'm out on the ocean in my boat, I can see them. I can feel them with me. They've always been with me. They'll always be with me." The house, the place, those memories, the presidency—quite a thing.

That was the beginning of the rock that began rolling downhill, and that's one of the largest reasons that it [the assassination] still has such a hold, such a grip on us even before you get to the various conspiracy theories that are out there. The hold that President Kennedy had was on the nation, but more powerfully on our imaginations. It instilled such pride in people, my mother, my father. My father had died shortly after Jack Kennedy was elected president. The pride they felt in having an Irish Catholic in the White House—because they were of an age and of a generation where they could recall and recite various elements of prejudice toward them because they were Irish Catholic, coming to this country from Ireland—the sense of pride it instilled in people, my mother especially . . .

My mother had a picture of John F. Kennedy on the wall with a palm from Palm Sunday. The palm had to have been fifteen to twenty years old before she took it down. But she never got over the pride she had in the fact that John F. Kennedy was president. Nor I think did she ever get over the sadness of losing him. She felt it was a personal loss. I think many Irish Catholics, especially around Boston, felt it as a personal loss. They took that from us. They took him from us.

> *Edward Kennedy said, "When I'm out on the ocean in my boat, I can see them. I can feel them with me."*

Harry Belafonte

Having risen to prominence in the 1950s as the "King of Calypso," Harry Belafonte leveraged his musical success and fame to emphasize civil rights activism. He had campaigned for JFK in 1960, performed at the inaugural gala hosted by Frank Sinatra, and become a key supporter of Rev. Martin Luther King, the 1961 Freedom Riders, and others fighting for the cause. Three months before Kennedy went to Dallas, Belafonte helped organize King's historic March on Washington, the setting for his famous "I Have a Dream" speech.

I was first really aware of John F. Kennedy during his [1952] run for the Senate in Massachusetts. He had been brought to my attention as a rising star on the Democratic horizon, and there was some question as to what he would mean to the black community up in Boston, one of two places in the North that were as extreme in their racial conflict as any Southern city. The intensity on race issues was quite severe. Based upon the racial conflict, our and Dr. King's focus was that it was one of the cities we'd have to have on our list of places that must be attended to.

In that area, there was enough liberal power for us to call upon to stir things up a bit and get us on point. When John Kennedy stepped in, there was some question as to who he was and what he brought to the table. We were to find out later that he wasn't all that we'd hoped he would be—things in the Senate he voted on troubled us, both on foreign policy as well as domestic issues. I didn't really get to know him with any great specificity until he ran for the presidency. Up until that time, tracking his record in Congress, it was rather—from our perspective—undistinguished. There wasn't anything for us to be terribly excited about. As a matter of fact, there were good reasons for us to be somewhat cautious as to how he might vote on civil rights, human rights, and other such issues.

When he ran for the presidency in 1956, I got a call from a young man by the name of Frank Montero. He was an African American out of Connecticut or Massachusetts, if I remember correctly. But I knew Montero, and he said that Kennedy wanted to see me. I was curious. I didn't know him. We'd not had any exchange, and why he wanted to see me was a curiosity to me. So I said, "If he's looking for me to have some relationship to him running for the presidency, that's off the table because I'm committed to Adlai Stevenson." Although the primaries hadn't fully played out and we were in a foot race, my loyalties were to the Stevenson camp. However, they were most insistent, and when I met with Kennedy he came up to my apartment in Manhattan on the Upper West Side. He had just left New Jersey, campaigning for the New Jersey primary.

Through Frank Montero, I had discovered before he arrived that one of the reasons he was very insistent on talking with me was that they had just lost Jackie Robinson as a favorite son, as somebody who'd be there for the Democratic Party, pushing the issues of the Democratic Party in relation to the black vote. But there was a conflict: Robinson was quite angry with the Democratic Party for certain racial slights.

As a matter of fact, in pressuring the Democratic Party for details on what would happen with the black community and the black vote, what they were offering to the black community—Jackie Robinson decided to break ranks and endorsed Nixon. This gravely challenged the Democratic Party and its sensibilities to the black vote. Although they were very cautious about how they treated the black vote, they were fully aware that they had to have it. By Jackie leaving, one of the great icons of the period and even now, they had to look around for who could fill that space—who could be a counterbalance to the fact that Jackie was leaving. A number of people of color

When I met with John, I was quite taken by the fact that he knew so little about the black community.

were called, and I was one of them. The Democratic Party strategist concluded that to have me in their camp would be a big plus in a response to Jackie Robinson's break. They would push me a bit to the front of their game. When I met with John, I was quite taken by the fact that he knew so little about the black community. He knew the headlines of the day, but he really wasn't anywhere . . . nuanced or detailed on the deep depth of black anguish, of what our struggle was really about. It kind of passed him in the night. He had some familiarity, but there wasn't a great deal.

I asked him in detail about Dr. King. He knew very little, just that somewhere there was this force, and he was out there making some mischief. He knew for a fact that the most important element within the Democratic Party, which was the Southern Democratic oligarchy, that vote was seriously threatened by Dr. King. Therefore he had reason to keep as much distance from King as he possibly could because he needed that Southern power, the Dixiecrats.

Kennedy was not only charming but also had a bit of a wit to him. He knew some things about me as an artist and some things about my career, but I could tell he wasn't a passionate fan. I understood that the evening we met in my home was strictly a political move and a political agenda.

In the final analysis, I told him that I wouldn't endorse him, that I wouldn't be in his camp until we knew more clearly and in greater detail what his platform would be in relationship to the black vote and black people in general, that I wouldn't even consider endorsing him because I was committed to Stevenson. I remember him saying to me, just as he was about to leave, that if down the road he was able to gain the endorsement for the primaries and became the official nominee for the Democratic Party, would I then endorse him? I said, "Let's cross that bridge when you come to it, and let's see where the whole political landscape resides."

I didn't talk to him again until I began to encounter people like Harris Wofford and Bobby Kennedy and more people in the Kennedy camp who began to move more vigorously toward the front of the game and began to dig more deeply into the black community. I had just come back from touring Europe, and the primaries had fallen his way. He had won it. Then Frank Montero again called and said, "We'd like to talk to you again." When they came that time, they had far more details on the black vote, what the platform would look like, and I said, yes, that I would help him.

I think there's absolutely no question that not only did history do more to make John Kennedy than John Kennedy did to make history, but that history was precisely the upheaval which this country had at its dawning. The black movement was very vigorous and beginning to move into a place that really had him imbalanced. He didn't quite know how to deal with us. The war in Vietnam wasn't quite the war it came to be, but it was beginning to bubble seriously during his watch. I think, between the peace movement and certainly during the civil rights movement, he was caught in a place for which he was completely ill prepared to lead. But as events grew, as things revealed themselves and he had to make decisions, there's just no question that he always fell on the right side of the question—that as he evolved and as he grew, he became more and more caught up with us. I think more than anything else, not the politics so much but the moral persuasion, the moral force of a cause, was what made him have to take a good, hard look at who we were. But I must say that, more than anyone else in that family, Bobby was the most effective.

Bobby had a big hand in shaping how the campaign would be handled, how we would deal with a lot of issues, deal with people of color—a lot of that fell into Bobby's space. It was Bobby who went down to Georgia and called the Georgia state legislator when Dr. King was imprisoned. John called Coretta, but it was Bobby who called the governor of Georgia and worked it out, put the game on the table.

I thought that Dr. King endorsing Kennedy was a place Dr. King didn't want to go or shouldn't go. We had no idea what this guy would do. We had no idea what his policy would really be, and one thing Dr. King couldn't afford was to endorse someone who, during his presidency, turned out to be not in the best interests of black people. If he had endorsed him, a lot of that blame would be at Dr. King's doorstep. So we mapped out a way to do it so that it appeared as though Dr. King was endorsing him but hadn't really, and that was an ad that we took out in the *New York Times*. The ad applauded John Kennedy for reaching in and saving Dr. King from the humiliation and the threat of being sentenced to life on the Georgia chain gang. That kind of gave the word that Dr. King was favorably inclined but hadn't officially endorsed him. The rest of us did.

We stepped in very vigorously, and I campaigned for John and got to know him. I wasn't as intimately engaged with him—although we had reason for meetings and exchanges—as I was with Bobby. Bobby and I had great traction and great moments together because the Justice Department and all that Bobby was about was directly in our crosshairs every day. It was extremely important to us to have America and the Justice Department on the side of the movement, because without the federal force, without the federal government, without the federal courts, without the Supreme Court, without those forces landing squarely on our side of the struggle, we had no other place else to go.

Not only did I share a feeling that the Kennedys were of our time and a huge look into the future of America, but we liked the style in which he [Kennedy] did it. He did it by identifying with an America that was far more energized with the possibilities of conquering the future. We're going to space. We're going to change the way in which all things are done. We're going to have a foreign policy that looks at the world differently. All of these things coming from the Kennedy camp were very refreshing and very promising for us. So though we had some areas in which we had issues, the vast canvas of the Kennedy period was a lot of things that were in our favor.

He had style. He loved the popular culture of the day. He not only loved what Sinatra and the Rat Pack and all of those with him did, but he showed up at my concerts, invited me to the White House, and made me know that what I represented culturally he found tasteful. Bobby and Ethel came very often, especially to the concerts I gave in Washington, DC, at the Carter Barron Amphitheater. With Kennedy, with his brother, and with the family in general, especially Sarge Shriver, there was a sense that the Kennedy family was our future, was what America and what certainly white America should be about and could be about.

We had a lot invested in who they were, and we enjoyed them as a family. A lot of the stuff came out about his handsomeness and philandering—that played a very little role in our interests. We were sure there was a lot of flirtation going on. Everywhere I went, especially when there was an entertainment clan, the Hollywood group, all the most popular actresses and actors were vying for space with the Kennedys. I had a friend who once said, "Popular people used to have things thrown at them by their fan base, handkerchiefs and underclothing and all sorts of things. But the Kennedys had women throwing body parts." That's how insane it was in our culture about the power and the attractiveness of this family.

That same year, Dr. King's "I Have a Dream" speech was for me, like for everyone else, an epiphany. To see that much passion contained, to see that much of America on display, to see people from every strata of life caught in this magnificent moment, displaying and letting the world hear their voice in relation to the best that was in the American profile was quite breathtaking.

I had been called upon to gather the international celebrity community of artists. There were huge political sensibilities at stake and certainly Kennedy's sense of jeopardy in his political ambition and all else that was at play, including J. Edgar Hoover, because I think he had a huge impact on this, pushed this to the edge. In the face of all of that, debating with the White House, trying to bring reason to the table, they were deeply concerned. They said there was going to be a lot of violence. Even if we thought within our own ranks they were lovely people and good of heart and there'd be no violence, we had no way of controlling external forces that might infiltrate, that had mischief on their minds. We had to assure them that we felt secure enough in the way we were doing this. We had massive labor movement players, and a lot of the security we had was heavily dependent on how well the labor movement and labor workers handled crowd control.

The voices of the high-profile artists of the day were very much in evidence. Needless to say, when that was pulled off with such great success, the windfall of good that came from that moment in our history did an awful lot to convince the Kennedys and certain forces within the Democratic Party that we were much better at the game than anybody had imagined. For us to be able to pull that off—the unification of labor, show business, artists, workers, blacks, and across the entire spectrum of American society, all in evidence in harmony—gave them greater faith for the future that was yet to come but was to be filled with so much tragedy, with the murder of [John] Kennedy, Dr. King, and Bobby, even people like Medgar Evers. The worst was yet to come.

When the president was shot, I was in Europe. I had just embarked on the first of several missions to ascertain the climate in Europe for our movement. We did it for two reasons: not only to broaden the base of international information on what our struggle was about but also because we were desperate for resources. We were drying up very quickly. Too much bail money, too much was being expended. It was a very costly movement. Too many bodies to move, too many cars to hire, too many people in different areas that needed funding for our cause. We needed to find other frontiers. There were a lot in the civil rights movement who resisted the idea of going to Europe. For some it was the edge of a betrayal that we took a domestic issue, as they called it, and put it into the camp of a neighbor's purview for them to have a commentary on.

But there were others of us who felt very strongly that betrayal was falsely concluded, that our mission had far more meaning than that narrow sphere of betraying the family. If there's a cruelty to the extent that black people were experiencing America's animosity toward us, what family were we supposed to be protecting?

On November 22nd I was in Paris reaching out to the arts community, and we eventually made a successful showing there. I was having a meeting with Yves Montand, Simone Signoret, Jules Dassin, and Melina Mercouri. They were in Paris shooting the film *Topkapi*, and I'd gone to the studio to watch them shoot. Afterward we were going to James Michener's house for a kind of a cocktail evening. Word came while we were at the studio that John Kennedy had been shot. We weren't quite sure of the accuracy of the information or what the details were. Some said he had died, and some said he was just gravely wounded. When we got the information, we were absolutely stunned, like the whole world was. And by the time we retired to the cocktail party, everybody was caught up in the news. It was on television, French television, and fortunately a lot of people spoke fluent French who could translate the details for those who were not so fluent. At that very moment, I tried to reach Dr. King. I tried to reach Andy Young. I tried to reach Stan Levinson, who was a real close friend and confidante on issues. I called Coretta King. We were not only caught up in the great tragedy of the moment but were desperate for information as to who did and what caused it. Our great concern was that someone of color may have done this thing. Certainly the mood and the anger and the rage that the black community was feeling suggested that somewhere in our midst there may have been an individual or a group that stepped into the space to have this act of vengeance. I needed to get back immediately and was able to get a plane that very evening, Air France, to get back to the United States and hook up with Dr. King. But I remember that I was in that environment, with these artists and friends, when the information came.

What made me concerned was that a little group had just been formed called the SNCC (the Student Non-Violent Coordinating Committee) in which I had played an important part. Ella Baker, who was one of the leaders in our movement, had reached out to me to talk about this young group, that they deserved to be funded and to be recognized and that most of them would perhaps be breakaways from the Southern Christian Leadership Conference and Dr. King's movement.

When I met these young people, most of them were teenagers, some in their very early twenties, and some younger, like Julian Bond, John Lewis, and Diane Nash. She was seventeen years old and with child. These are all young people, but in their midst is a group of very angry street guys. They belonged to different groups and were the earliest mobilization toward what became known as the Black Panthers. I was concerned that SNCC and some disgruntled young man brandishing a rifle, who

At that very moment, I tried to reach Dr. King.

had always said, "An eye for an eye, tooth for a tooth," would be found to be the assassin. So for us, there was a visceral, deep energy to quickly find who this was and how to prepare ourselves for it. We had a meeting with Dr. King, Andy Young, and others to discuss what happened if this turned out to be in our camp. For what this meant to our movement, meant to our people, and meant to America, I don't think we ever would have been forgiven had it turned out that a person of color had done that.

Regarding the assassination itself, something sticks in my mind that's almost indelible. Bill Moyers interviewed one of the high-ranking officials, if not the head, of the CIA, and in that interview, way back—I think color television hadn't even been fully introduced—Bill Moyers asked about assassinations and about foreign policy and the relationship to assassinations. The interviewee said that in the CIA and in the work they did, they couldn't be distracted just with political or moral consequence. When Bill evoked the moral question, the interviewee said, "We have no moral questions in the work we do," and Moyers asked, "But what happens if you get caught?" I'll never forget the interviewee. He said, "We'll never get caught." Bill pressed the point: "But what happens if somewhere the—" The guy looked at him, very calmly and very precisely, and said, "We will never get caught."

I don't know that what Malcolm [X] said—"The chickens have come home to roost"—had to do specifically with the vindictiveness of the moment, that you're finally getting paid back. I thought it was far more visceral. I don't think it was just a view of history. Malcolm was somewhere else. He saw it as an act of vengeance. He was also speaking, I think, for what is still a characteristic in American foreign policy. We are killing off a lot of innocent people, and there's a price being paid that Americans know nothing about because we're not in the middle of the anguish of daily losing innocent victims. When we do experience it, we go ballistic, correctly so, whether it's the Twin Towers or whether it's what just recently happened in Boston. When it happens to America, we are most passionate in our response. This goes on every day in the lives of tens of thousands of people, all over this globe. This goes on, and there's a deep hurt, a deep resentment and a great political loss for America. These things happen, and even back then I think what Malcolm was alluding to was that somehow justice was being meted out.

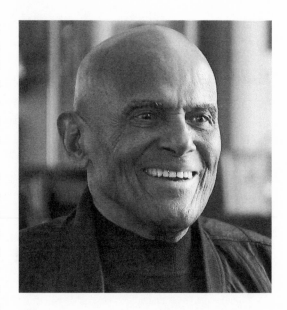

What saddens me is that America was made to witness its vulnerability as a nation that believes it's on a righteous course, that says it is morally powerful, morally precise. Those deaths did an awful lot to jolt us into a new space of thinking about ourselves as a people, as a nation, as a force. What is deeply saddening is that we don't seem to have learned much from that fact. Although other characteristics attest that we are on a correct path in the decisions we're making that affect human conduct and the personality of our country politically, we have still given much too much space to the mischief makers. We still give much too much in this country to those who would willingly put America into a bloodbath and are holding onto their impression of others. America is as deeply racist today as it was then. It only plays out that theme very differently because the success of our journey has been to change the law, to force the law to be enforced by the vigilant, but by and large there are still those who are quite willing and quite eager to put this country into a bloodbath because they feel theirs is the only cause and theirs is the correct mission for America. Racism is very much alive and very much at play.

I also think a lot of the criticism being laid out against Barack Obama that is ascribed solely to political differences is infinitely deeper than that. I feel a lot of it is precisely the fact that a big part of America has never been able to accept that a man of color sits at the head of our government, leading us to decisions they must abide by. That sticks in their craw. They're

America is as deeply racist today as it was then.

fiercely angry. Those Southern forces who were defeated during the days of Kennedy and Johnson have never forgiven the Democratic Party and the Dixiecrats. The Democratic hierarchy fled and became the new [conservative] wing of the Republican Party—that's being played out today. The hostage America became to those forces in the South that were deeply angered by that new experience is very much at play today. They haven't lost that sting yet.

Andrew Young

In 1963 Andrew Young was a thirty-one-year-old pastor and civil rights leader, about to be named executive director of the Southern Christian Leadership Conference in Atlanta, Georgia. Started by Martin Luther King Jr., the nonviolent SCLC aimed to end segregation in the South. Young's work in coordinating many of the key protests in the early '60s proved fundamental to the passage of the Civil Rights Act and the Voting Rights Act. Young went on to become a US congressman, ambassador to the UN, and mayor of Atlanta. In 2003 he created the Andrew Young Foundation to support and promote education, health, leadership, and human rights in America, Africa, and the Caribbean.

I was in Chicago, and Kennedy was making a speech in a black playground on the South Side. I went, and I have never seen anybody light up a crowd like that. People didn't campaign in the black community very much before him, but the fact that he was there, and to see him and the response—I thought that was a new day.

When Martin Luther King Jr. was arrested and Kennedy made a call to Coretta, nothing like that had ever happened before. For somebody running for president, being concerned about the wife of Dr. King—and he wasn't even thought of necessarily as a great civil rights leader yet; King was just a black man in prison—that Kennedy made a call got him elected. That plus Chicago. Dick Gregory used to say that people voted in Chicago like they'd never voted before. It was the turnout in Chicago that actually swung that election. Those two events helped make him president.

Kennedy was a man of vision, the vision that America has got to lead the world. That was at the end of the Second World War. I remind people all the time that what the Second World War did was stabilize the world, which had been destabilized by the printing press in the fourteenth century. When they printed the Bible in German and Latin and English—every time the printing press reprinted the Bible somewhere, you had a revolution and a new nation. It took the Second World War, the New Deal, the Great Society, and the Marshall Plan to make all that work. For the first time in five hundred years, by the 1960s the world was on a level playing field. Every nation on the planet was

growing at 6 to 10 percent, and it looked like we really had it together. Then came the combination of assassinations, which took away the visionary leadership, and technology. If it hadn't been for that generation of television journalists reporting on our civil rights movement, we wouldn't have had a civil rights movement.

We didn't expect a lot from him. Jimmy Carter, Lyndon Johnson, and Bill Clinton grew up in the South. They had black friends as children. But the Kennedys really had no contact with black people; they even had Irish maids. We knew their hearts were in the right place, but they just didn't know any better. It was mostly in the interaction with Bobby Kennedy. But the president and Dr. King always related very well. Whenever Martin went to visit him, he said that when you meet with President Kennedy, he asks you questions for an hour. If you meet with President Johnson, he talks for an hour. The truth of it was that Kennedy was a seeker in the

Whenever Martin went to visit him, he said that when you meet with President Kennedy, he asks you questions for an hour. If you meet with President Johnson, he talks for an hour.

human rights area. This wasn't naturally a part of his background, except that growing up Irish they'd had to fight through discrimination in New England when he and when his father were growing up, but they'd sort of come through that.

Once Kennedy came on the scene, he represented the future. I never missed a Kennedy speech. When the president spoke, everything stopped. It was like Joe Lewis fighting or Jackie Robinson starting in baseball. We hung on the words of the president just because he talked about civil rights, acknowledging it as something he was aware of as a deep-seated American problem. I saw pictures of John Kennedy and Dr. King in households in Kenya and in the artisan shacks of the carvers in Zimbabwe and Tanzania. The world identified with these men. They had a vision that could unite the planet. Now there were competing visions at the same time, and the Cold War view was competing with this global, universal vision.

I was at a training conference for voter registration workers in Frogmore, South Carolina, at the Penn Community Center. Septima Clark had developed a literacy program. We were teaching people to read and write, to register to vote. Dorothy Cotton and I were the staff, and we had fifty people from across the South, from Louisiana, Mississippi, Alabama; these were the leaders we were training, who later became the voter registration leaders. Their children became the elected officials, and for me that was the heart of the civil rights movement.

When we heard the news, everybody immediately stopped and got on their knees—those people, they were what the Bible calls "the salt of

the earth." They were not educated. When they prayed, it wasn't so much in words as in chants and song; and when we heard that he had died, the prayer continued for America. Dr. King was coming there. He was really shaken. He said, "If the hundreds of Secret Service men can't protect the president, then anytime they want us we've got to be ready to go, because there is no protection." He took the president's death as a sign of his own assassination. We preachers try to make something good out of every tragedy, and there's an old expression, "There's no remission of sins without the shedding of innocent blood."

Lyndon Johnson was ready, but we felt that Kennedy gave his life for us. It was the moral mandate that America had to change. I don't think anybody else could've done what Lyndon Johnson did. I'm almost ashamed to say that I doubt Kennedy could've gotten a civil rights bill through Congress, and yet without Kennedy's life and death, Lyndon Johnson couldn't have gotten it through. So in many respects, together they saved America.

> *Everybody immediately stopped and got on their knees.*

The conversations between Lyndon Johnson and Richard Russell are classic; the one thing Lyndon Johnson said that I disagree with was,

"This will cost us the South for generations." In a way that's true, except that
he became president, Jimmy Carter
became president, and Bill Clinton
became president. Eisenhower's judges
really paved the way for the civil rights

We felt that Kennedy gave his life for us.

movement, from the Supreme Court right on down to the Fifth Circuit,
but that period gave us a lift. It gave us a challenge. It set the stage for
modern America, for a modern world. At the same time, it led to the end
of what you call the Greatest Generation.

I don't think it drained hope; I think it produced a new generation. Bill
Clinton will say it was John Kennedy who inspired him, Jimmy Carter,
from rural Georgia. There is from the Southland, and from the struggles
we've had, an emergence of leadership and vision that was strengthened,
the revolutionary vision that all men are endowed by the Creator—not
by their wealth, not by their education or their color, but by the Creator.
We have the need. We have the technology, and we actually have the
money. There is no deficit in the global economy, but nobody's giving us
the vision or has put together the vision that would enable us to bring this
money to meet human needs in a safe, secure, and profitable way.

All of the pieces are there; we just don't have the kind of vision that
would've come out of a Kennedy—if he'd lived another fifty years or
another forty years—or Martin Luther King, Malcolm X, or any of the
leaders who were taken from us too soon. Each of these men stood for
something, and though they were killed, I say that the assassins' bullets
just freed the spirits. The spirit of John Kennedy is very much alive. The
strength of this country is that we do represent the whole world, and
these men somehow captured that vision.

Carlos Bringuier

Born and raised in Cuba, where he worked as a lawyer, Carlos Bringuier came to America in 1961 and opened a clothing store in New Orleans called Casa Roca. In 1963 he was a twenty-nine-year-old exile, activist, and delegate to the anti-Castro Student Revolutionary Directorate. On August 9 of that year, Lee Harvey Oswald was handing out "Fair Play for Cuba Committee" leaflets when Bringuier started a fight with him. Both were arrested. A week later, Oswald debated the issue of Fidel Castro and Cuba with Bringuier on the Bill Stuckey Radio Show. Tony Plana played Bringuier in the 1991 Oliver Stone film *JFK*.

I had great faith and expectations for Kennedy. I thought he understood the Cuban situation and that he was going to solve the Cuban problem—and ultimately the problem of the United States—because Castro, a Communist ninety miles from the United States, was a very dangerous thing for the US democracy.

I heard about the Bay of Pigs plan in Guatemala right before I arrived in America. One of my brothers was already in the training camp in Guatemala, and from Argentina I went to Guatemala to visit my parents. I learned about the invasion then because my brother was training as a paratrooper. When I arrived in Miami, I came looking for work, but then I got taken over by the romanticism of those years, about freeing Cuba. So I signed up to go on the invasion. I was waiting to be transferred to Guatemala, but that never happened. My father-in-law wrote a letter from Argentina and warned me not to get involved in it, and I thank him for my life.

April 17, 1963, was the day of the invasion. April 15 was when they bombed the military airports and air bases in Cuba, and April 18 and

April 19 were when the fighters ran out of ammunition. But they were brave people. I was not happy with the way the Kennedys treated the people who participated in the Bay of Pigs.

There were not too many Cubans at that time here in New Orleans. At the time there were only maybe six hundred, eight hundred, but there were several organizations, and I was the delegate of the Cuban Student Directorate. I was talking with two young Americans one day when this man walked into their store

and joined our conversation about Cuba. He explained that he had been in the Marine Corps in the United States, that he had trained in guerrilla warfare, and that he was willing to offer his services to us to train Cubans to fight against Castro.

I told him I didn't have anything to do with military events, that my job in New Orleans was only as an anti-Castro man. It was only about press and propaganda. I was not involved in military activities. Then he put his hand in his pocket and offered money to help. I said, "I cannot take the money. You have to send that money to our headquarters in Miami." The next day he showed up at the store again. I was not in the store. He left a guidebook for the Marines with my brother-in-law. His name was at the top: Lee Harvey Oswald.

When he was giving me the guidebook Oswald had left, my brother-in-law told me that Oswald looked like a very nice person. I said, "I don't know. I have something in the back of my head, in the back of mind; for some reason I don't trust him. I don't know if he's a Communist, an FBI agent, or whatever, OK? But there's something in him—I don't trust him."

I didn't know he had already tried to kill General Walker in Dallas.

That first meeting I had with Oswald was August 5.

The second time I met him in person was August 9—that was a Friday—in New Orleans. A Cuban by the name of Celso Hernandez came crawling to my store and told me he had seen an American on Canal Street with a sign that said VIVA FIDEL! HANDS OFF CUBA passing out some Communist pamphlets. So we went over there. We picked up another Cuban man, and we went looking on Canal Street. We could not find this American. We took a streetcar, and I had a big sign with me, with the Statue of Liberty stabbed in the back; it said DANGER! CUBA LIES IN CHAINS 90 MILES AWAY.

We took a streetcar, but we could not find him. Finally we came back, and I went back to the store. When I was in the store, a third Cuban, Miguel Cruz, came running into the store and said, "Hey, Celso discovered the American again on Canal Street, and Celso's watching him."

I took the sign again; we went down there, and I found Oswald in the 700 block of Canal Street after St. Charles. He was almost in front of the first store where I'd worked in New Orleans. Immediately I remembered him, and then he looked at me.

In the first moment he had a smirk on his face that looked like he was not happy with what was going on. But then Oswald extended his hand to shake hands with me. I refused to shake hands with him. And then, as Celso had been insulting him in Spanish—because Celso didn't know any English—I started insulting him in English, calling him traitor, Communist, and different things. It was around two o'clock, I believe, and there several Americans surrounded us to watch what was going on.

I was angry, and I was going to punch Oswald. I took my glasses off and approached him to punch him. But in that moment he put his hand down and said, "OK, Carlos, if you want to hit me, hit me."

That stopped me cold. My blood went cold. I said, "This guy knows what he's doing. He wants me to break the law by punching him." I decided not to punch him.

At that moment, Celso grabbed Oswald's literature, tore it up, and threw it in the air. There was a policeman who used to patrol in that block, and he approached me and said, "OK, let him do his demonstration. Go to your place." I said: "No! If in Cuba they don't allow us to do this, I am not going to allow them to do this here."

I turned to the people who were watching—there were maybe fifty or seventy of them—and I started explaining who Oswald was, that he had tried to infiltrate my organization. Then two police cars arrived, and we were taken to the First District police station.

In the First District station, they started questioning Oswald. At first he started answering questions. But when he was asked about the members of his organization, he refused to answer in front of me. Then he was moved to another room. That day we had to put down twenty-five dollars for a bail bond in order to get free.

The third time I saw Oswald was on August 12. That was the day of the trial at the Second Municipal Court. I thought that was the last time I was going to see him. I brought the guidebook for Marines to the courtroom. I showed it to the judge, and the front page where it had Oswald's name on it, and I explained to the judge that the person who had originated the whole incident was Oswald, when he tried to infiltrate my organization. If he had not done that, then nothing would have happened on the day we had the problem.

The judge—I saw his eyes, and I knew he understood what I was saying. The judge dismissed the charges against us and fined Oswald ten dollars. That was the only time in history that Oswald was charged in a court of the United States and fined. I thought that was the end of it, the last time I was going to see him.

But then the next day, Bill Stuckey, a newsman from New Orleans, contacted me because he wanted to find out the address of Lee Harvey Oswald, to interview him. I said, "I don't like that idea. They don't allow us to go out in Cuba and be interviewed." But then I sensed he had decided to do the interview anyway, and I said, "OK, instead of the interview why don't you make a debate? That way both sides have the right to say their opinions, and the people can judge over the radio who is right and who is wrong." That was a famous moment in New Orleans.

On August 16, a Cuban man left a message that Oswald was in front of the International House holding a demonstration. I went over there, but Oswald had already left.

A friend of mine from my school in Cuba, Carlos Quiroga, and I decided to send someone over to Oswald's house posing as a pro-Castro

Cuban. This was to find out what the Fair Play for Cuba Committee was planning to do here in New Orleans. Quiroga went over there and had a conversation with Oswald on the porch. That conversation was when we found out that Oswald spoke Russian. At one moment a daughter of Oswald came to the porch, and Oswald grabbed her and talked to her in Russian. Quiroga asked him if that was Russian, and Oswald told one of his many lies: Yes, that was Russian; he was learning Russian at Tulane University. He never attended Tulane University.

The last time I saw Oswald was on August 21 when we had the debate at WDSU radio in New Orleans. In the studio during the debate, I didn't feel at any moment that he was a violent man.

Before we arrived for the debate, we were in the lobby. At one moment the two of us were together, and I asked him why he didn't change sides and try to help his family and his country—because what he was doing was wrong. He told me, "Carlos, I am on the right side. You are the one who is on the wrong side."

Then we went in to the debate. I didn't know that another person in that debate—Ed Butler from the Information Council of the Americas— had discovered things about Oswald that I didn't know. They'd confirmed that Oswald was attempting to become a citizen of the Soviet Union as well as his defection from the United States to Russia. I was surprised by that. That was why I only spoke twice during the debate—I thought the other people had better weapons than mine, and my ego was not so big as to try to take over the debate.

But during the debate I asked Oswald one question that had never been asked of him before the assassination. I asked him if he agreed with the dictator, Fidel Castro, when on July 26 of that year he'd qualified President Kennedy as a ruffian and as a thief.

Oswald stopped for one second before answering: "I will not agree with that particular wording, but the United States government—" And then he started blaming the United States government. That was the only time before the assassination that Oswald was asked a question about President Kennedy.

After the debate, I issued a press release that I brought to the UPI, the AP, the newspapers, and the television stations. I asked the people of

New Orleans to write to their congressmen and ask for a congressional
investigation of Lee Harvey Oswald,
a confessed Marxist and an agent of
Fidel Castro in the United States.
Nobody paid attention to me.

Oswald as an agent of Fidel Castro? Yes.

At that time I had known Communists, and most of the Communists I knew, I believed, were dangerous. But I didn't categorize him at that moment as violently dangerous. Oswald as an agent of Fidel Castro? Yes. He'd confessed that he was a Marxist, and to me anyone who was a Marxist committed the same crimes of the Marxists who put innocent people in front of the execution wall.

A relative of mine was working in a stock market company. He called the store and told me that Kennedy had been shot. They'd received a teletype that Kennedy had been shot in Dallas. That was the first news I had.

Ten minutes after that, he called back and said the teletype said that apparently he had been seriously injured because they saw blood in his hair. At that moment, my illusions of going back to Cuba deflated completely because, in my opinion, the only person in the United States who had a moral obligation to help us recover Cuba was President Kennedy. That was my first thought.

After that, I received a call from the delegate of the Cuban Revolutionary Council in New Orleans, Frank Bartes. He wanted me to sign a telegram with him to Jacqueline Kennedy, offering our condolences. I refused to join him in that. I said, "We have to wait." I wanted to find out who was behind the assassination. In my mind, it could have been a stupid racist who was mad at Kennedy. It could have been Mafia people. It could have been Communist people. It could have been anyone from a spectrum of different ideologies. I said, "We have to find out who it is before we send a telegram of this type, because we have to word the telegram according to who is behind the assassination."

After that, I left the store and went to my house. I was living in one of the poorest sections of New Orleans, in the St. Thomas Housing Project.

I was having a late lunch over there, and I had the radio on. I heard the name Lee Harvey Oswald. I jumped from the chair and went to the phone. I called the FBI first to tell them who Oswald was.

Then I called the *Times Picayune* to tell them who Oswald was. The *Times Picayune* wanted me to go immediately over there, and I went over. They already had Ed Butler and Bill Stuckey over there. Butler told me to wait and don't be interviewed for a few minutes because Stuckey was trying to arrange a deal, a monetary deal, to provide information about Oswald. To me that was revolting. I never thought that, with the president killed, somebody would be asking for money to give information. I said, "No, Butler, I'm sorry. I'll give everything that I know free. I don't need any money."

To me, President Kennedy was the last hope that the Cuban people had to get rid of Castro. The day I heard that Kennedy was killed, those hopes went out the window—because Kennedy had the moral obligation. He had sworn in Miami in December 1962 that he was going to return the flag of the Bay of Pigs invasion, of Brigade 2506, to a free Havana. When Kennedy was killed, there was no one who was going to take over that statement from Kennedy.

Sunday morning, when Oswald was led down the hall, I was at the Secret Service office talking to an agent. He received a phone call, and he turned to me and said, "Oswald has been shot." It was like when you see the end of a movie. You're watching a movie and you see "The End."

I said, "Castro got rid of Oswald." I was thinking that when Oswald went to trial, the one who would be sitting there would be Fidel Castro. They got rid of Oswald, and everything was confused. Everything became "Who killed Oswald?"

On November 22 I was interviewed on local, national, and international television. I said, "I don't know if Lee Harvey Oswald is the assassin or not, but if it's proven that Lee Harvey Oswald is the assassin, the hand of Fidel Castro is behind the assassination."

I jumped from the chair and went to the phone. I called the FBI first to tell them who Oswald was.

My statement arrived in Cuba, and the next day Castro held a gathering of the masses in Cuba because he wanted to address the "lies" against him. He mentioned me and tried to distort what I had said. I am sure that day and the next day Castro was sweating very badly because of what I said.

I was interviewed by the Warren Commission, and I was told by several people, among them Ed Butler, not to be too outspoken against Castro; just tell, matter of fact, what happened with Oswald. That is what I did in the Warren Commission.

Secret memos from the CIA that never reached the Warren Commission but would come out in 1998 referred to two assassins Castro had sent to the United States in 1960 and 1961 to kill Kennedy. The Warren Commission never knew a lot of things about the assassination. The commission was just a seal of approval of an idea that was planted by President Johnson, who was convinced that Castro was the one who killed President Kennedy. Johnson said that several times to different people, but I believe that President Johnson wanted to close the case, say it was one person, not a conspiracy, and that's it.

—◆—

I know Fidel Castro. Presidents of different countries and presidents of the United States, they're presidents. They are politicians. But Castro is not a politician—Castro is a gangster.

The first person he ever killed, on February 22, 1948, was a cousin of mine: Manolo Castro, who was leader of the students in the University of Havana and was the person in charge of Cuban sports in 1948. Fidel Castro killed him.

On November 1, 1958, he killed another cousin of mine, Rosco Menyano—or at least he ordered the situation that ended with the assassination of my cousin. He was a pilot with the Cuban airline, and his plane was leaving Florida to Cuba. Castro sent some people from the 26th of July Movement to Florida. Those people hijacked the airplane before it reached Cuba. When they told my cousin they wanted the plane to go to the Sierra Maestra, my cousin said to them, "We don't have gasoline to reach the Sierra Maestra. We will crash." They said, "You have to go." He said, "I won't go."

They stabbed him to death. The plane eventually crashed in the Bay of Nipe. Several of the passengers were killed. Some of the mercenaries, terrorists, from the July 26th Movement were killed too, but some of them survived. One of them just recently died in Coral Gables, Florida. When I returned to Cuba in 1959, I saw a *Bohemia* magazine in which they were interviewing the survivors of that hijacking, and they were bragging about how they had to kill the pilot because he didn't want to reach the Sierra Maestra.

I am a Christian. I don't believe in falsely accusing a person. If Castro was innocent, I would have never blamed him. But I know him—he's an assassin. He had been doing that for years, and he had every motive to kill Kennedy. Kennedy was going to get rid of him.

I believe that is one of the problems Bobby Kennedy confronted after the assassination, that he felt guilty because, I believe, Kennedy was playing a game he could not really be involved in. Kennedy was not an assassin. Kennedy could have had various bad traits as a politician or as a person, but he was not an assassin. That was something in which he should not have been involved.

I was a lawyer in Cuba. I used to work in a criminal court, and I have never put blame on an innocent person. I believe that Castro is an assassin. Only an idiot could think that Castro is a saint, that Castro is not a gangster, that Castro is not an assassin. We are dealing with an assassin: a serial killer assassin. That is the man who has been in power for fifty-three years in Cuba.

I told that to Garrison, the district attorney of New Orleans, at the time of his investigation, and I told him that if he wanted me to work for him, I would work for him for free. I didn't want to frame a Communist, and I didn't want to frame an anti-Communist. What I wanted was the truth, because I knew the truth would blame Fidel Castro.

I learned about Jim Garrison's investigation because an American by the name of David Ferrie came to my store asking to meet with Dr. Carlos Bringuier.

I said, "I am Carlos Bringuier."

Ferrie didn't remember that we had met in 1961, I believe, for ten minutes at his house with Sergio Arcacha and Carlos Quiroga. Ferrie at that time was helping Arcacha with the Cuban Revolutionary Council. I had heard from Cubans that they didn't like Ferrie because of his tendencies. Then I wanted to meet Ferrie. We went over there and stayed for ten minutes. When we left, I told Arcacha, "If I were you, I would not like to be seen with this guy."

Ferrie forgot about that, and he came asking for Carlos Bringuier. He told me that Garrison was doing a witch hunt on him and that Garrison was going to frame him for the assassination of President Kennedy. He said something at that moment that I didn't like. He said that all the judges should be hanged.

My father used to be a judge in Cuba. I didn't want my father to be hanged. I got very short and said that I didn't have anything else to talk about with him, and he left. At that moment I was feeling great. I was thinking, *Okay, the district attorney is going to discover that Castro is behind the assassination.* That was my first thought.

After a few days I started receiving news from Cubans who were being interviewed by the district attorney, and the line of questioning was not in that direction. Then I called the district attorney's office and asked to have a meeting with Garrison. The next day they called me, and I went over there to meet Garrison.

Garrison was a very impressive guy. He was six feet something, and he looked like Perry Mason in a lot of ways. He was telling me his latest conspiracy theory. I don't know if it was conspiracy theory number three or conspiracy theory number thirteen, because he had a lot of conspiracy theories. He mentioned a lot of different names of Americans that never came out in public. I don't want to mention their names because they are very respectable Americans. When he finished explaining his theory to me, I said, "You are either stupid or you are a Communist."

He said, "I won't discuss anything else with you unless you take a lie detector test."

I said, "You can give me three lie detector tests! But I don't discuss with you until you give me a lie detector test."

He sent me to take the lie detector test. We went to the office of William Gurvich, who administered the lie detector test. A couple of days later I received a call from the district attorney's office that he wanted to meet with me again.

Garrison apologized to me and said I had passed the lie detector test perfectly. That was when I offered to work with him without pay. I didn't want to blame a Communist or an anti-Communist—what I wanted was the truth, and I knew where the truth was going to take me. Several times after that I was called to Garrison's office. One time I was called because a Cuban was brought from Miami who was going to identify Arcacha with Oswald. For Garrison, that was tremendous, a perfect thing for his theory.

Then James Alcock, who was the assistant district attorney, brought me into a room with a Cuban. I knew this Cuban. He had been living in New Orleans, and I knew him as a thief. His name was Emilio Santana, and Santana was identifying Arcacha with Oswald in a meeting on Washington Avenue of some people from the Alpha 66 Movement.

They wanted me to be the translator. I translated everything Mr. Santana said. When he finished, Alcott was all excited because now they had Arcacha. I knew that was wrong. Arcacha and I were not on speaking terms when Arcacha left New Orleans in 1962, and I knew Arcacha was not in New Orleans when this guy was placing him in New Orleans.

I asked Alcott if I could ask Santana a question. Alcott said yes. I said, "Okay, it could not have been where you said, on Washington Avenue and Madison Street, the service station of the Suarez Family." I knew the Suarez Family had the service station there and that they were with Alpha 66. Then I said, "The person that you said was there, the delegate of Alpha 66, his name is Miguel Bretos."

And he's like, "Yes, that's it! Miguel Bretos was the man who was there." I knew that Miguel Bretos had a lot of resemblance, physically, to Arcacha. You had to see Alcott's face—everything disappeared in front of him. When I finished he said, "I want to check that the translation of Dr. Bringuier has been completely accurate." He was testing me to see if I had changed something; he could charge me with obstruction of justice if I said something other than what Santana said to me.

After we left, I talked to Santana. I said, "Santana, what are you doing here? How did this happen?" He said, "These people from the district attorney showed up in Miami. They started questioning me, and they offered to pay for my trip here, to put me up in a hotel, and give me drugs if I testify."

In Cuba in 1959 I was part of the 10 percent of the people who knew what Castro was. Ninety percent of the people were for Castro; 90 percent of the people said, "Oh, Castro is the man." In New Orleans, when

Garrison was district attorney, 90 percent of the people were for Garrison. He duped everybody. Remember that New Orleans has always been a very corrupt city, and Louisiana has always been a very corrupt state. Garrison was the district attorney, and he had the dirt on all the politicians.

Garrison started his investigation because of David Chandler, who was a newsman with *Life* magazine. He talked to him about everything he had. The problem for Chandler was that Chandler was putting the blame on the Mafia, and Garrison was part of the Mafia. Garrison took all the information that Chandler was providing to him, and when he had all that information, he didn't do anything against the Mafia. That is when he broke up with Chandler.

To me, one of the most incredible things is how people sometimes cast blame on innocent people. Oliver Stone and Kevin Costner were able to carry that movie, *JFK,* by putting the blame on an innocent man like Clay Shaw.

I had the opportunity to meet Clay Shaw after he had been indicted by Garrison. I was invited to the reception he had in his house after he was acquitted of all charges by the grand jury in less than three hours. The man was a gentleman. I don't care if he was gay or not gay—that is his personal decision—but this man was a gentleman. This man was recognized by a lot of ambassadors and very influential people all over the world, and Garrison was able to blame an innocent man.

When Oliver Stone came to New Orleans with Kevin Costner, they invited me to his hotel; they wanted me to help them with the movie. When Oliver Stone finished explaining his movie to me, I told him, "You are going to do terrible damage to the young people of the United States, because what you are saying in that movie is wrong. You are not portraying the truth in that movie." He told me, "Carlos, you have to realize that I am not doing a documentary, that I am doing a movie. In a movie, I have the latitude of expanding the truth a little bit."

I told him, "I don't want to cooperate with you," and I walked out of that room. Kevin Costner was running after me into the elevator, asking me to reconsider. I said, "No. The damage this will do to the American people is terrible. The people will think that what he's saying in the movie is true, and it is not true."

One person who told me what was going on after the Garrison investigation was Oriana Fallaci. She interviewed me over at Casa Roca at that time and told me, "Carlos, when this trial is finished, a movie will be made about this. If Garrison wins, a movie will be made about how good he was. If he loses, a movie will be made about how much of an idiot he was." But she was wrong. He lost, and a movie was made about how good he was.

History changed when Lee Harvey Oswald fired those three shots in Dallas on November 22, 1963—not only the history of Cuba but also the history of the United States and the history of the world. If Lee Harvey Oswald was alive today, he would be very happy to see the way the United States is going.

I met the president of Guatemala, Miguel Ydigoras Fuentes. He was president of Guatemala during the Bay of Pigs invasion. I met him one time at a dinner in New Orleans, and he was sat next to me. He wanted me to tell him about Lee Harvey Oswald and my encounter with Oswald. I said, "I will tell you that if you tell me something about the Bay of Pigs that I am not aware of."

He told me, "One month before the Bay of Pigs, Kennedy sent an emissary to Guatemala, telling me to dismantle the camps, because the invasion was not going forward. I sent a friend of mine to Washington to give my response to Kennedy." Ydigoras said that when my friend met Kennedy, he told him what Ydigoras said: that that was the right time to get rid of Castro.

"If we don't get rid of Castro now, Castro is going to get rid of us." Fuentes told me that my friend Alajhos said that at that moment Kennedy had started moving in his rocking chair and after a few minutes told him, "OK, tell your president he is right, that I am sorry that I am surrounded by *fediches*." That was the word Ydigoras Fuentes used. *Fediches* are bad advisors, people who are bringing you only the bad news about a situation—and so the invasion would go.

Two of the leaders of the Bay of Pigs, Kennedy and Anastasio Somoza, were both killed by Castro's people. One in Dallas, Texas, and the other in

Asunción, Paraguay, by another Castro sympathizer, a communist Argentinean trained in Cuba and sent to Paraguay to kill President Somoza. I believe that one of the reasons that President Kennedy and even Bobby Kennedy were killed was because of Castro.

Sirhan Sirhan was a follower of Fidel Castro too. Sirhan Sirhan was identified as attending a meeting that was for Castro, where he had a confrontation with a Cuban exile also. I invited Bobby Kennedy to come to New Orleans during that campaign, and he sent me a letter promising that in the future he would be coming and meeting with us here.

I once presented one of my books, *Operation Judas,* in Miami. After the presentation, I saw a man in the first row. About two weeks before I went to Miami, I had seen his picture in a book he wrote.

After the presentation, this man came to me and asked, "Do you know who I am?"

I said, "Yes, you are Felix Rodriguez. You are the man who cut Che Guevara in Bolivia."

He said, "Yes."

I said, "I saw your picture in the book you wrote."

He said, "I want to tell you that I was a friend of Bobby Kennedy and that everything you said in your book is the truth."

I don't have any doubt in my mind that if Bobby Kennedy had become president of the United States, he would have gotten rid of the man who had killed his brother. So Bobby Kennedy could not be allowed to become president of the United States; that is one of the reasons Bobby Kennedy was also assassinated.

One of the other victims of Fidel Castro, in my opinion, was Martin Luther King. Martin Luther King was not a Communist. Martin Luther

King was looking for the advancement of colored people in the United States. Martin Luther King had been invited to Cuba several times, but he refused to go to Cuba and give his seal of approval to the dictatorship of Fidel Castro. Martin Luther King didn't want to be part of the revolution that Castro wanted to come inside the United States. He was a friend of the Kennedys. In my opinion, that is one of the reasons he was also killed, in order for the Communists to take over the black movement in the United States.

———

I am glad I had the encounter with Oswald to a certain extent, because I believe I was in God's hands. I believe that gave me the opportunity to destroy the myth that Kennedy was killed by right-wingers or conservatives or whatever—because I was there; I know what happened.

In regard to Garrison, I was glad to be there too, because I believe I confronted him. I believe he respected me, and he didn't want to confront me because he knew that I knew more about the assassination than he knew. I have read the twenty-six volumes of the Warren Commission. Every time Garrison was saying something on television in New Orleans, the television station would interview me after that, and I was saying, "What the district attorney said is not true because what happened was this, this, and this." Garrison would change everything.

I feel bad that thing happened to me, though, because as this was happening we lost a little girl. My wife was pregnant during the Garrison investigation. At one point I was thinking that Garrison was going to arrest me at any minute, so I sent her with the kids to her family in Buenos Aires—I didn't want the kids to be present if they arrested me. When eventually I thought Garrison was not going to move against me, I called her. She came back to the United States. Then she lost the kid. We lost that kid when she was seven months pregnant, and I believe we lost that kid because of the Garrison investigation. She was crying every night; she was very upset with the situation, and she was very afraid.

Unfortunately that is not what Oliver Stone and Kevin Costner think about the assassination.

Richard Reeves

Political biographer and news columnist Richard Reeves was a twenty-six-year-old reporter for the *Newark News* in 1963. An award-winning author, primarily writing on American politics, he teaches at the University of Southern California.

I don't think he was prepared, but I don't think anyone ever has been. The job is sui generis, and they make of it what they can. They have much less room for movement than I had imagined. John Kennedy obviously was well read in history and thought about it. All the sickness he had had as a kid, he read almost everything he could. He, like every other person I've ever talked to who ran for president—Lyndon Johnson and Adlai Stevenson were his real rivals at that time—had the answer, "Hell, if they can do it, I can do it." Then they get there. They come into this building that has been emptied out, every paper is gone, everything is white and what-not, and it's really a "What do I do now?" situation.

He did have, with some exceptions, the best and the brightest for him. He was a very tough guy. Politicians at that level have to be ruthless, and they have to cut away the people who helped them along the way but are no longer useful. Being rich probably helped in that. He saw them as servants, and he, more than other presidents I've looked at, made his own decisions in secret.

He organized the White House as a spoke-and-wheel, with himself as the hub and the spokes leading out to other people. No one in there ever felt fully secure, because they didn't know what he was saying to other people. He didn't do things as if it were a group. He talked about this himself. He wanted to keep total control over what he was doing. He did that by dealing along to spokes of that wheel.

He was used to doing what other presidents often had to learn to do— not to do anything himself that could be done by someone else. He was very used to people waiting on him. Some days he would change his shirts five times a day with someone else, Bobby or some stiff, holding it out. You talk about him being surprised about small things—he was stunned to find out that Ben Bradlee would wear shirts for two days in a row. That was totally alien to him. He lived in a world where there were lawyers, maids, cleaners, doctors, everything you

needed, in that same kind of organization around you. Eisenhower had the same kind of treatment, though he didn't have the money, because of his rank. You have to know that to be president. You can't go in there like Jimmy Carter and think it's like everything else. It's not like everything else. Rich people know that.

The fists were closed, but they were often swung at each other, and that was the way Kennedy wanted it. He wanted them to be competing against each other with only him knowing what the competition was really about. Jackie Kennedy's biggest worry was really about her children being exploited. As far as John Kennedy was concerned, there was a whole world out there to be exploited, including these two beautiful children. When her car pulled out of the driveway at the White House, he often grabbed a phone, called a photographer, and said, "She's gone, you can come over and take pictures." Of course when they got there, the kids were there, and some of those images are now indelible in our view.

If nothing else, John Kennedy taught us how to be postwar rich Americans, how to dress—he dressed differently—how to cut hair, what was important. Although he didn't think things like opera and the symphony were important, he thought it was important that Americans did because we had become a new people. Before World War II, before the GI Bill, people in this country lived very limited lives. After the war, for the first time many Americans—even if with guns in their hands—had seen the world. They recognized and he certainly recognized that we were going to be the leader of the world; he was going to lead by example, which was an easy thing for him to do.

Kennedy taught us how to be postwar rich Americans.

Conservative Republicans of course like to say that we probably could have been rougher on Kennedy, but he couldn't have been rougher on us because one of the Kennedy policies, strategies, tactics, was that all good news would come from the White House. Any bad news would be announced by the Agriculture Department, the Labor Department, or someone else. The press caught on to that—the action wasn't out in the agencies anymore; the action was all centralized in the White House. Kennedy was controlling it, and we really had no choice but to play the game his way. We were played very skillfully, and it wasn't because of any love affair between us and the Kennedys.

What we liked about the Kennedys was: They were good copy. They were a good story. We didn't think they were better than other people, but they were a hell of a lot more interesting than other people. That was part of a buildup. The man will live forever because he was a cultural icon. He was a competent politician who did some good things and some bad, but the fact of the matter is he changed the way Americans thought of themselves. The president was in our living room now, and so were some of the troubles of the world, particularly civil rights. We talk of the Internet today and all of that or Gutenberg and the press. The arrival of television was like that. It changed [the world]. Nothing was ever the same, and he understood it better than we did.

When it came to the press, he was not above picking up the phone personally and calling the press lords or even columnists and chewing them out or asking them for something—including calling the publisher of the *New York Times* when the *Times'* Tad Szulz had sniffed out what was going on in Cuba, though it wasn't as big a secret as we think of it now. Kennedy did pick up the phone, called the *Times,* and said, "How are you going to handle this?" To a certain extent he edited it, particularly taking out the fact that we had the time table—we at the *Times* had the time table. We knew what was happening.

Other stories were held as they are today because the president called and said, "It's in the interest of national security." The guy who took the most beating from him, who was one of the best reporters covering him, was Hugh Sidey of *Time*. Kennedy thought, *This is just free television*. When he was once asked during the campaign what was the most important medium in the country, he said *Time* magazine because it's all over the world, and people think it represents the government. *Time* obviously covered him with their best man, Hugh Sidey, but Sidey woke up many unpleasant mornings with Kennedy screaming at him—the president screaming at a reporter. How do we react when that happens? We want to dive under the bed. We know our place, but he knew his place too and was willing to use it. He didn't talk to Sidey for weeks because Sidey cited the fact that his picture, he didn't know why, was in *Gentleman's Quarterly*. Kennedy called him up and said, "That's a homosexual magazine. You're going to ruin me. Why are you doing this? Who's making you do this to us?" Of course no one was making them do it. They were covering what happened in front of them. The president of the United States was on the cover of *GQ*, and that was it. That was a story.

Rich people grow up with long driveways, with lawyers to buy their way out of situations. He had been bought out of woman situations with payoffs since he was a teenager. That's the way his old man, Joe Kennedy, handled his own life and handled his son's life. It wasn't a situation like Gary Hart, who got caught at it; the *Miami Herald* was sitting on his stoop when he was inside for a weekend with a young lady named Donna Rice. We couldn't sit on the Kennedy stoop. We couldn't sit at the White House. People came in cars; Marilyn Monroe came to the Carlyle. I'm going to plead innocent here because I worked for a small paper in the country at that time, but guys protecting guys and "guys will be guys" was a very large part of it. Even if we felt like reporting it, I don't think our editors would have run it. It was still considered private business. We didn't know enough about it, and who among us was going to be the first to throw a stone? We were afraid.

He was a very sick man, and one of the reasons he was so reckless and careless was that he always expected to die young—he lived life as a race against boredom. But the medical thing—someone could get elected with a woman thing today, and have been. But someone with the health profile that John Kennedy had would not be elected. Had he run in times where medical records were more accessible, where the reporters covering it were doctors like Larry Altman at the *Times* and whatnot . . . But they lied, they lied, they lied. One statement after another during the campaign; doctors would issue statements that there was nothing wrong with him. Whenever there seemed to be [something wrong], none of us knew. To my knowledge, there were only two or three pictures ever taken of him on crutches, and he was on crutches a good deal of the time. I don't think they were published at the time.

I don't know that he learned from what they [his military leaders and cabinet] did. What he did was stand fast in what he believed. The Bay of Pigs wasn't much compared to the Cuban Missile Crisis, and here there were two men who could conceivably destroy each other and a lot of each other's world.

His genius, and it *was* genius, was a great piece of leadership in the Cuban Missile Crisis, since he was the only guy who understood that Khrushchev was in an equally precarious position and wanted an out just as much as Kennedy did. Khrushchev had hoped to sneak all the missiles in and then announce it—but he didn't. We caught him at it. At that moment, both of them were the same. The advisors for both were saying, "Go get 'em. Push the button. Push the button." Both of them—seasoned politicians both of them, different systems but both politicians—knew it was disastrous and that they had to find a minimum path out of the thing. It was Khrushchev who gambled and lost.

There are two fine moments I think in the Kennedy presidency. One, which was a kind of extended moment, he was the first president to come to office when the United States could be invaded, the first time since 1812. Now with ballistic missiles, we could be reached by an enemy. The world was in better shape, closer to peace when he died than when he came in, which I think was a great achievement.

He was the first president to come to office when the United States could be invaded, the first time since 1812.

These two guys came to power knowing their own countries could be destroyed. Kennedy badly underrated Khrushchev; he also was taking a lot of amphetamines at that point in his life—he had an outside doctor, Dr. [Max] Jacobson, who was shooting him up. That probably helped his energy; it probably didn't help his judgment. But what did him in was that John Kennedy lied more than a bit about his growing up and his development. One of the things on his résumé was that he had been at the London School of Economics and that Harold Laski, the Marxist scholar, had been his mentor. Everyone around him who really didn't know very much about Communism thought: "He really knows about the dialectic. He knows how to deal with these people." Well, the truth is, he never went to the London School of Economics. He got sick; he stayed home. He thought he could win on charm, like many other politicians. They always believe they'll prevail one on one. He believed that. But it didn't happen in Vienna, and he was just crushed by it. He said, as we know now, to Scotty Reston, "We're going to have to stand up to them someplace because they think I'm a weak man, and I know the place." Reston said, "What's the place?" And he said, "Vietnam."

It was very rough. One of the things he did when he came out [to Vienna] was to meet first with Scotty Reston in a room; it had been arranged in advance. Reston, the Washington bureau chief of the *New York Times* and probably the most powerful journalist of his generation, was waiting for Kennedy in a side room. Kennedy came in—he was carrying a hat, which was unusual for him—and he slumped onto a couch and put the hat down over his face. Reston asked, "How was it?" He said, "Worst thing in my life. I'm going to have to spend a lot of time undoing that." What happened was that Kennedy obviously was a very rational fellow, but he had no experience at this level. Khrushchev did, and Khrushchev was, by nature, a thug—a likable thug, a funny guy, but he never let Kennedy get off the dime. Kennedy would say, "Why don't we do this?" and Khrushchev would jump on him, saying: "Do this with you after you put the missiles in so-and-so, and you did this, and you're oppressing that. You're the enemy; you're the one trying to start a war. Why should we deal with you? Why should we deal with any of you? You sent spy planes over."

It went on and on and on, and Kennedy wasn't used to being talked to that way. Beyond that, he was never able to pull himself together to mount an effective defense. One, he didn't really know much about Communism and Marxism; two, he was drugged up. He had been shot up with amphetamines by Dr. Jacobson for the pain, the huge pain he had in his back. What effect that had on his thinking and his ability to defend himself and the rest of us, we don't know for sure, but obviously it had an effect.

The other great achievement, which he doesn't get as much credit for from many people, is that America was being torn apart by a civil war, something it didn't want. He didn't want to deal with civil rights above all, but young blacks in places like South Carolina were listening to his words about doing and being and freedom. He meant those for Eastern European audiences, but it worked in Greenville, South Carolina.

Kennedy had been asking, "Why is this happening? Stop this." He told Harris Wofford, his civil rights adviser, "Get your damn people off those buses," and Wofford said, "It's too late for that," and it *was* too late for that. George Reedy, Johnson's press secretary, in a memo to Johnson, who then passed it on to Sorensen, said, "They're doing it because of you,

"We're going to have to stand up to them someplace because they think I'm a weak man, and I know the place." Reston said, "What's the place?" And he said, "Vietnam."

and this is going on because both sides, the Southerners in Congress, the white Southern establishment, and the black kids think you're on their side. The politicians think you're just doing this for black votes; the blacks think this is the revolution. Until they know which side you're on, this is going to continue and get worse and worse."

During the troubles at the Universities of Mississippi and Alabama, he went on television, gave one of the great speeches—almost without notes—in American history, in which he took the side of the minority, which is no small thing in a democracy. He said, "This is not a regional question, this is not a political question, this is a moral question. What kind of people are we, and are we the kind of people who are going to continually oppress and suppress some of us because they're of a different color? After all, who among us, given a choice, would choose to be black?"

That was almost as great an achievement as the fact that missiles weren't fired, that the president of the United States stood with a minority. At that point it almost didn't matter what he did, because then the black people took over, white civil rights workers took over, and we were a better country for it.

——

I was a reporter for the *Newark News* when the phone rang, and an editor said, "The president's been shot; get down to the office," which was in Morristown. I went down there, and I had this surreal scene where the first other door I saw opening at Ten Park Square, an office building in Morristown, belonged to Ray Manahan, the chairman of the Democratic Party and the mayor of Morristown. I walked in to talk to him about it. His window was being cleaned. I was just picking up quotes they might or might not use. His window was being washed, and there was a guy out there with the belt and whatnot, laughing and smiling at us. We were practically in tears, and I thought, *I'm looking at the only man in the country, the guy out there, the window washer, who doesn't know what just happened to America.* What happened to America was we lost our innocence. As the great Mary McGrory said to Pat Moynihan, "We'll never laugh again." And Pat said, "We'll laugh again; we'll never be innocent again." It changed the country, and Kennedy is partly to blame for all that. If there were another negative, it was that the Kennedys drove this aura of assassination that was in the air in the early '60s: Patrice Lumumba, the leader of the Congo, had been assassinated just before Kennedy became president. Trujillo was assassinated in the Dominican Republic with help from the CIA and American weapons, and as we knew, maybe even then, there was plot after plot to try to kill Castro.

It never entered our minds—I don't know if it entered Kennedy's—that the most vulnerable leader in the world was the American president. He was the least protected, particularly in those days, much less than today. Maybe it was inevitable that some screwball—in this case, with a gripe about Cuba, which we were pushing around—would try to get the president. I don't believe in any conspiracy theories on the president. I think Oswald killed him. He was nuts. He had a cause, Cuba, and he got lucky; and we all got unlucky and were never the same.

It was like lightning. I think that Vietnam and civil rights were what made young people lose faith in the credibility of their leaders. The people who ran to conspiracy theories are a different breed of cat. The conspiracy to them is more important than the event and its aftermath. I would put it down not to the Warren Commission but to public officials who lied to us that changed us. Public officials lied and lied to us about the war in Vietnam; that changed us as journalists, but it also changed citizens as people with faith in their system, their country, and their leaders.

There had been hundreds of books obviously, but in the end only two of them counted. A lot of them had to do with women, with attacks or defenses of his record. I had just finished reading a book called *The Emperor* by Ryszard Kapuscinski, the Polish writer, about the fall of Haile Selassie. It was this marvelous picture of talking to everyone around a major figure and figuring out from that what he was like.

I found myself thinking—I was living in Paris at the time—what did this seem like to Selassie? I didn't know anything about Ethiopia or emperors, and I thought I could do a book like this. I've been around the White House enough. I can do a book about this, about how life looks to an American president. I picked Kennedy because the two pillars of Kennedyana

Under our system, the presidency is really an act of faith on how the president will handle situations that haven't yet happened.

really were Schlesinger's and Sorensen's books, and it was twenty-five years later. Things had changed; people had changed. I thought that even though all these other books were out there, there was kind of an open field to try to cover him minute by minute, day by day—to know what was on his desk every day, to know what he said before he got to that desk and that kind of thing.

I was learning things. I learned big lessons, but they didn't come immediately, because immediately I was thinking about compiling material and building it up. The big thing that surprised me, and surprises me to this day, is how reactive the presidency is as a job. The campaign doesn't matter; in some ways the person himself doesn't matter. Under our system, the presidency is really an act of faith on how the president will handle situations that haven't yet happened. I'm sure Kennedy realized long before I did, since only thirty-five or forty guys really know what it's like to be president: You're constantly reacting to events you had no control over.

We would've eventually had a counterculture movement, but maybe "eventually" is fifty years. I do think he would've begun to cut back on Vietnam or at least assure young people. Young people were rioting because they were being drafted not because they developed a political ideology. In the beginning it was self-interest, and it became the '60s. John Kennedy came to office when people wore hats and three-button suits, and he left when they were tie-dying—well, they weren't yet, but because of his influence they ended up tie-dying—T-shirts and things. Because of the way he lived—glamorously, recklessly—we all took more chances.

I hate to say this, but I think it will turn out that Reagan, in political terms, will have been a more significant president. John Kennedy was a very good president and may have been on the edge of becoming a great president, although great presidents, at least in my lexicon, are created by the events they have to face. Suddenly an oil rig blows up and fills the Gulf of Mexico with oil. You can't anticipate that, but you have to respond to it. There were three out of four with Kennedy. He did a very good job in tamping down—and might have  been on the verge of doing more than that—the rhetoric of the Cold War, which was much stronger than young people today understand. People talked about bombing each other all the time. But the relationship with the Soviet Union was better and less dangerous when he left than when he came in. He took the moral stand on civil rights, even though the worst people in it—the worst segregationists and bigots—were in his own party, the Southerners in the Democratic Party. He chose the minority over them, which was important. He brought out the best of us in many ways, including the Cuban Missile Crisis, and it could be argued the only thing a president can do in this great democracy is to bring out the best or the worst in the American people. Richard Nixon failed because he brought out the worst.

The fourth thing, which is a negative to me, is that he got us into Vietnam—not Johnson, not Nixon. Once Diem was assassinated, with his permission we owned Vietnam, and we went through that pathetic group of generals who only wanted to steal. I don't know when he would've pulled out. He would've pulled out before Johnson, but he had a failing as a leader, which cost him in Vietnam: When things went wrong, Kennedy tended to think it meant we had the wrong guy in charge, so let's put a new guy in and see until we get to the right one. I don't think that's a valid assumption, particularly for someone who controls as many people in power as a president of the United States. Vietnam is the black mark on his record. With weaponry and civil rights, it verged on greatness. All in all, he was pretty good, and he was better at the end because he had some experience. He had much more sense of what he could do and what he couldn't do.

So was he a great president? I don't think so. He belongs in the near-great category—the best one-term president since James Polk.

Pat Buchanan

In 1963, native Virginian Patrick Buchanan was a twenty-five-year-old editorial writer for the *St. Louis Globe Dispatch.* He left to work in Richard Nixon's New York law firm and soon transitioned to campaign advisor when Nixon began his quest for the presidency. Buchanan served as an advisor in the White House under Nixon as well as Ford and Reagan. With Tom Braden he founded the influential CNN program *Crossfire* in 1982. In 2000 Buchanan ran as the Reform Party's presidential candidate; he continues to write and appear as a conservative analyst on MSNBC.

B ack in 1958 I was down in Fort Lauderdale, and my girlfriend and my brother and his girlfriend were there. My father had been an accountant for a very rich man, Page Hufty. Page Lee Hufty was his daughter, and there was Alex Hufty, who was getting married. Alex said, "Why don't you guys go up and represent me at the wedding," so we went to the reception, and I will never forget it: In through the door at the reception comes John F. Kennedy, looking like a million bucks. My brother said, "Isn't that Bobby Kennedy?" I said, "No, that's Jack Kennedy, the senator." He came through with tremendous charisma, immensely attractive, a tremendously likable individual, and a new-generation politician. He really had it.

When I was at journalism school, we were sent down to DC for what's called field observation week. We went to the White House one day, the Congress another day, and we got to go to the president's press conference—that was a press conference right after, I believe, John Glenn had come back from orbiting the Earth three times. This guy from the

Daily News got up and said, "Mr. President, the *Daily News* has recommended that there be a holiday for school kids when John Glenn—comes to the White House," and Kennedy said, "You know, this administration has always fol-

lowed the policy of the *Washington Daily News*. There'll be a holiday!" That was the charisma and the likability of him.

In St. Louis, we didn't have TVs in our offices or anything. There was one office, a side office, and we watched television there right off the newsroom. We all got together and watched his press conferences. I watched every one of them when they were televised, and they all were. We went in there, and, even if you disagreed with the guy, you had to come away admiring him. You'd say, "The Democrats have really got a candidate. They've really got a leader, and we've got to get our own candidate."

When I became an editorial writer in St. Louis, which was around August 1962, we were very critical of Kennedy, but we were very supportive of his actions in the Cuban Missile Crisis. We condemned him for the murder of [president of South Vietnam] Diem; we felt the administration had had a hand in that. They were in some way complicit with that, and that was appalling. We disagreed with him on a number of issues, but I supported Kennedy's tax cuts in 1962. The rest of the editorial board didn't.

On civil rights, it was our feeling that Jack Kennedy couldn't get anything done. He wasn't a terribly effective president in dealing with Congress. I'll tell you what, though: We supported Jack Kennedy, and I wrote editorials about the showdown with Ross Barnett, who was the governor of Mississippi. Very soon after I joined the editorial page, in October 1962, Governor Barnett basically tried to block the entrance of black students, specifically James Meredith, to the University of Mississippi. I wrote an editorial saying, "Governor Barnett says he's willing to go to jail, and that's exactly where they ought to put him." We supported Kennedy and the courts and everything they did against Governor Wallace as well in June 1963. What we were against basically was folks from the north going down south, but we were pro law and order up and down the line, whether it was demonstrators on one side or governors on the other.

What was it Harold MacMillan said? He came back from a visit to Washington and said, "The Kennedys remind me of the Borgias taking over a somewhat respectable, small northern Italian town." There's a great deal of truth to it. These were tough, somewhat ruthless politicians. Jack Kennedy was wiretapping the steel executives. Jack Kennedy ordered the wiretaps on Dr. King. Bobby Kennedy told Hoover to go ahead and do it. These were tough customers. Jack Kennedy used to joke about how his father told him, "Don't buy one more vote than you have to in West Virginia. I'll be damned if I'm going to pay for a landslide." That's the way they were. They were tough, irreverent politicians, and all three of them, Bobby Kennedy, John F. Kennedy, and Martin Luther King, wouldn't be in the pantheon they're in today had they not died the way they did, by assassins' bullets.

Jack Kennedy was admired at the Buchanan dinner table and by my father, who said, "We've got two good patriots running now." He wouldn't have said that in Truman's and FDR's day, but there was an admiration for Kennedy and for Richard Nixon. I preferred Richard Nixon, and I think my father did too. We couldn't vote in those days.

But I'd carried Richard Nixon's golf bag in Burning Tree Country Club, and we had watched him much more closely than we had Kennedy, so I would say most of us preferred Richard Nixon. When

> *Harold MacMillan said, "The Kennedys remind me of the Borgias taking over a somewhat respectable, small northern Italian town."*

> *Kennedy used to joke about how his father told him,*
> *"Don't buy one more vote than you have to in West*
> *Virginia. I'll be damned if I'm going to pay for a*
> *landslide."*

he lost, there wasn't great apprehension of what Kennedy was going to do. Arthur Schlesinger wrote *Kennedy or Nixon: Does It Make a Difference?* because the two of them seemed to agree on everything except Cuba, where Kennedy was tougher, and Quemoy and Matsu, where Nixon was tougher. There wasn't this dramatic difference, the way there was in the 1940s, with those candidates. We felt that either one of these would be a good man and a good president. It was a new generation, and Jack Kennedy wasn't a flaming liberal in our judgment. He was no Adlai Stevenson. We were glad to see Stevenson out and Kennedy in. Kennedy was a cold warrior. He was a tough customer. Back in the '40s, some of his statements about FDR and the loss of China sounded tougher than Richard Nixon.

Nixon had great respect for Kennedy. He had admiration for Kennedy. I don't believe I ever heard him really be derogatory about Kennedy at all. They had certainly been friends during the '40s. They had traveled together to debate up in Pennsylvania. Joe Kennedy had given money to Nixon's campaign. Nixon had liked Jack Kennedy. But whenever you go through a campaign, you can start off liking the fellow, but by the end you've got confessional material in your mind about what you think ought to be done to that guy.

We heard these stories about Kennedy when I was in St. Louis, but I would say, "Look, I don't believe this stuff. This can't be true." There was sort of an unwritten rule among journalists in those days that you just didn't write about those things. But I do believe this: If Jack Kennedy had lived, and had he won the election in 1964—which I think he would have—by '66 and '67, with all the assaults on the establishment and the way journalism changed, an awful lot of that would have come out. It would have been massively destructive to his reputation. John F. Kennedy is a mythological figure today because of the manner in which he died and the pageantry of his funeral. But if he had lived, there would be no Kennedy myth. There would be no Camelot.

On November 22, 1963, I had just finished writing a major weekend article of two thousand words for the *St. Louis Globe Democrat,* saying, "Goldwater is going to win this nomination; I don't care what the other folks say." It was around noon in St. Louis. Then word came over the AP or UPI wire, and there was just a bustle. We all rushed into the room where the only TV sat, right off the newsroom. We sat and watched, and some of the women in the newsroom were crying, openly crying.

It was really appalling. We watched for most of the afternoon, and we sat around and talked. The publisher wrote the editorial on Jack Kennedy's death. He was very conservative, but it was a good editorial. He put black lines on all the columns on the front page. I went back and took the piece I had written and threw it out. I said, "It's irrelevant now. This is a new world." My friend Denny Walsh and I saw the killing of Oswald a couple of days later, and then we watched that funeral.

That period, all of what went on, really made a tremendous impression on the heart and soul of the country and every individual here. You're never going to forget that. Those are the hours and those are the days that immortalized Jack Kennedy and created the great myth of today.

It was a dramatic change [in America], and I was appalled. It was a horrible thing. But the editorial editor—he was an old fellow, Hamilton Thornton—he said, "You know, this has happened, but Johnson's liable to be a better president."

But I was just taken by it, as I think young people were at that time. Kennedy had just changed the whole world. I was part of the Goldwater movement, and that suffered a crippling blow the day Jack Kennedy was shot because of the blame or the association that this

If he had lived, there would be no Kennedy myth. There would be no Camelot.

was Dallas, the right-wing atmosphere, and all the rest of it. It took a lot of the fun and joy and joie de vivre out of politics.

The Kennedy assassination is a marker of a period. The Eisenhower and Kennedy era should be put together as almost an era of good feeling after the Truman-McCarthy period and before the Johnson-Nixon period, and the death of Jack Kennedy was an exclamation point at the end of that time period. While Johnson had great successes from his presidency all the way through 1974, Richard Nixon's resignation from office really was a time of turmoil, hatred, and division in America; it poisoned our politics for a long time—and Jack Kennedy is on the far side of that. He's back in the good old days, if you will, and what followed was quite an incredible period and very rough.

<hr />

I don't believe the conspiracy theories. I tend to believe the Warren Commission. I believe Oswald fired the three shots. He had already attempted to kill General Walker. He was a Castro-ite. He was a radical. He'd been over in the Soviet Union. There was all the talk about the grassy knoll, but I never really believed it, and I don't think there is as much belief on the conservative side, or even on what you might call the radical right side, in the conspiracy against President Kennedy. I was not as conversant with that as some of the theories you heard on the other side . . . because why would they do it? All the talk later on about the New Orleans crowd down there and all that, I'd leave that to Kevin Costner. I discredit it. I've seen the movies, I've seen all the material, and I believe Oswald acted alone.

On Vietnam, what concerned us was what happened to President Diem; it was impossible or difficult for some of us to believe this could have taken place without the complicity of the government of the United States. Jack Kennedy himself had talked about "personnel changes," and we heard reports that when Kennedy got word that not only was Diem overthrown but that he'd been murdered along with his brother in that armored personnel carrier, he got up, ashen-faced, and left the room.

If Jack Kennedy had not died the way he did, if he had lived, if there had been no assassination, he would have gone through the same hell that Lyndon Johnson did—maybe worse. George Wallace had announced for the Democratic nomination several days before Kennedy died, and Kennedy would have been on the ballot in Wisconsin, Indiana, and Maryland, where Wallace did extraordinarily well. Without Lyndon Johnson in office, Wallace would have torn Kennedy up badly. We would have still gotten the nomination for Barry Goldwater. Goldwater would have been beaten by Kennedy, probably by ten points rather than twenty, but Jack Kennedy would have continued down the road into Vietnam, which was a very popular war in 1963 right on through 1964. His political end might have been as bad as Lyndon Johnson's, if not worse.

Kennedy was a good president. The Cuban Missile Crisis was handled correctly—even if he did give away the Thor and Jupiter missiles in Turkey and Italy and even if he did agree not to invade Cuba—because we really were there on the threshold of a possible mistake that could have led to nuclear war and the destruction of an awful lot of what we all love. That was handled statesmanlike, and he deserves permanent credit for that.

But do I think he's a great president? No, I don't think he's one of the greats. If you look at his domestic achievements, Lyndon Johnson's far exceed what he did. Kennedy got the Trade Expansion Act. He wasn't a strong president legislatively. He didn't get any civil rights bill. What Kennedy is famous for is that he has become an enormously inspirational figure in history for young people, for generation after generation. But again, that's got to do with the way the man died. Richard Nixon felt that he was always held to a more severe and harsh standard than the establishment ever held Jack Kennedy or Bobby Kennedy to, and I think he was right in that. I do think there was a measure of real resentment at how he was treated compared to what others got away with.

Frank Gannon

A twenty-year-old student at Georgetown University in 1963, Frank Gannon regularly played piano for President Kennedy. In the early seventies he worked as an intern to Donald Rumsfeld in the Nixon White House. With then-girlfriend Diane Sawyer, he helped organize Nixon's memoir, *RN,* and later became a conservative fundraiser in New York. In 1982 Gannon began segment-producing *The David Letterman Show* and videotaping interviews with Nixon, some of which proved too frank for public consumption. Gannon now runs the New Nixon website and the Richard Nixon Foundation blog.

I was a senior at Georgetown. For the last couple of years, I had worked my way through school by bartending and playing piano at 1789 in Georgetown. I had been discovered as a piano player earlier that year by Red Fay, the undersecretary of the Navy, who had had been President Kennedy's roommate at OCS at naval training. They were great friends. When Red became the undersecretary to the Navy he started giving parties aboard the secretary of the Navy's yacht, the *Sequoia*. I was playing in 1789 one night, and as I walked out to thunderous applause, he tugged my coat and asked, "Do you play for private parties?"

I said, "I haven't, but I would. Why not?" That was a Friday night, and on Sunday night I was aboard the *Sequoia* playing for the president of the United States. It was incredible for any number of reasons. First of all, I was young, and suddenly you're with a president and the whole panoply of it. We would board the *Sequoia* at the navy yard and then steam across the Anacostia to the air naval station. One of the most vivid memories I have is of him arriving. This was a new level of busy, a scary level of busy that I'd never seen—he's in the back of the limo with a desk, and he's signing things and reading things as they come up. Then he's piped aboard.

The concept of the pressure he was under was another impression I had—the intensity, almost in some cases near hysteria, of the people on the boat to relax him, to make sure he had a good time. It was quite an experience for a young college student.

I'm guessing that I played for him between a dozen and twenty times. I became briefly fashionable, because all the people who were on the boat then hired me to play on land for their private parties. The money I earned from that allowed me to go to graduate school in England. Looking back, I see he was working the room. I was part of the room, and he worked me to a tee. It's become a cliché that when a politician talks to you, he or she makes you feel that you're the only person in the room. That's how I felt. He would come over. His briefers had told him I was president of the student body, so he asked me about my campaign and what the issues were. He would always come over at the beginning. He would come over and ask, "How are you?" and "How are things at school?" And before he left he would come over and say, "Thank you." That was the extent of our relationship.

I was the only piano player, so if it was going to be on a weekend night, they would call in advance so I could ask the owner if I could take off. Early that week, that week of November 20, I got a call from Red's office saying the president was coming back from Texas. If he wasn't too tired, they were going to have a party that night; the *Sequoia* was going go into dry dock, and the next window of opportunity would be April. Every expectation was that it would be a go.

When I finished my noon class and walked down the street, there was a car stopped in the middle of the street, a white Buick convertible with the top down—it was a fairly mild day—and a growing number of students, to which I was added, listening to the radio turned up. That was the first news that the president had been shot. Then I went into a bar with a television set above the bar and listened. Twenty minutes later it was announced that he had died. It was impossible to believe. I was thinking that I was going to be playing for him that night, and then two nights later I was on the forty-block line at the Capitol, waiting to walk past his coffin. It was unimaginable.

Before Billy Joel coined the phrase, I was a piano man, and one of the things a piano man does for his tip jar is have songs that you play for people. Just as I believe that graphologists can tell you a little bit about somebody from their handwriting, I think a pianologist can also tell you something about people by their songs. I had a song for everybody, and the president's song, contrary to conventional wisdom, was not from *Camelot*. It was from the Pulitzer Prize–winning show *How to Succeed in Business without Really Trying*. It was the song "I Believe in You." I can see that. Robert Kennedy's song was from *Camelot*, "If Ever I Would Leave You," which is a more brooding, melancholy, thoughtful song. Mrs. Kennedy's song—I only met her in April 1964, after the assassination, on the *Sequoia*. I asked Red if she'd like a song. He came back about forty minutes later and said, "She does have a song. She wants to know if you can play 'Me and My Shadow.'"

It was a perfect storm in a perfect sense. At the time there was an exponential rise of [household] television sets, and by 1960, 90 percent of American homes had at least one television set. How perfect that, when the medium was in place to bring politics, to bring the first family into every American home, you had the most telegenic first family imaginable in history—and not just the president but the kids. I mean, everybody knew. Even if you weren't a Kennedy supporter, a Democrat, or a liberal, you knew John-John; you knew Caroline. It was an invigorating, inspiring time. You'd have to be either very cold or very unimaginative not to have been touched by that.

— ~ —

I helped Nixon on the research, organizing the research, and writing the memoirs, so it was a very interesting relationship. There's a wonderful handwritten letter in the Nixon Library in Yorba Linda that Kennedy sent to Nixon when Nixon was nominated to be vice president in '52. In it he says, "I always knew you'd go far, but I didn't think you'd go quite this far this fast." They had been friends when they were bookends on the House Education and Labor Committee in 1947 because they were the two youngest members. The Kennedys— Jacqueline and John—invited the Nixons to their wedding. As president of the Senate, Nixon did a number of things that were greatly appreciated by the Kennedys, and they

wrote numbers of letters to express that appreciation when Senator Kennedy was sick and had back problems. Nixon extended votes and did things in order to accommodate Kennedy's problems. They were very cordial, friendly—they were very different people and of different parties—but they had a thing. When Nixon was in Europe in the late '40s with the Herter Committee, the two Kennedy sisters, Jean and Eunice, were there, and Nixon went touring with them one day. There was this kind of relationship. Joe Kennedy had sent, via Jack Kennedy, a check for one thousand dollars to help Nixon in his House race in 1948.

I think the thing that changed it [their relationship] greatly, that was searing for Nixon, was the '60 campaign and coming up against the political organization—the money, the intensity, the ferocity was something. It must have been something to be on the receiving end of it.

On November 22 Nixon was [working] at a law firm on Wall Street. He had been in Dallas the night before and had left that morning. He talked about how when he drove out he could see signs—some not friendly—preparing for the president's arrival coming from Fort Worth that day. He got off the plane at LaGuardia, and they were driving over the Queensboro Bridge. They stopped at a light, and someone rushed out of the shop and said, "The president's been shot." The cab went to 810

Fifth Avenue, where Nixon lived, and he went up and called J. Edgar Hoover. As he describes it, he said, "Who, Edgar, who did this?" Edgar says, "It's a Commonist"—that's how he pronounced "Communist." That was how he found out, stopped at a traffic light on the Manhattan side of the Queensboro Bridge.

It's the most traumatic event for the nation, along with Vietnam, of the latter half of the twentieth century, and I don't think we've actually processed either of them yet. They're still open and raw and unsettled. It changed everybody. But it certainly changed the world for Nixon.

The Kennedy history is one thing, and historians and others for years are going to uncover, analyze, and deconstruct his record and his personality and his peccadilloes. That's not necessarily going to be positive, but that's history.

The Kennedy legacy is going to be the Kennedy mythology. We like to think we've grown out of mythology, but obviously it has a very long pedigree where human beings are concerned. The Kennedy mythology is almost archetypical—a young hero and beloved leader felled at the height of his powers and before his time while trying to lead his people to an exciting, challenging, noble new frontier. That's not necessarily true, but as long as we're still around, and I think for a very long time, that mythology isn't going to be changed or challenged. I think that's a good thing. That's certainly a powerful legacy for any president to leave.

What I think about is a card that's still on my wall from JFK's Navy secretary. A couple of weeks after the assassination, I got this Christmas card from Red Fay, and on the inside he had written: "Frank, you added to his happiness. Red." So in "the watches of the morning," when I finally wake up and surface, if I think about those days, that's what I think about.

> *The Kennedy legacy is going to be the Kennedy mythology.*

Kathy Fay and Paul Fay III

Kathy Fay and Paul Fay III are the children of Paul "Red" Fay Jr., one of President Kennedy's longest and closest friends, who served as undersecretary and secretary of the Navy during his administration. As a family, they spent many joyful days with the Kennedys in a variety of settings, and JFK served as their sister Sally's godfather. Teenagers at the time of the president's death, their father, who died in 2009, told them that he knew as early as 1943 that his friend would become president one day.

PAUL FAY: My father met JFK when they were in training for PT boats in Rhode Island. They went out and played a touch football game, and out walked this skinny kid, as my father referred to him, who had a sweatshirt that was inside out with an "H" on the inside—not showing obviously. All he remembered of the skinny kid who happened to be John Kennedy was that he was all elbows and was running into him the whole time. He was a very difficult guy to cover. That was the first encounter. The second encounter was in the Solomon Islands. My father wanted to change from one PT boat to another when they were doing maneuvers—practice, if you will. He decided to use the flag sign language they had in the Navy, but the message he gave to Kennedy's boat made no sense.

KATHY FAY: I first met President Kennedy in 1959, before my twelfth birthday, at our house in San Francisco. He came in with my father. I don't know the reason, but we were in the living room, and Dad said go sit next to the future possible president of the United States.

PAUL: Kathy and I were kids at the time we knew President Kennedy, in our teens. He had a special quality about him. There was something about President Kennedy that when he was talking to you, there was no one else in the world he was paying attention to. He was focused on you. He was interested in what you had to say in a way that was very personal, and I have yet to meet someone else who had that same quality to that extent. Jackie was a very special lady. She was very good to me, and what people don't realize is what a great sense of humor Jackie Kennedy had. Jackie was a very bright woman, very well read, with a great sense of humor. All I know is that we knew him and the way he treated us, the way we saw him operate with other people and the warmth and the kindness he showed. I never, ever sensed a

President Kennedy autographing photos for Kathy and Paul III

brute in that man. He was never that way. He was always considerate, always thoughtful.

KATHY: We saw intimate moments with him and Jackie. I mean, I saw them with their chaise lounges pushed together, holding hands by the pool, and I just felt a warmth.

PAUL: It was also a different time, and the press then was made up of all males. There were very few females in the press corps at that time. There was a club that certain things weren't spoken about. I don't think it just happened in the White House. I think all over Washington, DC, from senators to congressmen—this was part of the reason you got into office. But the man we knew, he was a remarkable, wonderful man.

KATHY: I was in Seattle with Mom and Dad and my little sister, Sally, who is President Kennedy's goddaughter. Dad was giving a speech to the midshipmen, and while he was giving the speech his aide suggested that we should go shopping. We went to this big department store, and my mother wanted to look at the antiques. I said, "I'll take Sally up to the toy department," because I wasn't interested in antiques. "I'll meet you back here, Mom." On the escalator up to the toy level, I saw one floor where all the televisions were sold. Everybody was gathered around the TV. I thought, *I want to know what's going on over there*, so I said, "Sally, just come with me." People were gathering and gathering; I squeezed into the middle and looked up at the TV, and it said something like "the president has been shot."

It was such a foreign thing that I thought, *the president of Seattle or the president of a bank?* But I was thinking, *Why is it getting so much attention?* Then I listened some more, and they said it was the president of the United States. I thought, *Oh, he's been nicked. That's kind of news.* So I said, "Come on, Sally. We have to go find Mom." I went racing down to the antiques department and found my mother, and I said, "Mom, you're not going to believe this, but the president was shot," and she went, "What?"

I tell her, "Mom, he's just nicked," and this woman comes over and says, "No, my dear, it's serious; it's very serious." My mother just came sort of unglued, dropped to her knees, and started to say a prayer, and this other woman dropped to her knees. I'm going, "Mom, I just don't believe this." I mean, it was just—everybody was really upset, and I was holding on to Sally.

I was still not focusing. This is just not happening. This is too weird. So we get back into the car to go back to where we were going to meet Dad, and on the radio it says, "The president, the thirty-fifth president of the United States, John Fitzgerald Kennedy, has died." My little sister looks up and says to me, "Kathy, does that mean I don't have a godfather anymore?" I didn't even want to acknowledge that.

My mother was crying, and I still was just not believing this. We get back to the headquarters, waiting around for Dad to walk in, and my father, who's so expressive and always had an expression in his face— anger or humor, warmth, love, or something—when he walked through the door and I took one look at him, it was like there was nothing there. He had lost his soul. That's when I knew the president had gone, and it was horrible, just devastating to us.

When he [my father] walked through the door and I took one look at him, it was like there was nothing there. He had lost his soul.

PAUL: I was in boarding school in New Hampshire, and that was the weekend we bought our skis, ski hats, et cetera. They were in the auditorium selling us these different items, and somebody ran in and said, "The president's been shot." We went into the one TV room, and that's when I heard about it. It was devastating.

KATHY: We attended the funeral. We also attended the very private funeral, where we all stood in line to greet Jackie. I was there with Mom and Dad. This was just private, where dignitaries and personal family friends got the opportunity to say a few words to Jackie. We were standing in line, and I could see the tears running down my father's face. But he said to me, "Kathy, whatever you do when you see Jackie, do not cry." That just increased the odds for the flow of tears. It was so upsetting. When I had my moment with Jackie, I just lost it. I hugged her and said, "I am so sorry," and she hugged me for maybe ten seconds, which is a long time. She whimpered and just held me. It was an incredible moment. It was like she was allowed just to release with someone. I was crying, and she was whimpering, and it was just an incredible moment, really close, that I felt very privileged to have experienced.

Not long after I wrote her a letter.

Dear Jackie,

I will never forget when I first met the president. I was sitting on his lap in San Francisco, and he was telling me about when he would become president. He invited me over to the White House. Even at that early date, I knew it would come true. It certainly came true, but it all went too quickly. I still to this day don't wholly believe what happened. The president to me has always been my dream man. Every time I saw him, I thought my heart would never calm down. When

Daddy told me to kiss him goodnight at Camp David, I shied away with embarrassment. Now I wish I could have kissed and hugged him a million times. I loved the president very much and always will, but I know I could never love him as much as you do. I hope that if a crisis ever hit our house I could carry on as majestically and beautiful as you did. What I have just said is not nearly as much as I feel. I only know that you and the president will always be in my mind, the greatest first lady and president the world has ever known. I will pray for you.
    Sincerely yours,
    Katherine Fay

PAUL: For me, President Kennedy was somebody who was inclusive as opposed to divisive. What we have today is: Everybody has very strong beliefs. President Kennedy obviously had very strong beliefs, but he was someone who was open to hear everybody. My father would tell me stories where somebody extremely conservative and very Republican would come in and meet with President Kennedy. They would walk away maybe not agreeing with President Kennedy but knowing that they had a fair hearing and that it was an enjoyable experience. To me, that's his legacy of a time when things weren't so polarized. For instance, my father campaigned for Dwight Eisenhower. My father, who was one of Kennedy's best friends, campaigned for Ike! President Kennedy understood it because he understood my father and understood his background. He had an understanding of people. That doesn't mean he would have changed his beliefs for that, but it shows he was a big man and a great intellect in my opinion. I think that was the legacy he left me: "Try not to be small, but try to be big."

KATHY: He wasn't judgmental at all. I think he was open to everyone, and you could feel it when you met him. He just paid attention. He was interested in everyone and felt everyone should have a fair shake at life. He was a great man.

PAUL: I had conversations with my father about the Warren Commission. I said, "Dad, don't you feel that maybe the Warren Commission was not spot-on correct, because there seems to be all this other evidence of possible outside influences?" My father said of course he had heard of that and read about it, but he said he thought the Warren Commission was correct. That is the most I ever got out of my father on that subject. My father and the majority of President Kennedy's best friends— and I would even say Bobby—accepted the Warren Commission and wanted to move on.

They didn't want to dwell on it. That was his attitude, and [it was] the same with most of his and President Kennedy's other friends, like Chuck Spalding. His son, Dick Spalding, is a good friend of mine. None of them really wanted to focus on possible other conspiracies. They all wanted to close that chapter of the book. It hurt them all so much. They just wanted to close the chapter.

KATHY: The same with me from Dad. He said, "Kathy, if any of this could bring him back, fine, but this Warren Commission—nothing can bring the president back, so I don't really want to talk about it. It's done." It wasn't his favorite subject at all.

PAUL: My father firmly believed that if President Kennedy had remained president, if he'd lived, we wouldn't have gone to Vietnam. My father was either on the *Sequoia* or the *Honey Fitz* with the president, and a call came in. It was one of the commanders. The president said, "Red, I want you to come with me to listen to this." We had sent some troops over there as advisors to Vietnam, and one of the commanders wanted to have the advisors get engaged in a firefight on the ground in Vietnam at that time. President Kennedy told the general for every man that he heard was engaged in that fight he would bring two soldiers back. He did not want us to get engaged in a ground war in Vietnam, and my father, if he were alive today, would have said categorically that President Kennedy would have done everything he could not to have gone into a war in Vietnam.

Bill Daley

Son of legendary Chicago mayor Richard Daley, Bill Daley was fifteen years old in 1963. He went on to become an attorney, bank executive, secretary of commerce under President Clinton, and White House chief of staff in President Obama's first administration.

There was that Irish Catholic connection between the families. We had different types of politics, different upbringings, but my dad saw in the president an opportunity for America to move forward and for Irish Catholics to get recognized by someone who was the best of the representatives at the time. There were lots of Irish politicians at local levels throughout America, but the idea of someone with John Kennedy's background having the chance to be president of the United States, along with the personal connection my dad had with him, was an opportunity that my dad saw that was unique. That added to the enthusiasm for the president when he ran.

My father may have had reservations early on, but I know he always talked of the convention in '56 when then-senator Kennedy made a run for the vice presidency and how close he came, and how excited my dad was to be part of trying to do that. My dad had been around for a while and knew most of the national political players, so I don't think he ever thought Jack Kennedy took second place to any of the national people, including Adlai Stevenson, who was a strong Illinois person and a very close friend of my dad. But by the time '60 came around, my dad was of the opinion that Adlai's time had passed and this truly was a chance to energize the nation and the party and give the Irish Catholics of America something to be proud of forever.

My father thought he [Joe Kennedy] was a tough guy. They made a major investment in Chicago years before with the Merchandise Mart.

A young Bill Daley (far left) with his father, Chicago mayor Richard Daley, President Kennedy, his mother, and five of his six siblings

My dad knew him well. Up until or even after the stroke, he used to come out to Chicago. He came out to Chicago once or twice to get the reports on what was going on with that investment, so my dad stayed in touch with them. He thought he was an extremely bright businessman and used to say that Theodore White's book *Making of the President, 1960* could've been a one-word book, and that word was "father." He believed JFK's father was the one who made him the president.

My father and John Kennedy were close. The first time met him I was something like twelve, and all of us were in a room with him. He had a great ability to engage even the young kids like us. He would ask us questions, and everyone was nervous as heck! He asked one of my sisters, "Do you teach in a Catholic school?" and she said, "Yes." About five seconds later she said, "No, I teach in a Catholic school." She was fumbling all over herself, and my dad was like, "What's going on here?"

But he engaged us as young people, and he was always very friendly. I remember once he called during the summer of the convention, before the convention in '60, and my parents were at a summer house we rented up in Michigan. I picked up the phone, and he said, "Is the mayor there?" I said, "No, he's not here," and he said, "This is Jack Kennedy. Would you tell him I called?" I said, "Do you want me to go get him?" He said, "No, just tell him I called." I jumped on my bike and rode down to where my mom and dad were and told him. Dad came back and called him, and it was all in anticipation of the '60 convention.

He came to Chicago quite a bit during that election. He came for the first debate, which was in Chicago. He helicoptered, which was new, from Indiana into Meigs Field, which at the time was a small runway right on the lakefront of Chicago. There must've been ten or fifteen thousand people out there waiting for him to arrive. Shortly before the helicopter landed, the crowds pushed the fence down, and these people all came running out toward the helicopter. It was kind of like you saw with the Beatles a few years later. It was that sort of hysteria. The police had to put sort of a circle around everyone. Kennedy got in a car and rode down Lakeshore Drive. It was absolute mania going on. Then on the Friday before the election, he came for what used to be called a torchlight parade, which ran from State and Madison downtown out to the old Chicago Stadium on Madison Avenue. There were a million people between State and Madison—and that's probably only two or three miles long at most.

It was unbelievable to see. He was obviously a very good looking guy. It was a whole new generation. He represented it more than anyone. He was a war hero. He had it all going on. This was as good a political operation in the beginning of the new media world that had ever been seen. But you started with somebody who, again, was incredibly good looking, articulate. He had a certain style about him that maybe Cary Grant had; there weren't many politicians out there who had that sort of style. Most were short, heavyset sort of politicians or Southern senators who walked around with Panama hats on, smoking cigars. Kennedy just had a whole different way that was very representative of that new generation, and it was amazing to see the hysteria in people.

The Kennedys went to the best schools in America. It was their wealth and the style, and the lifestyle that gave them was something no one had seen publicly, especially in the political world. He had his own airplane. There were lots of people who honored that and weren't so cynical about it as we would be today. They wanted to have it, but there were also people in our neighborhood when we grew up who were proud that somebody had that who was Irish Catholic, knowing that most didn't get that chance. It wasn't held against them—it was celebrated; it was great that one of us was able to do that and get there.

There's a famous picture we have of Kennedy in an open car coming down Madison; it's bedlam. Everyone in the picture has a stressful look on their face, from the press to his sisters in the car to my dad. There's great anxiety. Kennedy's got the biggest smile on his face, enjoying himself. It's a great picture, and it kind of summarized how much he enjoyed that. It was a great rally. I remember sitting there, listening to his speech; we were all out there, our whole family, and it was four days later that he was elected.

I remember election night. It was a long night: My dad came home around four or five o'clock in the morning, showered, changed clothes, and then went back downtown. It probably wasn't until about ten in the morning, I think, before they actually called it. The untold story is that when there were allegations about vote fraud—and this is fifty years ago—my father offered to pay for half of a statewide recount if the Republican Party would pay for the other half. They refused.

We were the first family on the day after the inauguration that Kennedy had breakfast with. Truman, and then us. You know that picture we have in our house? We were the first guests, and he took us for a tour. We all went to the inauguration, six of the seven of us. My brother Rich was a freshman and at a Catholic college, and they wouldn't

> *My father offered to pay for half of a statewide recount if the Republican Party would pay for the other half. They refused.*

let him out because he had a final exam, so the six of us went. It was great excitement, and my brother John and I—and I was twelve or thirteen—we had white ties and tails and top hats we had rented. Top hats! It was crazy. That evening after the Inaugural Ball, we were going back to the hotel. My dad said, "How'd you like to go to the White House tomorrow?" and I said, "Great." He said, "We're all going over early." So about 8:00 or 8:30 in the morning, we're there. I think the president had had breakfast with Harry Truman, and then Truman and the president came walking in from the residence, and we were all sitting in the Cabinet Room. My dad was close to Harry Truman also over the years, so we all said hello. Then Truman left, President Kennedy took us into the Oval Office, and we had pictures taken. He wrote a note to each of us, a handwritten note. When he came to me, he asked, "What's your name?" and I said, "Bill." My dad said, "*William*," so the note is to William.

Then he said, "Come on; I just moved in here yesterday. Let's go for a tour." So Kennedy took us for a tour of the White House, and he showed us the swimming pool. Then we went into the main building, the residence. We went upstairs, and they were having public tours on the main floor. The staff and the security people started to put curtains up, like bamboo curtains, to separate, and he said, "No, no, no; don't put those up." So the tours were going on in one part of the aisle, and we were walking down the other. Then somebody would say, "There's the Blue Room, there's the Red Room," and Kennedy said, "We can't go upstairs" because Mrs. Kennedy was upstairs resting; as you know, she had just had a baby shortly before the inauguration. So Kennedy took us for a tour, and then we went back to the Oval Office to say good-bye to him. My brother Rich came down to Washington with my dad six months later. Kennedy said to him, "You weren't here for the inauguration," and Rich said, "No." Kennedy said, "Come on, I'll give you the tour I gave them." So he took Rich for a tour of the place. It was great. We have a terrific picture of the six of us, my mom and dad, and the president on January 21 in the Oval Office.

When I left the White House under President Obama, he gave me a picture of my dad in the Oval Office with Kennedy and a picture of him and me in the Oval Office with a handwritten note to me, which was very kind.

My father thought Kennedy was doing great all the time. He was extremely proud, and he was supporting him from morning till night on whatever he wanted to do. He believed Kennedy was getting the country moving. He was focusing on urban America; he was going to try to get things done. He obviously had a very difficult Congress at the time, with Southern Democrats and Republicans, different than today.

I'm sure they talked about civil rights. I'm not sure which of the tapes relate to that, but the civil rights [movement], the whole change that was going on in America and in urban cities and the migration into the big cities, like Chicago, and the difficulties that were going on, was one of the reasons my dad wanted Kennedy to win. But it was a tumultuous time, even those three brief years, for America: on race and obviously on Vietnam.

We all went out to the airport when the president came to dedicate O'Hare. We did the whole thing with him, and then he did a couple of major Cook County Democratic Party fundraisers. He spoke at at least one or two of those. One time he was riding out to McCormick Place, and a new development had been built, a mixed-race development on the South Side, not far from McCormick Place, called Prairie Shores. My dad was in the car—this is the old days—and they diverted the motorcade because he wanted to show Kennedy the development. They were good friends and had a lot of exchanges. In early November '63 Kennedy was supposed to come out to the Air Force–Army game at Soldier Field in Chicago. It was the weekend that the assassination of the president of Vietnam took place, so he called that morning to say he couldn't come out for the game, which was rather disappointing—about three weeks later he was assassinated.

The last time we saw him was at the Mayors Conference in June '63 in Hawaii. My mom and dad, my brother John, and I went out to that. My dad may have been president of the Mayors Conference that year. They had a big hall for him to come in and speak, and my brother John and I were standing on the aisle. Kennedy came down the aisle, and there was a lot less security back then, but there was still a lot of security. But as Kennedy was coming down the aisle, shaking hands with people, we were trying to get to him like everybody else. He shook hands with us; he looked and went about two feet and then turned around and said, "What are you guys doing here? Where's your father?" We said, "He's up on the stage." All these people are looking at us like, *What the heck did he stop and talk to them for?*

Kennedy went up and gave his speech. My father had a tendency, as an Irishman, I guess, to get really red if he was out in the sun. He looked like a lobster. So on the way back out of the place, Kennedy came over and said, "Jeez, your dad's really sunburned. Take care of him. Have a good time in Hawaii," or something like that. But John and I were looking, and the people around us were like, *Who the heck are these two guys?*

—◆—

I was a sophomore in high school, and they announced on the PA system that he had been shot. We were in English class, and then they announced that he had passed away. We went to Latin class, and then they ended the day for everyone. We all left early in the afternoon. I got on the bus, and no one was talking. Women were crying as we went home. My brother and I were taking the bus home, and there was just a hush. When people did talk, they talked in hushed tones; there were women crying, and you could just see the stunned look on everyone's faces.

We lived in a very ethnic, Catholic neighborhood. Obviously all the churches opened up that evening, had some sort of prayer service. There was just an enormous pall over the city that I don't think I've ever experienced. It was probably somewhat similar to 9/11. That night, Friday night, my dad came home for dinner, and that was only the second time in my life I ever saw him cry: when his father died and that night. I think my father was of the sense that things were possibly spinning out of control. How could this happen? With all the other social changes going on, there was great fear that there was something—an undercurrent—here that was going to be very bad for the country.

We saw ourselves vulnerable as a nation to things that were foreign to us. At the time of the Cold War, the racial changes, the social changes in the country, Kennedy was making changes and represented a new way of doing things. But with his assassination, there began to be a real concern: Were these new ways going to spin out of control? Were we going to change things fundamentally and lose control in a disorganized way and not with a game plan?

Then you went into the mid-'60s, the war and the disturbances throughout many cities in America and the rest of the world, and then you stumbled into '68 and all hell broke loose—a president chased out of office, Bobby Kennedy assassinated, Martin Luther King, the Democratic Convention, the Russians invade Czechoslovakia—and nobody does anything, you know? You have the riots in Paris and the youth riots, and the whole world seemed to be spinning out of control that year.

My father was—in the sense that this person he had put so much hope in, and again this Irish Catholic thing—really strong. For someone with my father's background, who fought to come up into politics and government and leadership and to have the chance to work with an Irish Catholic president—someone he was close to, had known for quite a few years, and had known the father for many years because they had substantial investments in Chicago—it really affected him. You could just feel it. You could see it. He acted that way for a while, for quite a while, and that transferred in many ways to Bobby and then to Ted Kennedy even many years later. He stayed very close to them and with many of the people who were close to the Kennedys.

Swanee Hunt

A daughter of Texas oil tycoon H. L. Hunt, Swanee Hunt was thirteen years old in 1963. Her father was a right-wing firebrand on the radio, and after the assassination, some believed that ultraconservatives in Dallas, including H. L. Hunt, may have played a role in JFK's death. More recently, Swanee Hunt founded the Women and Public Policy Program at Harvard University's Kennedy School of Government, and President Clinton appointed her as his ambassador to Austria. She is also the Eleanor Roosevelt lecturer in public policy at the Kennedy School.

Dad was sixty-one when I was born, so he was in his late seventies as I was developing my own voice. It was actually my mother who—when she found out that Mark, the boy I wanted to marry, had voted for Hubert Humphrey—opposed our marriage adamantly, even though he was training to be a Southern Baptist minister. She opposed it and opposed it, but then when it became inevitable, she decided, "I'm going to get onboard. How do I tell your father?" She went into the library and told him. Mark and I were waiting, and then we went in, and he was very pleased. He said, "I think you ought to start having babies right away." He was thinking more about legacy than he was about what my points of view were.

My first memory of John Kennedy was when my dad was in the paper and the headline was "Hunt Backs Jack." It was so extraordinary because my father wasn't just an ardent anti-Communist; he was really a voice for the rightest of the right. But he felt very disillusioned when Jack Kennedy came to be president; he figured that the Communists at Harvard had ruined him. Dad was a huge admirer of Joe Kennedy, so he was quite disappointed in Joe's son Jack—but he just couldn't stand Nixon.

Dad wasn't vitriolic, but he was very convinced that the Communists had infiltrated our country. It's so interesting when we think about those times. The Soviets had instilled a reign of terror in Eastern Europe. Let's not forget that when Khrushchev was banging his shoes saying, "We will bury you," that was real. But dad had *Lifeline,* a series of radio stations with his program that he sponsored, and they were advocating things like getting out of the United Nations because it was Communist controlled—actually all the universities were

Swanee Hunt with her father, H. L.

Communist controlled. I went to SMU, ten minutes from the house, even though it was "Communist controlled." I really wanted to go to Radcliffe, but because it was run by Communists, I couldn't. And you know what? Fifteen years ago, when I went to Harvard to teach, Radcliffe asked me to come and speak there. I told them that story, that I really wanted to come to Radcliffe and my father wouldn't let me because it was run by Communists. Someone in the back of the room yelled out, "We were," so maybe there was more to it.

I didn't share his views, but we didn't argue with him—it was sort of a very old-style patriarchy. I'd say our family tree looked like a weeping willow. Of all of Dad's kids, and there were fourteen living, I believe I was the youngest to pull out of that point of view. I was a child of the '60s. I was born in 1950, so as I was shaping my own view of myself and also of society, Gloria Steinem was out there leading the women's movement; there was the civil rights movement, the anti–Vietnam War movement. I was really influenced by those in a way that my older brothers and sisters weren't.

Regarding the climate in the city, I went to an all-girls school that had an unusual number of what we would call liberal students because they were from the Jewish community. And yet I remember being on the playground playing tetherball, and we were chanting, "We'll have a World War III. We elected Kennedy." If you want to understand the culture, one of the good places to do that is on a playground, because the kids are soaking it up from their families at home.

I found out from John Kenneth Galbraith, who's now deceased but was a friend, that Dad called Galbraith and said, "Why don't we have a radio program, and you and I will represent different points of view." I think that's fascinating. My father had no formal education. He left home when he was about eleven, jumped on a railroad car, and laid railroad tracks. He planted eucalyptus, was a short-order cook, a lumberjack. He was born in 1889, so he was of the era of what we call self-made men, that American phenomenon. It actually did exist.

Everything about our upbringing was uncomfortable except for the First Baptist Church. I'm not now an evangelical fundamentalist, but at First Baptist Church you had the strong evangelical Christians, fundamentalists who were really reacting against the social gospel, which was saying we need to care about civil rights and things like that. They said, "No, it's your relationship to the Lord, to Jesus." Well, that was at a crossroads with political conservatism, the far right, and out of that came the religious right. It happened at First Baptist Church. I was there. First Baptist Church had two pastors in ninety-six years. My father was representing the political piece, and my mother, God bless her, was representing the religious piece, and it was happening at the church. We were at the church eighteen hours a week.

I was drawn into politics because it was political conversations every night. I would ask questions like, "Who is Alger Hiss?" and Dad was furious when I asked that. He said, "You don't know who Alger Hiss is. That shows you're being influenced by Communist dupes." You couldn't really ask a question even about a person I thought would show that I was engaged. But no, we didn't have that ominous feeling about Kennedy in my in my circle.

The week that Kennedy was coming to Dallas, there was a great sense of expectation—it was exciting that he was coming, and I wasn't afraid in any way. Everyone in the country knows where they were, what the room looked like, what the sounds in the air were when they got the news of the death. I was in a science class, and it came on over the loudspeaker at the school. I was thirteen. The teacher's face became ashen. I remember getting a beaker from the lab and getting some water to take to her, and then all of a sudden the principal knocked on the door and asked me to come out of the room. My sister Helen, who's a year older, was already in the hallway, and we were whisked off in a police car, an unmarked police car as I recall, and taken to the home not of friends in our inner circle at the church but of the next town. We were told never to tell anyone where we were. We didn't see our parents for weeks. My sister, who was in the university, was taken in by a professor. My brother stayed close to the frat house because of death threats against my family. That wasn't the first time we had had death threats. I remember being on an airplane. The plane landed, and everyone was asked to keep their seats, and then my family was taken off by security people, sort of guarded so that we wouldn't be shot by a sniper. That was part of our life.

My father disappeared, and my mother disappeared. We found out later that they had put on some sunglasses and essentially gotten the

We were whisked off in a police car, an unmarked police car as I recall, and taken to the home not of friends in our inner circle at the church but of the next town. We were told never to tell anyone where we were. We didn't see our parents for weeks.

hell out of Dodge. They went incognito out of Dallas and were gone for quite a while, but we didn't have contact with them. We didn't know what was going on. I never had a one-on-one conversation with him about what happened—we never had conversations. I don't remember Dad ever asking, "How was your day?" We saw each other every day; at six o'clock we were to be at the table because *Lifeline* was going to start, and the radio was on the table. After we heard the fifteen-minute show, he changed the dial and heard another fifteen-minute show. That was our thirty minutes at the table. But he adored Helen and me and my brother and other sister, and he had us sing for company every night. We always had company, five nights out of seven, and Helen and I would sing anti-Communist ditties: "Put on your thinking cap, and see the big booby trap and the mistaken

bait for you and me, and if we don't awaken we will all be taken, and we'll never more be free," instead of "Put on Your Old Grey Bonnet." It was pretty far out there.

Those radio programs were very popular in the rural South. We have our comparables now, but it wasn't mean; it wasn't a Rush Limbaugh name-calling. He didn't want to say "Communist" on the air, so it was "the mistaken enemies of freedom." I think that "mistaken" is a very respectful word to use as I look back on it. It's just that they were behind every door and under every rug.

My father's name continued to pop up, however, when there were conspiracy theories. It was pretty hard. Not long ago, in 2006, I was in doing some work at an inner-city school in Boston, where I live, and saw a chart the kids had made about the Kennedy assassination. How amazing is that? They showed the different theories, and there was H. L. Hunt. Like, whoa! Even now, there's that thought. But those ideas really didn't go anywhere; people have studied them, looked so carefully. I don't let it haunt me.

At the end of his life, Dad was still very concerned about the country, but he had passed that on. I was one of what he called "the youth freedom speakers," so there was a sense of his passing on the baton to people like me. He thought I would still be making speeches about the Communists and Cuba and how they're so close to our shores and that sort of thing. But you know what Dad was able to accomplish? He passed his zeal on to me, my two sisters, my brother, and others. He had a vision that he was going to save the country from the Communists. Can you imagine that kind of vision? I have a vision too. I'm working on how to double the number of women in Congress. I'm working on how to stop sex trafficking around the world. I'm working on how to stop war by elevating women's voices. That comes from Dad. It comes from Mom and her religious commitment.

When I was living in Heidelberg, in my twenties, I went to a movie with friends. It was on an Army base actually. We watched whatever movie was coming through. It was called *Executive Action*. We were half an hour into it, and I realized it was about the assassination of Kennedy, and they're talking about my father as having bankrolled this and that. I think they even called him "Harold"; my dad's name was Haroldson. Those kinds of moments probably happened five or six times, and they were gut-wrenching. But I've talked to people who've looked so carefully at this, and I am convinced that it is part of that whole conspiracy attraction, the seduction.

I heard about the Oswald letter to my father on the radio. No one told me that it was coming. It made big news where I was living in Heidelberg. Actually it was written to "Mr. Hunt." People who've looked at it very carefully over several years have discovered that it was actually intended for E. Howard Hunt, who was involved in the whole Watergate mess. It was also a forgery by the KGB. It was never even really for Mr. Hunt [or my father].

Jimmy Carter

In 1963 Jimmy Carter was a forty-year-old Georgia state senator and farmer. Having inherited his father's debt-ridden farm, he had to live in public housing while he studied agriculture at public libraries. He became governor of Georgia in 1971 and president of the United States in 1977. His post-presidency years, widely considered a model of humanitarianism and public service, have garnered him countless awards, including the Nobel Peace Prize in 2002.

Kennedy was popular in Georgia. In fact, when I was first campaigning in Massachusetts, I was asked, "Why do you think you're going get the votes in Massachusetts?" I pointed out that John Kennedy got a bigger margin of victory in Georgia than he did in Massachusetts when he ran for president, so he'd been pretty popular in Georgia except for some people who considered the race issue most important. Of course John Kennedy played a strong role in bringing about equality between the races, and that was not popular with a small fringe of people in Georgia. But I think he was popular.

In our family he was perhaps the most popular president in my lifetime—more than FDR. My father supported FDR in 1932, but he never voted for him again because he was basically opposed to government intrusion in private affairs; plus he was a farmer. When Roosevelt put a program into effect that required people to plough up cotton and peanuts, kill pigs, and initiate daylight saving time, my father felt that was an unwarranted intrusion. My daddy was a Libertarian more than a Democrat in those days, but my mother, I think, privately voted for Franklin Roosevelt because of Eleanor Roosevelt. I don't know for sure about that, but I think there was no doubt that before the 1964 Goldwater/Johnson

election, Georgia was overwhelmingly favorable toward Democrats, including John Kennedy.

I had been quite interested in politics, even when I was in the Navy, and when I resigned from the Navy to come home to work on the farm—I was a farmer for sixteen or seventeen years, growing mostly peanuts, cotton, and corn—John Kennedy was very important to me. My mother was a very strong supporter of the Kennedys. She supported Robert Kennedy also, when he ran for president.

I was working in my warehouse on the day John Kennedy was shot. I was on a tractor, as a matter of fact, hauling grain and peanuts back and forth. I unhooked my tractor from a trailer to weigh it and went into my warehouse where farmers were. Some of them were listening to the radio and told me that the president had just been shot. I was startled and grieved. In a few minutes the news came across—I think Walter Cronkite said it—that the president was no longer living. I went outside on the private porch and cried for a while. It was the first time I had really wept for more than ten years. The last time I had wept before that was when my father died. John Kennedy's loss was a great personal blow to me, and I grieved along with the overwhelming portion of people in my own community and throughout the South. Later I had a chance, as president, to speak at the dedication of his library.

I grew up in a segregated society. I lived in Orchard, Georgia, which is west of Plains, just a small community. We were surrounded by about 215 African Americans, so all my playmates, all the people with whom I grew up, were African Americans, and they made a heavy and beneficial impact on my life. I saw at an early stage, particularly because of my mother being a registered nurse and dealing with these families, the devastating impact of racial segregation, which at that time was supported by the Supreme Court, Congress, the American Bar Association, the churches, and everybody else, including the whole congressional delegation in Georgia and of other states as well. I saw the devastating, adverse impact of that very misguided thing that had lasted almost a hundred years after the Civil War, and I saw that John Kennedy and Robert were two of the people who were condemning it, maybe sometimes tentatively but effectively.

When he died, I didn't know how John Kennedy's replacement, Lyndon Johnson, would act, but he turned out to be a real hero. It was Johnson who actually put into effect the civil rights acts that have transformed our country, following in the footsteps of the Kennedys. I don't believe that John Kennedy, even in a second term, would've been able to get the civil rights acts passed that Lyndon Johnson did, because it was a narrow margin when Johnson finally got Congress to agree. But his inimitable way to marshal the decisions of Congress to accommodate his desires was really what made it possible for us to get the civil rights acts passed. Maybe to some degree, it benefited from the aftermath of the assassination of John Kennedy. I think the sorrow and appreciation that went into the political environment because of John Kennedy's death did help Lyndon Johnson put into effect the civil rights acts.

I had never thought about running for public office for those fifteen or sixteen years while I was farming, but I was always affected beneficially by the idealism and innovations John Kennedy brought to the presidency. He was the first president born in this century. He was young and vigorous, dynamic and eloquent. He was a Navy veteran, as I was, and as Lyndon Johnson and Gerald Ford were; we were all Navy veterans. He brought a good image and also good accomplishments to the White House. Those were the key elements that affected me: the Kennedys' idealism and eloquence, Lyndon Johnson's persuasiveness on Congress, and the need I felt to see racial segregation end in the South and throughout the nation.

I went outside on the private porch and cried for a while.

That said, the tinge of the Vietnam War and the attempted assassinations, the anti-Cuban factor, and the Bay of Pigs disaster provide some remnants of negative memory of John Kennedy. But I think they've faded into relative secondary importance [when measured against] the idealism, vivacity, and progressiveness he brought,  at least in my mind and, I think, in the general public's. There's a general feeling of good and gratitude toward John Kennedy.

Both Kennedy's and Johnson's administrations provided me not only with ideas but also with personnel. My secretary of defense, Harold Brown, has just written a book that covers a good deal about what he learned in direct meetings with John Kennedy on the nuclear issue, the Cold War with Russia, and the development of our nuclear arsenal. A lot of those top personnel who worked with Kennedy did work for me in the White House. I walked in his footsteps like I walked in the footsteps of all previous presidents in a way. But what John Kennedy brought to the White House has really not been duplicated, replicated, or even felt an element of competition. There's still that vivacity and that change from one generation to another, which really has not existed since that time.

The most direct effect of John Kennedy's administration was the Peace Corps. My mother, who worshipped John and Bobby Kennedy, went into the Peace Corps largely because of her affection for them. She was still in the Peace Corps when she was seventy years old, serving in India. Later, my oldest grandson, Jason Carter, my mother's great-great grandson, fulfilled that position as a Peace Corps volunteer. He served in the Peace Corps in South Africa. So both my mother and my oldest grandson have served in the Peace Corps, partially honoring the legacy of John Kennedy.

One thing we should remember is to address the key issues of our nation truthfully and forthrightly, which I believe he did. In my opinion, there is a legacy of John Kennedy that emphasizes human rights and peace. Our country has

Both Kennedy's and Johnson's administrations provided me not only with ideas but also with personnel.

gone backward tremendously in the aftermath of 9/11 in honoring the basic premises of human rights. There are thirty paragraphs in the Universal Declaration of Human Rights, and the United States is now violating ten of those premises. That would be inimical to what John Kennedy stood for.

Since the Second World War, the United States has been involved in conflict after conflict. John Kennedy was very heavily affected—as was I—by the need to avoid war because of a threat of a nuclear conflagration that would have destroyed the earth if we had gone to war with the Soviet Union. During the Cold War years, there was a great reticence to [get involved in] regional conflicts that could've led to a war between the two super powers. That was particularly on my mind when I saw the fighting between Israel and Egypt bring about a nuclear alert system when Nixon was in office. I tried to avoid that process by bringing peace between Israel and Egypt, and I think John Kennedy had that same feeling of foreboding that a regional war could erupt into a super power conflagration that would've brought a nuclear holocaust.

Bill Clinton

In 1963 seventeen-year-old Bill Clinton was the Hot Springs High School delegate to Boys State, where he was elected Arkansas's delegate to Boys Nation. While attending Boys Nation in Washington, DC, Clinton shook hands with President Kennedy in the Rose Garden. A photograph of that meeting, just four months before JFK was assassinated, remains one of President Clinton's proudest possessions. Having attended Georgetown and then Oxford, he won the Arkansas governorship in 1978 and, after a later term as governor, the US presidency in 1992 for two terms. Since leaving the White House he has devoted himself to public speaking and humanitarian work through his philanthropic foundation. His Clinton Global Initiative has helped improve the lives of more than four hundred million people around the world.

I doubt if he would have run without it [his father's wealth and drive], and he probably wouldn't have run if his brother—who by all accounts was a truly exceptional man—hadn't been killed in World War II. But I think that by the time he ran he was quite a gifted politician who was smart enough, able enough, and knew enough to get himself elected president. And in the new era, when primaries prevailed, he turned out to be quite effective in those primaries.

1960 was the second presidential election I followed. We got a television shortly before the 1956 election. I was really involved. I lived in a Republican county, and when the election was going on, my ninth grade English teacher let us debate the election every day. I was virtually the only one taking Kennedy's side. I was debating with my best friend, who came from a Republican family, who said, "Nixon has more experience, and he isn't bad on civil rights," which was true at the time. I said the country was sluggish; we needed new leadership. It was very interesting to me, how it all played out. It was my first real obsessive following of politics day to day.

For me what was interesting was that Kennedy came from a wealthy family, whose father was obviously much more conservative than he was. He was pro–civil rights, and he wanted an economy that worked

Photograph © Bettmann / CORBIS

for everybody. He seemed genuinely concerned about other people, and he was young and vigorous. You just had the feeling that if he got the job he'd do something with it, and I think he did.

The people he appointed clearly had deep convictions about civil rights. If you look at Burke Marshall, John Doar, and all those people in the Justice Department, they weren't playing games. They were serious. It may have been a political masterstroke when he called Coretta King when Martin Luther King was jailed. It certainly meant a lot to me and other Southerners who were pro–civil rights.

But it's important not to judge him now by the standards and the reality that prevailed then. He made a beginning, and some important things happened while he was president and before he was assassinated. President Johnson of course did much more and maybe felt it more because of his own upbringing. But it was made possible because Kennedy won that election and started the ball rolling.

He showed a concern for people who were dispossessed around the world. That's what the Alliance for Progress was about. It's what the Peace Corps was about—though I think his feelings were maybe not as rooted in his own experience as President Johnson's were. He was putting his toe in. He knew how much Harry Truman had angered the South while integrating the military and any number of other things, and we had Strom Thurmond's Dixiecrat Party in 1948. He could see, like anybody who had eyes then, that there would be a price to pay. Remember, just a few years later, when President Johnson signed the Voting Rights Act, he said he had created a generation in which the Democrats wouldn't win the South. It turned out to be painfully true.

When I go back to Georgetown, if I'm taking people there who are not familiar with it, I take them by the house and show them the stoop where he announced Bobby [as his attorney general] and said he thought Bobby ought to have a little experience before he went into private legal practice. It was a great line. But Bobby Kennedy had been counsel to the McClellan Committee, and he turned out to be one of finest attorneys general this country ever had.

I think he wanted Bobby because he knew Bobby would always have his back. I think you *should* want an attorney general who'll tell you the truth about the law and not let you do something illegal but also understands that the presidency as an institution needs to be protected.

They [the press] liked him. I think they identified with him. It was something new, and as it turned out, it wasn't only something new—there was substance there. At that time we were close enough to World War II, close enough to Korea—we were in the bulge of the Cold War—that the press knew the stakes were high, and they were a little more reluctant to troll the White House and play the "get-the-president" game. I think that happened more after Watergate happened and they became disillusioned.

We knew he was going to address us and all the Boys Nation people. There were a hundred of us, standing in the Rose Garden. We were lined up in alphabetical order, so I was near the front. I was bigger than everybody standing around me, and when it was obvious that he was going to come down and shake hands—I didn't know whether he'd shake hands with every-body—I got up there and made sure I shook hands with him.

I got up there and made sure I shook hands with him.

It made me feel good about my country, not just him: the idea that somebody like me, who came from a family without any money or political connections, could actually be in the Rose Garden shaking hands with the president. It's sort of like: That's the way a democracy *ought to work*. People ought to be able to have access to their leaders, and we ought to have leaders who aren't afraid of us. I was always so afraid after Kennedy got shot—and we did a much better job with security later on—that we would just keep pushing our leaders away from the people. He mingled with us that day and thanked us because we voted for a civil rights plank that the Senate wouldn't adopt. He knew there were four Southerners, including me, who voted for it, and he was very glad about that. It was really touching, the whole thing, and it made a real impression on me.

One of the things I did after I became president was that every year I could be in Washington when Boys Nation was there, I had them come [to the White House], Girls Nation as well, and I always took pictures with all of them. I was glad I got to shake hands with Kennedy; probably only twenty or thirty of the one hundred did, and so I always made sure we did that. The first time we did it, Al Gore told them, "You might want to make sure you get this picture. It might come in handy someday." It was really funny, but it was a moment in the life of a kid that I'll never forget. I was grateful to him and was grateful to my country.

I wanted to go into politics by then. I figured the best I could ever do was to be a senator, and I wanted to be a good one if I ever had a chance to run. Everybody wants to say they knew they were going run for president. I didn't. But I loved politics, and I believed in civil rights and in Kennedy's economic policy, which was moving people out of poverty. I thought the purpose of politics was to change other people's lives, and that's what he was trying to do. So that's what I was full of that day. I actually got to meet this guy I had supported, who was young and vigorous and was actually getting things done. I was just so proud to be an American that day. It made me believe in my country, believe in democracy. I was a true believer in everything that was best about America—and the fact that the president would come down there and shake hands with us made me think I was lucky to be an American.

———

I was in my calculus class, my fourth-period advanced math class. I was a senior in high school. It was right after lunch that I heard. My teacher, Doyle Coe, was the assistant principal, and he was called to the phone. He came in totally ashen-faced and told us the president had been shot. I remember it as if it were yesterday. I was heartbroken. I was hoping he would live. We didn't know in the beginning whether he was dead. I just remember being totally bereft. There was a lot of hatred of Kennedy in the South over civil rights. The people who hated him, the right-wingers in the South, didn't think he was being a pansy on civil rights.

I remember walking back to our main school building, and all these students were there. This girl who was in the band with me—I liked her, liked her whole family—said, "Maybe it will work out well for the country." I knew they were much more conservative than I was, but I was just appalled. I couldn't imagine why anybody would kill him. I didn't know anything then about what later came out with all the conspiracy theories about Cuba and the Mafia and all the stuff I read.

I just thought it was a tragedy for the country, because we seemed to be moving in the right direction. We were taking on issues that we hadn't taken on in a long time. I thought we were in good shape at home and around the world. For all the "best and the brightest" criticism he got, I thought he was pretty shrewd in making judgments about when not to take other people's advice. I thought the way he maneuvered through the Cuban Missile Crisis indicated that. I'm not sure he would have been as vulnerable to the people who said we just had to keep building up, and building up, and building up, and throwing good people after good people and good money after bad in Vietnam. I'm just not sure he would have. We'll never know, but I just was bereft. I felt that he was at the helm doing well, and I liked Lyndon Johnson.

I'm not like a lot of other people. I really was for him when he ran in the primaries. I just thought he'd really done a good job; he meant something to the country, and he symbolized the future. It was as if it was snuffed out.

They [Jack and Bobby] seemed young and beautiful and full of life and vigor, and they were killed on the job. I think that had a lot to do with it. I was older when Bobby Kennedy was killed,

and I also got to meet him once. He came to Georgetown and gave a speech at a deal I was sponsoring. I really was crushed; I thought he had the capacity to change the country.

Jackie had this curious combination of youth, beauty, and style. She really had a very pronounced diction, but she seemed like somebody you'd like to be with. Later in her life, after I became president and even when I was running, Hillary and I became friends with her. For reasons I never fully understood, she supported me in the primary in 1992, and she came to one of my early events in New York. One of my prized pictures is sitting with her at dinner in the summertime in Martha's Vineyard. I just loved her, and Hillary really was close to her.

In a way they symbolized our growing up, our aspirations. For my whole generation, the first time we looked at politics, there they were, and we liked what we saw. In her case, because I really got to know her, the more I knew her, the more I liked her.

I did [think about the parallels]. I think historically the time I served was more like the time that Theodore Roosevelt served, but psychologically it was the same thing [as the Kennedy era], with the generational change. You were assuming all these responsibilities, and you knew people would have questions about how you handled the security issues—probably more for me than for him, although he faced them too.

I always tried to find people who had different experiences than I did, who had different skills and different knowledge. I thought about that a lot. There's a huge danger in Washington, both within the White House and within the larger community, of groupthink. You've got to fight it all the time. The very first week I was in office, I told all the young people who were working for me that they should never come into the Oval Office and tell me what they thought I wanted to hear—otherwise I could run the place with a computer.

It's important not to minimize the fact that the Kennedy team's economic policy worked; that they built important things like the Peace Corps and the Alliance for Progress; that they and he did a good job handling the Cuban Missile Crisis. They were smart, and they did a lot of things well, but they were a little too prone to groupthink. They sometimes didn't know what they didn't know.

I'll remember how I felt when I was arguing for his election when I was fourteen. I'll remember how I felt when I met him the Rose Garden when I was almost seventeen. And I'll remember how I felt when he was killed. I will remember how well I thought President Johnson did when he took over, and I'll remember how badly I wanted Bobby Kennedy to be elected in '68 and how sick I was when he was killed. It was a rough decade. Things seemed to be coming apart. In some ways—socially, economically, and otherwise—it prefigured the kinds of unraveling we've had over the last forty years as we moved into a very different world. We now know of course that there were ambiguities, conflicts, concerns. It's never perfect when anybody's president, but I'll be grateful that he served. I think he did a lot of good.

Joseph Biden

In 1963 Joseph Biden was a twenty-one-year-old political science major at the University of Delaware. He served on the Delaware County Council before becoming a US senator in 1972. Reelected to the Senate six times, he served as chairman of the Foreign Relations Committee and the Senate Judiciary Committee. Barack Obama selected Biden as his vice presidential running mate in the 2008 presidential election. Biden is the first Roman Catholic and the first Delawarean to serve as vice president.

I was a senior in high school when John Kennedy was elected. To me it was all about possibilities. He always talked about everything, but you had a sense that there was nothing beyond our capacity. From his inaugural speech to the speech about the moon shot, it was all about possibilities. That's what sticks with me most about his legacy. His legacy is that that's what we are as a nation. We're a nation that attracts people because of the possibilities that exist. I was a Catholic schoolboy, Irish Catholic, Jean Finnegan's son, going to an all-boys Catholic school. I had two reactions. The first reaction was: My God, this may be the final validation of us Irish Catholics, that we're totally accepted.

I know this sounds strange, that Irish Catholics in the '60s would think somehow they were second class, but that's how it was. There was that sense of exclusion from certain areas of social and public life. But there was the other piece. The other piece was that I couldn't picture him at our kitchen table. I mean, John Kennedy was almost princely and very wealthy. That was different than the Irish Catholic neighborhood I grew up in. I lived in a neighborhood where I was one of only three Catholic families—a development, seventy-nine new homes built—and there was a

real division about President Kennedy. But there was this great sense
of pride about it. I had a professor
named Dan Carroll in what we
used to call Problems of Democracy, POD. I remember him talking about how consequential West
Virginia was and what this meant
for the American democracy, that
finally there was this mixed sense
of overwhelming pride. But it
wasn't the kind of connection I
had with Robert Kennedy as a col-
legiate law student. I could picture
Robert Kennedy at my table, but I
could never picture John Kennedy.

My sons, my daughter, and my granddaughter talk about it like this
guy was so overwhelmingly popular. We barely, barely won. There were
allegations, all the usual stuff. But today when they talk about it, my Lord,
everybody loved John Kennedy. But the interesting thing was, after his
assassination there was this sense of the country coming together. That
didn't exist in my memory as a junior in college, that it existed when he
got elected. There was a change in attitude almost immediately.

Concerning Cuba, if you think of his foreign policy, the Democratic
Party at the time was viewed as a robust internationalist party, taking on
Communism—the legacy of Truman—and John Kennedy was viewed as
being very aggressive and tough on foreign policy. I think the Democratic
foreign policy today, after we got over the Vietnam War, is much more
internationalist, less what we were when I first got to the US Senate in
'72. There actually are more similarities today, and my guess is that he'd
have a different attitude about Cuba. But Cuba was then part of a bipo-
lar world, and the question was: Was it essentially a pawn of the Soviet
Union? Was it a staging place, et cetera?

What resonates is that he was calm, collected, absolutely resolute.
Having gone through war personally, I think he had more confidence in

both assessing and challenging military judgments. So I think there was a sense of calm and resoluteness. I remember the Cuban Missile Crisis, sitting in what we called the student

It was almost like a frozen frame in time.

lounge and scrounge, the television on with fifty other people watching black and white, and John Kennedy coming on and explaining what the situation was. I remember the sense of real concern but also confidence. He communicated: "I'm in charge. I've got this handled. I'm OK. We're OK. But here's what it is." He was like the doctor who came in and said, "You have cancer, but I think we can take care of this. I've done this before. I know"—even though he had never done it before; it was just confidence. He exuded confidence, and it was contagious.

It was a Friday afternoon; I remember it vividly. I was on the steps of Hullihen Hall on the mall at the University of Delaware. It was a warm day; we had just come out of class. As we were walking through the hallways, we heard that the president had been shot. I had a car on campus—I wasn't supposed to, but I had a car on campus—and three of us we went to my car, got in the car, and turned on the radio. It was disbelief. I remember it was almost like a frozen frame in time. Instead of everybody on campus running and saying, "Did you hear?"—there were these quiet groups of people saying, "Can that be true?" You'd see five students in a corner. It was almost like if you said it out loud, he was going to die. Half an hour later, or almost an hour later, whatever it was, it was, "He's dead," and "How can that be? How is that possible in the United States of America?" If it happened today, you'd have great crowds gathering in the street, but then it was private. Whomever you were with, you just pulled aside and said, "Is this real? Is this really happening?"

I do think Bobby reflected the change that took over the country. With him, there was always a greater sense of urgency and the need to deal with it, whether it was the civil rights movement or the war in Vietnam. I always had the sense that Bobby Kennedy was saying, "This is who I am. This is what I believe. This is worth fighting for. Here I stand." There was more of a declarative sense of what this nation should be. Every-

thing had changed—not just because John Kennedy was assassinated but because the world was changing rapidly.

When I think of John Kennedy, I still find myself wanting to focus on his heroic sense of this country, his heroic sense of what his obligations were, about being able to absorb pain and suffering and move on—the resilience. My dad used to say, "It's not about whether you get knocked down but how quickly you get up," and John Kennedy was just totally resilient. The Kennedys, no matter what hit them, they got back up. They got back up. In that sense, in my mind as a kid, and even as an elected official, they came to represent the resilience of this country. When I think of Kennedy, I think about the notion of possibilities. There's nothing beyond our capacity. It's not naiveté; it's a sense of our capacity.

He'd feel a sense of vindication and surprise that there is an African-American president. I never doubted his desire to integrate African Americans fully into society. But, if I can compare him to his brother, he just thought that it would take a long, long time, that there was a process. I think he would be surprised at the additional complexity of the presidency. It's a very different world. In many ways there's a lot more on a president's plate than there was when he was president. I think he would be disappointed in an institution I think he cared about, Congress, the Senate. I think he'd wonder how it had gotten to this point, because when he was there, there were still real divisions in the country, like what I got the tail end of in 1972. There was the old segregation, the South, but it [Congress] still functioned. It still was viewed as the most responsible legislative body. I think he'd be surprised how it has lost that standing.

John Kerry

In November 1963 John Kerry was a nineteen-year-old, guitar-playing sophomore at Yale University. After graduation he enlisted in the Navy and requested deployment in Vietnam, where he was awarded three Purple Hearts, a Silver Star, and a Bronze Star. Returning to Massachusetts, he became assistant district attorney, lieutenant governor, and one of the state's US senators. He ran as the Democratic Party's presidential candidate in 2004 and is serving as President Obama's second secretary of state.

Kennedy's election was enormous. It was a huge transformative moment in my life personally as well as in our generation. It was sort of the breaking out of the 1950s. I remember it as transformative in many different ways. I was in Boston, going down to the dentist from school in New Hampshire, and it just by happenstance turned out to be the last night of the campaign at Boston Garden. I had to go to North Station to get a train back up to Concord, New Hampshire, but I played hooky for a couple of hours and waited for this rally to take place. I took reams of information back from this incredibly exciting event.

I actually wound up speaking before the school the next day, in a pre-scheduled debate with a Republican counterpart, doing a two-minute something before the morning studies. He represented Nixon; I represented Kennedy. It was my first political speech ever, first engagement ever. Of course he [Kennedy] won—he didn't win at the school, which was overwhelmingly Republican—but it was the beginning of a wonderful journey for all of us about the civil rights movement, the nonproliferation engagement in the world, the Alliance for Progress, the opening up of doors of opportunity for people in the world, and it excited us. It gave us a great sense of possibility and a lust for being engaged in the life around us in politics.

Did I think [the Kennedys] would define the rest of my political life? No, never had a clue. I graduated from high school in the summer of '62 and went to work for Teddy that summer, full-time as a volunteer, during the course of which I met President Kennedy, and it was transformative. It became almost natural in the sense that this was what you want to be doing.

This is the noble enterprise, as President Kennedy himself put it, that politics is a worthy undertaking. We all came into it with this tremendous sense of changing the world. It was before the revolution of '68. It was before Vietnam had a really pronounced impact on all our lives. It was filled with possibility until that dark November day of '63.

In 1962, while I was working in Boston for Teddy, I'd been told we were going sailing, and I raced to get down to Hyannis in time. I was late. I arrived at a very different summer White House from anything you see today. It was one little security thing at the front gate. I said, "Here's who I am," and they said, "Oh, go ahead, drive up." I drove up and got out in front. There was one guy in front. I walked into the house, and there was a guy silhouetted in the window, standing there alone, nobody else around. He turned around, and was the president of the United States. He walked over to me and said, "Hi." I said, "Hi," and, probably inappropriately, I think I said, "Mr. Kennedy." I didn't even know you call him "Mr. President" back then.

We talked for a minute. He asked, "What are you doing?"

I said, "I'm in between high school. I'm going off to college."

He said, "Where you going?"

I said, "Yale," and I grimaced, knowing he was a Harvard guy.

He looked at me, said, "No, no, that's great, you know, because I now have a Yale degree." He'd just gotten his honorary degree. He couldn't have been nicer about it and talked to me about the campaign and what Teddy was doing. Then we all raced out to go sailing, and it was totally surreal. What was it like? It was: Pinch yourself. "Am I really here? What's going on?" He disarmed me completely and made it meaningless that I was going to the rival school. He put me at ease and then exhibited all that charm, all that charisma that everybody saw in so many ways so many times.

Regarding his Cold Warrior persona, Vietnam hadn't risen to a level of awareness where it was a major choice in our lives until after he had been assassinated. It was really Lyndon Johnson who bore the brunt of implementing "Bear any burden, pay any price." Many of us opposed that at some later point in time, but with President Kennedy what we saw was the hope and possibility, and we saw his stand on civil rights. We saw him send the troops down to break the back of Jim Crow. We saw him with this exciting Justice Department and Bobby Kennedy, the challenge against organized crime, and all these efforts to set the world right. That was still in its most romantic, least impactful in any negative way, stage. I don't think we saw that. I didn't feel any confrontation with that at the time. Later, obviously, those words came back to be reexamined in many different ways at many different times, but it certainly wasn't manifest in his presidency at that point in time.

— ◡ —

The day he died is indelible, obviously, for all of us. I was playing in the Harvard-Yale soccer game, and I heard a ripple. I was playing, and I came out, sat down on the bench, and heard this ripple of conversation and concern and audible gasp go through the audience. The word was: "The president has been shot." We didn't know what had happened or anything. I remember just being completely disconnected from the game. It was just a shock. I mean everybody felt like, "What are we doing? We're playing a soccer game, and the president's just been shot."

We played out the game, and we learned before the game had ended that he had died. It was sort of a lost period of time. I can't tell you to this day who won. I don't know. I've never gone back and found out. It was such a state of shock for everybody that this could happen in America to the president. Notwithstanding that historically we've lost too many presidents to assassination. It's sort of stunning when you go back and look at it.

There was a sense of turning everything upside down, a total sense of the order of things having come apart somehow. I remember being with my roommates; we spent the entire weekend glued to the television. Then of course you watched this next moment of surreality, when Lee Harvey Oswald was killed by Jack Ruby. We were all trying to find some meaning in it. How do you find meaning in something like that? I remember walking around New Haven at two or three o'clock in the morning with a cousin who came down to spend some time with me because he knew I was involved in the politics and involved personally. At that moment I remember saying, "We have to make sense out of this. We, all of us, have to find a way to do something that makes it right." It was a very strong feeling of a responsibility to lead a life that made a difference somehow.

Regarding possible conspiracies, to this day I have serious doubts that Lee Harvey Oswald acted alone. I certainly have doubts that he was motivated to do that by himself. I'm not sure if anybody else was involved. I don't go down that road, with respect to the grassy knoll theory and all of that, but I have serious questions about whether they got to the bottom of Lee Harvey Oswald. I think he was inspired somewhere by something, but I can't pin anything down on that. I've never spent a lot of time on it. But I think, after a certain period of time, and that period of time may well have passed, it is totally appropriate for a country like the United States to open up the files on whatever history can be shed light on. I think that is appropriate. It has to be done in the right way, by the right entities or people, but certainly by a valid historian or for some valid analysis; I think that everybody would benefit.

How do you find meaning in something like that?

I enlisted back in 1965, not long after Lyndon Johnson's call for five hundred thousand troops in response to the Gulf of Tonkin episode in 1964. The America of 1965 was just dramatically different from the America of 1968. Even 1966, when I graduated, was a world apart from the universities and campuses of late 1967 and 1968. I think the first draft card was burned and the demonstration against the Pentagon were in 1967. I was in uniform. I volunteered because I thought it was important to volunteer. I thought that's what you should do. You should serve your country. You should spend some time in the military, and many of my classmates did: my brother-in-law-to-be; some of my best friends; my good friend, Fred Smith, who was in our class and later founded FedEx—they all volunteered. FBI director Bob Mueller, who wasn't at Yale but at Princeton, volunteered, went into the Marines.

Initially I believed that America needed not to quit on it [Vietnam], not lose. I saw it in fairly traditional terms. I had doubts as I went. I have repeatedly said to people that I had serious questions as I went, which was 1968, because we were hearing from a lot of people coming home. There was a new debate. There were new facts. A lot of people had a better sense of what was happening there. Then of course I went, I learned for myself, and came back very much opposed to what we were doing, believing that it couldn't work, that it was doomed almost from the beginning, because I had a better sense of what the reality was.

What would President Kennedy have done about Vietnam had he lived? I have no way of ultimately resolving it. But, like everybody who's followed that question, I do believe he was, himself, having serious doubts about any escalation. Most of the records indicate that after the election he intended to draw down and not get sucked into a larger war. But in the end, we can only speculate.

I didn't think at the time that Vietnam was Kennedy's mistake. It was much more the hubris of what went on in the years after that. We learned that the Golf of Tonkin incident wasn't real, didn't happen. We learned that we were interpreting things completely wrongly. We were just dead wrong about judgments being made about the Domino Theory, Communism versus civil war. There was just a host of things I learned later—observations of people like Bernard Fall and others of that time who had been completely ignored and/or distorted in order to fit this war into a compact theory that simply didn't apply.

A lot of us felt very angry about that as the years went on. Back in 1963, I can't remember the numbers now, but there weren't that many people there. By 1968 you had the height, around five hundred thousand, and sixteen thousand died in 1968. Then you had Richard Nixon, who ran on a secret plan for peace that, three years later, was still a secret. That's where the sense of bitterness and anger and frustration really set in. Back in the early 1960s, there was a kind of simplistic, fairly stereotypical, post–World War II, post-Korea view of the world. By 1968 it was hard to say there was an excuse for that anymore; and by '72, '73, and certainly '75, there was none. Henry Kissinger and Richard Nixon understood that, which is why they worked so hard ultimately to get an agreement that drew down and pulled out.

President Kennedy was, I think, not allowed to fulfill his prospects of being a great president in substance, in terms of legislation accomplished, bills passed, changes implemented on the nation. But in terms of his impact on the nation and his leadership for those brief years, he was a great president—he motivated, inspired, and left an indelible mark in a very short period of time by virtue of personality and presence. That's a big deal in today's world or by any standard. Certainly Lyndon Johnson passed far more impactful legislation and had a much greater legislative legacy than John Kennedy was allowed to have. I've read many analogies to the first years of other presidents who followed him, who really came into their own in their second term or later in their presidency. We never got to see the full measure of what might have happened legislatively, but we certainly are still living with the legacy of a president who had a profound impact on the world.

Chris Matthews

In November 1963 Chris Matthews was a seventeen-year-old college freshman from Philadelphia. After moving to Washington, DC, and joining the Capitol Police force, he became an aide to four Democratic members of Congress, worked as a speechwriter for President Carter, and served as a top aide to Speaker of the House Tip O'Neill. Since 1997 he has hosted *Hardball with Chris Matthews* on MSNBC. *The Chris Matthews Show* aired on NBC from 2002 to 2013. Among other topics, he has written two books on JFK, Kennedy, and Nixon: *The Rivalry that Shaped Postwar America* and *Jack Kennedy: Elusive Hero*.

Pat Moynihan once came up to me and said, "We've never gotten over it." He looked me in the eye and said, "You've never gotten over it," which was to me almost like an ordination. He was bringing me into the brotherhood because he knew Kennedy. I try to explain to people just in a big-world sense: You don't know what politics in America was like before Kennedy. It was guys in three-piece suits, the smell of cigars on them, musty characters like Taft—they were boring people.

For the party chairs we used the word "politician," which meant backroom guys. It didn't mean candidates. It meant backroom guys with

You don't know what politics in America was like before Kennedy. It was guys in three-piece suits, the smell of cigars on them, musty characters like Taft—they were boring people.

cigars, Adolphe Menjou types. That's what politics was. Probably the most interesting guy would be Ike. At least he was happy. He had a nice smile. Everybody else was sort of an indoor type—and along came this guy, Kennedy. Although it wasn't the colorized version we got after his death, the Camelot thing, it was pretty amazing to watch.

That was the day when people had a million people at a rally in New York, half a million people in downtown Philadelphia on a Wednesday at lunchtime. People had torchlight rallies, like in Connecticut at two o'clock in the morning, or in Michigan when he announced the Peace Corps at two o'clock in the morning at Ann Arbor.

It was a participatory democracy in those days. People had voter hats and buttons, not just lawn signs, and we were all into it. For the American people to vote like they'd never voted before—everybody voted, thirty-three million [votes] apiece—and then to have the guy taken away from us, the guy we picked? The guy who fought for the job and won it narrowly and clean, he wins, and then he's taken away from us.

I think nobody's gotten over it. It's not supposed to happen that way. One minute he's riding in a car, looking like a million bucks with his beautiful wife, and everybody's waving at him, and the next minute he's on a gurney.

—❧—

Hemingway's comment about grace under pressure fits [Kennedy during World War II]. It's in the middle of the night; it's completely black. There's no moon or stars. We're in the South Pacific, and his little balsawood boat gets cut in half. Eleven feet from him, he sees a Japanese destroyer go by—eleven feet from him in the boat—and his back is hurting. He said,

"This is what it feels like to die." His back was already bad, and he hits the deck, and it gets smashed again. In that split second, he decided basically to roll and dive into the water. They're in the ocean, the high seas, and he swims to the other part of the boat, which is drifting away, finds Paddy McMahon, who's badly burned, convinces him to try to come back and save his own life. Then he finds another fellow, who wants to give up too, and says, "You're putting on a bad demonstration here for our fella from Boston." Gets him to save his life, gets his thick sweater off, and carries him back to the boat. He gets the guys onto the boat. He decides, "This boat's already turned over in the middle of the night. It's not going to make it to the next day. We've got to swim."

Four miles away, there's an island called Plum Pudding. The key is they have to find an island the Japanese wouldn't be likely to come by, because the biggest fear of those guys, as we know from the book *Unbroken*, is to be captured by the Japanese. You don't want to be captured. It's worse than anything else, worse than drowning, so he has to find an island that is far enough away from them yet reachable. So what does he do? He takes the four guys who couldn't swim and the five guys who could, and he makes sure they all stick together on an eight-foot plank they found. He gets his EO, his executive officer, to take charge. He puts them together, so he saves everybody—and he's operating as a commanding officer.

Then he puts Paddy McMahon on his back and carries him for four hours in the water with a bit of the guy's life jacket strap in his mouth, just pulling him the whole way. Paddy has no idea that Kennedy had a bad back to start with and it has been hurt again. He gets them [onto the island] and pukes on the sand when he arrives there.

Half an hour later, he recovers and says, "I'm going out tonight." He puts a revolver in his pocket. He's got a lantern. He swims out into the ocean again, tries to wave down some other boat—he's scared to stay there another minute because of the Japanese. He gets washed away to some other sandbar. He wakes up on his sandbar, swims back to the island, and then says, "I'm going out again." He swims to another island. Finally they get to the third island, and he finds water. He finds a Jeep can with some water in it from the Japanese and some candy. He heads back, gets the crew, and keeps them going.

It's thrilling to think about this courage and leadership from this rich kid. Where'd it come from? He never had a life like this. He never had to be this kind of person. He certainly wasn't Joe Kennedy's kid. Joe Kennedy wasn't much of a patriot, [nor] much of an American really. Jack was the American. It's an amazing thing. It's almost like *The Godfather* in a good sense. He was the assimilated son who loved this country and was going to fight and maybe die for it.

Bobby wasn't happy with the LBJ pick. Bobby, I think, wanted to be vice president, though who knows what he wanted? He couldn't have been vice president.

I think [John] Kennedy had this feeling about Johnson. He just didn't feel comfortable in the room with him. He always felt that maybe this guy wanted to be president, and Johnson would admit, later in his life, that he calculated his best chance of becoming president was to become vice president. What did that tell you?

But Kennedy felt this sort of ogre-ish presence around Johnson. He said, "There's something about the guy." He told that to people like Ben Bradlee—but he always tried to treat Johnson with respect, and Bobby didn't.

I think Kennedy respected the rogue quality of Johnson as the guy who may have won an election under questionable counts back in 1948. I think he liked the way he ran the Senate, but they weren't close, and in the end it was pure calculation not to pick Scoop Jackson or somebody he might have gotten along with. There's the ruthless calculation: that he knew he had to pick Johnson or he was wasting his time.

Kennedy was the first Catholic [presidential nominee]. He was going to lose a lot of the South because of that. He was going to lose a lot the Midwest because of that. He did hope he'd get California. He did hope he'd get Ohio. He didn't get either. He needed Texas. He needed states like Texas and Georgia, and even looking ahead to '64, he said, "I need LBJ on the ticket. I have to pick him because I need Texas and probably Georgia." Even then, Kennedy thought he needed Johnson.

The Cuban Missile Crisis to me is astounding in terms of how Kennedy got us through it. There were both Churchill and Chamberlain involved in terms of this, Churchill in the heroic stand he took and Chamberlain in the deal he cut. If Kennedy hadn't found a way to cut the deal for the Jupiter missiles in Turkey and found a way to allow Khrushchev, who came off pretty well in that, to be able to pull back and take on his generals, we wouldn't have gotten through it. He had to find a way to do something under the table.

June '63 is Kennedy's greatest month, when he was able in three great speeches to come out for a nuclear test-ban treaty; the "Ich Bin ein Berliner" speech, the best speech of the Cold War; and the civil rights speech.

Whatever else people say about him, he was the first president in history to go on national television and say, "It's the Bible. It's our Constitution. It's what we believe as Americans," and to raise [civil rights] as a moral issue, which actually LBJ recommended that he do, to make it a moral issue. Certainly Martin Luther King was out there ahead of him, but I think he was the first president [to do it].

—⁓—

I grew up in a pretty Republican family, and I was [part of the] out-there libertarianism of Goldwater back in the '60s. By the time Goldwater ran in '64, I was turned off to him, but I was very much in that libertarian mode, like a lot of people.

I always wanted to meet Kennedy. It was a weird thing; even when I disagreed with him politically, I wanted to meet him. I always found him to be the most interesting politician of our time. Nixon was something; I liked Nixon. Goldwater was interesting; I liked him—he was romantic as a hero. But Kennedy was the one I found the most interesting as a person. I wanted to meet him because I couldn't quite figure him out. He did things that were so smart and almost brilliant politically; he always hit the mark, and I was just fascinated with that one. When I was conservative, he was too liberal, but he was also a liberal with balls, as we used to say about him, compared to Stevenson.

The other part of it is the longer courage. Imagine you're born and have every illness there is. You have scarlet fever; you have your appendix taken out. Then you have something that you can't quite figure out. It's a knot in your stomach—and we've all had nervous knots—but a knot that's inside your stomach; it never goes away, you can't figure it out, and you have to eat light foods and soups. You can't eat anything heavy or anything fried; it keeps getting worse and worse, and then you find out you have leukemia, which means you're going to die young. You're having your blood count [taken] all the time. Your mother calls but never visits you. The mother, Rose, was kind of remote.

He's away at Choate, constantly thinking, *I'm going to die. All they can do is keep my red blood cell count [up] and everything.* That's going on, and finally it turns out that he has colitis, which is bad enough. To have all these sicknesses and the bad back, which he had congenitally. . . . One of his legs was three quarters of an inch shorter than the other. He was wearing corrective shoes later in life. The bad back of course should have kept him out of the Navy. It did keep him out of the Army. He basically went through an intensive campaign of learning how to work his back and get through.

He managed to get into the Navy with some political help. His dad said, "This guy's going to be on one of these bucking broncos"—the PT boats, which we all know from fast boats, are pounding you all the time. He had to sleep every night on a board. He could never sleep on a bed his whole life. It was always on a board because of his bad back, and then they butchered him after he came out of the war. He spent a year in a hospital. They never fixed it.

Then in 1953 he [was diagnosed with] Addison's disease, which gets so bad. The first episode is in 1947. He's over with Pamela Harriman—Pamela Churchill at the time. She takes him to her doctor, who says, "This friend of yours isn't going to last a year." Then he gets another episode in the South Pacific with Bobby, who saves his life and gets him to the Okinawa Air Force Hospital, and that's sort of when their bond begins. The third time he has the last rites of the Church, in 1954 when he goes in for his back operation, which goes bad with complications. He barely survives. Even Nixon, who was in the [Harvard] class with him in '46, was crying in the car. I talked to a Secret Service agent.

This guy was so close to the edge of life all the time, and I think that explains his carpe diem behavior with women, his "hell's a-poppin', let's

The inner Jack Kennedy was far less romantic and far tougher.

have some fun" attitude about everything in life. "Let's get through the day, that's all we're going to have."

They lied—Ted Sorensen, all the rest of them, and India Edwards, remember she came from Johnson's campaign. They were putting out the fact he had Addison's disease. If we had known that and it had the full [coverage] like Page Three today in the papers, if it had been all over the place, he wouldn't have gotten through. The irony of the 1960 campaign is that Jack Kennedy was probably the only Democrat who could beat Nixon; Nixon probably would have blown away a Humphrey or a Stevenson. It must've driven Nixon completely crazy that this guy he thought was a playboy could beat him and nobody else could beat him. But that was a fact.

Jack Kennedy used the pictures to cover up who he was. He loved the glamour shots. He loved being handsome. He loved Jackie being beautiful. He loved all that photography. He loved the kids. He loved Macaroni the pony. I think he liked that idea because it created a certain thing he could manipulate and use. The inner Jack Kennedy was far less romantic and far tougher. Think of Jack as Bobby; think of Bobby as Jack. Bobby had to be the henchman. Bobby had to go into the room with Governor Mike DiSalle of Ohio and beat him up, and he had to go to Governor Tawes of Maryland and basically beat him up. It was Mob behavior. This was a Mob scene—not a mob scene with a crowd; it was a mobster type of event, where they really scared these guys. Jack would say to Bobby, "Make sure he's publicly for me, and don't bring my name up," and then Bobby would do it because he loved his brother completely.

Jack was the guy giving the orders. In fact, when you talk to all the old Irish Mafia, they say they came to love Bobby. Like Richard Hardwood, all those guys came to love him, the guys who covered him. Jack scared you, he was so tough, so brutal. He knew what he had to do, so he made these decisions to put Johnson on the ticket, to pretend he'd never met Richard Nixon. They'd been friends for twelve years, but he acted like he never met him when he debated him. It's cold, ice—he cut him. What he did with cutting the deal with Khrushchev: "Okay, I'll give you the missiles in Turkey. I won't tell anybody about it." That takes a real level of toughness, even ruthlessness if you want to call it that. Bobby was accused of it, but Jack was guilty of it. That's the big difference.

The hard thing about studying Jack Kennedy is to understand his brutality toward Jackie. Why didn't he feel some sympathy toward her, in the way that he not only cheated on the marriage but he didn't seem to care that she knew about it? [When Jackie had a miscarriage at eight months and JFK remained on his sailing trip] was the first time he showed real coldness. He didn't even come back. In fact, George Smathers, his friend from the Senate, said, "I told him to go back or forget his political career" because he would lose the marriage and everything, and he'd never be able to explain that kind of cold behavior.

We all live in compartments, and it's healthy in some ways. We go to the store, and we go to the dry cleaners. We know the fellow or the woman there, but we don't have parties with them. We meet people in certain places at work whom we don't hang out with. We live in different compartments. Most people live like that in a benign way. Jack Kennedy lived in compartments, almost like a *Titanic,* each compartment sealed off from the others. The Irish Mafia weren't Kennedy's social friends. Dave Powers was a handy man to have around, but he wasn't a pal socially. Ted Sorensen was his intellectual blood bank but not a friend socially; he never got invited at night.

The pals Kennedy hung around with—Ben Bradlee, Charlie Bartlett, David Ormbsy-Gore, Smathers—they were his friends, and then you can separate that group: the happily married, faithful husbands and their wives, who were couple-friends of him and Jackie. Then there were the guys he screwed around with, like Smathers. Smathers is a good example of a guy he had another kind of relationship with.

Everything was subdivided, and that's the way he lived. These various

> *Jack Kennedy lived in compartments, almost like a* Titanic, *each compartment sealed off from the others.*

people never met one another. The only one who could walk from compartment to compartment, from Jack to his serious girlfriends, like Mary Meyer, and to the ones that weren't serious, and to Jackie, was Jack himself. He could do this by the hour. He would have a relationship with one person, and then he'd go right back to Jackie. How can you explain it, except that's the fact?

Imagine these Knights of the Round Table, the Camelot image. Everyone in that world Jack lived in had his sword pointed to the center of the table, like the Knights of the Round Table. That's why they're round, to keep them equal, and he was in the middle. Everybody related to him. Jackie didn't relate to Mary Meyer, but he related to Mary Meyer, and he related to Jackie and the girls, Fiddle and Faddle, at the office, and whoever else was around, like Mimi Fahnestock or someone like that.

All those relationships were all pointing to him, but they never met. The Irish Mafia never met the WASP friends. The WASP friends socially never met the intellectuals. Arthur Schlesinger and Galbraith and those guys were possibly hanging around with Ted Sorensen, but they weren't hanging around with Dave Powers and Billy Sutton. They never got to know each other. It was Jack's world. Maybe it was a principality, but they all seemed to like it. Red Fay's daughter once said to me, "Nothing was as thrilling as to get the phone call" that Jack's on the line to talk to her dad. He made that family light up, because Jack was the best buddy from the old days, and the guys who were in the Navy with him said he was great company. They liked him. The thing about Jack [that] we keep forgetting about our politics, it's about liking the guy, and this country liked him.

— ·—

I try to capsulize what the '60s were like for me and the Kennedy experience. A friend of mine in the Peace Corps, in Swaziland, was in the village right next to mine, and we hung out a lot together. He teaches at the University of New Orleans right now. One night he took his village out onto the side of a hill, the people he'd been working with in world development. They all sat there, and he said, "I want you to see something tonight." As they were sitting there in the dark—this is in Africa—he pointed to a little light crossing the horizon. He said, "That's us going to the Moon." That was Kennedy. The wonder and romance and idealism of the Peace Corps and the magic of going to the Moon, that all happened because of him.

The Peace Corps was a great thing for me. The Peace Corps was the greatest thing in my life because what happened was: You go from being a grad student somewhere to all of a sudden you're out in the middle of Africa, all of a sudden you're on a motorcycle, bopping around, teaching business to a lot of African guys who are about fifty years old, who become your best friends. You're like a son to them, and you establish all these relationships. Then you hitchhike through Africa alone, and you do things like go to Israel for a month—all different places I went. You get to have the adventure of your lifetime. I would never have imagined the Peace Corps without Kennedy. Jack Kennedy came in, and he was so much the Peace Corps. It was his idea: adventure, fun, foreign travel, doing good. Run it militarily in terms of discipline; do everything right. It was great.

—◆—

I was up at Holy Cross, and everybody's Irish or Italian, a few French Canadians—and all Catholic. We were up there in Worcester, Massachusetts, the heart of Massachusetts. I was going to check my mail, which we always did after lunch, and some guy came up to me and said, "I'll bet you five dollars Kennedy was just shot," and I go, "What a terrible thing to say."

I walked over to Mr. Power's world history class, and he said to the class, "The president's been shot. Anybody who wants to take a cut right now, it won't be counted against you." I think we had three cuts a semester. I zoomed over to the Carlin Hall, a dorm, went down to the basement, and found Cronkite on TV. I watched what everybody watched, and I believe I watched him say, "He's dead." I watched it right through the night and the whole weekend. I was just taken with the whole story.

I have a very simple take on the Kennedy assassination. What you don't know, you don't know. But what we do know is this, which I think is critical: Lee Harvey Oswald had the job at the Book Depository weeks before the motorcade route was established, so it was a crime of opportunity. He had this infatuation with Castro, having become disillusioned with the Soviet Union when he was living there. Oswald came back [to America] and became infatuated with Castro. Before the crime in Dallas, he had gone down to the Soviet and Cuban embassies in Mexico City, perhaps trying to put together an escape route. Who knows? I'd like to see those records someday.

Oswald was caught apparently without a great plan. But that he was there at the time of the route, the president going right under that window, shows it was happenstance. Oswald had a point of view. He'd gone after Nixon at one point; he'd gone after Edwin Walker. He had a certain left-wing view of things that was pro-Communist but disillusioned with the Soviet Union. That's all I know.

When I was writing my book on Kennedy, I came across this wonderful little bit of film of this beautiful woman chasing after a guy and a gurney. You just see the gurney, and she's racing behind it. That last sense of life and then after all that, it was just: "Well, he died. He was killed." But the tough thing to do is to remember him when he alive and to remember the New Frontier—not Camelot but the actual New Frontier and how bracing politics was.

242

PART FOUR
CONTROVERSY

Mort Sahl

In the late '50s and early '60s, Mort Sahl was one of the hottest night-club comedians on the circuit. While most comedians were delivering stock jokes about wives and mothers-in-law, Sahl turned to the newspapers for material. Joe Kennedy personally recruited Sahl to write jokes that his son could use in his presidential campaign. In August 1960 *Time* magazine put the political satirist on its cover and called him "the patriarch of a new school of comedians," which also included Lenny Bruce and Jonathan Winters. He was thirty-six years old when President Kennedy was killed.

I was being managed by the same fellow who managed Peter Lawford; he managed just the two of us. Peter said his brother-in-law is going to go for it. I was very friendly with Adlai Stevenson, who was theoretically the heir apparent, and I knew Mrs. Roosevelt, who said to me, "Kennedy is going to try and get this, and he's more profile than courage." Then his father, the ambassador, called me at the behest of Milt Ebbins and Sinatra, who I saw every day, and he said to me, "I understand you can write political humor better than anybody and that you have the skill"—this is almost his words—"to put a stiletto between Nixon's fifth and sixth ribs instead of bludgeoning him. I want you to work for Johnny." That's what he called him, by the way. So I said OK. I took that call in the cutting room at Dick Carroll's men's

> *Mrs. Roosevelt said to me, "Kennedy is going to try and get this, and he's more profile than courage."*

haberdashery in Beverly Hills, so it would be confidential. There were no cell phones.

I went to work, and I can tell, as an old political script-writer, that Republicans pay you. They believe in business, so the old man called me without humor, without anything, and just engaged me.

JFK had a great streak of irony in the way he talked. He was very cautious. All the things people said about his reckless-ness—it wasn't like that at all. He said, "You like Castro?" I said, "Oh, yeah. I'm a young guy.

I love the idea of revolution." He'd say, "You don't find him unstable?" He was like an inquisitor. He answered questions for me. When some-body said, "Who are you after, and what are you pursuing?" Kennedy said, "Everybody." Like that. Or he said, "You know, you can profess loyalty to me, but I know guys like you. You love Adlai Stevenson, and if you can't get him you still won't go to me. You'll get Chester Bowles."

I said, "You don't like Chester Bowles?"

He said, "He still wears button-down shirts. Why should I like—" He switched what was at stake when you talked to him, and he had different personas. For partying, he liked Gene Kelly. Talked politics to me, and they hired me, and I wrote some jokes.

He was extremely bright and very aware that the liberals were going to be more trouble than the other, conservative, party. He got that right away. He was very smart, and he had a great sense of humor. There's nothing I put in front of him that he couldn't pick up and run with. He understood all the material. I wrote for a lot of people relatively, but he understood all the material, and he never objected. The old man objected on religious grounds, but he never objected. I gave him that joke where he said, "Is it going to hamper you to run as the first Catholic candidate?" and I said, "You say to them: 'It's not the hereafter that concerns me, it's November 4th is driving me out of my mind.'" He took it right away, put it on like a cloak that fit. And: "You're going to meet the pope. Are you going to kiss his ring?" "No, we've made a special arrangement. I'm going to call him 'Jack,' he's going to call me 'John.'" He took all that, you know. It was playful at the beginning, and then we had some good arguments too. I asked about his friendship with Nixon and everything. He stressed to me that you can learn from everybody. He was very sharp, even gave me romantic advice. I was going out with an actress then named Phyllis Kirk, and he said to me, "Bad pick. Is a mover. You don't pick chicks that way." I never asked him for any romantic advice.

I was home having breakfast when I heard he had been shot. In California, in the living room, I heard it, and then of course it plays out very fast. The next day Ruby is there. I used to talk about it in the show: "He shoots Oswald while he's being guarded by twenty-four members of the Dallas police force, or twenty-five if we count Ruby." I was dangling the bait even then. JFK was killed by a powerful domestic force. I believe it's such suppression that we can't get on with the job of being America until we clean our own house. Yeah, I do believe that. It's cost marriages and friendships and work.

I read Vince Bugliosi's book. I know him very well, by the way. He wrote that at Hefner's house. Hefner gave him an office. I used to see him up there all the time. You may notice that the book criticizes Garrison

I gave him that joke where he said, "Is it going to hamper you to run as the first Catholic candidate?" and I said, "You say to them: 'It's not the hereafter that concerns me, it's November 4th is driving me out of my mind.'"

quite freely and gives me a pass. He characterizes me as a fair-minded guy who tried to do his best. But I endorsed that investigation. In fact, I was in it.

I had my own show on Metromedia, and I challenged the Warren Report repeatedly. John Kluge said to me, "This is kind of redundant. You've got to have new evidence." So I went to New Orleans and met Garrison, and I became an investigator in the office. We went to the trial of Clay Shaw. I was very much his champion. If he [JFK] were here, we would not have been at war in Vietnam. I don't think there would have been a war. Our thesis in New Orleans was that he was removed because he was ending the Vietnamese War. We operated on that thesis, and we got in heavy water. It was very tough, career-wise. It was tough with your friends. They found it hard to accept.

As far as Garrison doing it to advance his career, I can think of other ways to advance yourself than saying the government killed the president. I can think of better ways to take advantage of your career moves.

We had a back channel to Bobby through one of his college roommates, and I saw Bobby. Walter Sheridan was in there with Frank McGee, taking arms against Garrison before he went to court. He might not have been that militant if he didn't run into all that opposition. The family wasn't much help to us, although I did run into Jackie in New York after we started the case, and she said to me that she knew. But they always thought they had the privilege of when to say they knew. They didn't much say anything. They said clouded things to me. Sargent Shriver said, "After all you've done for us—" Teddy said the same thing to me, but I was operating pretty much alone in show business. They knew that the whole thing was a cover story. The lone assassin; nobody believes that, but they know that it's unwise to say this. It's taking on a sea of troubles. But if you don't get justice for Kennedy, you can't get justice for the country. I didn't realize that when I met him. He came to be because he was a man of peace,

Our thesis in New Orleans was that he was removed because he was ending the Vietnamese War.

and the last speech, at American University, is documentation of what he was trying to do.

Who was responsible? A powerful domestic force, which has more power than ever? Oswald was an FBI informant who was used as a patsy. You know when we got him—or when they got him—in his wallet was the unlisted number of the special agent in charge of the FBI office in Dallas. No, he was just there to make noises. I mean, it's almost insulting: passing out Communist leaflets in New Orleans, establishing an identity, trying to buy a car in New Orleans. You don't have any credit.

But we have to look back on that time. Bobby told me that General LeMay raised his fists to President Kennedy in the arguments over Cuba. What's happened is, in the interim, art has characterized guys like that, like LeMay, as crazy and willful rather than working toward another goal. Look where war has taken this country. Look at the lack of humanity since Kennedy and where it's taken the country. We betrayed him. The American University speech, remember? "We breathe the same air as the Russians, and we all treasure a future for our children, to end all wars." What are there, sixteen thousand men in Vietnam when he's murdered? And wound up with that being our major effort. Of course the clincher is that you can't see the material.

The president's brain is missing in the archives. You can't see any of this. What did Johnson say, seventy-five years? And the way the thunder came down around Garrison because he opened up—the only law enforcement officer who opened it up. I don't know. Have people forgot what America was like, how optimistic it was?

Clay Shaw got acquitted because he perjured himself about Oswald and about David Ferrie. Who were they? Who were the Cubans? Who were the guys who drove to Dallas the night before in an ice storm? Why did they have to be there? Who was Ruby? Characterized as a patriot by the press, sent in to silence that guy. Ruby begs Warren to take him to Washington so he can tell the truth, and Warren says he doesn't have that power. A commission to solve the death of the president that never met as a body. We owe Jack Kennedy the truth, and we owe the American people the truth. There's going to be no future for our kids if we don't do it. We've become somebody else. It's an expensive lie.

I thought it took priority. It was a tough decision, but the money won't do you any good, and the good-looking actress won't do you any good if you sell your country out. You can't do it. You come home with a different country under your arm. I became a different person because a lot of different people didn't want to employ me. The William Morris Agency didn't want to book me. People turned against money because that's an  expensive lie. It involves the aristocracy of this country, who took part in an unlawful act. Until we clean that up, we'll never be who we were. But he set the tone. I wasn't a worshiper, as you know. I kidded him pretty good too. But I brought that up because I thought it was imperative. It did cost me a lot of work. Ironically enough, the liberals made me unemployable. They didn't want to hear that. They used to be people that would fight for their rights. They were eroded.

Garrison's the bravest man I ever met. That they've continued to discredit him and haven't looked into what he brought up only underlines to me that we were on the right track then. We were ready to go, but the people weren't ready for it. I mean certain people in positions of power. Look what happened to the country. What happened to me, that's minor. What happened to the country? We're not the country that does that to other people. We bought into perpetual war and brutality and a general mediocrity. That never would have happened when he was there. He's the guy who brought Pablo Casals to the White House.

Sixteen thousand men in Vietnam and aiming to get out. McNamara knew that too and didn't say it. Then we have the tapes of Johnson saying to McNamara, "Now is the time to go in and take them out, or all countries will go." Who benefited the most from Kennedy's death? Who suppressed the information? By the time we get to Chicago, it's Berlin, not Washington. I think it's very evident, or I never would have done this. You know, I'm not a Kennedy worshipper. He doubted I was even going to vote for him, and of course he was only ten years older than me—

Jim is like Jack. He stands up for what he thought was right, and the credentials of Garrison are where he came from. He was an FBI agent, a colonel in the Army. He got radicalized at forty-five because his president was murdered before his eyes and he wanted to know why. That's why he's genuine. The social democrats were born on the left and didn't have to earn their way over there. They had to earn their way over to the right. That's why they're so careful. That's why there are no candidates.

A lot of people thought I went crazy. But by the same token, I wondered why they don't go crazy, why they can rationalize with whoever's there. It's the same thing that happens when you work at a network. If somebody's son gets the job, you say, "Maybe it'll work out." You can't do that. You can't be a moral man and do that. Every moral man knows this. If he's Jewish, he thinks only they know it, but everybody knows it. We are formed by our families. Bobby was the toughest guy I ever knew, and it's because the old man made him the enforcer. He had to bring home a head on a stick, make sure it wasn't blamed on Jack, and he never got thanked. That's what happens. If you're left to be free and do good things, you wind up like Sarge Shriver, one of the most heartbreaking things that ever happened.

When Garrison was at his worst off, I went to George McGovern and said, "We're in a terrible spot. We want the truth, whatever it is. Doesn't have to be our truth, but we want the facts." He listened to me, and he said, "I'm sorry, Mort, but, your hero Jack Kennedy wasn't a very good president." I said, "Is that

> *A lot of people thought I went crazy. But by the same token, I wondered why they don't go crazy.*

251

punishable by death?" That was the end of my relationship with George McGovern.

I was an unlikely guy to be a comedian. America's an unlikely country to emerge, but I took it at its word. That's why I'm here, and that's why I won't abandon it. It will sink us all. I may have a temporary financial advantage out of it, but that isn't going to do it—that's nothing you can leave your kids. You can leave them money, but you've got to leave them more than that. You've got to leave them a thirst for the potential of this country. The president was willing to do that and become a traitor to his class to do it. That guy I met on a very random afternoon I didn't think would have that influence.

I'm surprised that all the people who benefited by being there didn't speak up. Schlesinger, McGeorge Bundy—they didn't behave like his friends. On one very sorrowful night, Garrison said to me, "None of us ever knew him, Mort, except you." I said, "Yeah." He said, "Well, for God's sake, didn't he have better friends than that?" I asked that of the audience too.

Cynthia Wegmann

In November 1963 Cynthia Wegmann was a fourteen-year-old student at the Academy of Sacred Heart School in New Orleans. Four years later her father, Edward Wegmann, defended family friend Clay Shaw against charges brought by District Attorney Jim Garrison that named Shaw as a ringleader in a conspiracy to kill the president. Cynthia assisted her father in preparing the case; she is now a successful New Orleans defense attorney.

I was at Sacred Heart—third prep or fourth prep, we called it—seventh or eighth grade, and we were getting ready for what is a Sacred Heart tradition of bringing Christmas baskets and presenting them to the archbishop to give away to the poor. Every family or every girl at the Heart would make a basket that would feed a family for Thanksgiving and then give them something for breakfast and lunch the next day. We were sitting there on the bleachers in the gym, and Mother Johnson came out with her little wooden clacker and said, "Excuse me, quiet, quiet," and told us that the president had been shot. I do believe that we were then sent home, so we went home and watched the TV for the next—forever.

The president had come here before, and I think I was one of the girls who presented him with roses, but we felt like we were all giving him flowers. It was like you'd lost a friend. He was so handsome, and she was so beautiful. It was just terrifying. *What's going to happen to the world? What's next? How can this happen?* Just terrible—and then the poor children, little John with his little salute and black jacket with the boots on backwards? That was just not good.

I don't know. It let LBJ do what LBJ did, but Kennedy himself was a great equalizer. He could talk his way out of anything or end anything, and I think the civil rights movement might have been easier if people could have looked at him and followed his lead. The country was totally stunned. We'd won two world wars, and then we named our first young president, who didn't like to wear a hat. It definitely changed the way the world thought or the way we felt. We no longer felt invincible. If somebody could kill our president on our streets in the South, then what else could happen? And then what?

~~~

Clay Shaw was very much a gentleman. He had a wonderful booming voice— we sometimes call it the old-fashioned "Creole voice," with that modulation I wish I could imitate. He was brilliant. He wrote plays. He restored the French Quarter—he really started it. He was, along with friends, responsible for them not tearing down the French Market. He restored, I think, at least seven houses. That's how my father and he came to know each other, because Daddy was an estate lawyer and transactional lawyer. He was Clay's attorney to do all the real estate turns that he did. He'd buy one, flip it, spend the money on the next one, and restore that one. He really had a sense of style.

Clay Shaw at Tulane

Clay tried to figure out why he was targeted, and the only thing he could think of was, OK, he had an international reputation, which would make Garrison's persona or reputation go all across the newspapers internationally. More particularly, he describes in his diary—and he did in *Esquire* magazine as well—two incidents: One, he witnessed Garrison throw a glass of wine in his wife's face at Galatoire's—a serious faux pas, a no-no. The other was that he stopped Garrison from molesting a twelve-year-old boy at the New Orleans Athletic Club.

Who knows what Garrison thought? All you know is that he concocted this miasma of lies and stories, a lot of which was based on Mark Lane's "triangulation of crossfire" stuff. He had to have a scapegoat. Because Clay Shaw was such a ginormous man in international circles, as well as in stature, and because Garrison knew that Clay was alone but for his mother, who was in Ruston, he went after him, hoping he could hound him and that he might commit suicide or something before Garrison could be shown up to be a fraud.

What he [Perry Raymond Russo] did afterward in the press was to say, "I was under hypnotic suggestion." They put Perry Raymond Russo under sodium pentothal and hypnosis three times by the then-coroner, whose name was Chetta. He said in the beginning, and you can read the transcripts that he said, "I don't remember," "No, I don't know any Clay Shaw," "No, I don't know any Clem Bertrand," "I don't know." Finally, by the third time, he was like, "Okay, okay. I give up." But Russo did recant. It was three times under hypnosis, and if you read those transcripts, it's pretty incredible. Russo being put under hypnotic suggestion not once, not twice, but three times before he put him on the trial was pretty amazing. All of that came because Bill Gurvich, who was working in the DA's office, said, "I can't take it anymore." He quit his job—he had five children or more—and brought Daddy this information. He was pretty phenomenal.

The man [Garrison] came on television during the trial and before, and he just looked so earnest. Everything he said sounded so convincing. I remember asking my daddy, saying, "Daddy, he doesn't look like he's lying," and Daddy said, "He makes it up on one side of his head, shuts that side off, and believes it on the other." I went to law school after Clay was acquitted to save the world from the likes of Jim Garrison. My only problem was, when I went to work in criminal court, I believed everybody.

I went to law school after Clay was acquitted to save the world from the likes of Jim Garrison.

I can't say [why Garrison did it]. I should know better than to say what I think somebody else thought, but I think Garrison had cleaned up the prostitution in the French Quarter, and he needed some other mission. In '67, four and a half years later, he comes across this Mark Lane book that connects Castro to New Orleans and comes up with this story. Kennedy was killed on November 22, 1963, and Garrison arrested Clay on February 27, 1967—I think he was only booked on March 1, 1967. But by that time, Garrison's sweep of the prostitution on Bourbon Street was over, so he had a new mission.

Clay actually talked about the fact that he didn't know why he had been targeted. There was, if you read the transcripts, some mention of some "Clem Bertrand" meeting with Oswald and this guy [David Ferrie] with carpet fibers glued to his head to make eyebrows. Somehow or another, "Clem B" and "Clay S" became "Clay Shaw."

Daddy had gone to Atlanta or right outside of Atlanta to open or to seal the deal for the building of a restaurant, Brennan's of Atlanta, which I think subsequently burned. He came back, he'd been on the plane, it was raining, he had walking pneumonia, and Mother greets him at the front door. We all did. Daddy didn't take his hat off—and Daddy always took his hat off when he came in the house. He goes to the phone because Mother had told him, "Clay's been calling you. Billy's been calling. You have to answer the phone." Daddy picks up the phone, and he says, "I'm in no mood!" and hangs up.

The phone rings back, and whoever's on the other end—I assumed it was Clay—says, "Don't hang up, Edward. This is no joke. I'm at the DA's office. They're about to arrest me for conspiring to assassinate the president of the United States." Daddy says, "Okay, I'll be right there," walks out the door, and goes two blocks, and comes back around, and he goes, "Where's the DA's office?" He was a civil lawyer.

When Clay was arrested, I was seventeen. I was a senior at the Academy of the Sacred Heart, which is on St. Charles Avenue—wide-eyed and innocent. It seriously made life different. I was followed by two men in Garrison's employ. Daddy was followed. Even my brother, who was twelve, was followed. I think they gave up on Dirk after a while. They sat outside Sacred Heart, and of course the first thing I did when I got out of Sacred Heart was—didn't even change my shoes—just took my bag and went over to Ottoman Stables, where I rode and taught every afternoon. They sat outside the barn and waited for me to come out. I don't know what they thought I was going do. But once you realized who it was, it would be too much fun to get on my little fat red Arabian and take off the other direction and leave them like, *"Ahhhhh!"* They never turned around, though, and went the wrong way, down this street. I don't get it, but they didn't. You know, you have these suspicions. Like, okay, so the seventeen-year-old-at-the-convent girl is going to be doing what?—smoking pot? I have no idea. Instead I was riding horses and chewing hay straws.

It [Shaw's trial] was like a three-ring circus. It was in Judge Haggerty's court, and there was Daddy, Billy Wegmann, Irving Diamond, who had this wonderful voice too, and the jury. It took them a long time to seat a jury, but after the jury was seated, I think the whole thing lasted six weeks. Garrison gave the opening statement, but Jim Alcock, Garrison's assistant DA, ran the trial and did the closing statement. It was amazing because, as it went on, more and more news people became more and more on the side of right, not of might. I met some very nice people, lots of reporters. I don't think Mom went except maybe to hear some piece that Daddy did.

When you heard Garrison after the trial was over in the afternoon, I said, "Daddy? How can he say that?" Daddy said, "Just don't worry. Just wait."

"Don't hang up, Edward. This is no joke. I'm at the DA's office. They're about to arrest me for conspiring to assassinate the president of the United States."

I believed in Clay's innocence completely. What did I think when the jury went out? I said, "I'm pretty sure it will be fine." Then I called my friend who was sitting there with me at that time, Tennessee Lynn, and she was like, "We were holding hands and praying and promising God that if he'd just get Clay off, we'd do charity work for the next twenty years." She said, "I didn't do any of it, but I think you did some."

The jury went out, and forty-five minutes later, enough time for everybody to go to the bathroom, have a cup of coffee, and take one vote, he was acquitted. Three weeks or so after that, Garrison arrested him for perjury. Then Daddy started, and luckily I was able to help him with that—even though I wasn't a lawyer yet—to do a civil rights complaint, which was filed in federal court, an injunction against him for going forward with this next heinous trial.

Daddy thoroughly believed in what he was doing. He believed him. He believed in him, and he was going to stand there and stand between Clay and anybody who wanted to smear him. So for two years, from the time that Clay was arrested until the trial was over, and then even further, when we filed the complaint in federal court for the injunction to stop Garrison from persecuting him for alleged perjury, that's all Daddy did.

The jury went out, and forty-five minutes later, enough time for every-body to go to the bath-room, have a cup of coffee, and take one vote, he was acquitted. Three weeks or so after that, Garrison arrested him for perjury.

He asked me not to go away to college because he wanted me to stay here. He wanted the family to be together. It took a little longer than we thought.

The trial to enjoin Garrison from going forward, it was based on a civil rights violation, where Garrison had to know that he was wrong and that Clay was telling the truth because of this, that, and the other thing. I think Daddy's complaint was fifteen, twenty pages. It lays it all out. Christenberry took testimony. Christenberry was a very careful judge, and he wrote a thirty-page opinion that ripped Garrison up one side and down the other and said, "No, you can't go forward." Then that was appealed by Garrison.

We sided with Christenberry of course, and that went up to the Fifth Circuit Court of Appeals. They decided with us and stopped the perjury trial. Then we filed a complaint—I

Edward Wegmann

think I was a lawyer by this time—to recover damages from Garrison and his buddies, Truth or Consequences, which had put up money for the prosecution or persecution, if you prefer, of Clay. In the midst of that, seeking damages to restore Clay to the finances he had lost during all this time, Clay's mother died, and then Clay died, and since Clay had no children, no descendants and no direct ascendants, under a quirk of Louisiana law the perjury action or the defamation action was considered a personal action, which could only be pursued by ascendants or descendants directly. That has been changed since then, but if not [for that] we would have won. We made it through the Fifth Circuit, and the decision was very heavily weighted in our favor. They said no because it's a civil rights action; Louisiana law doesn't govern who can inherit. Then the next thing was to go to the US Supreme Court. We lost by one vote, five to four. It [Christenberry's language] was extremely strong, and he excoriated him. It was like a vindication.

In the beginning, he [Shaw] was fine. He once described it as a Kafkaesque experience. He couldn't live in his house for two months because Garrison had people stationed outside of his house. The news people were hounding him too, so he lived with a widow woman, as she described herself. He said everybody was very kind to him. He said he wasn't a religious man, but he ended up going to The Sentinel, which is a retreat house, and felt a great lifting of his spirit during the middle of this persecution. Toward the end, he lost his spirit, but during it he was sure that he would be acquitted and that he might be able to get back some of his calm and go back to writing plays and

short stories. He had retired in order to write.

He had an off-off-Broadway play. He then sold one of the properties he had in the Quarter in order to fund the costs. He meant to travel and enjoy his life before that long. His mother was older of course, and she died the year before he died. Clay died in '74. The stress is definitely attributable. He died of lung cancer; the stress probably exacerbated that. His chain-smoking didn't help, but the stress certainly had an enormous effect on that. He was quite a good man.

Daddy had Clay cremated because he knew, given Garrison's propensity and what Garrison had claimed all along, that Garrison would have had the body exhumed in order to try to prove he was killed or committed suicide—because he kept saying, "Everybody's dead. This person's dead, this person's dead." They were all old. They were dying. That's why Clay was cremated, and he was buried in an unmarked grave near his mother in Ruston. I don't know if it's still unmarked, because the stigma has left, but he was buried in an unmarked grave next to his mother. People were still making threats as Clay was dying of lung cancer. Daddy didn't want him to be disturbed in any way.

They reelected him [Garrison], just "Yep, no problem." Then they elected him to the Fourth Circuit Court of Appeals, on which he served,

How can you think the most heinous crime of the century could be committed by a group of Looney Tunes and one nice man?

but I don't think he ever wrote an opinion. I appeared in front of him once, and he didn't ask me a single question.

People thought he must have something. The conspiracy theorists abound, and where it comes from, I don't know. How can you think the most heinous crime of the century could be committed by a group of Looney Tunes and one nice man? But they did, and I still, since this time, have gotten phone calls from people saying, "Explain this." It's like, "All I can tell you is: It's wrong." How can you keep something like this under wraps with that many people involved? You can't. Clay was so well known that, if you and I were in a restaurant and he walked in, he would tower over us. I think he was six-foot-four, giant shoulders, big barrel chest, a shock of white hair, and a voice that had this wonderful timbre to it. You couldn't mistake him for anybody else. I don't get it.

Rosemary James

In 1963 twenty-six-year-old reporter Rosemary James was in Charleston, South Carolina, working for the *News and Courier.* Afterwards she moved to New Orleans and became a reporter for the *New Orleans States-Item* and WWL-TV. From 1966 to 1969 she covered District Attorney Jim Garrison's trial of her friend Clay Shaw. She later cofounded the Pirate's Alley Faulkner Society and wrote a book about the Big Easy. Today she and her husband, Joe, own Faulkner House Books, an independent bookstore, and live in William Faulkner's old apartment in Pirate's Alley.

I didn't move to New Orleans until the end of December 1963, about a month after the president was assassinated. I had come down here to visit friends and fell in love with the city, went by the *States-Item,* asked for a job. When I got home, I had one, so I arrived here and went to work on the first day of 1964. When the president was killed, I was in Charleston. I was working for the *Charleston Evening Post* and the *Charleston News and Courier* at the time. I was on my way home for lunch, and I turned the radio on. That was the first knowledge I had of it. I didn't believe it at first. I was shocked. I just didn't believe it at first. I was sort of like Walter Cronkite; he didn't want to believe it when Dan Rather called him and said that he was dead.

It all happened because New Orleans District Attorney Jim Garrison, a very flamboyant character, who had national ambitions, was on a plane ride back from Washington with Senator Russell Long, and Long was on the Warren Commission and wasn't satisfied with the conclusions of the Warren Commission. He thought they didn't go far enough with the investigation, and he suggested to Garrison that he should pick up this investigation and go full speed ahead with it. He told him he thought that the New Orleans jurisdiction would work because Oswald had been here. He told Garrison quite frankly that this could make his national reputation, so that's how it got started.

Jack Dempsey was our police reporter at criminal district court, and every day he sent these little dispatches by teletype—that's how long ago it was—and he said, "Such and such is going on, and I keep hearing that Garrison is investigating the assassination of John F. Kennedy." After about three of these messages, the then–city editor and managing editor suggested that we look into it more seriously. We tried to talk to Garrison, and he wasn't available; he wouldn't make himself available. The criminal district court judges had what's known as a "finds and fees" fund, and the district attorney had access to that fund. He was using that fund to finance trips to Dallas and for investigative purposes, and we were able to go to the records of that fund and find that he was indeed spending a lot of time in Dallas and other pertinent places. We did a very brief story, not much longer than a couple of pages. I finally got him on the phone. I said, "I have something I would like to show you. May I come and visit with you?" He said yes. I gave him the story. He read it, and he smiled and said, "I will neither confirm nor deny." That's all he would say.

I said, "Well, we're going to publish this story." Then he said, "I'll neither confirm nor deny." So we went with it the next day, and we believed that he wanted us to publish this story. If I had to do it all over again, we probably wouldn't have published. I would have said, "You know, this is a bunch of—"

All the news people came in from various and sundry places, even from *Izvestia* and *Pravda*. He had a major news conference, and then

If I had to do it all over again, we probably wouldn't have published.

everything died down. People went back to their respective news organizations. He really loved a headline, he really did love it. He loved all the attention, so he would have a new news conference, and he would give us a new theory about what actually happened. This went on and on and on. I didn't make a judgment that he was really nuts until he arrested Clay Shaw, and then my suspicions were confirmed by that action.

Garrison had a very convoluted, byzantine sort of mind, but he had a history that wasn't particularly pleasant. First of all, for many Garrison was considered a closet gay. That wasn't generally known in the community, but a lot of people who knew him thought he was. Here's Clay Shaw, whom I knew; he's socially acceptable, he's doing all kinds of wonderful things business-wise. He's getting a lot of positive attention, and he's gay. Even though that was not a subject that was generally discussed, there's a feeling that Garrison was maybe a little jealous. Also, Garrison had a known reputation for beating up his wife. He was a wife abuser. One night, Garrison and his wife were having dinner at Brennan's, which was at the time operated by Ella Brennan, as opposed to the other branch of the family. Ella and Clay were very close friends, and they were having dinner together. Garrison slapped his wife rather brutally, and Clay got up and went over and stopped it and asked them to leave. Garrison was very abusive. There were harsh words then.

Garrison was the kind of guy who craved headlines. For example, it was well known in the city that he had a relationship with and hung out with working girls, but in order to get crusader kind of headlines, every once in a while he would round them up and put them in jail, which is about as hypocritical as you can get, because the next night he'd be drinking with them, and Bourbon Street had classy drinkers back in those days and classy strippers. He spent a lot of time down there. We all knew that side of Garrison, that he was hypocritical and also that he was a headline chaser.

There were two people I knew very well who were very good sources of mine when I was covering Garrison. One was an investigator, an ex-cop named Pershing Gervais, who was a really interesting character. He had been Garrison's chief investigator, and he was the first person who told me the whole thing was a crock. The next person who told me that was a criminal district court judge who had been Garrison's first assistant DA, and he said, "That is such a crock; I can't even begin to tell you how stupid you all are to be covering it at all." Those were his words, but the coverage went on because he would come up with some exotic new theory.

He had a triangulation of crossfire. Then he had some right-wing Texans. Another theory was that David Ferrie, an ex-pilot, was part of a conspiracy, that he had been killed off. In fact, Ferrie probably killed himself by his diet. He did nothing but drink black coffee and eat Jell-O. That was his total diet. I interviewed him, and I know he was a real kook. At first Garrison had dismissed him, but once he died of a heart attack according to the coroner, Garrison said he was the most important witness and maybe his case had been destroyed. That brought a whole new flock of headlines. Those were just a few examples. There must have been at least twenty different theories that he proposed, and that's why people with any judgment early on thought the guy was a kook. Then when Clay Shaw was arrested, they washed their hands of the whole thing because he [Shaw] was so respected in the community in so many ways. The people Clay Shaw hired to represent him were first-class and had a great reputation in the community. Half the community, at least, abandoned Garrison as a serious investigator.

The reason it came to trial? You need to look at the law of Louisiana, which gives district attorneys enormous power, more so than most states. For example, a district attorney without a grand jury indictment can file a bill of information against someone and bring that person to trial. Generally speaking, district attorneys can do what they want in Louisiana. There are few stops on their power. Another reason was that it was entertaining news coverage for the general populace—this has been a community and a state that really enjoyed politicians who would entertain them. Garrison, whatever else he was—nuts, cynical, whatever—he was very entertaining. I think it was allowed to get that far because of his personal charisma.

New Orleans history was a great piece of it. When he arrested Clay Shaw, you got a real dichotomy in the community: those who thought he was seriously nuts, and those who were still in his corner for whatever reason. For example, there was a group of businessmen that formed something called Truth or Consequences to fund the DA's investigation so that he wouldn't have to get money that had to be reported. This was strictly against the law, but they went forward with it anyhow, and that's how he was funded for a lot of his foolishness. I think they were just political supporters of Jim Garrison's frankly. They were actually formed before Clay Shaw was arrested, but it may have been that Garrison talked to them and asked them to fund him so that he could continue his investigation without oversight.

Every time someone would mention that possibly the Mob was involved in this, Garrison got all out of sorts with them, tried them before the grand jury, and got them cited for contempt or jail for something or another. Garrison was threatening to haul a *New York Times* reporter before the grand jury who strongly believed that the entire conspiracy was initiated and funded by that whole crowd. They had a great motive because they had lost a lot of property in Havana and had put a lot of faith in the Bay of Pigs event, which turned out to be a disaster. There was strong feeling that they had the best motive of all, but if you mentioned that, Garrison would get all up in arms and try to punish you. He came to me and said that he was going to bring me before the grand jury. I said, "If I were you, I wouldn't. I have a lot of stuff I've never reported about you." That was the end of that.

The day after Clay was acquitted, Garrison filed a perjury charge against him, and federal judge Herbert threw that out. After it was all

---

Garrison said to me, "If I were you, I wouldn't. I have a lot of stuff I've never reported about you." That was the end of that.

---

over, I never had harsh words with him again. In fact, I once had some dealings with a civil court judge represent-ing a client; I remarked that this judge would sign any-

It was a terrible miscarriage of justice against Clay Shaw.

thing that was put before him on behalf of the opposition, and he cited me for contempt. By that time, Garrison had become an appeals court judge, and he ruled in my favor. He could have been really mean. He had a great ability to keep a conversation going with a person, but it was a ter-rible miscarriage of justice against Clay Shaw.

After Clay was acquitted, he died not long thereafter, a broken man. He was worn out from the whole thing. Clay had been ready to retire as a gentleman. He wasn't wealthy, but he had put aside a lot of money; he had restored a lot of properties and had them as income-producing properties. He planned to spend the rest of his life writing. He had written a couple of plays, and he was actually a good writer. That's what he wanted to do with his life, but this investigation and the ultimate trial and the cost of attorneys bankrupted him. He was just worn out, and I think the stress possibly caused him to succumb to cancer earlier than he would have otherwise.

Regarding the movie *JFK*, Oliver Stone and I had some verbal con-frontation via the *Times-Picayune*. He bought Garrison's line of gar-bage hook, line, and sinker, and the film he produced was exactly what I expected—a travesty. First thing he did was cast Kevin Costner, who is known as a kind of all-American good guy, as Jim Garrison, which was the beginning of the travesty as far as I'm concerned. It was a terrible film. Oliver Stone is another nut. He and Garrison were in good company.

I never spoke to Stone personally after the film was made. My only exchanges with him were through letters to the editor of the *Times-Picayune*, but if I had been able to see him personally after seeing the film, I would have told him what I thought. I'll tell you what Pershing Ger-vais said. He and I went to see the film together at the *Times-Picayune*'s request. Pershing Gervais had been Garrison's chief investigator at one time, an ex-policeman, someone who had been a great information source throughout my journalistic career, and a great critic of Garrison. They wanted us to go and see it and then be interviewed after the film.

When the film was over, the *Times-Picayune* reporter said, "Mr. Gervais, what did you think of the film?" He said, "It was a pile of shit." Those were his exact words, excuse my French. Then he asked me my thoughts, and I said, "Ditto." Those were our comments about the film. It portrayed Clay in a way that wasn't indicative of the man. It made him seem like a flamboyant queen who was involved in orgy-type dinner parties and things of that nature. It gave a false impression of a really decent man. Not that he would have been against costuming for Mardi Gras or anything like that—and in fact he did. He was a full member of the community, but Oliver Stone just completely distorted the truth.

The whole thing now seems so surreal; it really does. I think about all the Damon Runyon-esque sort of characters who were part and parcel of the whole drama, one of whom was Dean Andrews, who was a two-bit lawyer who probably couldn't earn a living if it hadn't been for representing lesser Mob figures or Mob-oriented figures at least. I'm completely convinced that Dean Andrews was called by someone and told to go to Dallas and represent Jack Ruby. I'm completely convinced that he told the truth about that. I'm also convinced that he made up the "Clay Bertrand" name to avoid telling the FBI and other investigators who questioned him who actually called him. I think he knew precisely who that person was, and he was trying to protect that person, but it backfired in that Clay Shaw was judged to be Clay Bertrand by Garrison for whatever reason. Before he died, Dean Andrews told me it definitely wasn't Clay Shaw. The other thing was that no one ever looked for another candidate other than Clay Shaw because they believed that Garrison just made it up on the spot.

My best friend at the time in the journalism world was David Chandler, who had been on the *States-Item* with me and then went to work for Time-Life as a reporter for *Life* magazine. He was on the inside of the Garrison investigation at the time that we broke the story and was thinking that he had an exclusive for *Life* about Garrison's investigation. He was also there during all the talking about Clay Shaw and why Garrison thought he should arrest Clay Shaw. Thereafter he would have nothing to do with Garrison, because he said it was such a ridiculous piece of phony logic that he used to try to get Clay Shaw as another headline-producing event.

I believe the Mob was the best possibility of a conspiracy, and there may have been some other ele-ments involved such as the Teamsters—that's what I believe—possibly even some disillusioned right-wing Cubans: some elements of the thing that Garrison kept presenting here and there and yonder as individual theories, like fourteen Cubans shooting from the storm drains. That was one of the theories du jour. Every day there was something new, so it became harder and harder to give any credence to Garrison. However, I do think there was a conspiracy, and I think that, because of Garrison, it was never fully uncovered. I think the Mob put together a scheme that he was part of. That's what I think.

I do feel that Marcello was treated unfairly in several instances by the feds. There was one trial, for example, involving a nightclub called The Crash Landing. The evidence and the witnesses presented by the fed-eral prosecutor in that case were such a put-up job that it was obvious to everybody in the courtroom and certainly obvious to the journalists covering the thing. I did some reporting on that after the fact, and one or two of the witnesses stated that. The federal judge in the case said: "I agree with what was said by the media last night—that the witnesses are sus-pect." That was one example of how Marcello was treated unfairly. I think he was deprived of his civil rights when he was deported to Guatemala. They just grabbed him, put him on a plane, and dropped him in Guate-mala, and if it hadn't been for one of his friends, Lisa Mosca, the owner of Mosca's Restaurant, he might still be cooling his heels down there. She sent him money. She was able to get him a big sum of money, and he was able to get back into the country as a result of her help. There are lots of reasons to think Marcello has been treated unfairly in many instances because if an ordinary citizen were treated that way, there'd be a public outcry. Whether he facilitated a conspiracy, I don't know. I really don't.

I'm a Yellow Dog Democrat. I've never voted for a Republican, and I love my life. Kennedy was a wonderful image for America at a certain period in our history that was well needed, very much needed. We needed a heroic character and someone to fall in love with politically, and he seemed to fit that bill perfectly. I don't think he was the greatest president we've ever had. Despite all we've learned, I still think he was a good man. I think he had enormous challenges to face while he was president, including the Cuban Missile Crisis. He made a terrible mistake with the Bay of Pigs, probably. He should have followed through on the commitment. He made some enemies then, and Bobby Kennedy made a whole lot more enemies for him with his pursuit of the Teamsters Union and several other avenues of investigation that he worked on. Given the John Kennedy I know today, including all of his peccadilloes with women, I would still vote for him.

Mike Kettenring

In the 1960s Mike Kettenring was a reporter for WDSU television in New Orleans, but in the summer of '63 he worked at Reilly Coffee, where one of his coworkers was a twenty-three-year-old machine greaser named Lee Oswald. At WDSU Kettenring worked on the Oswald investigative team, interviewing many Cubans in New Orleans, and in 1967 he covered the Garrison-Shaw trial. In later years he served as news director then general manager of WSMV-TV in Nashville—often cited as the best station in the nation—before becoming a man of the cloth.

We worked together at Reilly Coffee Company during the summer before the assassination, and I walked with him a couple or three times. He was a fellow worker. He was sullen, low-grade anger, a loner. Didn't really join in, certainly wasn't going to come talk with me. The few times I had conversations with him, I had to go to him. We'd mostly kibitz. The only thing we ever talked about that related to the assassination was he told me that he had lived in Russia; I just thought that was a lie, that he was just trying to inflate himself. I just dismissed it.

After the summer, the next time I saw him was on television after the assassination, right before he was gunned down, and I'm looking at him and saying, "My God, that's Lee." I thought, *He's an angry enough man, he probably did it*. Like so many people, we all remember where we were when we heard about the assassination, but it's become part of me because it wasn't just being stunned at the assassination, it was: "I know him, and, yes, I believe he may very well have done that. He could have done that."

I was in a student council meeting at college, and my immediate thought was *Camelot's gone. We're in trouble.* In my opinion, that's exactly what happened to our country. We got in trouble because Arthur died and Camelot fell. We lost innocence. We went immediately from *Leave It to Beaver* to *Easy Rider* and *Apocalypse Now*. We went from June Cleaver, sweet little June, to strident women legitimately looking for their rights—but very stridently. We went from

Martin Luther King and nonviolence to H. Rap Brown and burning cities down. We went from saluting our war veterans to spitting in their faces. We literally went from innocence, from childhood to adolescence, and it was an ugly adolescence. It was with a great deal of anger and attitude.

It was obviously a confluence of [many] things, but I think the level of anger, the attitude that the country took on was far greater because we had lost our great hero. We went from being a country that John Kennedy called us to serve—"Go into the Peace Corps. Don't ask what you can get from the country, but what can you give to the country?" And all of a sudden, it was a "me" country. We lost that sense of hero worship, someone who would lead us to serve. I'm a priest in my life, and all great religions, every one of them, stress service. That's what humanity is all about, we think. John Kennedy thought that. He had some problems in his life. I wish he would have come to me for confession for one or two of those little sins, but he was a great man because he understood leadership and he understood service, that people who serve come together. We didn't come together after his death. We split wide apart.

⌒⌒

I was a reporter at the time, and I was part of a little three-person investigative unit that looked into these things. Everyone we talked with was a typical New Orleanian—off the wall. We interviewed a man at the time, David Ferrie. He came in for the interview with pieces of orange carpet taped above his eyes because he had no hair and he wanted to be interviewed with eyebrows. Only in New Orleans, I submit, would that happen.

Jim Garrison was an egomaniac. I covered the trial, the Clay Shaw trial. Every day, I got up and I said, "Today's the day there's going to be a little

> *David Ferrie came in for the interview with pieces of orange carpet taped above his eyes because he had no hair and he wanted to be interviewed with eyebrows.*

bit of smoke coming out of his gun. There's going to be something today." Never happened, but he would go before the cameras after court, every day, and keep saying how he had all the evidence in the world to prove that this was a conspiracy and that Clay Shaw was deeply involved in it. Never found a single piece of evidence as a reporter about any of that. Jim Garrison: a big, tall, imposing man physically, but he just had this ego. He wanted to be on the world stage, and I believe with every fiber of my being that's why he did it.

He picked on Clay Shaw because Shaw was easy. He was a gay man at the time when being a gay person was not widely accepted, and he felt he could use that to his advantage. Clay Shaw was an involved person in the New Orleanian business community and in the social and cultural communities as well, so the movers and shakers of New Orleans all knew Clay Shaw. If he could tie Clay Shaw to the assassination, he would be bringing down a person who had clout in the city. Until the very end, virtually the entire city felt that Jim Garrison had evidence to prove what he was saying—to the very end. The jury came back right away because there was nothing there, literally nothing there.

Carlos Marcello was on my beat at the time, so I frequently talked at him. If he was getting off a plane, I was there. He never responded to my questions. All I wanted at that point was to find out how deeply involved he was in the Mafia. There was little question that he ran criminal activities, but there was no evidence that he was like the Mafia dons in New

York. There was no evidence that he was involved in anything that was violent, no evidence that he committed murders. That was an aspect of it that I wanted to explore, and then, when the assassination occurred, questions arose as to whether the Mafia was behind Lee Harvey Oswald. Then I wanted to interview him about that.

This was pretty much like the Clay Shaw trial. We found nothing to link Carlos Marcello to the Kennedy assassination. Marcello was part of the fabric of Louisiana. Louisiana was comfortable with criminals running their government. They were comfortable with criminals having deep influence within the city, and I think that if you asked one hundred people in New Orleans, "Was Carlos Marcello a criminal?" one hundred people would tell you, "Yes, he was." If you asked them, "Should he be going to jail?" probably one hundred of them would say, "No." Conspiracy and intrigue are part of the culture of the city. Still are today, even more so back then. Conspiracies intrigue New Orleanians in a way they don't intrigue lots of other people in our country, and it was easy for them to believe there was a conspiracy to kill the president.

I couldn't find anything that indicated Marcello had any problems with the president. He may have had it, but we couldn't find anything of that nature. I think Carlos Marcello always felt like he didn't get a fair shake, that when he was deported it was on the flimsiest of reasons. That certainly got under his skin, and when the Kennedy assassination occurred and he was being linked with it, that got under his skin as well. It just rankled him. I think he felt it was unjust. Now maybe a Mafia person saying, "This is unjust" is pushing the envelope just a little bit, but I think that's how he felt.

Pretty early on, I was convinced I would not [unravel it] because we kept running into

> *Conspiracies intrigue New Orleanians in a way they don't intrigue lots of other people in our country, and it was easy for them to believe there was a conspiracy to kill the president.*

brick walls. There wasn't anything really substantive that we could find, and I was the rookie on this three-person team. The other two were really seasoned, veteran reporters, very good reporters. We just didn't find anything.

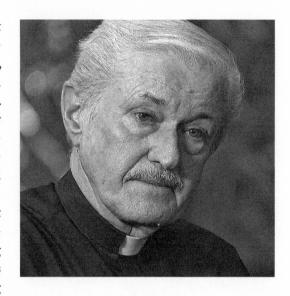

I got a call one night from one of Carlos Marcello's lieutenants, telling me, "Mr. Marcello has finally agreed. He's going to talk with you. You got to show up at two o'clock tomorrow morning at the parking lot at Smiley's Restaurant on Jefferson Highway." I worried about that, didn't tell my wife I was going. I slipped out, and I got there, waited about two hours. No one showed up. Never knew whether it was a friend pulling my leg or whether it was Marcello pulling my leg, but, no, I never got the interview.

Marcello never told his side of the story because the world wouldn't have believed him. He was a Mafia don. He ran a Mafia family, and who was going to believe the Mafia don coming out and saying, "I didn't have anything to do with this"?

I think the chances are so small that we can dismiss them. I never say never, but the chances are so small that I would be shocked. I'd be shocked. It's fifty years. A conspiracy? Somebody would have talked by now. Somebody on their deathbed would have talked about it. Someone would have written a book to make lots of money about it. To think that anyone who was involved in a conspiracy was going to keep his or her mouth shut for fifty years? Boggles my imagination.

I believe the Warren Commission. I believe there was no conspiracy. There's nothing that we surfaced to indicate there was a conspiracy, and other than the huge number of books that came out with conspiracy theories in them, mainline media and television news did a good job, because I don't think television news ever really pushed the conspiracy theory.

⌒ ⌒

President Kennedy was a man of vision. He was a man deeply steeped in service. He founded the Peace Corps. God bless, it's still here today. He looked upon everyone who had rungs of the ladder to climb as someone to help, as someone to serve. I am a priest, and my God doesn't judge any of us on the last bad thing we do, doesn't judge us on the worst thing that we do. He judges us on the totality of what we do. Add up all the morally good and neutral on this side of the scale and the bad on that side of the scale, and John Kennedy is still a hero.

> *Add up all the morally good and neutral on this side of the scale and the bad on that side of the scale, and John Kennedy is still a hero.*

Well, maybe not at twenty-nine, thirty-nine, or forty-nine would I have still thought him a hero, but at sixty-nine, with the reflection of sixty-nine years, yes, I would, and how we all change in life. I have changed, and I no longer look at judging a person on the narrowest part of his life but on the totality of his life. It's what I think is so wrong with cable news today, because that's what we do in cable news. We try to tear everyone down into the worst thing they've done rather than looking with perspective at the totality of what they've done.

It [joining the clergy] was a very tough decision, but I'd thought about it for years. If the Church allowed married priests, I'd have been a priest a long time ago. My wife endorsed it. Toward the end of her life, she knew she was dying, she told me, "Look, better God than another woman. Have at it."

Robert Groden

Turning eighteen on the day of JFK's assassination—at home, playing hooky from Forest Hills High School—Robert Groden was so moved by the tragedy that he decided to devote his life to exposing what he believed to be a government conspiracy. In the ensuing years he "liberated" a copy of the Zapruder film from Time-Life, keeping it in a safe for five years before showing it on the college circuit with comedian-activist Dick Gregory. They brought the film to Geraldo Rivera, who broadcast it on national television for the first time in 1975, which caused an uproar and helped lead to the 1978 formation of the House Select Committee on Assassinations. He has coauthored a number of assassination conspiracy books and worked as Oliver Stone's chief Dallas consultant on *JFK*. On most days he can be found near the grassy knoll, discussing his theories and selling his publications and videos to visitors.

B ack in the '60s I wasn't into politics per se, but I was fascinated by history, especially questions of history, and when this happened on my eighteenth birthday, I gravitated to it immediately. I've been working on this case since the day it happened and am still doing it now forty-nine years later.

I admired President Kennedy. My family were all Republicans. It was President Kennedy who made me realize that it's not the party but the president, the man, who really creates the office, and I admired him, especially after the Cuban Missile Crisis. I was absolutely shocked; I took it very personally when he was killed, so I started studying it, and a little while later I visited his gravesite and made a promise to him, a silent promise that I would do everything within my power for as long as it

took to try to find the truth—
because even at the beginning,
I didn't believe that one person
did it alone.

The president was set up; he
was brought here to Dallas. Lee
Harvey Oswald was given the
job in the Depository. He had
always shown up for work, he
had never missed a day's work.
They knew he'd be here, so it
was easy to blame him. Shots
came from the front, they came
from the rear. The president was
killed; Governor Connally was
injured, whether on purpose or

by accident we don't really know. Immediately, when the president was
taken to Parkland Hospital, the witnesses there, dozens and dozens—the
ones that saw the head shot—all said that the shot came from the front.
They were unanimous about it at the time; nobody said anything differently. The throat shot and the head shot came from the front. That alone
should lead us to want to know more.

[Who did it?] I don't know the answer to that. What I do know is
the House [Select] Committee [on Assassinations] after three years said
it was the Mob. The Senate Intelligence Committee implied that it was
the covert actions branch of the CIA. A lot of people have stated that
Lyndon Johnson was involved in it. I don't know that he was—maybe
he was, maybe he wasn't—but that issue is there. I don't think it was the
Russians. I don't think it was the Cubans. Our issue in this case has never
been to try to find out who wanted the president dead. We know that. The
question is to find out who succeeded.

I worked for a company in New York. We did some optical work
on the [Zapruder] film for *Life* magazine. We blew it up from 8mm to
35mm. I obtained an extra copy—one that was supposed to be thrown
away and wasn't, and it was given to me. I worked on it myself at night, in

the middle of the night, on my own time, at my own expense. I stabilized the film. I took the original film, which was very shaky, and I stabilized on the president's head and just shot one frame at a time until the film was over. When I

> *Our issue in this case has never been to try to find out who wanted the president dead. We know that. The question is to find out who succeeded.*

ran it back, it was obvious that the president had been shot from the front. You see the bullet enter the right temple area, and the president's thrown to the rear and to the left. There was no question that he was shot from the front.

I use the word "liberated" because the Zapruder film should not have been in private ownership from the very beginning. It is the single most important piece of evidence in the Kennedy case. That, and the next thing after that is the medical witnesses. I have eighty-seven medical witnesses who said that the shot came from the front. That's very important; I can't throw that aside just in favor of the Zapruder film; but they're both very important.

They [the autopsy photographs] needed to be out there; they were illegally classified in the first place. There was a game played between the Kennedy family and the government to hide the autopsy photographs. The government didn't want anyone to see them for political reasons. The Kennedy family didn't want them seen for personal reasons. So they made a deal together where the Kennedy family gave the photographs to the government on paper.

Then the government gave it back to the Kennedy family. The Kennedy family then gave it under a deed of trust to the National Archives. These are pictures that are key evidence in the Kennedy case. There were 152 pictures originally, now there's only about fifteen of them left. Ninety percent of them have disappeared from the National Archives. That's pretty weird. Not only are they missing, but the president's brain is missing, the skull fragments are missing, the microscopic slides that were created of the wound margins, they're missing. How can they be gone? These were left in the National Archives for safekeeping for history. They're all gone.

Back in 1975, I was asked to appear at a symposium in Boston called the Politics of Conspiracy; I showed the Zapruder film there, and it was picked up as a major news story by all the networks. I received a phone call from Geraldo Rivera while I was testifying about this to the Rockefeller Commission. Would I appear on his show, *Goodnight America,* and show the film of the assassination?

I immediately agreed, and we showed it. Two days later I received a call from Washington, DC, to please bring the evidence down and show it to the House of Representatives, and I did. To my absolute amazement, Congressman Thomas Downing of Virginia introduced legislation just a few days later to reopen the case. Then he called me up and asked if I would be the staff photographic consultant to the committee. I agreed, but my showing the film on *Goodnight America* was a very iffy thing. We didn't know if there would be any legal repercussions. As it turns out, *Life* magazine, which owned the film at the time, said we couldn't show it. Their lawyers sent a letter to ABC saying, "You can't show it," and Geraldo said, "We're showing it, or get yourself a new boy." So we showed it.

The last official investigation was the House Assassinations Committee, and they ruled that there was a conspiracy. They knew it. Every single one of the doctors at one time or another, usually through their whole careers, said that the fatal shot came from the front—all of them. But it was [an entry wound at the throat]. Dr. Robert McClelland, he's still alive. He's the one who was standing at the president's head, and he said that the shot came from the front. When I worked for the House Assassinations Committee, I interviewed more than twenty of the doctors. I've got the videotaped interviews with all of them, and every single one of them said that the shot came from the front. Every one.

They never looked into who the front shooter was. They never tried to find out. The question is: Who was the shooter from behind? You want to believe it's Oswald? Fine. I don't believe it was Oswald. I found a witness who testified to the Warren Commission; her name was Geraldine Reid. She was talking to Oswald when the shots went off. She's the one who made the change for him for the Cola-Cola machine on the second floor. There are two basic questions: Was there a conspiracy, or wasn't there? Was Oswald a shooter or the shooter? Do you believe he shot the policeman? Officer Tippit was killed with an automatic. Oswald had a revolver.

This is a controversy that's been going on now for half a century. People believe what they want to believe. I believe what the evidence shows. I worked for the House Assassinations Committee; I testified before every investigation since the Warren Commission. I worked on the inside. I saw what went on, and I saw what the evidence was. If you don't want to believe there was a conspiracy, fine—because I'm not going to change your mind. But the evidence is there that it was a conspiracy, and the government admits it.

The Warren Commission was a cover-up. There's no question about that. The reason for it, I believe, is that they were presented with the option of admitting a conspiracy and following the evidence that Fidel Castro was behind it. If they'd have done that, then we would be forced to go after Castro, and that would probably lead to World War III.

The main issues in this case are not so much, "Was Clay Shaw guilty or not guilty?" We may never know that completely. I believe he was; I believe he took a tremendous chance by lying at the trial, saying he didn't work for the CIA when he did. I always have to wonder, *Why did he do that if in fact he didn't have something to hide?* In any case, the main issue here is: Was there a conspiracy? And as a side issue: Was Lee Harvey Oswald part of that conspiracy? I don't know that we'll ever know the complete truth, but we do know there was a conspiracy, that there was more than one shooter. How deep does the conspiracy go, how wide? We don't know, and thanks to the cover-ups that have gone on through the years, we may never know. But we do know there was more than one shooter.

Some of the original broadcasts on television and radio were giving different stories, different aspects of this, than what came out even later that afternoon. There was a situation where a major network, as a matter of fact NBC, stated that a man was seen running

The Warren Commission was a cover-up.

behind an office building across some railroad tracks. I'm from New York, and in New York everything is a grid, so in my mind's eye I had pictures of buildings right next to each other and railroad tracks running behind it. We hadn't seen any pictures of the knoll then; we didn't know about Dealey Plaza. Clearly we've got the depository building here, and there are the railroad tracks. The man they were chasing was over there. That disappeared, and it was years and years until that broadcast again. That made me start to wonder: If the guy is up there, how is he running over here at the same time? It didn't fit.

I can't answer for you the actual reason I've spent half a century doing this. I admired President Kennedy. The world changed, America changed, everything changed because of this particular event. I felt it was important to do it. I just gravitated to it, and I've been doing it ever since. If I would have lost interest in it, I don't know what . . . I probably would have done something else. But I really felt this was important. It gave me a mission in life, and I feel it's important to everybody. We have been lied to for so many years, and it wasn't until the House Assassinations Committee that we learned the truth.

The truth was: There was more than one shooter. Whether you believe Oswald was involved in it or not, there was more than one person firing, and that means conspiracy. People still deny it, and it's beyond me. More than 70 to 80 percent of the American people have always believed that there was more than one shooter, and they were right. Yet the majority of the news stories that we've gotten through the years tell us a different story against the evidence. What can I say? I need to do this.

Children, teenagers in school, aren't being taught the issues of the assassination. They're being told the original Warren Commission story: Lee Harvey Oswald acting alone killed the president. It's not true—but the teachers don't seem to care, and the textbooks are inaccurate. It took years and years for even the *Encyclopedia Britannica* to change it from "Oswald the assassin" to "He was the alleged assassin." I wrote to them, and they said, "You're right," and they changed it. Now it says, "alleged assassin," which is closer to the truth. There's not much I can say about kids, except when they come out here in the plaza, many of them, even little kids, are fascinated by it. They look around; they have questions.

We've had kids, eight- and ten-year-olds, that know more al most adults do.

I started doing this in 1963. I never stopped; and here it is nearly fifty years later, and I'm still doing it. I don't know ai who's still doing it. I know there are people who are alive that c.. about the case who were doing it back then too, but I have an advantage—I was only eighteen when this happened, so I started a lot younger than most of the other serious researchers in the case, and nearly all of them are dead. I think there are fewer than a dozen original researchers in the world still left alive, probably far fewer than a dozen.

—～—

Oliver [Stone] is a perfectionist. He wanted to get it done as well as he could. Even though the scenes in the Depository were mostly in black and white, he changed the color of the window frames to the color they originally were back then in 1963. They're green now, but they were sort of like pink then.

He took care with details that nobody would notice or even care about. He cared about the case. He put a lot into it, and of course the government started to attack him right away. This film was challenged, and it was attacked in the editorial pages rather than the entertainment pages. That's never happened before or since. Oliver expected that the Hollywood community would back him and support him. They didn't; they ran for cover. He did a movie, *JFK,* which was a very important movie historically. It's made a tremendous difference in this case. It got the files opened in the National Archives. Oliver is owed a tremendous debt of thanks. As far as the movie goes, it is a percentage of the evidence. It starts at the time of the assassination and a little bit before and goes through to the finding of not guilty—not "innocent" but rather "not guilty"—of Clay Shaw in New Orleans.

There should be another movie. There needs to be *JFK 2* to tell the rest of the story from 1968 until now, because more has happened now than happened in the time frame covered by *JFK.* But what is told in that movie is Jim Garrison's story. It's based on my book *High Treason;* it's based on two other books, including Jim Garrison's book *On the Trail of the Assassins,* and it tells what happened to him, what he experienced. That's what the movie is.

Oliver Stone's take was actually Jim Garrison's take. It wasn't his own take; he was telling Jim Garrison's story. The title of the movie is *JFK.* It could just as well have been called *The Jim Garrison Story.* Garrison lived it, he went through it, and I'm glad he got his story told before he died. His conclusion was that Clay Shaw was involved and Oswald was set up, and that I must agree with. The one thing Garrison couldn't prove at the trial was motive. The jury was absolutely, completely convinced there was a conspiracy. What they were not convinced with was Clay Shaw's involvement because Jim couldn't show motive. He said, "The motive is simple, Shaw is a CIA agent. He worked for the CIA." Of course Shaw denied it, and it was years until we found out from the director of the CIA that Shaw had lied, that in fact he did work for the CIA at the time.

The largest sacrifice I've made personally in all of this is giving up my career. The second biggest is giving up my career as a motion picture optical effects expert. But the biggest challenge and the biggest sacrifice was back eighteen years ago. My wife and I made the decision that I would come down here to keep the issues alive because we had lost about a dozen people in eighteen months. The other side in this case was winning by default. The Sixth Floor Museum, which has been lying through the years—telling people the Warren Commission was right even though they know better—had nobody to challenge them with any credibility. So my wife, Kris, who sadly passed away just two years ago, and I made the decision. She stayed up there with the kids and the grandkids. I moved down here to keep the issues alive. This matters to me. It really matters to everybody, but it particularly matters to me.

I would like to see the truth be known before I die. Today I'm sixty-eight years old. What can I tell you? I don't know about how much time I've got left, but I will be doing this as long as I'm alive. Dallas has ticketed me eighty-one times here in the plaza. They've thrown me in jail twice, and I haven't broken any laws. Two of the judges who defended my point of view in court were fired. Know what message is sent from that type of

thing to the rest of the judges? If I ever have to go back to court again, how am I going to get a fair trial?

The case needs to be reopened; there are many leads. Yes, they're cold, but the possibility of following through on some of them is still there. We changed history when I released the film in 1975—it did the impossible. It changed the course of history in this case; it's not over yet. There's still a lot more to learn. I have a new book coming out that's called *JFK: Absolute Proof,* and it is that; it is absolute proof. In it I have a lot of brand-new evidence, things that have never come out before. I found a witness who was talking to Lee Oswald when the shots went off. I've found documents within the government's files when I worked for the government for the House Assassinations Committee.

There's a lot of stuff that people haven't seen, and they need to see it. This may be the last book I ever write. I've done fourteen publications already, one of them hit number one on the *New York Times* bestseller list. They said it was number two, but even so it was number one—they told me that. In any case, I don't know where this one's going to go, but the public needs to know; they have a right to see this evidence. It can't go on being suppressed.

My favorite ally in all of this through the years was Congressman Thomas Downing of Virginia, who I showed the films to back in 1975. He realized there was a lot that needed to be answered, and he created the House Assassinations Committee and asked me to be on the staff himself, which I was. People like Tip O'Neill and others realized we were right. There was a legitimate question that needed to be answered. Now people want to know the truth. They'll go into the Sixth Floor Museum; they'll just shake their heads. They'll go down to the bookstore and want to find books on any side of the issue, and they won't find anything on our side because it's censorship. They won't allow any of these things to be in there, and they should. They should let people know the truth. They want to know the truth. They are attracted to the questioned history. About 95 to 99 percent of the people know that there is a conspiracy. In their heart of hearts, they feel they know it. About 1 to 5 percent believe there's an open question about it, that maybe there was, maybe there wasn't.

I'm here Friday, Saturday, Sunday, and holidays.

Vincent Bugliosi

In November 1963 Vincent Bugliosi was the twenty-nine-year-old president of his class at the UCLA School of Law, due to graduate the following spring. He was already working in the L.A. District Attorney's Office, where he later rose to prominence for his unparalleled conviction-success rate (105 convictions of 106 felony jury trials), including that of the Manson Family in 1969. His book on the Kennedy assassination, *Reclaiming History*, researched and written over a span of twenty years, consists of more than two thousand pages and tackles every theory of the case in minute detail.

I was going to UCLA law school when JFK was elected. I admired him. You know why I admired him? The guy was a war hero. He talked his father into getting some doctor to prepare a phony medical report so he could fight in the war. A destroyer cut his PT boat in half, and for four hours he swam to shore, taking with him one of his crewmembers. So the fact that the guy was a war hero who didn't have to fight at all—his father was ambassador to England—impressed me about him.

A couple years later I was trying one murder case after another down at the L.A. District Attorney's office. I was walking down the hall at UCLA law school in front of the business office, and one of the secretaries called out, "The president's just been shot." Because I happened to be president of the class at that time, I went into all the classrooms and announced to the students, and the professors excused everyone for the day.

The assassination of course shocked everyone, and I was just totally shocked like everyone else. The main emotion at the time by far was shock. However, there was another emotion: of hope. You know, he didn't die until about half an hour later, so many people were saying, "Maybe it's not going to be fatal."

There was also the
thought that maybe,
lost in the transmis-
sion, he really wasn't
shot, that someone
got it messed up.
But it was a terrible
blow to the Ameri-
can people.

My life at that
time was trying one
murder case after
another, so I hadn't
studied the assassi-
nation at all. My life seven days a week—I didn't take vacations or anything—was going from one murder or robbery or rape case to another.
Up to that point, what I had heard from the conspiracy theories was that
the Warren Commission had bias, distorted the record, and fabricated
evidence. What came through to me, and I didn't have any opinion, but
one thing did bother me: I kept hearing that the Warren Commission
had sealed the records for seventy-five years, the natural inference among
people being, "Why did they seal the records unless they have something
to hide?"

I didn't get involved until 1986 when I "prosecuted" Oswald posthu-
mously in London. According to *London Weekend Television*, the American Trial Lawyer's Association had their national convention in London
of all places in 1985; they started taking a survey, not just in London,
but they flew over here, and they went to bar groups all over the country
and asked them, "Who should oppose each other?" According to them, it
should be me. When they first asked me to do it, I said no because I had
been asked to do other things like this in artificial courtroom settings.

But they replied, "Wait. This is totally different from anything you've
ever been involved in. We know about your love affair with your yellow
pad. There's not going to be any script. Your yellow pad's the script. We're
going to have the real Warren Commission witnesses, no script, a regular

federal judge, a regular federal jury chosen from the jury rows of the Dallas Federal District Court."

I said, "This is really something."

They promised me twenty-eight hours because, how do you put on the Kennedy assassination in a couple hours? It ended up twenty-one hours unscripted. It was a mock trial, but it was kind of like a docu-trial. *Time* magazine said it was the closest to a real trial the accused assassin would ever have.

Gerry Spence defended Oswald. His name came up as a criminal defense attorney, and I came up as a prosecutor. I have to say, though, that when they met with me they asked me, "Should we choose Spence, Racehorse Haynes, or F. Lee Bailey?"

I told them F. Lee Bailey had a brilliant criminal mind. "Tremendous experience, but he doesn't do his homework." I said, "Racehorse Haynes, that name is a misnomer. According to what I've heard, he puts people to sleep."

They said, "We just came back from Houston, and we heard the same story."

I said, "Spence, I've come up against him in a debate in Wyoming, where he's an iconic figure. I think he's the best one who could stand up to me in final summation." So that's how it came about. Twenty-one hours, no script, regular federal judge, federal jury—and the jury convicted Oswald. The trial was a mock trial, but it was totally different from any other mock trial. Where do you have a mock trial where Gerry Spence and I work for close to half a year preparing for it? Spence will tell you that he prepared for this trial as much as any other murder trial in his entire career.

One of the first things I did when I was assigned to handle this case in London is get to the bottom of the sealed-records allegation. What did I find out? The Warren Commission didn't seal the records. The investigation was closed on September 24, 1964, and all the documents that hadn't been incorporated into the twenty-six volumes were sent to the National Archives for safekeeping. A cover letter by Chief Justice Warren, which I found, told the National Archives that he wanted them to have the fullest disclosure possible of these documents to the American people.

So it had nothing to do with Warren and the Warren Commission. It was an old National Archives rule that whenever documents for a federal investigation were turned over to them for safekeeping, they sealed them for seventy-five years, believed to be the life span of an average person. Since that time, because of the Freedom of Information Act of 1966 and the JFK Act of 1992, this seventy-five-year rule has been totally eviscerated; 99.9 percent of those documents have been made available to the American people. People say, "What about that one-tenth of 1 percent?" G. Robert Blakey, chief counsel of the House Select Committee on Assassinations, and Judge John Tunheim, chief counsel of the Assassination Records Review Board, both told me personally that their staff was shown all 100 percent of the records. They both assured me of that, and there's no smoking gun in there. The smoking gun doesn't even make any sense.

If there was any group that was bold and criminal enough to murder the president of the United States, surely they'd have the lesser immorality of removing any incriminating documents from those National Archives, so it's all just sublime silliness. There's nothing in those archives that's going to explode the case.

When I got into the case in 1986, I found out that it was they, the conspiracy theorists, who were guilty of the very things they accused the Commission of—distorting evidence and so forth—and I decided to do a book on it. *Reclaiming History* is a result of about a twenty-year effort. The only conspiracy in my opinion that had any merit at all—but there was no evidence—was the one with anti-Castro Cuban exiles. They were under a misimpression: Kennedy clearly said, "We're not going to support you at the Bay of Pigs. We'll get you there, we'll train you, but we're not going to get involved." But they said, "He's just saying that to the public. Obviously he's going to get involved." In their mind, Kennedy betrayed them at the Bay of Pigs by not giving them air support. So their brothers, their fathers, et cetera, died. If anyone had

> *There's no smoking gun in there. The smoking gun doesn't even make any sense.*

a motive, it was they. But there was no evidence. Then there was a recon-
ciliation between Kennedy and anti-Castro Cuban exiles at the Orange
Bowl right before the assassination. Both Jackie and the president were
there, and they presented him with the flag of their brigade. He said,
"This flag is going to raise itself once again in Cuba, and I'm going to be
with you." That was the only theory that gave me any thought. All the
other conspiracy theories made no sense whatsoever. Likewise, Castro
didn't have anything to do with it. Castro's not insane. He told the House
Select Committee, "You think I'm crazy? This would have been the greatest pretext in the world for them to blow Cuba off the face of the Earth."

The House Select Committee was in existence for about thirty
months. After the twenty-ninth month, with 250 investigators, what did
they conclude in a draft of the draft of their final report? "No conspiracy."
That was their draft of the final report. Then two fuzzy-headed acoustics
experts from Queens College came forward at one second before midnight. They told the House Select Committee—which was running out
of money anyway but wanted to keep the investigation alive—that they
had listened to a police Dictabelt recording from an open microphone,
presumably by a Dallas police motorcycle and presumably in Dealey
Plaza. They didn't hear any sounds of gunshots, but they did discern what
they said were impulse sounds, four impulse sounds, one of which, they
said with a 95 percent probability because of their mathematical compu-
tations, came from the grassy knoll.

Now the HSCA already knew that three shots were fired by Oswald
from the Book Depository building, so any fourth shot, of necessity, would
have been a conspiracy. They sold the HSCA that incredible bill of goods,
but it was a hotly contested House. Four of the members of the House
Select Committee wrote strong dissents; two of them that were in favor
of it were very, very weak. The conspiracy community was levitating with
joy. What brought them crashing down to Earth was that in 1982, twelve
of the leading scientists in the country and physicists—under the auspices
of the National Research Council and headed by Norman Ramsey, a professor at Harvard—looked at those same tapes. They also discerned these
impulse sounds, but what did they also find out? That at the identical
moment of these impulse sounds, in the background they hear Sheriff Bill

Decker giving instructions to his troops, and that was proven to be one minute *after* the assassination, when the presidential limousine was long gone down the Stemmons Freeway on the way to Parkland Hospital. So those impulse sounds could not have been any fourth shot.

By the way, to show you how silly the conspiracy theory is, their main idea is that the CIA hired a Mob hit man to fire from the grassy knoll. Whoever fired that shot, supposedly from the grassy knoll, the head shot's only forty yards away and the guy is so bad a shot, not only can't he hit Kennedy, he can't even hit the presidential limousine. It's just crazy. I have to say this: The House Select Committee did a good job, but they really stained and blemished their record tremendously. It was very unprofessional what they did, to seize what these two acoustics experts had. That's all they had to go on, the acoustics evidence. Twenty-nine months of investigation showed no conspiracy.

Oliver Stone shouldn't even be invited to the table of discussion on this. I'll give this to Oliver—you know, I've got to be fair to him—he did have the correct date. He had the correct city. He had the correct victim. But other than that, his movie, and I'm choosing my words carefully, was almost one continuous lie, and he had the audacity to fictionalize history. Fine, but you call it fiction. He didn't. He bought the fringe conspiracy theories, all of their theories, even though it was rebutted by everything else. However, there are certain areas where we know flat-out that he knew he was inventing evidence. It's the consensus of everyone except Oliver Stone that Jim Garrison framed poor Clay Shaw. How did he do it? He literally had his staff bribe, intimidate, and hypnotize witnesses. The jury came back—they had a cup of coffee of course—they came back in about twenty minutes. It was ridiculous. He's [Garrison's] a disgrace. Then Stone came along and resurrected him from his legal grave. There's no merit whatsoever to the prosecution of Shaw. Totally innocent.

Billions of words have been written about the Kennedy assassination, more than any other single one-day event in world history. But to summarize it, I learned as a prosecutor, you don't have to be a pro; it's just common sense: If a person is innocent of a crime, chances are there's not going to be any evidence at all pointing toward his guilt. But now and then, because of the nature of life, the unaccountability of things, there may be one piece of evidence and in unusual, rare situations, two, three pieces of evidence that point toward guilt even though the person is innocent. But in the Kennedy case, all the evidence, without exception, points toward Oswald's guilt. In *Reclaiming History,* I set forward fifty-three separate pieces of evidence that point toward his guilt, and under those circumstances it wouldn't even be humanly possible for him to be innocent—not in the world in which we live, the world where there's going to be a dawn tomorrow. Not in that world. Only in a fantasy world can you have fifty-three pieces of evidence pointing toward guilt and still be innocent.

Let me quickly give just a couple pieces of evidence. The murder weapon, a 6.5mm Mannlicher-Carcano, was proven by firearms tests to be the murder weapon. So, one, Oswald owned and possessed the murder weapon. Two, he was the only employee at the Book Depository Building who fled the Book Depository Building after the shooting in Dealey Plaza. Forty-five minutes later he shoots and kills Officer J. D. Tippit of the Dallas police department, who stopped him on the street for questioning.

Half an hour later at the Texas Theatre, he resists arrest by pulling a gun on the arresting officer. During his interrogation over a three-day period, he told one provable lie after another, all of which showed a consciousness of guilt. It's not even possible for this man to be innocent. I have no doubt that he's guilty. I'm satisfied beyond all reasonable doubt that he acted alone.

People say, "Ruby silenced Oswald for the Mob." Doesn't that presuppose that Oswald killed JFK for the Mob? If he hadn't, there'd be no reason to silence him. Jack Ruby had all types of problems. He had organic brain damage. He'd be the last person to use as a hit man. He loved the Dallas Police Department. He'd hang

All the evidence, without exception, points toward Oswald's guilt.

out at police headquarters. He loved them. He was a big blabbermouth. Again, you don't use a blabbermouth as a hit man, constantly going to the Dallas Police Department to talk about things he had heard at his girly club, the Carousel Club. Someone who knew Jack really well, Jack Revell, who was a detective for the Dallas Police Department, told the House Select Committee, "Jack Ruby was a buffoon." He said, "If Jack Ruby killed Oswald for the Mob, and if he was a member of the Mob, then the Mafia needs someone new to be their recruiting officer."

Why did he do it? Jack Ruby loved JFK. When I say, "loved JFK," his psychiatrist also said it, and he wasn't talking about in a loose layman's sense but talking about how he literally loved the man. He cried over the assassination weekend, cried constantly over the death of JFK. He thought JFK was the greatest man who was ever born. His sister Eva was there at the time. She moved to L.A., and I used to talk to her from time to time, and this is what she said: "Jack cried harder when Kennedy died than when Ma and Pa died." He hated Oswald. When he shot him, he said, "Someone had to kill that SOB, and you guys couldn't do it." He loved Kennedy. That's one of the reasons he did what he did.

The second reason: Jack fantasized about being a hero. He used to tell people, "I can dream about the Dallas Police Department being overcome by some terrible bad men, and then I come and I save them." If you talk to people who knew him at the Carousel Club, you know what they say? "Jack wanted to become a hero." The prosecutor in his trial told me, "Jack wanted to become a hero." Several members of the jury said, "Jack wanted to become a hero." He asked his lawyer, "Where's the author that's going to write a big book and a movie about me?" He thought he was going to get a slap on the wrist because he killed the guy who killed the president, and there was all this animus against Oswald. He thought that within a short period of time, he'd be back at the Carousel Club greeting people at the door from all over the world, wanting to shake the hand of the man who killed the man who killed the president. But he was a man of rather low intellect, with a violent temper. He was constantly getting in fights at the Carousel Club. He was not a hit man for the Mob. No evidence. The FBI checked it out. No evidence that he was ever associated with the Mob.

As far as the people are concerned, there's been a decreasing trust by the American people in their government down through the years, and it all started with the Kennedy assassination and the conspiracy community's allegation that the US government was concealing the truth from the American people. At the time of the assassination, polls showed that about 76 percent of the American people had trust in their government to do the right thing for them. That number dropped precipitously after the Kennedy assassination, all the way down to 19 percent in the early '90s. Today I think I've heard it's somewhere around 40 percent, so I don't think there's any question that it hurt the American psyche. When you have the trust and the confidence of the American people in their government undermined to the extent that they actually believe, in effect, that their government was an accessory after the fact to Kennedy's murder—in the sense that the government was concealing the truth to protect those involved—that has to have a deleterious effect on the nation's psyche that has manifested itself through the years, and that distrust was fortified by subsequent events like Watergate and Iran-Contra. But it all started with the Kennedy assassination.

Now as far as what happened having an effect on history, it's my belief—no one knows—but we may never have had the Vietnam War, whose cataclysmic consequences resonate to this very day. There's a substantial division of opinion among Kennedy's advisors and close associates as to whether he would have gone to war. Whether he would have gone to war is a question whose answer is lost to history. However, let me give you one strong piece of circumstantial evidence pointing to the direction that he would not have gone to war. On October 11, 1963, about a month and a half before the assassination, he issued National Security Action Memorandum number 263, which ordered one thousand American troops in Vietnam home from the 16,500 who were already there, and he wanted them home by the end of the year. Now that may not be dispositive or conclusive, but it certainly shows he was not eager at that point to escalate our involvement in Vietnam. Of course he said contradictory things, but he actually believed at that time, as most American leaders did, in the Domino Theory. They take South Vietnam, and next thing you know they're at our door ninety miles away in Cuba. It wasn't real, but it was perceived to be real at that point. But he said many contradictory things. He talked to people like Sorensen and Schlesinger. They actually heard him say, "Withdrawal is the viable alternative here."

⌒⌒

There are two realities in the Kennedy case. One is that at its core this is a very simple case—not just simple, it's a *very* simple case at its core. In fact, within hours of the shooting in Dealey Plaza, Dallas law enforcement, I'm talking about the Dallas PD, Dallas Sheriff's Office, local office of the FBI, they already knew—not believed—they already knew that Oswald had killed Kennedy. Within about a day or so thereafter, when they learned who he was and his background, they were convinced he acted alone. That reality exists at this very moment. This is a very simple case.

However, there's another reality here: Because of the unceasing and fanatical obsession of thousands of Warren Commission critics and conspiracy theorists, not just in America but around the world, who put this case under a high-powered microscope and examined every conceivable piece of evidence from every angle, and split hairs and then proceeded to split the split hairs, and made hundreds upon hundreds of allegations, and along the way deliberately distorted the official record, this simple case has been transformed into its present form. What's that form? It's now the most complex murder case by far in world history.

One example: In my book I found it necessary in one end note—I'm not talking about the main text now, one end note in manuscript form—to allocate about 120 pages on acoustics, with fifty footnotes. It's gotten totally out of hand. Right now, there're many, many people around the country who are looking at some document from the archives or elsewhere for some inconsistency, some discrepancy, some contradiction, something that doesn't add up, which in their mind equates to conspiracy. When you have thousands of people examining every word and comma of thousands of documents, otherwise intelligent people—now I'm choosing my words carefully again—when it comes to the Kennedy case, they're certifiably psychotic, and I'll say that publicly. When you have otherwise intelligent people looking at every word and comma, they can create a lot of mischief. You follow? And that's precisely what they've done.

Now there are many reasons people believe in a conspiracy, but I'll tell you the main one is the conspiracy theorists. On September 24, 1964, the Warren Commission issued their report. The conspiracy theorists had already been screaming conspiracy since the final bullet had come to rest. So they had about ten months of trying to poison the American public before the report was even issued. But still, when the Warren Commission came out with this report, only 31.6 percent of the American people rejected the findings of the Warren Commission. The majority accepted it. But over the years, and through their constant torrent and blizzard of books, radio and TV talk shows, movies, and college lectures, the shrill voice of the conspiracy theorists finally penetrated the consciousness of the American people and convinced the majority of Americans.

Right now the figure is around 75 percent that Oswald was either a member of a high-level conspiracy or just some patsy who was framed by an elaborate group of conspirators ranging from anti-Castro Cuban exiles to organized crime. I think it was Joseph Goebbels, propaganda minister to the Third Reich, who said, "If you push something at someone long enough, eventually they're going to start buying it, particularly if they're not exposed to any contrary view."

An example of how dominant the conspiracy theorists have been is that of the thousand books written on the assassination, I would wager that the percent of pro-conspiracy books is around 95 percent. That's all they've heard basically, and it's eventually taken its toll. The thing that occupies the American mind more than anything else is not even Oswald's guilt. But if he is guilty, was there a conspiracy behind him? I can knock that out in about two minutes. That is what you hear people talking about: Conspiracy, conspiracy, conspiracy—he was part of a conspiracy.

I can summarize that in three points:

(1) The Warren Commission, the FBI, and the House Select Committee all conducted extensive examinations of the evidence in this case and concluded that there was no credible—let me italicize the word "credible"—no *credible* evidence that any of these groups like the CIA or Mob was behind the assassination.

One little footnote to this: In London, Spence was raising all these conspiracy theories and all that, and I told the jury, "Folks, let me tell

you something. I'll stipu-
late that three people can
keep a secret, but only if
two are dead, and here
we're talking about fifty
years later not one credible
word or syllable has leaked
out. Why? Because there's
nothing to leak out."

(2) There's no evidence
that Oswald ever had any
association of any kind
whatsoever with any of
these groups believed to be
behind the assassination—

by meeting with them in person, letter, phone, carrier pigeon, it didn't
make any difference. No evidence that he had any association with any
of these groups. The FBI covered just about every breath Oswald ever
breathed between the moment he came back from the Soviet Union on
June 13, 1962, up until the day of the assassination, twenty-five thousand
interviews. They found no evidence of any connection between Oswald
and any of these groups.

(3) Let's assume, just for the sake of argument, that one of these
groups—and this is a prodigiously unlikely assumption—decided to kill
the president of the United States. Oswald would have been one of the
last people on the face of this Earth they would have gotten. Why? He's
not an expert shot; he's a good shot, not an expert shot. He had a twelve-
dollar mail-order rifle. He's notoriously unreliable, extremely unstable.
Here is a guy who defects to the Soviet Union, pre-Gorbachev. Even
today, who in the world defects to the Soviet Union? He gets over there.
He desperately tries to become a Soviet citizen. They turn him down.
What does he do? He slashes his wrists, tries to commit suicide. Just the
type of guy—I'm being sarcastic now—just the type of guy the CIA or
Mob would want to rely upon to commit the biggest murder in American
history.

Let's take it a step further. Let's assume that one of these groups for whatever reason wanted to kill the president. They decided they want Oswald to do it. Let's see where that takes us. I'll tell you where it takes us. There are two scenarios. I'll give you the least likely first: After he shoots Kennedy and leaves the building, the least likely thing that would have happened, there would have been a car waiting for him to drive him down to Mexico, Guatemala, or what have you. They, the conspirators, certainly wouldn't want their hit man to be apprehended and interrogated by the police. That's the least-likely scenario. The most-likely scenario by far is that, if the CIA or Mob got Oswald to kill Kennedy for them, there would have been a car waiting for him to drive him to his death. You know that would have happened, and yet we know that Oswald's in the street with thirteen dollars in his pocket trying to flag down buses and cabs. That fact alone tells any rational person that he acted alone.

> *It's all sublime silliness.*

Even the presidential motorcade, which took the president right beneath the sixth-floor window of Oswald, wasn't determined until November 18, four days before the assassination. It wasn't made public until November 19, three days before the assassination. Does any rational person believe that a conspiracy to murder the most powerful man on Earth, the president, would be hatched just three days before the assassination? Again, it's all sublime silliness, but it took me the equivalent of thirteen volumes of four-hundred-word pages, not because it's not a simple case but because of the conspiracy theorists—and they never end. I got sucked into the abyss. I couldn't get out. Finally my editor said, "Vince, we're going to press." If he hadn't, I wouldn't be here now. I'd probably be up to twenty volumes.

PART FIVE
CULTURE

John Glenn

Born and raised in Ohio, John Glenn enlisted in the Army Air Corps after Pearl Harbor and fought in the Pacific Theater in World War II as well as the Korean War. Recruited by NASA, he became the first American to orbit the Earth on February 20, 1962. Six weeks after the president's assassination, Glenn resigned from NASA to run for public office, eventually serving as US senator for his home state from 1974 to 1999. The recipient of the Congressional Gold Medal, Distinguished Flying Cross (five times), and the Presidential Medal of Freedom, he became the oldest person to fly in space in 1998.

I grew up at a time when the word "astronaut" hadn't been invented yet. It was something new. If I had a hope at that time, it was that I could learn to fly. My dad had taken me up in an old two-seater, a biplane, and I was hooked on aviation from that time on. But we didn't have much money, and to take flying lessons was something in the future.

In 1946 Stalin said that Democracy and Communism couldn't live in the same world together. The Soviets set out to do us in, and there wasn't any doubt about it. They were active in that. China went Communist; we had the Korean War and later the Vietnam War. All these were parts of the Cold War, a deadly competition. Between 1946 and the early 1950s, a lot of people thought maybe Communism really was the wave of the future. They [the Communists] had had a lot of success around the world. When they wanted to take over a country, they just did it: Hungary, Czechoslovakia, Poland, the Berlin Blockade. I don't think people knew for sure what direction this whole thing was going. The Communists were helping a lot of third-world countries, trying to get their support, and sometimes with great success.

Then it came time to have a space program, and lo and behold: In 1957 they sent up *Sputnik*, which they had in Earth orbit while we were still trying to get ours off the launch pad without blowing up. Castro aligned himself with them, ninety miles off our coast down here, and we had the Cuban Missile Crisis later on. We look back now and think, *That was destined to happen*, but we didn't know that then at all.

Kennedy wasn't in office very long till he decided to activate the program to put Cuban refugees back into Cuba, which resulted in the Bay of Pigs. He had made the decision, [but the plan] started under President Eisenhower originally. Right after that, the Russians put up Gagarin and made an orbit around the Earth. We thought our first person in space—Al Shepherd on the suborbital flight—was going to be the first in space. But the Russians beat that by about three weeks. It was against that backdrop of a dual failure that President Kennedy made a very gutsy decision, as we looked at it then—to establish a program for Earth orbit, which we hadn't learned how to do yet. From that we established a program to the Moon, which came after Al Shepherd's suborbital flight and before my orbital flight.

Kennedy knew what he was doing. I don't think we'd have someone stand up today and say, "We're going to Mars. We have X billions, and we have to do that." We had the background of the Cold War, from shortly after the end of World War II, and we had the Korean War and the Vietnam War, where we had been opposed by the Soviets.

> *We were behind in the manned space program because we were better than they were technically.*

It was a positive objective. It wasn't just responding to something the Soviets had done, like the Berlin Blockade or the Wall. This was setting a positive objective, and we kept it open for everybody around the world to share in that. That had been the policy from the start, and it was very important. Kennedy announcing the Moon program startled me and a lot of other people. Some of our high government officials and the president, I believe, had downplayed *Sputnik*: Don't worry about this beeping pineapple or grapefruit or whatever it was going around the world. But that attitude quickly changed, and we had to be competitive.

The problem was that in some respects we were behind in the manned space program because we were better than they were technically. That sounds backward, but the ICBMs built for nuclear weapons were the ones that we had to convert and use for manned space flight. We had been able to miniaturize nuclear weapons, but the Soviets hadn't. They still had to build big nuclear weapons, so they had big boosters. When you convert that over, they could practically put a house in orbit if they wanted, where we were limited to about four thousand pounds, which is the reason the *Friendship 7* was so small. We couldn't put a bigger one up there because we didn't have a big enough booster to do it.

We were very conscious that this was a competition with the Soviets for big stakes. I didn't believe the United States was second-best, but for a long time they had been playing up this idea of the United States being second-best technically. They were having success in space while we were still all too often blowing up on the launch pad. We felt that and wanted to get going as soon as we could. It was quite a shock when Gagarin made that flight and beat us into space.

The first time we got together with Bob Gilruth, director of NASA at that time, he said, "We're all feeling our way." We were experienced test pilots, and seven of us were selected. He wanted us to work on the program and help in the design and all the things we needed to do to find out how we were going to go into space.

The program was there, Project Mercury. They had outlined and put together the ideas for the capsule and the limitations we'd have on it. Kennedy had already set the path. It was some eight years later before we actually landed on the Moon, but the path of what we had to do—to let Neil [Armstrong] and Buzz [Aldrin] go up there and do that—was pretty well set.

We had to do some of the first steps, though. We didn't know how to orbit yet for sure. We'd done a suborbital flight, but we had a lot to learn. We put a little eye chart with different size print on it on the instrument panel because the ophthalmologists thought my eyes might change shape and I wouldn't be able to see. It's still in there, as a matter of fact. It was twenty-three inches from the bridge of my nose to that chart—I remember that figure for some reason. Then we were supposed to report feelings of dizziness or nausea, vertigo from strange movements in the inner ear. There was a lot we had to know, so we were working as hard as we could to learn these things so we could go ahead with the lunar program.

As far as doubts about participating, I didn't have any. Gilruth told us at the first meeting, if any of us ever had doubts, just say the word. We were on loan from our individual military services, and we'd go back with no questions asked. There was an escape pass if we wanted, but of course nobody even thought of going back.

Anybody who didn't like to be in small spaces would have been eliminated early on. We'd all been fighter pilots and test pilots; we were accustomed to being in small, cramped spaces, but it wasn't very big. We had some camera cases covered up with a little cloth thing with Velcro on the end of it that came down and then the control handle. The board switch was over on the other side with a little plunger on top. If we operated that during launch and turned that handle inboard about forty-five degrees, it would set off an explosive thing that detached us from the booster going up and activated the escape tower that would pull this up and away from an exploding booster if we had a problem. The "abort handle" is the name; everybody called that the "chicken switch."

We practiced and practiced so that everything was automatic. If we had a particular emergency, a drop in pressure or something, we knew exactly what to do. I did have trouble with the automatic stabilization control system, the SCS.

I had reservations. I can't say that I was 100 percent convinced, but it was important for the country. You just train for it and do it. I'm sure the confidence of the seven of us who were in training as astronauts was higher than the average person in this country because we'd been trained. The more you know about something, the more confidence you have in being able to deal with it. But there were moments when I thought, *What if this thing blew up?* We'd seen some blowups. We'd watched some of the missile failures. But we were also convinced that those problems had been solved and that this flight was going to be OK. So we went ahead and did it, whatever risk there was. We accepted that risk as we did during test flying in new airplanes.

I had met Kennedy at a reception here in Washington, and we had shaken hands. I didn't know him well. I got to know him better when I had been selected for the orbital, the flight of *Friendship 7*. He asked me to brief him on the plan for the mission. I went in to brief him, and I thought it was going to be a short few minutes, and that would be it.

But he was really interested; he had a real curiosity about exactly what we were going to do and how we were going do it. I finally said, "Mr. President, you're asking questions that I would like to answer, but I'd like to do it with a model and some graphics. What if I came back in ten days or two weeks and went through this in real detail?" He said, "Absolutely." When I came back, he asked questions, and we spent about an hour in the Cabinet Room at the White House.

We had things planned minute by minute for the whole flight. But of course we got up there, and we couldn't see out there. Where we saw out—the little window we looked out of—that's only about fifteen inches. We looked out, and we looked down, and we saw all nations at a glance, even though we weren't up as high as they go now. It was very impressive, and we had time to think a little bit about it. But it was very busy; the whole flight was planned very carefully.

They were a steady, luminous, greenish glow, like fireflies on a summer evening.

When I looked out at the first dawn, it looked like there were millions of fireflies, not blinking on and off but turned on. They were a steady, luminous, greenish glow, like fireflies on a summer evening. We didn't know what they were. I reported them, and that happened each dawn. The scientists determined that they were little water particles coming out of the heat exchanger on the spacecraft, as they're supposed to do, and they were collecting and then freezing.

Scott Carpenter, on the second flight, saw the same thing. He tapped the side of the spacecraft, and a whole shower of them went out. They'd been collecting on there, and they were water particles, I'm sure. But why the glowing yellow color? I don't think we know to this day why that first light of sun coming through the atmosphere and then back out to the spacecraft going around the Earth had that glowing, luminous color.

After the flight was successful and the spacecraft had been returned to the Cape, Kennedy came down and they had a celebration. The hatch was off to the side so that he and I could both stand and look into the spacecraft I had just used. He was recalling what I had briefed him on about a month or a month and a half before. He was a very curious person, and I've thought a lot about that since. Most people who accomplish a lot are people like that, who are really curious about everything around them.

When I came back from the flight, he was very curious about not only my personal experiences but also how this was affecting the rest of the world. Other nations were very interested in this. We talked about that some. This was something that was very important for the country, and he was much more confident then that we could actually accomplish the goal of landing on the Moon.

After Al Shepherd's successful suborbital flight, there was a parade in Washington, DC. There were hundreds of thousands of people out that day,

and we began to get an idea that this was really important to the people of this country and that they were really excited. I expected some attention, but I didn't expect all the super attention to it. It's hard to believe that I was in the middle of that. I sometimes looked at myself almost in the third person, as though I was looking at someone else out here. *Was that really me?*

It wasn't just in this country. The decision, made early on by Eisenhower and continued by Kennedy, of making our [space] program public and open to everybody was a very wise decision. I have a stack of newspapers that someone collected and sent to me from different capitals all around the world. All the headlines are on *our* flight of the *Friendship 7.* That there would be that kind of worldwide interest was almost unbelievable to me. They didn't do it with the Soviet flights, but they reported our flights in a "We did this" type presentation. The free world had done this together. That was good.

The Soviets had kept their program secret. We said we'd share the results of [our program] with everybody, and we did. We've continued that with the International Space Station now. Fifteen other nations besides us are involved in the space station. Ironically the Soviets—the Russians now—participate in our space flights. It's amazing how things change over a period of time.

Gherman Titov, who was their second orbital astronaut, came to this country in the summer of 1962, right after my flight. We had a reception at the Russian Embassy and were told, "They finally have accepted your dinner invitation for this evening," even though it had been turned down a couple of days before." So, I thought, *We'll put on a dinner.*

I told their [the Soviets'] driver to drive halfway to Baltimore and get them lost a little bit on the way out to the house. I sent a

> *"I don't know how things work in the Soviet Union, but over here sometimes you have to work for your dinner. Take off your coat and help."*

couple of policemen off to get frozen peas at 7-Eleven, and Annie and I went racing home and canvassed the neighbors for steaks. They were supposed to arrive any minute, so I had two of these little round barbecue things with charcoal in them, with fans on them, getting very hot. We were going to put on a dinner one way or another. Just about that time, the cars pulled up out front and Titov and the Soviets who were with him—the ambassador and everybody else—started walking up the driveway.

One of the little posts on this barbecue thing burned off and dumped the steaks in there. I tossed water on it, and smoke and steam were coming out the carport. As Titov came up, I told him through the interpreter, "I don't know how things work in the Soviet Union, but over here sometimes you have to work for your dinner. Take off your coat and help." He did, and we had a great time. The next time I saw his wife at that time, Tamar, she had her shoes off and was with Annie and Louise Shepherd grinding Planters peanuts to put on the salad. He told me later that was the best time he had while he was in the States on that trip.

Bob Kennedy came to me about six months after my space flight and said he and the president talked and wondered if I would be interested in running for the Senate. He and Ethel, we had dinner out at Hickory Hill and talked about this. I thought about it, but I turned it down. I thought my flight wasn't far enough in the past, and I owed it to the program and everybody to plow all my experience back into the program that would help train new people.

I turned down that opportunity, but Bob and Ethel, we became very good friends. They invited us up to Hyannis Port a number of times. On some of those weekends, the president was up there. That's where we really got to know him. We went sailing on their yacht, the president instructing my teenage son on sailing and things like that. He was a warm, friendly person. If there was a definition of charisma, he'd be that definition. He just exuded personality. We got to be good friends.

I water-skied, and of course the president, with his back, didn't. Jackie was a good water-skier. She and I skied together sometimes, and the press made a big deal out of that with pictures of us out there, the two being towed at the same time. One time I fell—I had a longer tow line than she did. You'd cross back and forth and toss the line over the person ahead of you. I hit her wake, which dumped me, and I went into the water. She kidded me about that for a long time.

I was driving from Ellington Air Force Base in Houston back out to the Johnson Space Center and heard [about President Kennedy's assassination] on the car radio. That was a real blow. Along with the rest of the country, I reassessed my responsibilities to the country. It was hard to believe, like it must be some mistake—the same way it was hard to believe when Bob Kennedy was killed. We had been campaigning with him. I often wonder what would have happened had he been president, but we'll never know that of course. Shortly after President Kennedy's death is when I decided to run for the office that he and Bobby had talked about.

It was devastating. The goals he had set, things he was doing, what he was standing for, and where he wanted the country to go—that was hard for the country to accept. There was a lot of excitement about the Kennedys, Camelot, and the future of the country. People couldn't believe we had changed direction, and then all at once it was cut short by this assassination. It was a tremendous blow for the whole country.

The Soyuz is over our heads right here, as we speak. Tom Stafford and Deke Slayton, who were directly involved with the Apollo-Soyuz Test Project, were good friends, still are—or Tom is; Deke's gone now. That was a good thing, a first effort to get our programs together and cooperate. Early on, Kennedy had suggested that we work together. The response from the Soviets wasn't all that favorable; it wasn't completely negative, either. I always did think there were hopes that we could get together with the Soviets and do some of the things we're doing now, combine programs as we're doing on the International Space Station. The more we keep the space program and other technical programs on an international basis, the better off we are in the long term. The advantages may vary from one country to another temporarily, but the more you share information and the more you work together with other people, the better off you are yourself.

Ending the shuttle program was a very poor decision.

Ending the shuttle program was a very poor decision. It was the most complicated but the most capable vehicle ever built. As John F. Kennedy said, "We are the leading space-faring nation." For us to have to pay the Russians to launch our people up to our space station, one we built and put up there—with some help, of course—I don't like that at all. The biggest opportunity that followed the Lunar Landing was the International Space Station. When I was in the Senate, I supported that fully and debated that every year on the Senate floor for appropriations. Wherever we travel in space, we're well advised to do research that benefits people right here on Earth—wherever we go. The International Space Station is the most unique laboratory ever put together.

On the shuttle in 1998, we had eighty-three research projects on that one flight—on medicines, growth, aging, all sorts of things. Before it burned up, *Columbia* had ninety research projects. To cut off our only means of getting to that [space] station and to take heavy equipment back and forth was wrong.

We have three different groups working on building craft that will take people back and forth. We will resume that. But right now, if something happens to Russia's launch system, our human space program ends. That's it—until we build a new way of getting back and forth. We could have maintained that. When President Bush made the decision to discontinue the program, he wanted to set another goal of having a permanent presence on the Moon. But it's expensive to do that. He didn't want to increase the budget, so in order to pay for it, he said, "We'll cut out the shuttle program." Each shuttle launched, it was estimated, costs somewhere around four hundred million dollars. That's a lot of money.

But [cutting the shuttle program] cut out our only way of getting back and forth to this station, which I see as so valuable for the future and for research in the future. To come down to paying sixty million, seventy million dollars for each astronaut launched up to the station and back by the Russians, that's wrong. If we're going to be the space-faring nation that John F. Kennedy envisioned, I would like to have seen the shuttle replaced only after we had its replacement in hand and ready to go.

I went to see President Obama after he took office and tried to get him to reverse that decision. He said, "We're in the midst of the recession"—the beginning of the recession at that time. He said he couldn't put the money back in the budget. I'm sorry we couldn't do that. But the original decision to do away with the shuttle was announced at NASA in 2004 with a cut-off date of the shuttles by 2010 and ending the space station by 2015. The [Obama] administration has extended the life of the space station out to at least 2020, with some possibility that we're going to extend beyond that time period. I hope we get our own means of transportation back and forth to the space station—and get it soon. It's important for the future.

I also hope we can instill in our young people an appreciation of what this country is, what it stands for, and what it does. Over the past fifty or sixty years, there's too often a forgetting of these things that led up to why we even have the country we have today. That has to be appreciated—it's not something that is written forever and will be there forever unless we nurture it and stick with it.

I have put my things, my memorabilia, to be archived at Ohio State University, where we have a John Glenn School of Public Affairs. We have about six hundred students who are going to be there this fall—undergrad, master's, and doctoral programs. If we can instill in some of these young people a feeling about this country that isn't just "What's in it for me, and how can I get better ahead?"—what's good for the country instead of the individual still applies today, even more than it did in Kennedy's time, because we have greater separations of our people in political life and public life today than we had back then. Right now we're at a very bad time here in Washington. We are at a time of opposition just to oppose, not for any sane, good purpose. I'm hoping that we'll see a change in some of that attitude with the younger generation.

The feeling of Camelot, what this country can be, the future we can have—it doesn't come automatically. It comes because people work at it, because you have people like President Kennedy and others who work at this thing, have worked at it in the past and given us some of the directions that would be better for the country in the future. The idea of Camelot is still there. You look at a movie and you think of the objectives of a Camelot, a perfect society. Can it develop? Will it have problems?

President Kennedy was holding out this hope that, yes, we can rekindle some of that feeling and some of that responsibility in almost every American to participate and do the things that need to be done. That's how this country moves ahead. It doesn't move ahead by everybody taking interest in just what's good for them alone.

I was fortunate enough to make two flights, the first Earth orbit for this country and then later on. As I age here on Earth, the effects of aging are similar, in many ways, to what happens in space flight after you're up there four or five days. Not a day goes by that I don't think something about what happened in space.

When you're looking at the Earth, you're going over whole nations. You can look down and see a whole country at a glance. It gives you a different perspective of things. You've gone clear round [the Earth] and back again every hour and a half. You're starting over again and looking at different scenery the next time around because the Earth has turned under you while you were up there. I wish everybody could go up there and look down. Maybe there'd be some different international attitudes if everybody could [go up] into space and look down.

Nancy Olson Livingston

Paramount Pictures signed Milwaukee native Nancy Olson in 1948, and soon thereafter Billy Wilder cast her as Betty Schaefer in *Sunset Boulevard*, for which she earned an Academy Award nomination for Best Supporting Actress. In 1950 she married her first husband, lyricist and librettist Alan Jay Lerner. They divorced in 1957, three years before the Broadway debut of *Camelot,* for which he wrote the book and lyrics. A year before the assassination, Olson married music exec Alan Livingston, who had signed Frank Sinatra and the Beatles to Capitol Records. In November 1963 she was living in Los Angeles with him and her two daughters by Lerner. In the decades since, Olson has stayed mostly out of the spotlight, making only a handful of appearances on television and film.

I had been in a play at UCLA, a Molnar play, *The Play's the Thing.* I played the lead, and the talent scout from Paramount saw it and said, "We'd like you to come out and do a screen test." I did it, they signed me, and I kept going to school. I was a client of Famous Artists, and Charlie Feldman was the head of the agency. I was a twenty-year-old student while I was doing some things at Paramount.

I had just finished *Sunset Boulevard,* and it wasn't going to be released for at least a year and a half, but nevertheless I had worked with Billy Wilder, and I'd gotten a real taste of what the motion picture business was all about. One day I got a call from his secretary, and she said, "Miss Olson, Mr. Feldman would like you to come to dinner on Saturday night at seven o'clock." I had never met Mr. Feldman, so I thought, *Is that appropriate?* Being a Midwestern doctor's daughter, I wasn't quite sure, so I explained this to her, and she said, "Please. Can you please be there at seven o'clock?" So I went.

I walked in, entered a sitting room, and sitting on a sofa at the other side of the room, with two little white poodles, was Joan Crawford. She tried to introduce herself to me, and I said, "I know who you are, Miss Crawford."

I sat there, and I realized this was going to be a challenging and strange evening. Charlie came in, and behind him was this tall, very thin young man. He kind of shuffled. He had a detached air about him—as if he wasn't really interested in even being there—but he sat next to me and said his name was Jack. I was kind of uncomfortable, and I said, "Where are you from, Jack?" He said he was from Massachusetts, and I said, "I've always wanted to go to Massachusetts." Then I said, "What do you do?" and he said, "I'm a congressman." I said, "Are you a Democrat by any chance?" and he said, "Yes." I said, "Fabulous. So am I." That's how things started. To me he was slightly distant. I think he was very amused by me. I don't think this is what he expected.

The maid said there was a phone call for Mr. Kennedy from England. He said, "Please start your dinner, I'll be brief. I'll join you." So we had dinner, and Miss Crawford went on and on about how terrible men can be. I was trying to reassure her and say, "Please don't feel that way. They can be really quite wonderful."

The plan was that we were going to go to the Beverly Wilshire to see Kay Thompson and the William Brothers. I was going to drive Jack in my car and then leave from there and go to the Palisades, where I lived with my aunt and uncle. Joan was going to go in Charlie's car. I said, "Could I use a powder room, please?" They directed me down this long bedroom hall, and on my way back I'm putting on my little white kid gloves, and I had my little pearl earrings on, which I still wear. An arm came out of a bedroom door, pulled me in, and pulled me into a very suffocating embrace. I was absolutely dumbfounded, out-

> *An arm came out of a bedroom door, pulled me in, and pulled me into a very suffocating embrace.*

raged, scared, furious. I thought, *Who is doing this to me?* and then *Good God, it's Mr. Kennedy.* I reminded him that we had just met. He said nothing. I retrieved my glove from the floor, and I went back to the foyer with my heart racing.

I didn't know what to do. Should I just go? Should I stay and take him, as planned? I stayed, he got in my car, and we drove to the Beverly Wilshire in total silence. Nothing was said. We saw the show, and now Miss Crawford, who lived in Brentwood, said, "You must come to my house for a drink." That was on the way for me, it was right off Sunset Boulevard, and so Charlie said, "Nancy, Jack will go with you, and I'll go with Joan." So we get back in the car, and we drive to Brentwood in silence.

We were shoved up the stairs and woke all the children—but this is interesting, this was when Jack and I kind of bonded, because we were both very, very concerned about the children. We both pleaded with Joan please to let them go back to sleep. That was interesting, that somewhere we did identify and had the same emotion about what was going on.

We went down the stairs, and I said goodnight. I got in my car and went home. About a month later, I answered the phone. There were nickels clinking down in a pay phone machine, a phone from somewhere—it turned out to be the airport, and it was Jack. He asked would I like to go to the movies, and I said, "No." Now, I was dying to get out of my aunt and uncle's house. I would've loved to have gone to the movies with almost anyone. But virgins have amazing strength, and he was a formidable opponent. He called again; he tried one more time, and I had to say no again, I was busy.

> *There was something about him, with his relationship with women, that was very strange, something I had never actually encountered. It was like a craving for chocolate—and just as emotionless.*

The next time I saw him was at another party at Charlie Feldman's. I had the feeling that he barely tolerated me, and I was eager to have a conversation. He was a congressman; he was a Democrat. I was interested in the world; I was interested in politics. He put up with it. I realized there was something about him, with his relationship with women, that was very strange, something I had never actually encountered. It was like a craving for chocolate—and just as emotionless. Once he had that first delicious taste of rich fudge, then he could go on and take care of his real cravings. It was an incredible ambition mixed with a real and very visceral intelligence—that, combined with a sense of this country, where we should be in the world, what I always thought was his core understanding, that it was part of his destiny. I knew he wanted to be president of the United States. I accused him of it by the way, and he was annoyed. I said, "Don't fool me; I know what you're after." He didn't like that, but because he had been so rather aggressive with me, I felt I could have that kind of a conversation.

As time went on, I learned about his reputation with women. People in Hollywood were involved. He was seeing a lot of people out here. I think he and Charlie, the first night they invited me, they went through the book and said, "Who's new at Paramount?" And they said, "There's this little girl, Nancy Olson. Why don't we have her?" They had no idea what they were getting into.

By 1961 Alan Lerner and I were divorced. I spent time with Oleg Cassini, friendly time, so I spent a little time with Jack and Jackie when they were married and when she was having Caroline—it was before he became president.

After the second convention of Adlai Stevenson, Jack made a real play to get the vice presidency spot. He lost to Kefauver. There was a brief time, right after the convention, when suddenly people thought perhaps Stevenson had a chance. Alan Lerner and I had dinner with Jack, with a very small group one night, and Jack—I'd never seen him like this before. He was wounded. He felt he had strived for something, he'd lost out on it, and it was an opportunity that was lost. That was really devastating, that he had lost. I reminded him, I said, "Hey, 1960, you've got a great shot at it then." And of course that's what happened.

May I stop for one minute? That was for me a revealing moment, that I'd never seen Jack be actually affected. He was always so smooth. He was the quintessence of cool. To me that's what he was all about.

But anyway, he won the presidency. I wrote checks, Alan Lerner and I wanted him to win very much. He won, which I thought was absolutely fantastic, and I found myself in Washington for the inauguration. I was with a small group going from ballroom to ballroom, and Teddy Kennedy joined us at one gala. Afdera Fonda, Henry Fonda's wife, was there. Joe Alsop had given somebody in my group a key to his house and said, "I'm with Arthur Schlesinger Jr. We're going off to our parties, but here's the key. Whoever gets to the house first, you know, light a fire, open a bottle of brandy; we'll be with you as soon as we can."

We got there first. We lit the fire, opened the brandy, and I'm passing through the front hall when all of a sudden there's a terrible rapping, thumping on the front door. Nobody's paying attention, so I said, "There's somebody at the front door." They said, "Nancy, open it." It was stuck, so I yanked it open—and there was Jack, the president of the United States. He said, "Good evening, Nancy." I said, trembling, "Congratulations, Mr. President." He came in, and I thought, *How did he get here?* He didn't have a hat or a coat, and there was swirling snow.

He went into the living room. Afdera Fonda was standing there, not looking the least bit surprised. It turns out that she went to one of the balls, got into the box where the first lady and president were seated, whispered into Jack's ear, "We're going to Joe's," and that's how he got there. But Jackie's back with the children at the White House. She had just had baby John, so she was tired, and he wanted to keep going. Maybe he had a date, I don't know, but he showed up. He knew everybody in that room. There was a small group from Palm Beach, his family friends. There were people I really didn't know. There was Emmett and myself. Peter Duchin; Peter and I see each other every four or five years, and we say, "Will you ever forget that night?"

Jack sat by the fire in an armchair. Somebody gave him a glass of brandy. He lit a cigar, and he sat there and started to reminisce. He was very touched by Frost, the poet, and he had laughed about going to the White House in the morning and seeing Eisenhower in a top hat. He said he looked like an Irish Mick from Boston. But what he was most interested in was what Nixon was going to do. He'd heard that he might run for governor. Did anybody know if that was true? Imagine, the first night of his presidency being interested in four years down the road.

He turned to me at one point, which so surprised me. He said he had gone to the play *Critic's Choice* in New York to see Henry Fonda, and he said, "Nancy, I thought of you. You should've played the role of the wife, opposite Henry." I said, "Thank you." That was very generous, and very dear.

There was one moment that was, to me, possibly the most dramatic. It was toward the end of everybody's talking. He was looking in the fire, and he was drifting in his own thoughts; he was thinking, kind of to himself, and he said, "You know, I had a briefing with the State Department this morning. They left a mess in Vietnam." Vietnam? I sat there and thought, *Who cares? Where is Vietnam?* "It's in Southeast Asia, the French—" Can you imagine the night that he is president not one day, and he's already worried about Vietnam? It's on nobody's radar. None.

November 22, 1963, I wasn't feeling well. I was lying down; it was in the morning. The phone rang, and it was my husband, Alan Livingston, from Capitol Records. He said, "Nancy, are you watching TV?"

I said, "No, of course not."

He said, "Turn it on; the president has been shot. I'm coming home. We're closing the company."

Within two seconds, the phone rang again. It was the school, the John Thomas Dye School, where I had Jenny and Liza, and they said, "We are closing; come and get your children." I had a carpool with Judy Balaban, who was then married to Tony Franciosa, and she said, "You're not feeling well; don't worry about it, Nancy. I will pick up the children."

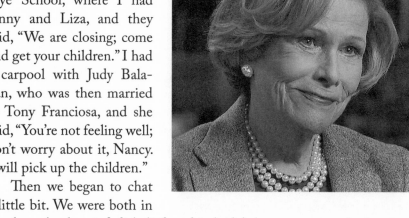

Then we began to chat a little bit. We were both in absolute shock, grief, disbelief, and it hadn't been announced who shot him or that that he was even dead yet. He was on his way to the hospital, and I started ranting and raving with her and said, "Those miserable, conservative, Southern, right-wing—" I went on and on and on, and she said, "Nancy, it may not be any of those people. For instance, there's that young man in New Orleans—he's got three names. It's something, something, Osborn, Os-something." I said, "Whoever it is, please, dear God, get him." We hung up. Within half an hour, they were at a theater ambushing a young man they were after, Lee Harvey Oswald.

To this day, it gives me shockwaves to try and understand how she knew. First of all, she's the smartest woman I know, and she reads everything, the *New York Times*. Both of us, we talk about what we read in the *New York Times*. She said there was a page printed at that time, just before the editorial page, that talked about news roundups from around the country and had a picture of Lee Harvey Oswald on the street corner in New Orleans. There was a story about him leaving the Marines, that he had gone to Russia, and he'd come back, and he lived in Dallas. So she said, "It could be anybody. It could be someone like that." Can you imagine?

I have a feeling about his legacy. He was president for such a short time, a thousand days. When the Russians sent *Sputnik* up into the heavens, he very resourcefully and creatively thought of something. I saw him on television, and he said to me and the world, "We are going to the Moon." It's like a fairy tale: We're going to go to the Moon, and dance, walk, and look back at our world—and he actually put in motion the funding for NASA. He meant it. It happened, and there has been an explosion of science that has revolutionized the world ever since; it hasn't stopped. When I think of him, I bless him for that. I'm very grateful that he was president. We learned something from him. We learned something from that family, the magic of that family, the beauty. It was a remarkable period to remember.

My first husband, Alan Jay Lerner, wrote *Camelot*. After the president's assassination, Jackie was interviewed by William Manchester among others and she said, "I kept thinking about *Camelot*." I thought she of all people understood the poetry not only of *Camelot* but of her life. She had a kind of literary wisdom. She was extremely well read. She had an appreciation of things that were beautiful. She was an interesting person. She had the instincts of a great movie star.

Rose Styron

In 1963 Rose Styron was a thirty-five-year-old poet, journalist, and human rights activist married to Pulitzer Prize–winning novelist William Styron. She had first met Kennedy years earlier when he campaigned on her college campus, but the president and first lady invited the Styrons into their inner circle after the literary couple attended an April 1962 White House dinner honoring Nobel Prize winners. Rose was a founding member of Amnesty International USA and has since served on the board of many nonprofit organizations, including Human Rights Watch, Equality Now, and the Project on Justice. She is also an overseer for New York University's Faculty of Arts and Sciences and a member of the Council of Foreign Relations.

When I first met John Kennedy, he was running for Congress. It wasn't his first time, but he came and talked to those of us who were in the Wellesley center, the little political group. Of course we thought he was incredibly attractive. He looked you directly in the eye and seemed to be listening just to you and to be really interested in what you were saying. The magnetism was right there in the eyes. We liked everything he said, and we were rooting for him for reelection.

When my husband, Bill, and I went to the White House for the Nobel Prize dinner, it was exceedingly glamorous, and I, as a poet, was very excited to be there because he was the first president who had ever asked a poet, Robert Frost, to be at his inauguration. I remember Frost with his hair blowing on that very windy day, trying to read this wonderful poem. Robert Frost was at the dinner, so as a poet I was particularly impressed. On the other hand, there were all Nobel Prize winners, and there was Linus Pauling, who had been out picketing the White House that morning. He went back, put on his tux, came to the White House, and got up and danced to the Marine Band, which I don't think anybody had done before. All of it was quite amazing.

We knew some of the other people there. There were a couple of our neighbors, like Frederick March. Bill kept saying, "Why are we invited? Jimmy Baldwin and I are the only young writers." Then he said, "I bet I know. The son of a bitch is after my wife." Which was, of course, not true at all. That was a sea change for the White House, to have those kinds of evenings: Pablo Casals playing at the White House, making it welcome for artists and Nobel Prize winners. That was the night the president made that wonderful remark about how there was more talent and intellect in the room than there had been possibly since Thomas Jefferson dined alone. He got a big cheer from all of us at dinner for that. He made everybody incredibly comfortable, and so did Jackie. You felt you were with a couple of friends, even if you weren't friends, because they were so gracious and down to earth and brought you up to their level.

At the end of that evening, as we were about to leave, we were invited back—quite to our amazement—to the private quarters. It was very impressive being up there with Arthur Schlesinger, Pierre Salinger, and other Kennedys, waiting for the president to come in. Bill, who had been quite sick and was on heavy antibiotics, of course had had all the wonderful wine and champagne that was served that evening and sat down happily in the presidential rocking chair. When the president came in, someone nudged Bill to get up, which he did, greeted the president, and sat back down. The president very graciously nodded, sat on the couch with Robert Frost, and began to talk with him.

The president was particularly interested in what Bill was writing. He had just begun *The Confessions of Nat Turner* at that point, which Jimmy

Baldwin pushed him to write in the first person, I think. That was when Jimmy was with us, and they had long evenings together by the fire. Jack Kennedy really wanted to know more about it. He himself may not have been a profound reader of novels, but he read poetry. Jackie of course read everything. She was really liter-

> *The very last time we saw President Kennedy, which was in New York, he said to Bill, "How's the book going?"*

ary and cared tremendously for all the arts, but Jack did too, and he had a very wide-ranging mind, a variety of interests, and a tremendous appreciation for the need of arts support in our culture. It was music, literature, dance, movies, all of it. He really saw the United States as a place in which life could be enhanced by free-wheeling artists.

After we'd been to the White House, we were lucky to go out on the presidential yacht with him from Hyannis to Martha's Vineyard or around Martha's Vineyard. They talked about what Bill was writing. The very last time we saw President Kennedy, which was in New York, he said to Bill, "How's the book going? Where are you now?" and "Do you think you might want to come down to Washington and give me advice on who to talk to about what's going on in the South, and about the racial problems we're having there, which we're really trying hard to solve?" He was killed a week or two later, so that conversation didn't get finished.

I was in the chair at the dentist's office in Woodbury, Connecticut, when I heard the news. The dentist had a little spray of water that he was putting in my mouth. We heard on the radio that Jack Kennedy had been killed, and the water went all the way down my throat. I went home to Bill; we turned on the television, and I don't think we turned it off for a week. We sat and watched, and watched, and watched, and then Bill's father came up from Virginia, and we watched the funeral together. We all sat and cried, as everybody in the nation did. We were all so stunned and so grieving. Bill said, "I guess we'll never see the likes of him again." We were very down. We couldn't imagine what would happen. Then President Johnson was anointed, and we still couldn't imagine what would happen.

The assassination of John F. Kennedy triggered a series of events that changed the country. He had laid the groundwork for remarkable things. Of course he was hemmed in by the need for anti-Communism, for safety in the United States. But while he was securing that, which he did admirably in the very short time he was there, he was determined to open up America to the voices of intellectuals, environmentalists, and people who had something to say that would make America better. Johnson came in and tried to follow out those policies, and Clinton came in and enhanced those policies tremendously, so I think he had a great influence on us.

I became much closer to Jackie than I certainly had been to Jack Kennedy. We saw each other socially, but we never talked about her life with Jack. I saw quite a lot of her on Martha's Vineyard and sometimes in New York. She came up to visit us the summer after her husband was killed, bringing Caroline and John-John with her, and stayed at our house. We had a couple of very funny incidents that happened, but Jackie really had to keep an eye on everything: on her husband's legacy, on her children, on her life to come. She had quite a difficult time deciding, in both the family ways and her own personal life, travels, romance, and so forth. She kept it all going in an amazing way. She was a remarkable mother to those children.

She remained very close to Bobby and to Teddy and, I assumed, the sisters. I knew Teddy better than I knew any of the rest of them, and I knew Jean—those were the two I knew the best. But Teddy was very close to Jackie, and so was Bobby, so she had those two as anchors. But there were so many Kennedys that by the time she moved to Martha's Vineyard, she kept them at a bit of a distance, except on Labor Day, when the entire crew of all generations, from everywhere, came up to her beach. That was probably the most glorious day of the year on Martha's Vineyard, when we were all there with her. She was fun and gracious and invited us all. It was quite informal. Caroline and my daughter, Alexandra, became very close friends.

The last summer before Jackie died, the end of the summer in Martha's Vineyard, she said, "Let's go sit on the beach." We did, and she said, "I really want you to write a book about all your human rights adventures. I think it's important to do that."

I said, "I would like to write about all the extraordinary people I've met and things they said to me or they accomplished."

She said, "But you have to put yourself into the book."

I said, "I don't know how to do that. I don't want to do that."

She said, "You have to, to make it a successful book." She gave me some outlining stuff, and she said, "You think about this over the winter, and we'll talk, and then we'll meet here when I come in the spring. I hope you'll say yes."

I thought about it over the winter, and I decided I would do it with her. But she died before we got to meet again, so that book was never done. She was a really good editor and had a good eye for stories. I don't know how I would have done that, but I trusted her and would have loved to have worked with her.

We were all young and private together; some of us got to meet the rest of the impressive people in the world who were quite extraordinary, and that produced a lucky life for me. John Kennedy ranks pretty high among those people. I was in human rights for a long time, as well as poetry. The Archbishop Tutus came in from a different angle, and the poets came in from a different angle, and I admired all the human rights activists and survivors in other countries under tyranny that I visited on

He once said: "When power corrupts, poetry cleanses."

missions for Amnesty. But Jack Kennedy just stayed as a pure, fine figure for me. He once said: "When power corrupts, poetry cleanses." That stuck with me.

I've been fascinated by all the things I've read since. I knew a great many people who were very close to him, so some of the things I knew before, but I read things in Chris Matthews's new book, *Jack Kennedy*, which I hadn't known at all, especially about his youth and about what was going on in his mind, the conflicts and decisions he always had to make. It only enhanced and deepened my feeling for him as a person. I hadn't realized, until I read this book, how much he had suffered medically and physically as a kid and as a very young man. I knew what he had done in the war, and *Profiles of Courage*, and what he had done after he was a public figure, but I hadn't known some of the private stuff. It deepened my respect for him.

I'm not a myth-maker, but the results of the myth-making are quite real in that we have a National Endowment for the Arts and the Humanities, which was in his speech at Amherst when Robert Frost died. He gave a wonderful memorial up there and talked about the importance of artists, of writers of all kinds, and those words for the nation inspired whatever arts and culture came after he died, which Johnson and others promoted. In my memory, he lives both for his foreign policy and his national policy and for his caring about the arts. We thought he was a very fine man, and it was exciting to have him for a president. It was exciting to have him and Jackie and Camelot, not for the glamour but for the promise. Fifty years on, what lingers is the feeling of hope for all of us, for artists, for civil rights activists, for political campaigners, which we all were. It was a time of incredible hope and promise for the future; I don't think we ever had that again.

> *It was exciting to have him and Jackie and Camelot, not for the glamour but for the promise.*

Jane Fonda

The daughter of Hollywood legend Henry Fonda, who had campaigned for JFK in 1960, Jane Fonda had appeared in just a handful of films by 1963, but with her first Golden Globe nomination as best actress, her star was on the rise. That summer, the twenty-six-year-old actress had gone to Paris to shoot a crime thriller with legendary French actor Alain Delon.

I knew John Kennedy because my father, Henry Fonda, had supported him, had worked for him. When he was a senator, I would sometimes be out on a date at the El Morocco, and he would be there with Jackie. Then my father married an Italian, so we would spend some summers in the south of France, and Senator Kennedy and Miss Jackie would come over. I was just a little kid—kind of like, "Oh, my God. He's so handsome." When I got a little bit older, anything my father thought was good was OK by me, and I knew that my father thought he was an important person to have as president.

He impressed me with his handsomeness and with his activities. Because I studied with Lee Strasberg and I knew some actresses—well, put it this way: When I made *Klute* and played a call girl and a would-be actress, I had a photograph of Kennedy signed to me—my character, "Bree"—on my refrigerator. That had meaning for me because I knew another acting student would go to see JFK on a fairly regular basis, but nothing was said about that in those days.

I dated Teddy Kennedy a few times, so I knew the family. I had met Joe Kennedy when I was with Teddy Kennedy in the south of France, when I was about sixteen. Everything I knew about Joe came from the way Teddy reacted to his presence. Teddy and I were on the beach. It was toward the end of the day, and he said, " Come, I'd love you to meet my father."

From the moment we stepped into the house, Teddy became a different person: very timid, scared of this man who was sitting in the living room. He never got up; he was sitting there, and he was a patriarch in the total sense of the word. I knew I had to be on my best manners, and Teddy was on his best manners. This man was the ruler of the clan; that was for sure. I don't remember charm; I remember fear on the part of Teddy. That was what impressed me. I was siding with Teddy, and I was just like, "OK, the sooner we can get out of here, the better." I don't remember charm. I'm sure he was charming though.

I began to pay more attention to JFK simply because I was in France and I was with people who were very political and sophisticated and talked a lot about Kennedy and their hopes and dreams for America. Besides, his brother-in-law Sargent Shriver was the US ambassador, living in Paris. Because I knew the family, I would go and see him. In fact, he became the godfather to my daughter, Vanessa. It wasn't that I spent a lot of time at the embassy, but Sarge was a joyous human being. It was the opposite of Joe: He'd wrap his arms around you—just a lovely, wonderful, charming, life-affirming human being.

We'd finished work, shooting that afternoon, and I was coming home from the studio. I was staying at a little boutique hotel on the Left Bank, overlooking the Seine. I walked into the lobby, and I saw the actor Keir Dullea from *David and Lisa*. He was making a movie in Paris, as was I. He was standing at the reception desk, holding a phone, and his face was the color of a white shirt.

I said, "What is the matter?"

He looked up, and there were tears pouring down his face. He said, "Kennedy's been shot."

I just—we just both stood there and cried. It was impossible to believe. I remember then going upstairs to my room by myself and realizing I would probably never feel totally safe again. It just seemed so impossible that this great president, who was so adored by the world, was dead. It's like everything became unsafe and never has been, ever since, quite as sure about the world. It shook my worldview. Simone Signoret—a very close friend of my family, and I had become very close to her—called me up and asked me over for dinner because she knew how I was feeling and how she was feeling. She had a home in Île Saint-Louis. I walked, and all I saw were French faces crying. All the cars on the street stopped and pulled over to the side while people cried.

A friend of mine here in Beverly Hills when it happened said the same thing. They were driving home from the studio, and all the cars were pulled over to the side of the road while people sobbed. I went to Simone's for dinner. It was Simone; her husband, Yves Montand; and their very close friend Costa-Gavras, who subsequently directed some great films. Everybody was just crying and talking about what an unthinkable tragedy it was. That made a big impression on me because, again, I had been living in Paris during the Eisenhower administration, and it wasn't that way, hasn't been that way since. But I realized then the important place the United States played in the world even more than I ever had and that this man represented everything that people wanted to love about this country—and he was gone.

I think the Vietnam War would have ended had he not been killed, and here's why: Johnson, perhaps, accomplished more on the civil rights level than JFK might have, but Johnson didn't end the war. He told his biographer, Doris Kearns, "It was because I'd be seen as an unmanly man." I think that was true for a number of subsequent presidents.

All the cars on the street stopped and pulled over to the side while people cried.

I don't think Kennedy would have had that problem, this "premature evacuation."

He wouldn't have been scared to end the war, and I think he was coming to know that it was wrong. Some people even feel that was why he was killed, but I don't want to get into that because I can't say. But I do think he would have ended the war. I'm not 100 percent sure, but I think he would have. That would have been very important for the United States, all those people on both sides who died, and what it did to our global reputation—that would have been very different.

Shortly after Kennedy was killed, I met the man who would become my first husband. I lived in France for eight years. I was there during the so-called Tonkin Gulf incident. I was there for the Tet Offensive . . . in a country that had already fought the Vietnamese and lost. They knew. But we saw things on television in France that people in this country couldn't see, the bombing of churches and schools. There were American soldiers in Paris who were resisting the war. They had been over there; they had fled, and they were looking for compatriots to help them with things like doctors, dentists, clothes, and so forth. I met them. I became friends with them, and they told me what they had experienced in Vietnam. They gave me a book called *The Village of Ben Suc* by Jonathan Schell, and that's the book that changed my life. I read that book, and I said, "If my country is doing this, I have to go home. I can't do this anymore. We're being betrayed by our government."

My life has changed so many times in some ways, but going to Hanoi— more than three hundred Americans had gone to Hanoi before me. I was far from the first, but I was the first big celebrity, and being an American in a third-world country of peasants and fishermen that were winning was mind-boggling. You had to look very carefully to understand, "What's going on here? What does strength mean? How can the United States, with all our military might, not be winning this war?" It changed me, and it made me think about things very differently. I was there all by myself. That was the huge mistake I made. Then the picture—the most horrible thing I could have done in my whole life. I didn't think what I was doing. It was the last day there; I was emotionally drained. There was this little ceremony. I tried to sing in Vietnamese, and people were laughing. I sat down, and then I realized all those cameras—there were a lot of cameras, and I wasn't paying attention, which wasn't always the case. I guess it was a setup. I hadn't thought about it, and then I begged, I said, "Please—" because what it looks like is not what was in my heart or who I was. I'd been working with American soldiers for several years before I ever went there. I

knew more about being in the military than most laypeople do, most civilians do. But the image says what it says, and I will go to my grave regretting that terrible, terrible—

I don't think any president will ever again be able to manage the message like that. Technology has changed everything, whether it's WikiLeaks, whether it's Tweets, whether it's cell phones, whether it's just whistleblowers. Those didn't exist back then, and I think that's good. We're not perfect, none of us; we're human, and he was human. He was the right person at the right time with the right kind of guts, and maybe a majority of the right instincts. Someone I mourn as much, if not more, is Bobby. Had Bobby lived, given everything, that could have changed the world.

We need heroes, and they were beautiful, they were wealthy, they were sophisticated, and they were exciting. And the way he spoke. [Speechwriter Ted] Sorensen, he was really good. The speeches were poetic. I think part of what was so exciting about them all was that you had the sense it was natural. Whether it was the wind blowing in his hair in Hyannis Port when he was at the helm of his sailboat, or he was in Washington, or whatever, it wasn't studied; they were as close as we'll ever get to royalty. It just was in their blood. That Joe, he made it happen. "You are going to be historic," and they were. It was there. It wasn't premeditated or set up or staged; no matter whether they were playing touch football in Hyannis

Port or whatever they were doing, they were perfect for the time; they were beautiful, they were smart, and they had great taste.

I've never felt as safe as I used to before Kennedy was killed. It made me, me as an American, and America as a country in the world, feel less secure. That's one thing. The other thing: You can never really know what it means to be an American until you've lived outside America. To have lived in France at that time, when that president was killed, made me understand profoundly the importance of this country—what we do, how we behave, who our presidents are, and how important it is for whoever we elect to be able to be respected by countries around the world.

In other words, to understand differences. Because Kennedy was sophisticated, he understood differences. They didn't scare him the way they scare some of the subsequent presidents. I tend to be drawn to politicians who I think can be global and not nationalistic, always rooted in America as being a country everyone in the world wants to love and should love, which means we have to behave in a way that deserves the love of the world. That's what Kennedy's presidency taught me because I was living outside America at that time. That was important to me, and it continues to inform the way I vote.

Peter Yarrow and Noel Paul Stookey

New Yorkers Peter Yarrow and Mary Travers and native Michiganer Noel "Paul" Stookey, all in their mid-twenties, were on the top of the musical world in 1963. After planting their folk flag firmly in Greenwich Village two years earlier, their careers were rocketing: As President Kennedy headed for Dallas, Peter, Paul, and Mary had three albums in the top-ten charts simultaneously and remained there for the next four months. Apart from a brief interlude in the seventies while they pursued solo projects, the trio continued to play to sellout crowds until Mary's death in 2009. Peter and Paul continue to perform together.

NOEL "PAUL" STOOKEY: 1959 was my first awareness of Kennedy. I was a young kid and had just moved to New York. I was not a political creature. I had come from a very affable, Midwestern background, and I was so into meeting girls and having fun that I didn't pay much attention to politics. I was barely twenty-one in 1959, but I had an apartment on the fifth floor of a Lower East Side building, and it was really a hot, sweltering day in August. I opened the window, and I heard a noise. I looked out the window, and, through the narrow crack on East Fifth Street, I saw a limo go by with JFK in it, who was coming up the Lower East Side to advocate for his candidacy for presidency. That was my first awareness of JFK. Whoever thought, as a young kid looking out that window, that we would have a personal interaction with him just two and a half years later?

PETER YARROW: At the time we didn't realize that he and his perspective would change America so dramatically. In 1959 I was at Cornell. Many of the things that needed to change, that he began to change, were ruling the roost. For one thing, success was all about how much you got: how much stuff you got and how much status in the hierarchy you got. It wasn't about success as a human being, to be a caring, giving participant-citizen of democracy, who gave to their country.

STOOKEY: It was the size of the fins on your car. That's what it was about in the late '50s.

YARROW: It wasn't about who you were internally. If you were black, you were a second-class citizen. Women were very much second-class citizens. What

he opened up by virtue of his point of view was the idea that, hey, we really have to be together, all of us, of all genders, of all backgrounds, of all religions. There was so much that to me, in Cornell, was oppressive because it was so unfair. It was so inequitable, so mean-spirited, and so hierarchical.

I was pretty much what they called then a "turkey"—kind of like a nerd without the cachet. A turkey was condemned to turkey-dom, and I was until I sang in a class as an instructor. That's when I saw that the people, when they were singing these folk songs, these traditional songs, that their hearts were reachable. The music was creating a sense of connec-

It was the size of the fins on your car. That's what it was about in the late '50s.

tion that struck me and moved me because these are the people who considered me a turkey, and all of a sudden the turkey was leading the band. They were coming in droves. First hundreds and then up to one thousand people. To do what? To do what we did right here at the Bitter End.

STOOKEY: The accessibility of the music was a metaphor for the accessibility that Kennedy was introducing into the world of politics as well. Nixon and the Republicans had a certain kind of royalty connected to the presidency. Although the public still gave it to them, even

> *The accessibility of the music was a metaphor for the accessibility that Kennedy was introducing into the world of politics as well.*

when the Kennedys were in "Camelot," but from the top down, the perception when Kennedy took office was, "Between my family, between playing touch football, between showing you my humanness and my policies, I'm showing you that government is of the people, by the people."

YARROW: Which was not the case before, in the Eisenhower years. In the Eisenhower years, God bless him, he did say some powerful things, but the mood of the country and the perception of each other was so constrained with the idea of separating people into groups and into who was in and who was out. All of a sudden, JFK united this country in a way that I, in my life, had never seen. I had never seen people feel *We're on the same page together* and *We love this guy.*

STOOKEY: Where people might play the power card to remain aloof and have their agents or their people speak for them, Kennedy didn't. When we had just performed for the second anniversary of his inauguration, Kennedy made a point to come to each one of us, the performers, and ask a question that in a sense betrayed a certain naiveté that he had, sweetness too.

YARROW: Our contact with the president started at a performance at the National Guard armory, where we, in a very unlikely way, were asked to join the likes of Yves Montand, Carol Burnett, Gene Kelly, and a lot of stars. Here we were, barely beginning our career, but there was somebody in the administration who said, "We've got bring these folks in." We had just had our first and second hits, and one of them was "If

I Had a Hammer." The other one was "Lemon Tree"—pretty, but it certainly had no sociopolitical agenda.

The audience was very receptive and warm to us, and then afterward we went to a gathering at the vice president's house. This was only for the performers, the president, the vice president, and the staff who had worked on it, including Mrs. Evelyn Lincoln, the presidential secretary. We started out by sitting down and having dinner.

STOOKEY: Somewhere in the course of it, the idea was introduced that each of the performers would perform what they had done onstage at the armory again.

YARROW: Mrs. Lincoln came over to me and said, "Would you sing for the president? The president would like you to sing. Would you consider doing so?"

When she asked me that, I said, "We will if the president really wants us to."

She said, "Let's ask him." She took me by the hand to the president, and she said, "Ask him the question."

I said, "Mrs. Lincoln has said you'd like us to perform for you. Is that something you really want us to do?"

He said, "You better, because if you don't, you're going to have to endure my singing, and you don't want to have to deal with that." His naturalness and his warmth were so clear.

We went upstairs, tuned up our guitars, and came down to the sunken living room. We started to sing, and the song that galvanized everybody was Mary singing "500 Miles," and Mary didn't move in time to the music. She moved in time to her emotion. Her passion about this song, when she was singing, she was saying with urgency, "Come home, America, to yourself." That's the way David Halberstam perceived it, and he was right. When they saw her singing like that, they went gaga.

STOOKEY: There is a vulnerability to folk music anyway, and when Mary reached out with just one voice and these two guitars backing, it has a way of connecting. After all the flush was gone, after everybody had performed, the president, in his inimitable way, made sure to make contact with each of us. He came over, and he was recalling that at the armory, when we had begun the chords of "If I Had a Hammer," the audience broke into a cheer. He asked us, "I notice that the audience knew the song you sang. What was it?" Peter said, "If I Had a Hammer," and he said, "Yes, I was really surprised"—and Peter, wanting to help the president out of any kind of awkwardness, I think, began to volunteer the fact: "That was a top-ten single." I was thinking, *What does "top-ten single" mean to the president of the United States?* It was on a 45 record, and Peter was holding his hand up like so, trying to describe what a 45 record was, and the president put out his hand and said, "Yes, yes, I understand. It's just that I don't get a chance to listen to the radio much, driving to work."

YARROW: This was only a couple of years after we began to perform. The audience wasn't aware of the quality and the tone of what folk music was asking. We weren't entertaining them per se; it was asking for participation and unanimity of spirit and sensitivity. At a certain point, I said to the audience that was assembled, "This is called folk music, and it's very common when people sing folk music that they sit down on the floor together in a very informal way. Since I think you might get tired standing, may I suggest that you consider doing that?"

The first one to sit on the floor was the president. He sat down. Of course everybody else sat down, and then we sang. One of the songs was a new song for us, "Puff the Magic Dragon." Later I received a copy of a *Time* magazine article about that gathering, and at the top Lady Bird Johnson wrote, "We loved Puff too." But what happened because of that music, sitting on the floor, the humanizing effect of it, was emblematic of what folk music was doing every time people encountered it, whether it was from us or the many other performers of that time. It was noted that this was the first party that Jackie had attended in its entirety rather than leaving because it was so boring and political. Folk music dispelled the formality.

STOOKEY: I was a Johnny-come-lately to the political process. I inherited much of my perspective through my partners, who had an understanding of the political process and also the communal aspect of politics. There was no doubt in my mind that Kennedy's motives were very aligned with those of Martin Luther King, and perhaps during the war years there might've been more of a reluctance because he had a sense of the global community and what the concerns were vis-à-vis the Cold

War. You could say that Kennedy was a Johnny-come-lately, but it was just a process of being able to put ideas into action through the democratic political process.

YARROW: Kennedy's heart was there, and that's what inspired us all. But there's distance between having your heart there and becoming a leader in a political sense that challenges the political balance of power and challenges your less-progressive support. What you're talking about in the seat of power is the capacity to lead, but you need the groundswell of support to validate your point of view, so you can say, "See? The people want that." What we had come to believe was that it was our job not to be so much involved in electoral political efforts but to be a part of that groundswell and march in Washington in 1963, which was subsequent to this gathering we're talking about. We know from history that Kennedy had to be pushed. We know that ultimately that letter from Birmingham by Martin Luther King and the call to his brother Bobby were important. Bobby was undergoing a metamorphosis. Bobby became a different kind of leader at the end of his life and career.

JFK was also undergoing a metamorphosis from being a quintessential politician who had an extraordinary charisma but had to walk the walk of what presumably he espoused, in terms of ideals so that on the ground those changes took place to rid America of this horrific prejudice and hierarchy of human beings, whereby people of color weren't only second-class citizens but could be lynched with no judicial repercussions, who in the nation's capital couldn't use a water fountain unless it said FOR COLORED ONLY. We're talking about a time of extraordinary change, in which JFK laid the groundwork with an ideological perspective that inspired us all to feel that we are one and we want to reach for a better, more equitable, more moral country, and to provide him with the grassroots basis for being able to act and move in that direction.

STOOKEY: Peter had flown earlier to Dallas. On the day of the assassination, the bass player and Mary Travers, we had a concert there that night, and about halfway through the trip the announcement was made of the president's assassination. We couldn't believe it. Our thoughts ranged everywhere from *Is this like an H. G. Wells* War of the Worlds *hoax? Was this some kind of joke?* We changed channels. Pretty soon everybody was talking about it. Then of course came the secondary part of it, the part of denial, which was, *Okay, he was just wounded, but he's going to be better. He's been taken to the hospital.*" Then within the hour and a half or two hours left of the trip, the announcement was made that the president was dead. It was so unreal, and yet, as shocked as I was, when we finally pulled into Dallas, we went right to the hotel and canceled the concert right away.

We canceled the concert immediately and made arrangements to get out of town. But I remember not really feeling the impact of it until about a week later. It's like when you lose a parent, and you get through the funeral OK, but then a week later when you want to call them to tell them something and they're not there—that's what it was to realize that we had lost one of the great presidents of our time. That was amazing.

YARROW: We had done a concert the preceding night in Houston, and we were scheduled the next day to do a concert in Dallas, which we canceled. That doesn't really matter, but for me, I've wiped out the memory of the moment when I heard. All I remember was saying, "I'm getting out of here." I was so traumatized by it that I rented a car and started driving. I wanted to get out of there. As I drove, I began to be able to breathe again—because it was unthinkable. We adored JFK; we didn't just admire him. He was more than a president, however esteemed and honored the term "president" might be. He was somebody who gave us hope, direction. He had a heart that we felt was embracing us all, and we loved him; we didn't just admire him. Years later, people said, "You can't personalize the relationship and deify a president. You have to look at them as guys or gals with a job." But at the time, we didn't have that kind of perspective.

There had been other moments when I've felt that I really love somebody who is in office, Gene McCarthy being one of those people, and with a

> *We had done a concert the preceding night in Houston, and we were scheduled the next day to do a concert in Dallas, which we canceled.*

lot of people to one degree or another—but not like this. JFK was in people's hearts, their own flesh and blood. He was America personified, and to lose him was unthinkable. It wasn't something that you could grasp. It took a long time to accept that it had occurred and to process it in any way that we could even start to grieve because, as far as I was concerned, I was scared, I was panicked, and I wanted to get the hell out of there—and I did. It took a long time to begin to process this loss.

STOOKEY: If I was reading this as a mystery novel and I got to the part where Jack Ruby shot Oswald, I'd say, "You've solved that one; you've solved the assassination," because I don't think Ruby acted out of a pure motive of revenge to avenge the death of the president. That's the key. The Warren Commission did what they had to do—but they did it probably with tainted and/or limited resources. There's more there that we don't know about.

YARROW: For me, as much as we needed to get a handle on how this happened, at this point whether it was the Mafia or whether it was something completely out of the blue that was internal to the political system—which I totally cannot imagine and won't subscribe to—what's important isn't unraveling that secret. The only thing that would make that important is if we found that there was a further danger to the United States and the things we believe in that we need to eliminate, so for that, but not in terms of letting John Fitzgerald Kennedy rest in peace. God bless him; he did extraordinary things for all of us in this country. What he initiated, not just in terms of a heart space but also in terms of the pieces he put in place, like the Peace Corps, those have changed America in ways that still allow us to see ourselves as inherently committed to doing the right thing, to helping other people, whether it's our own or all over the world. That remains immutable. That's part of our memory of it, and that sustains. That gift is part of all Americans who somehow inherit that legacy.

STOOKEY: The impact of Kennedy's assassination, added to that of Martin Luther King and Bobby Kennedy, created a wall that shut out all the sunlight that had been coming in. To the extent that I was a progressive liberal, and aware now of the good that some political and community work could do, the obvious message to me, written on this wall created by these three assassinations, was: "Don't do it. People who care get shot at." I didn't feel that so much in the music, but, boy, within a year's time, it seemed like music stopped talking about those things we shared as a community and started saying, "Dance. Just get out and dance. Life is frivolous; it has no meaning, no purpose. Get out and dance. Dance, dance, dance." For the next ten years of our lives, with the exception of "Abraham, Martin, and John," I didn't hear any music that was deeply convicting or moving.

YARROW: Life separated itself more and more frequently. To those who, for whatever reason, say, "No matter what, we carry on," there were a lot of people who were exhausted by these losses; there were a lot of people who felt consequently disaffected from the process. They felt mangled by the sense of disappointment, as if all those people who are aspiring to good are living in great jeopardy. "They will not survive." This was the way it was going to be.

There was another impulse that came to me from the years prior to the trio, that I actually wrote about in a song at a later time, when I asked myself, "Is what we've been doing really consequential, or is this all something we've made up? Are we accomplishing anything, and did we get anywhere?" So I wrote these lines:

> You remember when you felt each person mattered
> and that we all had to care or all was lost,
> but now you see believers turn to cynics,
> and you wonder: Was the struggle worth the cost?
> And then you see someone too young to know the difference
> and the veil of isolation in their eyes,
> and inside you know you've got to leave them something
> or the hope for something better slowly dies.
>
> So carry on, my sweet survivor, carry on, my lonely friend.
> Don't give up the dream; don't you let it end.
> Carry on, my sweet survivor. You've carried it so long
> so it may come again.
> Carry on.

Music stopped talking about those things we shared as a community and started saying, "Dance. Just get out and dance. Life is frivolous; it has no meaning, no purpose. Get out and dance. Dance, dance, dance."

STOOKEY: If it was at all like my personal experience, the country went through an incredible period of denial, where for the first couple of hours they hoped that it was not true. For the next several weeks, they hoped that whoever did it could be punished. For the next several months, they kept their hopes alive by reading *National Enquirer* or pulp magazines that appeared next to the checkout lanes that said Kennedy was alive, living on some island in Cuba or off Cuba or in the Bahamas or in long-distance grainy telephoto shots where people looked like the Invisible Man, wrapped in gauze. There was just a spiral of stupidity that was kept alive by the press for a long time until finally it disappeared, and what we were left with was, "Okay, where do we go from here?" It's amazing that Richard Nixon got elected president. Is that what we came to? In a sense, though, he was the representation: "We'll take a firm wall, and no one's going to get past it, and that's what I'm standing for, and that's why I'm going to be your next president."

YARROW: The legacy of it also was that it made people not trust other people and institutions, that now we don't trust the government, we don't trust the CIA to be telling us the truth. We don't trust the information we're getting. We basically have to see every issuance of a piece of information from the news media or from the government itself with skepticism. In a sense, that was a loss of innocence and a coming of age, because we needed to be more rigorous in our evaluation of the information and the ideas that were offered by magazines and newspapers, where we now know that a lot of that stuff was made up to sell. But it also served us in good stead when people questioned the validity of the Vietnam War, which we now know was based on a whole cloth of lies, where what was reported was success and what was happening was the decimation of the Vietnamese people, of

our own young men, to no end, because, as Robert McNamara specifically told the president, it was not winnable. Part of the legacy made us healthily more careful about what we bought into and believed.

STOOKEY: It's a thin line between skepticism and cynicism.

YARROW: Some people wandered back and forth, and they felt, *I don't know what I'm doing in these vineyards, working in them*. But it was very important for us to step back and reassess that part of the mythology of America as a fountain of wisdom and truth that didn't have to be examined, to see if that was verifiably the case.

STOOKEY: There is a certain strength in vulnerability insofar as it reveals a process that other people can have access to: "Oh, yeah, you're making a mistake," or "You've made a mistake—I can do that, I can learn from your mistake." Something as abrupt as an assassination carries with it the realization that you can terminate a life, but you cannot stop an ideal that is of its time.

When you live your life for an ideal, it is the ideal that is communicated. A young person looks at this streaming past them, and they don't think in terms of their own death or their own mortality, but they are looking farther down the road at those ideas and those values worth holding onto. Insofar as Kennedy's legacy suggests a transparency that has been inherited by the Obama presidency, that it suggests a youthful

345

ardor that is available to all of us and a dedication to a broader, longer term principle, that is a great gift that Kennedy left us.

YARROW: Framed in my terms, I would say to young people: Do not give up even though it seems as if you are surrounded by enormous challenges that are insuperable. We have seen

Something as abrupt as an assassination carries with it the realization that you can terminate a life, but you cannot stop an ideal that is of its time.

extraordinary things happen in this country, many of them emerging from the ethos and heart of the Kennedy administration and what the person John Fitzgerald Kennedy was. We have seen extraordinary change in this country. Where people of color walked the streets in fear and couldn't vote, and [now] we have a black president. We have seen women come closer and closer to equal power, position, prestige, and respect in this land. We have seen the people rise up to stop a war that should not have been entered into, that was unethical, that was based on false principles.

The second thing I would say is that we need to continue to believe in and study about these events so that we can harness them in our lives, learn about them, and learn from them, because we have to not recapitulate our mistakes. We have a predisposition in this country to just forget about what we did that was wrong. I don't think, if we really had the kind of open, heart-to-heart commonality of national examination of what we did in Vietnam, we would have easily gone into Iraq, which was parallel in too many ways.

If you're a young person watching this or listening to this, hang in there, but also try and fathom what was good and what was faulted historically, and realize we have had huge victories that will need to come again in terms of the struggles of your own time. Do not be afraid to love someone you respect. It will empower you. Do not see them simply as functionaries. See them as an expression of your heart. Embrace them as that, carry them in your heart, and it will empower you as you go forward.

Judy Collins

Starting as a Denver-based piano prodigy before discovering the guitar and the powerful lyrics of music icons Woody Guthrie and Pete Seeger, Judy Collins in 1963 was a Grammy Award–winning twenty-four-year-old folk singer and Greenwich Village staple, with three acclaimed albums already under her belt and many more to come. As her career blossomed, Collins devoted more time to social activism. These days, in addition to touring, she is also a UNICEF representative.

The '50s altogether were very Hollywood: very big bands, big orchestras, the "moon, June, spoon" music. The politics were pretty rigid in terms of you did "this and this and this"—although in my family we didn't do "this and this and this" because my father was in the radio business. He spoke openly about the Vietnam War and about McCarthy, but there was the terrible McCarthy scare. Many people were hounded out of their jobs, accused of being Communists, and had their careers tainted.

It was a very conservative time. I had a bob like Dorothy Collins, and I wore a little poodle skirt when I was fourteen, fifteen, and sixteen years old. But suddenly I found folk music, and that sort of cut through all of that for me. When the music began to kind of bubble up, it was 1959, and the "Folk Scare" was happening, and that cut through all these other things that were playing on the radio. Previously you had "Wee Small Hours of the Morning" with Frank Sinatra, "Earth Angel" and "One, Two, Three O'clock, Four O'clock Rock," and other songs, but then came the folk music, and that began to carry the political changes right along. People were beginning to wake up, because we got into Vietnam early. We had advisors there with the French. Indochina was a problem during those years people didn't talk about. A lot of people didn't know about that, but it was happening, and it was sort of secret, sort of covert, and there was a lot of that going on.

There was a combination of things going on in the run-up to JFK. Kennedy's father was a patriarch who was the ambassador to England; he wasn't so terrific politically and had a lot of sympathy for Hitler. He was also a huge, wealthy industrialist. He was a bootlegger, a skirt chaser who had affairs with Gloria Swanson and others. It was a very aristocratic family, but it was an aristocratic family with very high ideals of behavior not on the dad's part but on the kids' part. They were certainly raised with a great deal of devotion to the Constitution and devotion to human rights. I think it was already there. I've read many indications that they were well-read. They were well educated, and they had service in mind.

Perhaps that paved the way. Perhaps they had suffered from the 1950s in the way a lot of us had—that closed-down state where you don't tell the secrets. You don't talk about alcoholism in your family. You don't talk about the affairs our politicians were having, including Roosevelt. You don't talk about those things.

Joe Kennedy certainly had aspirations for his children of doing the right thing and also being in power. He wanted to see his family in power in politics. JFK didn't do much as a senator really. He was sort of like an LBJ when he was in Congress. He just sat through a lot of things, but he was building his idea of what he wanted to do. Kennedy was suffering a lot. He had a lot of pain, and that's always a good teacher. But he was also, I think, ready for what was happening.

I do think that's one of those incredible historic moments where so many things come together. They were coming together musically, culturally, and socially in every way. The war was out there by the early '60s, and by the time Kennedy was elected it was going strong. The music was beginning to tell the story. In all the little places in Greenwich Village, Chicago, and Los Angeles, there were singers with guitars cutting through with lyrics that had stories, that had a point of view, and that in many cases had a political edge. People like Woody Guthrie and Pete Seeger were doing all kinds of things, helping to get the news out that there was something else going on, and it was very powerful.

It was very exciting to have this new presence in politics because he was talking about things that had value and had immediacy, and he was closer to our age. He was a young president; he was a young man. He had a young spirit. He had young, youthful ideas. He had ideas that could cut through, at least what we thought was, a lot of the fog of confusion and secrecy.

He was, I thought, doing many of the right things. We were so involved in the marches against the war in Vietnam, against the advisors, because the first death in Vietnam actually was in 1957, perhaps earlier. But he was taking actions, doing the right thing. The terrifying situation with the Cuban Missile Crisis he handled brilliantly. He didn't take the advice and just open up and fire away, which was what he was advised to do. His advisors were hot on the button to get it done and get it over. But he didn't do it. He put it off. He made the right decisions by being cautious. Whatever happened between him and Khrushchev resulted in this dialogue in which Khrushchev actually opened up a conversation. They'd opened up a dialogue after the Cuban Missile Crisis passed. That was a huge relief. People were terrified. People were expecting to be bombed out of existence.

He was on the right side of the arts. His wife, Jackie, the first lady, was very involved with bringing the White House into the social and cultural milieu that was happening. She was beautiful. She was intelligent. She spoke eloquently. It was a big showing of all the things we all believed in: art and culture and doing the right thing, treating humanity with dignity, and that everybody has dignity and should be respected.

I had been in the hospital in Colorado with tuberculosis for a number of months, and they let me out. I'd already made my debut in New York, but I was also in a divorce. I got a call from my manager saying, "They'd like you to come to Washington to sing for the president of the United

States." It was a big dinner at the Shoreham Hotel, an honorary dinner for President Kennedy. He was being honored by B'nai Brith. The people on that show were Josh White, the Clancy Brothers, me, Lynn Gold, Will Holt, and Dolly Jonah. It was incredibly thrilling to sing—and there he was, sitting there, listening to our music. I couldn't believe it.

Afterward, we all got to meet him, and the charisma was unbelievable. I'd met some stars. I'd met some people in Hollywood. My father was a big star in his own pond of Denver. People were very fond of him. He was very famous, and we as his kids got that; it rubbed off onto us a little bit. But I never met anybody with that kind of allure and power and sparkle, where also you felt that he was on your side and he was going to do what was right for you.

The civil rights movement was still in big trouble. The first big bill to pass in 1957, which LBJ pushed through, was the stepping-stone, I suppose. It wasn't what everybody wanted. There were still problems that had to be addressed. But I think everybody had the feeling that Kennedy was going to get it done somehow. America of November 21, 1963, was a place filled with optimism.

It was a cold day but not terribly cold. I got a bus to go to LaGuardia Airport to get on a plane to go down to Washington, DC, where I was working at a club called The Shadows. I got on the bus at about the time of the shooting, and the driver said, "Our president has been shot."

Then we had to drive to LaGuardia, and during that drive I was thinking, *Please, God, don't let it be somebody who's black.* That was my first thought, because we were already in trouble. There were some riots going on. We had a lot of problems with the racial division and the racial tension in the country. Then, when I got to the airport, the driver said, "He's gone." It wasn't very long—an hour, maybe. I continued my flight to Washington and went to see my friends Beverly and Lee Silberstein, who had an art gallery in Georgetown, and we sort of buttoned ourselves up around the television set and watched this drama unfold of the murder of Kennedy and the murder of Oswald by Jack Ruby in that police station. It was unbelievable.

By the night of November 22, we were crushed. It was over; we were done. This exciting, young, optimistic activist in a lot of ways— imaginative, artistic, articulate, stirring in his speeches, eloquent in his discussion, with an ability to move around in the world, help us not

All performances, all shows, all joy it seemed were canceled.

to be blown to pieces, and help us find our way—was gone. The feeling was devastation really. The Shadows and The Cellar Door in Washington, DC, were where I was going to sing—in the days immediately after the assassination, all performances, all shows, all joy it seemed were canceled. Everything stopped. It was like the world came to an end.

We didn't know there was a communication between Khrushchev and Kennedy, which had become quite extensive and had been initiated by Khrushchev. We who were marching against the war in Vietnam didn't know that Kennedy had proposed bringing one thousand troops home at the end of 1963. We didn't know that. Christmas was the date, and they were coming home. We didn't know that he'd proposed a civil rights bill—I think we might've known that it had been on the table. We didn't know that his nuclear disarmament agreement had been agreed between him and Khrushchev. We didn't know that. We didn't know those things. We were still devastated, but we didn't even know all the seeds of what he had been planting, what he was going to do.

Then Lyndon Johnson has become president in this bizarre scene on Air Force One, where Bobby is feeding him the lines for the words he has to say when he's declared president, and he's gathered Jackie into the picture, who's still dressed in her bloody dress. These were the images we were seeing. He's taking the oath of the president of the United States. We didn't know what we know about Lyndon Johnson today. We certainly didn't know that history in depth, and we would soon know, before the ninety days were over and the State of the Union was given, that he was not going to adhere to the withdrawal of troops, that he was going to conduct a build-up of troops in Vietnam, that he was going to get President Kennedy's Civil Rights Bill done—which he did and which was genius. We soon knew that Lyndon Johnson had his foot on the pedal along with his generals and his bloodhound associates in his cabinet, that he was going to go forward in Vietnam with a will to win and that he was going to follow through with President Kennedy's Civil Rights Bill.

He'd had all the experience in the Senate before, where he learned how to manipulate them in the most extraordinary way, which few people, if any, have ever been able to repeat in my lifetime, and he did force it through. That was the first real breath of hope and hallelujah that came out following the assassination, because we finally had a civil rights act passed. In that year, in 1964, the Mississippi summer is going on, and I and a lot of people I knew were going to Mississippi to help register voters, so it was a year of momentous change and tremendous activism on the part of many people.

There was a whole bursting of the bubble with the death of President Kennedy, and it was that now all our illusions were really gone. We didn't have illusions anymore. We now had the reality of the war, which was going on and on and on, and which most people I knew were marching against and speaking out against. The music was so diverse. It started to become just bubbling with contrast. That kind of eclecticism that was going on with Elektra Records was happening all over the country, as it was happening all over the world. The English rock scene was coming on. The Doors, the Beatles were coming through. We could dance to them. We could listen to them.

My career was solid, but I made a lot of decisions based on my own need to grow. I was already reaching into the orchestral world to bring myself into doing material that was new and different. When I recorded "Pirate Jenny" from *Threepenny Opera*, it was extremely political and extremely edgy. You had an incredible amount of choice, and it was all this bubbling talent, with this necessity to talk about things in a musical form. I always loved folk music, and I fell in love with it

We didn't have illusions anymore.

because of the stories, but it had personality and integrity, and it told you, "This is what's going on in certain parts of the world with certain people."

It's changed our country. It made possible some of the things that have gone on since. I don't think these things disappear. I think secrets kill. I think secrets demolish a certain central goodness in the country, and in the world, and I think they did that. I don't think this will be settled in the American psyche until they find out names: exactly what happened and by whom. Will we ever see that? I don't know. Certainly a lot of the information is right out there to see. There are certain things, like all the witnesses who died: dozens of people gone, unaccountably, in suicides, accidents, heart attacks, gunshots, and car wrecks—you name it. That in itself is pretty unlikely.

Our hearts were broken, and our trust was broken, so our inability to sit back and be comfortable with what was going on in the world ended in some kind of cataclysmic way. Not to mention that now the lies begin to come out. We knew there were things that weren't right about this, the manipulation of the Zapruder film, and the fact that somewhere in there something was diabolically wrong with the story. It's still something that preoccupies me from time to time, especially now.

Some books have come out very recently that talk about the background of these murders. One of Kennedy's mistresses, Mary Meyer, who was Cord Meyer's wife, was murdered the year following Kennedy's death, and it tells us a lot about the manipulation of people who might be dangerous because they knew too much, and they certainly knew things they didn't want us to know. All bets were off after this.

Robert De Niro

In 1963 twenty-year-old New York actor Robert De Niro had just completed his first starring role, in Brian De Palma's *The Wedding Party* opposite Jill Clayburgh. He has since garnered numerous distinctions, including two Academy Awards and the Kennedy Center Honors. Known for collaborating with director Martin Scorsese, De Niro's body of work includes *Bang the Drum Slowly*, *Casino*, *The Deer Hunter*, *The Godfather Part II*, *Goodfellas*, *The King of Comedy*, *Mean Streets*, *Midnight Run*, *Raging Bull*, *Silver Linings Playbook*, *Taxi Driver*, and *Wag the Dog*. He is considered one of the best actors of his generation.

I remember that everyone I was around had a good feeling about him. I wasn't really into politics or anything, but I also had a good feeling about him. They were an elegant couple, and that's why there was Camelot. We were all young. Everybody was hopeful. It was before the war was getting into a darker place and everybody was opposing it, so it was a good time. It was just what it was. For me, at that age, he was a guy who looked like he'd be a good president. He was charismatic, and that's why you noticed him. I feel the same way about Obama. He's the same: young, optimistic, energetic, hopeful—I feel the Obamas are the closest to the Kennedy legacy.

One thing I remember very clearly was the Cuban Missile Crisis. I was in a classroom, going to night school at the time. I think I was eighteen. I was sitting in a history class, of all things, and hearing it on the radio. I was of the generation where you got under your desks for the air raid drill, which is

totally useless, but anyway the whole class was listening to him, and I was very nervous. You felt that there could be something not good happening. I felt certainly that the world would change. I was not that aware of exactly how it would affect everything in the future. Obviously, it would.

At the time he was killed, I was on the subway, getting off on 42nd and Lexington in New York. I remember as soon as I got off the subway, people were talking, standing around, and so on. People everywhere were just standing around, kind of stunned, and I think that's when I knew. I was stunned. One of the reasons I was so stunned, as we all were, is that he was assassinated. You just never felt that that could happen. I remember watching the funeral all weekend on television, black and white.

When he was assassinated, it was kind of like that was it. It's over. Whatever that was, it was just over. When people say, "We lost our innocence," in a way that could be true. You could say that. There was an end to something. You didn't know where you were going to go after that. It makes me think of 9/11. I did whatever I had to do, but it changes everything obviously.

I used to think it was what it was, and now, being a little more aware of history and so on, I wonder if maybe there was more to it. I haven't really read the conspiracy books. I'm aware of them, been given the gist of what they are. So I start to think, *You know, maybe there was some sort of, not necessarily a conspiracy, but something that kind of led up through all the things that Bobby Kennedy was doing—and somehow that made it possible in some way.*

Sonny Jurgensen, Carl Kammerer,
and Bobby Mitchell

In a controversial decision by NFL Commissioner Pete Rozelle, games were played on the Sunday after the assassination. One of those games pitted the Washington Redskins—featuring recent 49ers transplant Carl Kammerer and former Cleveland Browns halfback-turned-flanker Bobby Mitchell—against the Philadelphia Eagles, for whom North Carolina native Christian "Sonny" Jurgensen quarterbacked, at Philadelphia's Franklin Field. The year after the assassination, the Eagles traded Jurgensen to the Redskins, for whom he played until his retirement in 1974. Kammerer retired from the NFL in 1969, going on to work in the Office of Congressional Relations of the Department of Transportation and later at the Nuclear Regulatory Commission. For many years he worked with both the Special Olympics and the Wounded Warrior Project. Mitchell retired from the field in 1968 to become a pro scout for the Redskins, at manager Vince Lombardi's behest, eventually rising to assistant general manager. The Pro Football Hall of Fame inducted both Jurgensen and Mitchell in 1983.

MITCHELL: Coming to Washington from Cleveland was a shock to me. When we'd come to Washington to play the Redskins, we'd see all the black people, just looked like for miles, and we said, "Boy, whoever comes here is going to be having it made." I never thought it'd be me. I was shocked when it ended up being me, but I just never thought of it as a Southern city, Washington DC, I don't know why. But then I can't go in the restaurant? My little kids couldn't go in the ice-cream shop. I said, "What kind of place is this?" This is Washington; the denial was just mind-boggling. I couldn't understand it.

I felt a sense of that change, though, because Bobby Kennedy and I were pretty close—from '62 to until his death. In fact, I was invited to the White House for a state dinner, and my wife and I were wondering, *How did we get here?* because the other black couple there was Sammy Davis Jr. and May Britt. It wasn't until much later I figured that Bobby probably told everyone about me. A big contrast: I can't go into some restaurants, but I'm at the White House.

Sonny Jurgensen

We're standing down by the East Room, and at that time the stairs from the president's upstairs apartment were right there by the entrance to the door. It's now been moved around to the front. People crowded when they said, "The president's coming down the steps," he and Jackie. I grabbed my wife, pulled her over to me, and said, "Let's get back here." We stood back against the wall, which was facing the steps. We were about five deep, people crowding in, and this is the honest truth: When they came down, and they were working their way through the people—now they still haven't gone in the East Room—he walked through them as he was shaking hands and walked straight to me. He walked over to me, and he said, "We thank you for what you do." So I knew Bobby had said something to him. There's no other

Carl Kammerer

Bobby Mitchell

way I'd get invited there. That was the only time I actually talked to him or was around him.

JURGENSEN: Just having someone that young in the White House, the family itself. The NFL was growing in leaps and bounds at that particular time. It didn't hurt it for them to want to attend games and for Ethel Kennedy to sit in the box up here with Jack Kent Cook and Edward Bennett Williams. It helped, and I know the players were aware of that.

KAMMERER: Everybody was aware of the changes going on, but many of us were involved with the Kennedys out at their farm, watching the children competing in horse games and hanging the ribbons around their neck at the end. My wife and I were scheduled to meet with the president. This appointment was made through William "Fishbait" Miller, who was the doorkeeper of the House of Representatives for, I think, thirty-five years. He was a friend of my two roommates, Eddie and Bobby Khayat from Mississippi, and I met him through those two guys. They set up a meeting for us. Then, just as the week was progressing, the doorkeeper called me and said the president needed some more time to work on his speech and so we'll do it when he comes back [from Dallas]. Well, he came back, but not vertically.

Joe Mooney, the groundskeeper, was always a funny, telling-jokes kind of guy. He saw some of us coming out, and he said, "Hey, the president's been shot." We thought, *Okay, he's going to give us a punch line,* and then in tears he said: "No, he's dead." We all gathered around the radio to listen to what was going on. That was the first occasion of us hearing about the death of the president.

As far as playing or not, we pretty much would take whatever decision was made and make the best out of it. But even right up until the game itself, we weren't sure whether we were even taking the field. The decision was made kind of late by Commissioner Rozelle to go ahead and do that. I respected the decision and supported that, but out in the stadium, here you are, you make a first

> *Even right up until the game itself, we weren't sure whether we were even taking the field.*

down or you do something, which normally you'd have the crowd giving some sort of response and cheer or whatever, but it was pretty quiet during the game.

> *Most of the players didn't want to play.*

JURGENSEN: When we heard about it, we were leaving practice at Franklin Field, and there was a little truck where we get something to drink, sitting up on the sidewalk for the students at the University of Pennsylvania. We heard it then, and it was a shock. We had a team meeting on Saturday night, where the discussion was whether they were even going to play the schedule of NFL games the following day. Most of the players didn't want to play. There were other things being canceled all over the country, and here our commissioner was saying, "We're going to go ahead and play the full schedule." People who were fans of the president, they were very shaken by it. Other people who weren't, they said, "We have to play football. Let's just play football." There was give-and-take and people hollering in the meeting and everything. It actually broke into a fight, a real battle royal—I've never seen anything like it in my life. It just split the team. Nobody wanted to play the game.

We walk on the field, and there was no buzz in the crowd. The players weren't motivated. You're just going through the motions. It looked like a bad Pro Bowl game—people just kind of trotting around out there. The Redskins won 13 to 10. I don't think I've ever played a game where there was no emotion, no passion for playing the game, and it's a wonder a lot of people didn't get hurt, because that's when you have a lot of injuries, when people aren't going 100 percent.

There was give-and-take and people hollering in the meeting and everything. It actually broke into a fight, a real battle royal—I've never seen anything like it in my life.

I felt it was best to go on.

KAMMERER: That particular game was quite different and quiet, reserved, down-played. I come from kind of an old-school type of mentality, and that is: Football's played in the rain and in the snow and in all kinds of conditions. I felt it was best to go on. But in retrospect, after many years, it easily could've gone the other way, and I would've respected that as well. We as a team dedicated the game to the president and sent the game ball off to the White House following our "major" victory.

JURGENSEN: All the teams wanted to do something, because everybody was in shock. They wanted to do something to show that we were involved and that we cared. They took a collection from each player. There was a decision made to collect some money for the Tippit family. It was just very moving not only for the football players who were in the NFL but for the entire country. None of us had ever experienced anything like that before.

MITCHELL: [A few weeks after the assassination] I received a call at home. Bobby wanted me to come to downtown Washington. We had a playground that was going to be named the John F. Kennedy Playground. It was the groundbreaking ceremony, and his office called and said he wanted me there. Well, I'm nervous because of all the stuff, and I didn't want to go, so they said, "We'll send a car for you." I said, "No, no, I'll drive."

But I want to get to a point that was really tough for me. When Bobby arrived, I had moved to the back of the group. The mayor of Washington and Bobby were up front, and the mayor told him, "Bobby Mitchell is there, Bobby." That's when he told me, "Get up here. Get up here." I came up there, and when we leaned over he said, "I want you to help me with this shovel because I'm weak." I remember leaning over with him to pick up the dirt, and I had his arm. It felt like his arm was about that big—tiny. He was so drained, and he was shaking, and I was shaking. I'll never forget that, what it had done to him in that very short time. We were close right on up until the end.

KAMMERER: I was struck with Kennedy's speeches and the way he put things together, "A rising tide lifts all boats," tax reform, reductions,

Mitchell, Jurgensen, Kammerer

and all the rest of that. I'm a conservative, and so I kind of like those points. But he touched the entire nation while he lived and profoundly after his death. Our country has moved way out on the right and way out on the left; there doesn't seem to be somebody who's in the middle who wants to sit down and discuss and negotiate and represent our people, our voters, our country. It seems like they're polarized, and I don't know how we're going to get back.

JURGENSEN: The assassination seems like yesterday to me. It's still fresh in my mind, and when you called us that you wanted to talk about this particular period, then it really started refreshing itself. It brings it back so much: the game itself, how the game went, people who were involved, the decisions that were made during that time. It was an experience you certainly don't want to go through again. You see things on the Kennedys, the different members of the family, and it all flashes back to you immediately; you think of that family and what they've had to experience over the years, the tragedy they've gone through, time and time again. It's unbelievable, the strength and the intestinal fortitude that family has and the things they have been able to overcome.

KAMMERER: Doesn't seem like it was fifty years ago. I pretty much close the book on events that are of the past and try to leave them in the past, but, as Sonny mentioned, the call to come and talk about it touched some emotions. I still stayed involved with the Kennedy family, and later on, in 1968, I was an official out at the University of Maryland, hanging the ribbons on the winners of the Special Olympics. It was just a marvelous thing the Kennedys did. I'm still involved in Special Olympics. One of my roommates, Eddie Khayat, has a Special Olympics tournament in York, Pennsylvania. I've been there twenty-five consecutive years.

MITCHELL: You never forget, on a yearly basis, what advancements have been made for my people. We live with everything every day, but when it comes to the National Football League, I'm very happy. From where it was when I came into the league in 1958, where we were lucky to have two blacks on a football team—when I came in it was two blacks, now it's two whites—but what it all boils down to is that everything has changed. But it's all been for the good, and everything is just so great now, until I get upset whenever there's something being said against the league or whatever, because so many good things have happened to us.

Oliver Stone

In 1963 seventeen-year-old New Yorker Oliver Stone was attending the Hill School, a college preparatory school in Pottstown, Pennsylvania. After an Army tour in Vietnam, he graduated in 1971 from New York University's film school, where director Martin Scorsese was among his teachers. Stone won his first Academy Award in 1979 for *Midnight Express.* In 1988 he bought the film rights to Jim Garrison's *On the Trail of the Assassins,* and directed the controversial conspiracy thriller *JFK,* which Warner Brothers released in 1991. He has won three Oscars and four Golden Globes among many other awards.

Kennedy inherited Vietnam from Eisenhower. Eisenhower supported the French war there. We paid 80 percent of the French expenses during that war, from 1947 to 1954. After that, Eisenhower kept talking about the Domino Theory in Asia. Kennedy very much inherited a situation that was fraught with peril. It was not only Cuba; there was Laos, there was Vietnam. Ike was the older man. He was the one who was trusted. It was very hard for John Kennedy to go against Eisenhower. With the Bay of Pigs, he committed to that policy—that Allen Dulles had put into effect—of invading Cuba through proxy groups. With Vietnam, he continued the policy of containing Communism. He put noncombat advisers into Vietnam, and he took the number from eight hundred to about sixteen thousand in 1963. But there was no combat role assigned to them, and he was very clear about that. He didn't want to put ground troops in. He said it repeatedly. He was pressured, but at the end of the day, he signaled his intention to withdraw. He was withdrawing the first thousand. He said to his friend Kenny O'Donnell, "I cannot do this, withdraw from Vietnam, until after the election of '64. I can do it in '65. I'll be very unpopular, but we won't have a crusade like a McCarthy crusade against me. I'll be the most hated man in America, but I can do it then." Everything hinges on that second election of 1964, everything, the whole balance of his presidency.

Kennedy was gambler, but he would only go so far. He was very conscious of being elected, because he'd just been barely elected in 1960. However, against Goldwater, how could he have lost? You have to ask, looking back now, when you realize how unsettling Goldwater was to the majority of Americans. Kennedy would have swept in a landslide, and it would have given him far more juice for the second term.

My father was very much against Kennedy and was a Nixon man and an Eisenhower Republican conservative. He thought Kennedy was on the left. It came up at the dinner table more than once. My dad was very outspoken and a very powerful, intelligent man. I supported Goldwater in '64. I was conservative, and Kennedy was definitely seen as a person who was selling out to the Soviets—signing the nuclear treaty, the partial test ban—and was seen as a shaker-upper and pro-Cuba even. Those feelings were in the air, and I felt them.

I liked Goldwater because he was outspoken. He was a man who said what he thought. He seemed like he wasn't slick. He wasn't charming. He was sort of a prototype of the rugged John Wayne Westerner. As an East Coast boy living a rather limited life, I fell for it. Goldwater was my candidate in '64. It's unbelievable now that I'm saying this, but you have to think about the mood of the country and where I came from. I had movie heroes, and he seemed like a movie type. He knew what he wanted. I didn't realize the danger implicit in his words at that point. I read a few of those John Birch manuals, and I thought, *It kind of makes sense.* Not that I was against godless atheists, but something about the United States seemed to lack a resolution, a spark. We seemed to lack will, and my father would talk about that.

I respected my father a lot, and I had those feelings probably, but as the years went on and my parents got divorced, I moved out. I went to boarding school. I saw another Kennedy. I started to see a young, handsome president, very gallant and moving. But I had no strong opinions.

This Kennedy group was something new and special. He was hatless at the inauguration. It seemed like everything was different about him. He was a young man. Nixon, Eisenhower, and Johnson, all these people were the older generation from World War II. Something about Jack Kennedy said young. The Kennedys were highly glamorous, and I fell for that too. My mother was French, and she was glamorous, and because Jacqueline Kennedy evoked France too, she was very much a darling. No, if anything, they were in the upper class of American society, because we always had a menu. We lost our upper classes at some point in the World War II era.

Kennedy's eyes were too large in his head, but he was very handsome, and he spoke beautifully well—his oratory, the way he handled himself, the grace under pressure. As I said in my documentary *The Untold History of the United States,* he was aloof from fear. Despite all the pressure that came down on him, he stayed, like Roosevelt, above it, away from it. He didn't seem to be bothered by it. I'm sure he took home his fears and his doubts, but he never expressed them.

I don't think Oswald shot anyone that day. He was on the second floor, where he claimed to have been having lunch, when the shot went off. He was put there. There were people on the sixth floor, absolutely, more than one. There were people in the Dal-Tex building. I do think he shot at Walker. You have to look at Lee Oswald as a jigsaw man. He was put together, from the time he was in the Marines and he studied Russian, when he was sent to Russia, when he came back from Russia, he worked at a series of jobs that were assigned to him. Nothing is very clear. When you follow the Oswald path, you're going to end up in a maze. But what's

You have to look at Lee Oswald as a jigsaw man.

interesting about Oswald is he was definitely an informant for the FBI, and his links to the CIA are the most confusing of all. We don't have all the information.

But there's no question, based on other facts that have emerged, that he had a good relationship with the Office of Naval Intelligence, which is military intelligence—ONI they called it. There were phone calls made to North Carolina from Dallas when he was in detention there with the police. He was trying to get through to this guy, John Hurt, in the ONI. Oswald has a very fabulous history. Marina herself is also questionable because of her ties to intelligence in Russia. But it seems that Oswald was used, and he wanted to be. Oswald's favorite TV show was *I Led Three Lives* with Richard Carlson. He wanted always to be one of those guys. If you really wanted to be known and you were that crazy, you would come out like a John Wilkes Booth, an assassin of a president and say, "I did it" and be proud of it.

He was in the Texas Theatre to meet somebody. Oswald was controlled all the way through, all the way through New Orleans, and all the way through Dallas. He had handlers. He had people he knew, that he was in contact with—a mysterious life, but he was definitely there to meet somebody.

I believe there was a phony defector program put together by either ONI or CIA. There were several at the time of Oswald, from around '57 to about '61, who went to the Soviet Union, garnered a profile as being anti-American, and came back to the United States and were used, as they were used throughout, for whatever nefarious purposes the CIA wanted to use them for.

This is a black op. Now, no one said that when Oswald went to Russia in 1959 or whatever, "He's going to be assassinating the president." No, no one knew about Kennedy until this decision to kill him until probably in '62 or '63, after Kennedy had shook up the government with a series of moves that were completely outside the mainstream of American policy up to that point. He was looking to end the Cold War. He was looking to alter our relationships in Asia with Laos and Vietnam. He was looking to find a new relationship with Castro and Cuba but above all with Khrushchev. Khrushchev is the other key player in this drama. Kennedy's intentions if he were reelected—and I have to say that becomes the hinge point here, the reelection of '64—were vast. It would have been a completely new world.

There's so many things that are off about that day. You might ask, Why so many conspiracies? CIA covert ops are war. It's a form of war. When you deal with war, you have what they call "conspiracies" that are so bad. For example, a heroic action such as D-Day couldn't have happened unless it had been a conspiracy by a few Allied planners to put together this very huge event, cross the Channel, land troops successfully. What they did was put decoys out all through the summer. They had false landings. They had fake intelligence. That's the way you get things done at a high level. Conspiracy is really called "planning."

But it's the nature of an event where there are so many witnesses to that killing. So many people show up who know something or know a snatch of something, who have a glimpse of something that went wrong. Most of that testimony isn't in the Warren Commission. On top of that, you have a situation where almost two and a half hours after the assassination, you have a solution. You have the killer. He's already being announced by some hack in Washington who puts out an announcement about Lee Harvey Oswald's profile, two and a half hours after. They hardly have apprehended the man, and they know all about him. Imagine all the people he intersected with. We never really got to know any of them in the Warren Commission. They were never really interviewed. So many people knew Oswald in so many different settings that, as I said earlier, some of them knew him as an anti-Communist. He seems to have liked Kennedy by what he told people, and if anything he was a bit of an idealist—the guy who saw *I Led Three Lives* and wanted to be an intelligence agent and work for the government. You may have known about Oswald, but you wouldn't have known that amount of detail. It seems to have been a cover story, which is typical in black ops.

I was in the Hill School in Pennsylvania when he was killed. I was very shocked and surprised. We followed the events that weekend—the whole procession, the funeral, the shooting of Oswald. It was ingested and we moved on with our lives. We didn't really think about it that much. That's not to say that when Kennedy died I wasn't shocked and sad and like the rest of the country. I responded conventionally. I bought the whole story about the Warren Commission.

Right before Oswald was shot, on Sunday morning, Johnson was already calling Fritz and Curry (from the Dallas police office) and saying, "I want to get a full confession from this guy, Oswald." This is the president of the United States. What's his rush? In other words, there was a rush to judgment. We were so scared of I don't know what, but we needed to get somebody who killed the president and who would admit to it. Then you have Oswald walking down this hallway (I love that), and he goes and he does a press conference. He denies his guilt. He says, "I'm just a patsy." I believe that he was truly stunned. He knew that something had gone down much bigger. He was involved in this thing, didn't quite know what it was about. But it was such a big thing, to be accused of killing a policeman first, that surprised him. Then a reporter asks, "Did you kill the president of the United States?" He's surprised because this thing is far beyond his scope of what he thought he was getting involved in. He was a pretty scared young man at the end of that day, that Sunday.

I went to Vietnam because I felt it was the right thing to do, to fight this war, and because my parents had divorced and there was no home for me left, really. I had very mixed feelings about attending Yale University, which I had gone to for about a year when I pulled out. George Bush was in my class—the class of '68—so I was surrounded by people who were really privileged, who were entitled. They felt themselves smug in a way or smug to the military, smug to the whole concept of the rest of the people. I felt strongly that I didn't have that experience in my life. I needed to get with real people. I needed to get away from this class of people around me.

I didn't think about the Warren Commission, but when I came back from Vietnam, let's say I was in a state of being numbed out and burned out as a person. I was a young dropout in a sense. It took me a while to integrate back into the American system. I went to NYU film school and got a sense of mission and purpose back. It took some time.

I wasn't involved in the protests like my peers. I did a movie about Ron Kovic, *Born on the Fourth of July*. He got involved right away. I saw it happening, but I was staying outside it. I had neutral feelings. I was shocked by how the civilians in our country were indifferent to the war. That's what shocked me—nothing different I guess than the Iraq wars and Afghanistan. People didn't care. They were making money. The economy was booming. So I never talked about it. You never talk about it because you were considered an oddball in our society.

The problem with that war is that the middle class and the upper class didn't send their children to that war until much later. The volunteer draft got to them, and eventually they protested. But it took many years of many casualties. I didn't turn against Vietnam until the '70s, around Watergate, around the revelations of the Church committee. When this rot started to come out about how corrupt some of these decisions were, I started to think about this thing. I turned around. I went to Central America. I did Salvador and Central America. I started to see the same thing as Vietnam happening again in Nicaragua and Honduras, and that turned me around. That was the mid-'80s.

By the late '80s I met a woman who gave me Jim Garrison's book *On the Trail of the Assassins* in an elevator in Havana. It was an amazing story, and it made me think about the Kennedy thing all over again. I took about a year and a half (I was making another film) to read as much as I could about the assassination, to talk to people. I got to know Jim Garrison and got to know a lot of people. I interviewed most of the people from the Dealey Plaza and policemen, and in 1991 we went ahead with the film. Then? Then my life changed.

Jim Garrison was going up against one of the biggest white whales of all time. He was going up against the government. He was going up against a covert operation, what they call black ops. These things are very different from what normal

I met a woman who gave me Jim Garrison's book On the Trail of the Assassins *in an elevator in Havana.*

Then? Then my life changed.

civilians are used to, and they don't understand them. Garrison was saying some things that were indeed exaggerated, but he had a case.

Jim wrote two books [about the assassination]. He went back to the same subject thirty years later, and the second book is a repeat of the first book. It's better, but he goes into the same detail. He's a passionate and very much liked district attorney in New Orleans. He served in World War II, and he served again in Korea. He loved this country. He, like me, didn't have an opinion about the assassination. It was only when he was talking to Senator Russell Long in '65 or '66 that he came back around to thinking about this thing. He read the actual Warren Commission [report] from beginning to end, and he started as a very smart man who was a prosecuting a case, as a district attorney. He questioned the veracity of the Warren Commission.

If you read his [Garrison's] book, he makes it very clear: His book is about the motive for killing Kennedy. Who takes power after someone is killed? He makes the point that the Johnson policy was quite different from the Kennedy policy all over the world and especially on the Cold War. Johnson went back to the old Cold War days. Garrison is looking for motive, which a prosecutor always does, and he tries to prove it in the book. It's very hard to prove in a trial against a covert operation run by the government.

Garrison has a limited view in New Orleans, but it's an accurate one. He found many witnesses, and I think Clay Shaw knew more than he [Garrison] ever knew. However, the movie is not just about Garrison—it's also based on Jim Marrs's book as well as my own research.

New Orleans was a very interesting middle ground in this whole assassination background. Garrison had quite a few of the witnesses there, including David Ferrie and Guy Banister, an ex-FBI chief. He was running the operation for the right wing in New Orleans, and also Clay Shaw. Out of those people, two of whom died before he could get to trial, he brought Clay Shaw to trial, which is probably the only chance he had left. But he is, at the end of the day, the only public official to have brought the case in the Kennedy killing.

Clay Shaw's background was CIA. He was a contract agent for them. He worked in Italy. He was in anti-fascist organizations all over Europe. He came back to New Orleans. He ran the Trade Mart, which was often used for political purposes because it's a huge business—you got to know everybody in South America. Shaw had a history of knowing David Ferrie, and he denied it at trial, and he has a history of knowing Perry Russo and various players who played out in this. He lied through the whole trial. The judge himself, Mahoney, who I met, tough little Irish guy, said to me, "I didn't believe a word that Clay Shaw said through the whole trial. He perjured himself all the way through." This is a judge talking, but Shaw was a smooth liar because he was trained to be.

Shaw's relationship to this assassination is a very obtuse one, and it's hard to prove these things, but there's reason to believe he was more involved, far more involved, than the surface would let us believe. His history of using a false name—most people knew him as "Clay Bertrand"—played into our movie. That was part of the reason that he perjured himself. Garrison was onto something, but he certainly couldn't go to Dallas because he wasn't a Dallas person. He did interview some of the people from Dallas, but Dallas was where the playground really took place. A lot of the players showed up in New Orleans. They also show up, by the way, in Miami and Chicago—previous attempts to kill Kennedy.

The research we did for *JFK* was as good as we could get at that time. We tried to make it as exciting and different in its style as we could. We kept to what our research told us. I believe that Kennedy was killed by forces that had to be fairly powerful in order to control the mechanism that could control the parade route, control the security that he got that day, could control the autopsy. One of the things Garrison isn't given credit for is that Pierre Fink showed up at his trial. He was at the original autopsy and told about the behavior in the autopsy, detail by detail, at the end of the movie. Watch it. It's amazing what happens. It's a controlled autopsy—and, by the way, the logistics of the bullet don't match.

My life is a process, but every one of these movies, *Nixon, JFK, Salvador, Platoon, Born on the Fourth of July*, taught me something about history. I researched each one individually. I guess by the time I was sixty years old I had decided that I'd like to just take a stab at the beginnings of my life in 1946, because that's the year after the atomic bomb was dropped. My life was lived under the shadow of that atomic bomb. America grew very powerful, a sovereign empire based on that bomb. It was the founding myth of our new Constitution, and I wanted to go back to the beginning, to that era. My life in films is about the building up of an American empire from World War II on to today, where we're a global security state, promising dominion over all. I'm proud of the movie *JFK*. It's a beautifully put together piece of work, and it's also solid in its research.

I didn't associate the assassination and Vietnam until years later because I went to Vietnam, and I would go again. I was that kind of boy. I came back another kind of young man. I changed over the years. Life is not like the movies, where you have an overnight change. It takes time to change. I became, I suppose, in the second half of my life, more progressive, more liberal. I think back about my life, and I can see where I thought America was going in the right direction in the '50s [when it] was going in the wrong direction.

In Vietnam, we were definitely going in a far worse direction. I didn't see Kennedy's killing as part of that until I read up and did my research. When you look at Lyndon Johnson, he takes office that day. Everything starts to change. The message goes out: "We're in Vietnam. We're staying." He sends troops within one year of Kennedy's death, he's got combat troops—he's got the Gulf of Tonkin Resolution in August '64. By the next year, in '65, he's got combat troops in Vietnam. It's a huge change in direction. South America, there's a coup in Brazil. Kennedy never would have taken part in that coup. That affected the rest of South America for many years.

Some people will say, "Wow, great movie," but some people will say, "I don't believe it." There's a younger generation coming. Maybe they'll be looking back at it. No film is the definitive version, either as a history or a book. It's a beginning. I'm very proud of the movie, and in two or three generations from now, if someone is still taking the time to look at it as an introduction into this world, I would be very honored and proud. But it's the beginning. There are many things more to learn. You should learn the

other side. You should learn some of the bad sides of Kennedy, but at the end of the day, the balance is in his favor.

If I hadn't done that movie, there wouldn't be a marker for JFK, and he needs one because he was a great president. I don't think he *would* have been a great president. He *was*. His behavior at the '62 nuclear crisis that we had with the near end of this world was very brave and very courageous. He looked into the abyss with Khrushchev. Khrushchev deserves more credit. But the truth is that Kennedy had been in war. He had experience with his military. Remember *Seven Days in May*, the [attempted] coup d'état? He didn't believe them. He had doubts about their intelligence, about what their intentions were, and didn't feel good about it. He was very conscious of his military. He was very conscious of the CIA. He fired Dulles and Cabell. That's a huge deal. Allen Dulles was an institution in Washington, so for him to do that was to signal his intention to change things. He made huge enemies with that, and with the military, by him not going to war in Cuba, he antagonized [them] to a degree that they would have cooperated with his removal.

We made a series called *Untold History of the United States*, which was very successful. In the middle of that series is a chapter on Kennedy. We don't go into the assassination. We go into what he did in office before and after, especially after the missile crisis of 1963. We show you the change in thinking about the military, about how he made enemies of the intelligence community, of the military, of the business community, and certainly of the racists. What he did in the South angered many people. They saw him as a guy who was changing the social order of things, and don't forget the anti-Castro Cubans, who despised him for having backed off the Bay of Pigs invasion, which he did. At the October '62 missile

If I hadn't done that movie, there wouldn't be a marker for JFK.

crisis, many Americans wanted him to go ahead and invade Cuba and nuke the place. When he didn't do that, General LeMay was furious with him. So were the other Chiefs of Staff. That's documented. He had many enemies when he went to Dallas.

He was a great president because he had the courage to be gentle and to be soft and to be weak at a time when everyone was demanding him to act strongly and to bomb Cuba, to go in and invade. It takes great courage for a man who has all the power in the world to not use it. It was a great lesson for mankind. He's not quite given the credit he deserves, but I'm not sure I would be alive [had we invaded Cuba] because I was living on the East Coast then. I think the world was much closer to destruction at that point than we know.

Steven Spielberg

In 1963 future film director Steven Spielberg was a sixteen-year-old high school junior living in Phoenix, Arizona, soon to move to California. He had already won prizes for his 8mm amateur movies and had just written and exhibited *Firelight*, a 140-minute feature that became the inspiration for *Close Encounters of the Third Kind*. The three-time Academy Award winner is a keen observer of world history and has produced or directed many historical narrative features.

Kennedy's election was the beginning of the new hope. It was very much a part of my life. I remember the inauguration, watching it on television with my parents. The only time I could remember a similar rebirth of the American dream, the way I define the American dream, was the election of Barack Obama.

I especially remember the Cuban Missile Crisis, which was the first time that something truly scared the life out of me, the living daylights out of me. We did a lot of duck-and-cover drills. Even before the Cuban Missile Crisis, we were doing that—but it was the actual crisis itself, when he came on television and said to the nation how close we were to being on the brink. My parents actually had gone away to a kind of a party in the neighborhood, and I was alone with my sisters. I remember looking out the window at all these contrails of B-52s flying over our house, the whole sky filled with contrails, because the big base was in Tucson, and I was in Phoenix. I remember filling the bathtub up with water and the sinks up with water, thinking this was the beginning of the end. I felt we'd have to start digging a hole in the backyard to move into.

I was in school on the day Kennedy was killed. I was in class. I don't exactly remember what the class was, but I was in school when the public address system came on in the classroom. We listened to the principal saying that the president had been shot, not that the president was killed, just the president of the United States had been shot, and then there was just a stunned silence. I remember not hearing anybody saying anything for a while, and then the teacher left the room. While the teacher was out of the room, the PA system

came on, I think about twenty minutes later, and it was announced the president had died.

The first reaction I had was: I wanted to go home. That was my first reaction. I wanted to go home and be with my mom and my dad and my sisters. That's when we got the news that class was dismissed, and we were all told to go back to our homes. I didn't need a bus to get home—I always took my bike to and from school—I jumped on my bicycle, and I rode home. I got there in ten minutes. My mom was in the kitchen. She was sobbing at the kitchen table. She was alone. There was no one else in the house. My three sisters hadn't gotten back from class, and my dad was still at work. I remember going over to my mother, and the television set was on. I remember putting my arms around my mother, and she just turned around, she just embraced me. I remember standing up above her because she was at the table and I was standing. She was just holding onto me, shaking and sobbing.

When it first happened and when I first got home, I began watching it on television; it was coming to me from the television, where reality was abridged by the medium. It took the event a while to sink in with me, and it really only sank in when the funeral occurred. We all sat as a family watching the funeral on our black-and-white television.

There's been so much written about it. There have been so many documentaries made about it. Oliver Stone made his movie *JFK,* and there've been documentaries on the Kennedys, on Jackie Kennedy—soap dramas as well. There hasn't been the one definitive movie about the Kennedy family, the Kennedy dynasty, the Camelot that once existed in our country.

I began watching it on television; it was coming to me from the television, where reality was abridged by the medium.

The Kennedys were the closest we ever came to having American royalty in this country, and in a sense, when Kennedy was brought down, it was really the end of the dream.

The end of Norman Rockwell's idealistic vision of America ended when Kennedy was shot and killed. Rockwell of course has had his tremendous resurgence in popularity and revival of popularity because we still believe in the great American dream. When Kennedy was killed, Rockwell went into his studio, and he painted Kennedy, a great portrait of Kennedy at the convention, when he was speaking after winning the nomination. I own that painting, and you can see the inspiration and the tragic sadness inside Rockwell's entire being. His art was so expressive in the way he drew Kennedy. There was a sadness in Kennedy's eyes, and here Kennedy was: He had won the nomination, and there're signs in the foreground of all the states that had voted for him, and there's Kennedy standing there with this kind of anticipation of a very sad ending in that painting.

It did change the country profoundly, but I was only really aware of how profoundly it changed the country years later when I was in college, because Kennedy's assassination started a chain reaction—a kind of house of cards started to come down, not immediately but gradually over the next decade.

The revelations about Kennedy since then don't temper my view of him at all because Kennedy was so iconic. He did such good for our image and for all Americans—"Ich Bin ein Berliner," standing toe to toe with Nikita Khrushchev, having the ships turned back around, go back the other way during the missile crisis. Amazing things occurred in his short,

Kennedy could have been a movie star—absolutely would have been a movie star—and he would have made some great movies. Probably one of them would have costarred Marilyn Monroe.

professional life span. He's Teflon. He's immortal, I think. He's been immortalized by history because he was so handsome. He was movie-star handsome. He could have been a movie star—absolutely would have been a movie star—and he would have made some great movies. Probably one of them would have costarred Marilyn Monroe.

Conspiracy theories follow all assassinations. A conspiracy is always a part of some national trauma. The reverberations are like the aftershocks of a great earthquake, and it seems inevitable that there're going to be conspiracies. I don't 100 percent subscribe to the multiple-gun conspiracy theory, but I also don't quite understand how Lee Harvey Oswald was able to get so accurately so many shots off with the rifle that he was shooting—to shoot so accurately, and kick back the bolt, and re-chamber a round, and fire again. That's really confused me.

But I've never been tempted to make a film about it. Oliver [Stone] made the defining film about the conspiracy. When it first came out, I thought it was outstanding. Then the controversy started, and the great test about whether you still think a film is outstanding is: Does the controversy taint your first impression of the picture? The controversy didn't taint my impression of how great a picture that was. I'm talking about cinematically. The best cinematic achievement of his career was the way he directed *JFK*—better than even *Platoon*.

The thing about doing a piece on Kennedy is that there are so many compelling moments in his life. Probably the most compelling moment for me in Kennedy's life is the Cuban Missile Crisis. That would be a pretty good film.

After Kennedy died, people were more open to looking at the unseemly side of the democratic process, which is all the things that creep and crawl in the shadows of our democracy, sort of unseen forces at work, unwinding things that are seemingly perfect, yet behind the scenes there's some insidiousness happening. Paranoid cinema was spawned by the Kennedy assassination. A lot of those films came directly as a result, I believe, of Kennedy's assassination.

When we were making *Band of Brothers* and *Saving Private Ryan*, what conjured up memories of Kennedy were two things that happened to me when I was beginning my career. The first thing was that the very first movie set I ever visited was *PT-109*, when it was in production with Cliff Robertson playing Kennedy at Warner Brothers. I was there, just part of a foot tour. This was before all the organized trams and buses and things like that. My dad took me on a tour of Warner Brothers because I was making little 8mm movies back in Phoenix, and he knew I was interested. We went to see the shooting of this movie, and it was the scene where the destroyer cuts *PT-109* in half. They had this full-size bow of a destroyer constructed and a breakaway full-size *PT-109,* and we waited for an hour and a half, watching them get ready for the big special-effect moment, the big physical effect. Just before they rolled the cameras, they cleared all the eyewitnesses from the sound stage. It was Stage 16 at Warner's, and we were all told to leave. I never got a chance to see it until the movie came out.

Then the first script I ever sold with a writing partner, Claudia Salter, was a movie called *Ace Eli and Rodger of the Skies,* which Cliff Robertson starred in. Fox hired me to do the rewrite of my own script, and I went down to West Palm Beach to meet with Cliff and spent about three weeks down there. Even though I was writing and rewriting this kind of barnstorming, post–World War I story for Cliff and the studio, all we talked about was Kennedy, and he said to me, "The greatest honor of my entire career has thus far been playing that president."

Paranoid cinema was spawned by the Kennedy assassination.

I've talked to my kids about the Kennedy years when they studied Kennedy in school. They've all brought back stories, papers they had to write about presidents—"Pick your favorite president." A couple of my kids picked Kennedy as their favorite president without ever being a part of that era or that generation, only what they knew about him. With this generation, anything that's five years old is ancient history, let alone something that happened in '63. But for a student, history is a gateway to understanding who we are today, and good history students really appreciate that you're building a bridge to the past and building a better bridge to the future by knowing your history.

The important thing to understand whenever you're recreating the past and there's source material that you can dip into—no matter how accurate you are to your source material—we're still making historical fiction. It's still a movie. Whatever you do, it's still historical fiction, which means that, even though we can quote chapter and verse what Kennedy said, what Lincoln said, the moments in the nineteenth century when there was no one, no secretary taking down verbatim notes of what was happening in cabinet meetings, it's up to the writer to be inventive and be creative. Based on how steeped the writer is in history, the way Tony Kushner was when he did six years of research and writing on Lincoln that he so understood the sort of the idiom of the nineteenth century he was able to create entire scenes that actually happened but nobody was there to tell us exactly what was said—that is the license that a screenwriter has when we're telling true stories about the past.

It was difficult for me imagining how I was going to make *Lincoln* without Daniel Day-Lewis. He so became Lincoln that I really felt for a long time that I was actually sharing three and a half, four months of shooting space with the sixteenth president of the United States. That was a great honor for me, to feel that I was in cahoots with Abraham Lincoln and still be able to go home and realize that I'm in the real world. But with Kennedy, it's just as difficult. There are actors, I'm sure, out there who could do a great job acquitting his personage, but it's not for me. No, the recreation of the Kennedy dynasty, the Kennedy Camelot, the Kennedy legend isn't something I would rush to as a filmmaker, but it is something I would rush to as an audience.

Jay Leno

At the time of the president's death, thirteen-year-old James "Jay" Leno was living in Andover, Massachusetts, with his family, soon to embark on a successful comedy and acting career. In spring 2014 he will step down from *The Tonight Show* after a twenty-two-year tenure as host.

I was in school. I went home, and my mother was very upset. But the part that really got her—and this was a few days later—we had seen Oswald get shot on TV. They showed that. I don't think anyone had ever been shot on live television before, at least certainly not in my lifetime. It didn't look anything like how people got shot on *The Rifleman* or *The Big Valley,* where they would do this and fall over.

The thing that really did it for us kids was a guy named Vaughn Meader. He put out an album called *The First Family,* and nobody had ever done anything like this before. The record was so popular, and all the radio stations played clips of Vaughn Meader doing John F. Kennedy, Jackie, and all the other people in the White House. We all recited the lines. My mother would go: "Stop doing that voice. Stop. That's annoying, stop that." It was the number-one record, I think, in the country at the time—I don't know if a comedy album has ever done that well again—so consequently we knew it as pop culture more than politics.

I was kind of a student of comedy at that time. Lenny Bruce had a show at Carnegie Hall. It was a couple of nights after the assassination, and his opening line was, "I guess Vaughn Meader's career is over." There was a silence, and then a huge laugh. It broke the ice a little bit, if that was even possible. In fact, Vaughn Meader was never heard from again.

But I remember watching the TV and the funeral procession and little John-John doing the wave, then the salute—and my mother in tears,

"Oh my God, what's going to hap-pen to that little boy? Oh my God." I remember looking at my mom and then looking at the TV, and then, when you're a kid, how do you keep your mom from crying?

Flash forward to thirty-five years later. I have John F. Kennedy Jr. on the show. I'm in the dressing room. I say hello to him. "Good to see you." Very nice guy. Jerry Seinfeld had just been on. I go, "Please welcome John F. Kennedy Jr.," and he walked out, I shook his hand, I looked in the mon-itor, and I saw my face and his, and I

almost started to cry. I got very emotional because I could see my mom saying, "Oh my God, what's ever going to happen to that little boy?" and it was almost as if I wanted to say, *Ma, he's OK. He's on the show. I'm with him right now, he's not—*

It didn't affect me in the dressing room. It didn't even occur to me, but the minute I shook his hand and just glanced at the monitor and saw him, our two faces together in the same shot, it was all I could do, really, to keep from tearing. I said, "Sit down. Good to see you." It was just really overwhelming.

A lot of people lived that Kennedy kind of life, but they didn't neces-sarily do things for the people who didn't live that kind of life. That was the great difference. When you would see a Kennedy show up at a rally to help people get home heating oil or to do something for the poor—that was the difference. Nobody who had yachts and boats really did much for people who had kayaks and canoes, that sort of thing. I think that was the big difference—when a Kennedy would show up at a union rally or do something to help African Americans, that was the new part, I think.

Google "*I've Got a Secret*, Lincoln." Remember the TV show *I've Got a Secret*? There's one episode where this old man comes out—and there's Dorothy Kilgallen and then the usual panel—and his secret was that he

I looked in the monitor, and I saw my face and his, and I almost started to cry.

was the last living witness to the assassination of Abraham Lincoln. He was five years old, his mom put him in the box next to Lincoln, and he saw John Wilkes Booth. I said to myself, *Wow, I'm watching somebody on TV who witnessed the Lincoln assassination.* I suppose to a young person now, someone who was at Dealey Plaza would probably seem just as amazing, but that just struck me as so bizarre, because when I was a kid, to me Lincoln might as well have been a thousand years ago as just a hundred. It was just fascinating.

When we do "Jaywalking," we find most people think women got the vote in 1966. They know Kennedy was president. They're not sure if it was before World War II or after World War II. It's so funny because it's as clear as a bell to me because I grew up in that era. But we asked people, "When did women get the vote?" The most common answer? 1966. They tend to confuse it, I think, with the Civil Rights Act. Most people aren't even aware of a Civil Rights Act. It seems preposterous to them that—"What, you mean black people couldn't—? What, it wasn't equality? When was that?" You know, they look at you like that. They think it was 1860, not 1964. We don't really talk about the Kennedy assassination in those segments, because there's not humor there.

I don't know if the assassination could be a subject of humor. Are there people who have joked about it? Sure. I mean, it's not for me to say whether they should. Am I a good enough comedian to do a joke about it? No—and I wouldn't want to. I think there are certain subjects—abortion is one, the Kennedy assassination—that aren't humorous because there's no hypocrisy involved. There are a lot of jokes about conspiracy theorists and things of that nature. Comedy works if it's based on certain hypocrisies.

He would have been an excellent guest on *The Tonight Show*. He had a great sense of humor. He was a guy's guy; he was kind of a raconteur. It's interesting how guarded and sheltered he was, because that was an era when the press protected politicians. If a president said, "Listen, this

ही

ही

is now secure. I don't want anybody to report this," you didn't report. Things have certainly changed a lot since then. It was sort of an old boys' club, where if there was a party going on and there were women—*wink.* The reporters were in on it too. I don't know if that's better or worse. It's probably worse.

But if he were on the show, I would have asked him: "When you said it, did you really think we could put a man on the Moon in ten years? Or did you just say that to inspire the country?" Because, don't forget, we had had failed rockets, and we looked like North Korea at that point. The Russians were ahead of us, and the idea of leaving our atmosphere was sort of brand new and controversial. The idea of going to the Moon and coming back . . . I mean, it takes four or five years to come out with a new car, with just new designs and new features. "To go to the Moon and come back in ten years? Did you think, or were you just saying that? Or did you just say it to inspire the country?" I probably would have asked him that.

JAY LENO

Tom Hanks

Living in San Mateo, California, Tom Hanks was seven years old in 1963. He later studied acting at the California State University at Sacramento before becoming one of the most successful film actors in history as well as a writer, director, and producer. Best known for starring roles in *Apollo 13*, *Big*, *Cast Away*, *Catch Me If You Can*, *Charlie Wilson's War*, *Forrest Gump*, *A League of Their Own*, *Philadelphia*, *Saving Private Ryan*, *Sleepless in Seattle*, *That Thing You Do!*, the *Toy Story* franchise, and *You've Got Mail*, he has won two Academy Awards and produced the 2013 feature film *Parkland* about the hospital where Kennedy was taken after the shooting.

I turned seven that July. I remember exactly what I was doing and where I was. I was at Lakeside Elementary High School in San Mateo, California. We were living with my aunt. My dad was between marriages. We were sleeping on sofa beds. My dad was sleeping in the vacation trailer they kept in their backyard. It was second grade during art class. The boys always drew the same picture over and over in art class: a strip of blue, which was the water, and we all knew how to make the outline of a ship with two little guns on the front of it, and then we would draw little airplanes—all we did was make naval battles. But it was like watching a movie when we did it, because it would be active. So eventually, with the explosions of the planes and that, you just had a picture that was just a bunch of flames. It looked like a Rorschach test.

We were doing that, and the principal came into the class. Seeing the principal was like seeing the senator from the State of California. He came in, wore a suit and tie, glasses, and he went over and whispered something to our teacher. Then he left the room, and we went back, and all you heard was the drawing. Then all of a sudden we heard tears, weeping; we looked over, and our teacher was crying. To be seven years old and see any adult who is overcome with emotion and is weeping is a very upsetting thing.

We immediately felt as though something horrible was wrong, and we were all very uncomfortable. She broke out—literally these words: "They killed him. They killed the president," and we thought, *They?* We were seven years old. How can anybody . . . and president of what? I didn't know where Dallas was. I didn't know how big the country was, but there was a sense of permanence to America and certainly to the office of the president of the United States that made it seem as though it should've been impossible for something like that to happen.

The principal's voice came over the loudspeaker and spoke to the entire school. He said, "The president of the United States has been shot, and—we are going to send everybody home." A lot of parents came and picked up kids, but our dad was a single dad. I don't know where my aunt and uncle were, so I ended up walking home by myself at a time when usually you're in school.

It wasn't a long walk home, but it was a walk through total suburbia that was a landfill community. All the houses were housing development homes. They were kind of nice. We had these vast empty fields with surveyor stakes in them, with the little orange ribbons that say where it's going to be. Everything was different. The lighting was different—I remember the light was different because it was early in the afternoon. It wasn't when school usually got out. The buses weren't there; there were fewer cars on the roads, and the ones that were seemed to be driving slowly. There was no hustle and bustle to it. I got home.

I'm sure we were gathered around the TV when Ruby killed Oswald. I wasn't watching it; I was in the other room, but I heard the kerfuffle. By that time, my aunt and uncle had made a bit of a shriek, so the TV was on when that played live, and it was just days from that walk home from school to being in an apartment of a friend of my dad. I was alone then too, because I was parked there for the day when Kennedy's body was in state in the Capitol Rotunda. I recall being overcome with emotion. There was just something that was so oppressively, viscerally, inherently sad about the way it was playing out. I had never seen anything that somber. I've never seen anything on TV that had that gravitas—the black-and-white images and the sound of the horses' hooves as they were going through the streets bearing the caisson with the president's casket on it.

I was alone then, and I didn't even know why I was crying. There was just something so oppressively heavy and sad about it. Of course every human being, every adult, every caregiver I saw was incredibly burdened with sadness and confusion, and it bled down even to a seven-year-old kid.

He was the first president I remember, and everything he stood for was the best of the United States at that very moment. He was young, and he was gorgeous. His wife was gorgeous. He had little kids. But we were between fifteen and twenty years after World War II, which had been, up to that point, truly the defining conversation that I heard constantly over and over again. My dad was a veteran, and my teacher was married to a veteran. Everybody talked about their lives in three distinct passages. They talked about their childhood. But they always said, "When I was a

I've never seen anything on TV that had that gravitas—the black-and-white images and the sound of the horses' hooves as they were going through the streets bearing the caisson with the president's casket on it.

kid before the war, *dah dah dah*." Then they came of age. My dad was a machinist in the Navy. He studied hydraulics in Pocatello, Idaho, and was somewhere in the South Pacific, and those five years were: "Well, that was during the war." "When I was in the war, I was here." "During the war, I was here." Then the rest of life after was always: "Well, that was right after the war." "Of course, back after the war happened, *dah dah dah*." Even then, my personal history was shaped by those three acts of the American story: before the war, during the war, after the war.

Kennedy was all about after the war. The country was so positively proactive and doing great things, and even when you're seven years old that positive spirit was reflected every day in school somehow. We talked about the American dream. We talked about our way of life. We talked about democracy. But we also talked about what the country was doing, how hopeful it was, how there was the Peace Corps, and there was the space program. There was this proactive sensibility that we had entered into the next phase of life as Americans, in which we did good around the world, if only because we were the beacon of goodness. We had these bad guys who lived on the other side of the Iron Curtain, and we were in direct competition. Not only that, we were the polar opposite of everything they stood for. Here you can do anything you want to; there you can't. Here you have the freedom to pursue every degree of happiness; there happiness is prescribed and doled out. Even if you were a seven-year-old, it was all about: We are on the cusp of a brand of greatness that we have earned, that we have fought for and saved, and that we are consciously choosing to go ahead and pursue.

We weren't at the mercy of any events. Instead, we are powered by our own abilities, our own dreams, our own choices. That's what I got. We even had a publication that was given to us every week, *My Weekly Reader*. It was a little mock newspaper that we had, and when we got it we would study it. We would have a moment where everybody read, and Mrs. Castle, who was my teacher after the assassination, would talk about what they were talking about. The things that were in there were stories, for example, about the great hospital ship *Hope*. It would travel around to the Third World and would heal the sick; it was about the Peace Corps. It was about the space program, which was, in and of itself, a lesson in science, engineering, politics, history, and art. It was embodied by the president of the United States who was killed in Dallas in November '63.

What always lingered from the John F. Kennedy assassination was not so much a question of how but a question of why. It didn't make sense that anybody would want to murder the president of the United States. Therefore, how was it possible for some individual guy to decide to do it? From that begins this kind of stewing pot of all the aspects of what the country sort of fell into by then. Vietnam was going on. There was the huge social revolution that had rightly come along as a generation decided to make its own questions, answer its own questions. I didn't get into the particulars of it all until some time in the '70s. Suddenly all the rules were off the board, and everything—everything—the questions seemed never to stop, whether they were motivated or not.

Regarding conspiracy theories, you would go through a phase where you hear shaky details. What about this, what about that, and what about that? It becomes almost fun to partake in it. It becomes almost like a parlor game. When Ouija boards first came around, you invested this power in a Ouija board. Then you start having goofy séances to see what can happen. It was all the same sort of game that went along with it, and it didn't matter that there were answers to the questions. The questions were far too much fun to ask.

Even a seven-year-old becomes a thirteen-year-old at some point and realizes: Hey, some of those people on TV aren't telling the truth all the time. By the time we got into Vietnam and everything else was going on, well, it sort of made sense. If they're not telling the truth now, did they tell the truth back then? I certainly fell into that idea. All these fun things that are kind of Rorschach tests: What about the badge man? What about that guy with the umbrella?—and all the other things that go along into it that become just part of a fun, distracting, and very complicated game that seems to have no end.

I will get all sorts of mail for saying this, but without a question, Lee Harvey Oswald acted completely alone. He did it all by himself, and all the other stuff that comes along with it is a very fun kind of connect-the-dots that don't really make any sort of shape. The thing that's very hard for people to accept is that it was possible to do. Lee Harvey Oswald had read the paper and knew the president's motorcade route because it was on the front page of the Dallas newspapers two or three days prior to it. The sad aspect of it all is that we lived in a world at that time where the president of the United States routinely rode in an open car so that he could wave to the crowds who were delighted to have a picture of the president—because why would John F. Kennedy do it any differently than Roosevelt did or Truman or Herbert Hoover? When you put together a few simple understandings of what basic human nature is, the sad conclusion is that not only was it possible, it was easy.

I'm sure the Mob wanted something to happen like that. They didn't like the Kennedys, without a doubt. The thing you end up falling into is: Let's go with them all. Mob, sure. Why not? Wait, wait, wait. The Castro people, sure, yeah, the Castro people. Wait, wait, wait. What about the military industrial complex? How about—sure, they—*Whoa*, wait a minute, what about those Indochinese people who wanted to have . . . There are so many people. Of course you go back in now, in retrospect, and say, "Was it Colonel Mustard with a lead pipe?" or whatever. Again, the fun continues in that way because the possibilities are endless, but you come back to a number of concrete facts—let's call them facts that are also part of the story—and it all just breaks down because all of the conspiracies don't take into account the very basic aspects of human nature.

I was sitting with my good friend Bill Paxton, who was in *Apollo 13* with me—we have these powwows every now and again. Bill lived in Fort Worth, Texas, and the president of the United States was going to be in Fort Worth, Texas, so his father said, "Boys, we're going to go see the president of the United States," and he was up on his shoulders. His dad put him on his shoulders when Kennedy came out of the hotel in Fort Worth just before the breakfast, and then he took the plane to Love Field and went into Dallas. Years and years later, Bill went to Dealey Plaza and saw the museum that's there. He was

Of course you go back in now, in retrospect, and say, "Was it Colonel Mustard with a lead pipe?"

looking at raw footage from the media of that day, and he says, "God, you know, I wonder if they'll have any footage of outside the hotel where we saw the president of the United States." Sure enough, the camera panned right past him on his dad's shoulders. That fostered in him a conversation that we had about that day and what it meant to us as Americans—literally little boys as Americans—where suddenly an aspect of our country and our consciousness was snapped in two, and for us it was now forever: "That was before Kennedy was killed," and then, "That was right after Kennedy was killed," which is one of the acts of our lives we go back over and over again in one way or another.

From that we read Vince Bugliosi's book. Now understand: Bugliosi is a prosecutor. He's not an author or a journalist per se; he is a prosecutor. That's how he wrote this book. It doesn't take a rocket scientist to go through the facts of what went on that day and all the theories that slowly get broken down. Eventually questions are answered every step of the way that always bring it back to this concept: There is an evil aspect of human nature. There is a sad part of ourselves that is broken up into individuals, and when it lands in an individual as it did with Lee Harvey Oswald, you have to throw up your hands and essentially curse divine providence that makes this happen.

There's an amazing story I read about Robert Oswald. If you ask your average American about Lee Harvey Oswald's brother, no one knows that Lee Harvey Oswald had a brother who lived in Dallas, who hung out with his brother all the time, who saw him regularly and knew, "My brother's a weird guy." I'm paraphrasing here, but this is essentially what he was. I don't know why Robert Oswald never appears in any of these conspiracy theories, but he picked up his brother when he moved to Dallas with his Russian bride. Lee Harvey Oswald went to Russia. He was a big celebrity for a while, then he stopped being a big celebrity, and he was just working at a radio factory in Minsk. I'm going to guess that anybody who spends a lot of time in the 1960s working at a radio factory in Minsk might want to get out of Minsk. His beautiful wife, who was also working in Minsk and probably wanted to get out of there, and Lee Harvey Oswald came back from Russia. They had been interviewed a little bit, and he was used to being the guy who had a microphone shoved in front of him. When he went to Russia, he had all the Russian media saying, "You are a true wonderful man, and thank you for coming, and you're a bit of a hero, and isn't it great to have you here?"

When Robert Oswald picked up his brother at Love Field, when he flew in from New York City, Lee Harvey Oswald came off the plane and said to his brother, "Where are the reporters?" He was anticipating his return to Dallas as being a much heralded news story, that he would be something of a big shot. Robert said, "Lee, you're just some guy." You hear that kind of story, which tells me, as an actor and as a guy who tells stories, that is human nature. It's no surprise, nor should it be any shock when you come around to the idea of, well, that's the man who shot the president of the United States.

Parkland Hospital was/is staffed by folks who were good at what they did. Everything was standard operating procedure. There was a staff on who came in, and all they did was have their morning coffee and flirted with each other, and the day wasn't going to be anything more unique. They weren't going to see the president of the United States, even though it was in the papers; it was on the radio. They were just going about their day. Lo and behold: Before they knew it, the shot president of the United States was in their care, was in those rooms, was in their hospital, and was forever a part of their lives, and only a few hours later the man who shot the president of the United States was in their hospital and in their lives and in their care.

History is made up of those types of witnesses who weren't the principal players, who weren't the strategists, who weren't the people that made it happen. They were literally the witnesses who saw it all come down. If my life was changed as a seven-year-old who found out about it because the principal walked into our art class in the afternoon, their lives were forever altered by the fact that they were good at what they did. I don't think you could find a better microcosm or a better example of what happened to the United States of America as a whole than what happened to those people in Parkland Hospital that day. That's a fascinating story. There are four stories that we tell in *Parkland*. It's about the people who were there, but it's also about Robert Oswald. It's about James Hosty, the FBI guy who had a brush with Lee Harvey Oswald a few weeks prior. It's

I don't think you could find a better microcosm or a better example of what happened to the United States of America as a whole than what happened to those people in Parkland Hospital that day.

also about Abe Zapruder, whose life was turned upside down by the fact that he had this new movie camera with the latest version of Kodachrome film inside it.

I remember reading what could we have expected from the rest of the Kennedy presidency. He was having trouble getting legislation passed in Congress. He had this brewing hot spot that was halfway across the world in Vietnam and Indochina. He would've—might've even—had a tough reelection campaign in 1964, but at the end of the day, that doesn't nearly fill me with the same brand of satisfaction as going back through the actual historical record, because what really happened, to me, is always infinitely more fascinating and never stops being a source for the mirror being held up to human nature.

I was fascinated by the movie *JFK*. I thought it was great; I thought it was brilliant. I thought it was filled with moments of very sharply perceptive questioning. At the same time, it's filled with more hooey than you could possibly imagine. Oliver Stone is a great filmmaker—he won the Academy Award for that film, and rightly so, because it's one crackerjack piece of filmmaking. But there's a scene in it where Donald Sutherland, as Mr. X, is explaining in the grimmest *veritas* possible and asking the question, "Why was the Washington, DC, telephone exchange shut down immediately after the assassination of the president of the United States?" You know why it was shut down? Because everybody was on the phone! All the circuits were busy—something that happened all the time if everybody tried to use the phone. You would pick up, and you would dial, and they'd say, "all our lines are down. All of our circuits are busy. Please try again later." You got the recording. That's part of that fun thing

that says, "Here's some-
thing that happened, and
isn't there a diabolical
answer to this very simple
question?" Well, not a diabolical answer at all. It's
loaded with those types
of things that you have to
chalk up as just being part
of the parlor game: The
Assassination of the President of the United States.

Making a movie of
the Kennedy years? This
comes along a lot in my
business: Can making this story up—re-creating it, having look-alikes
and all the other necessities of making a theatrical film—be better than
just the greatest documentary ever made, that you can do on *American
Masters*, that *NBC News* could do about the thousand-day presidency of
John F. Kennedy? I don't think you could do as good a job of it. You're
going to be falling down into some degree of melodrama, which at best
can be quasi-accurate, and that's not as good as being accurate or quite
simply turgid. I'll spend my time other ways.

His personal weaknesses haven't altered my opinion of him. No, we're
all cracked vessels, including all the presidents of the United States. We
had a guy who was complicit with the press in hiding the fact that he was
in a wheelchair: Franklin Delano Roosevelt—and he drank. He loved his
martinis at the end of the day. Not all that stuff goes into the hopper of
"Human beings are odd, folks." Nobody's perfect; we all have feet of clay,
and it's only some other kind of outrage machines that want to hold up
the worst aspects of our weaknesses as being the definition of our total
selves. Yeah, without a doubt, those Kennedy years could be described as
being racy all right, but so are our baseball heroes. They end up having
the same sort of individual lives that don't diminish the fact of what they
meant to this society and what they mean to us in our individual concepts

We're all cracked vessels, including all the presidents of the United States.

of them: Kennedy and his family, extraordinarily wealthy, very charismatic and handsome, and dysfunctional to a fault, yes.

That what's great about it, and one of the reasons we're so fascinated is that they're a clan. They have this great commonality in that they were part of that generation—Joseph and Rose Kennedy gave birth to this phalanx of people who ended up doing incredible things and being part of us all. From that comes this concept of service that you render. Not all of them, not all of the Kennedys have gone into the same degree of public service, but that first or second generation did. They have massive amounts of sad history and, at the same time, of incredibly impressive achievement, and yet we'll be turning to them again and again for aspects of our human nature. The best and the worst is all right on display right there.

Acknowledgments

The compiling editors would like to thank NBC News senior executive producer David Corvo, former news president Steve Capus, and veteran correspondent Tom Brokaw for their initial faith in the television project on which this book is based. At 30 Rock, everyone working on the *Where Were You?* special performed with tireless professionalism and good humor. They include coordinating producer Clare Duffy, associate producer Loren Burlando, coordinating producer Kallie Ejigu, associate producer Nick Johnson, and talent coordinating producer Jennifer Sherwood. The members of our technical crew likewise performed smoothly at the top of their craft, especially Greg Andracke, Rich White, Shawn Sullivan, Rick Albright, and Everett Wong. Endeavors such as this could not exist without the able assistance of staff interns, and we were most fortunate to have the services of Amanda Hari, Courtney Marmon, Kaila Ward, and Charlotte Lewis. Show editor Pascal Akesson crunched a massive amount of material into a seamless finished product, and Kathleen Berger at Transcript Associates saw that accurate interview transcripts were turned around quickly. Special thanks go to NBC News correspondent Anne Thompson for the use of her pad.

N. S. Bienstock Talent Agency found a home for the book and then performed yeomen's work in negotiating a complex multiparty agreement. At NSB, special thanks go to agents Steve Sadicario (TV) and Paul Fedorko (book) and able assistant Sammy Bina.

At Lyons Press, editor James Jayo, project editor Meredith Dias, copyeditor Paulette Baker, and publicist Laurie Kenney all performed remarkably on a seemingly impossible deadline. Research assistance and general support for the project were supplied by "Genius" Lucas Lechowski, Dr. Agnieszka Szostakowska, Aaron Sichel, Dale Myers, Jay Greer, Brendan Kennedy, Karen Stefanisko, Randy Lehrer, and the countless archivists and librarians whose expertise and assistance make these projects possible. Jem, Watson, and Z kept things in perspective as always.

Last but not least, sincere thanks go to all of the interviewees who trusted us with their memories.

INDEX

About the Editors

Gus Russo is the author of six books, including *Brothers in Arms: The Kennedys, the Castros, and the Politics of Murder,* winner of the New York Book Festival's History Prize. An investigative reporter for *ABC News Special Reports* ("Dangerous World: The Kennedy Years") and *CBS Reports,* he served as lead reporter for *Frontline*'s landmark "Who Was Lee Harvey Oswald?" He has written for *American Heritage, Baltimore Sun, Book Forum, Huffington Post, The Nation,* and *Washington Post.* He lives in Baltimore, Maryland.

Harry Moses has written, directed, and produced numerous primetime specials for all major networks and cable channels, including nearly one hundred stories for *60 Minutes.* He has received Emmy, Peabody, and Directors Guild of America awards as well as a lifetime achievement award from the National Academy of Television Arts and Sciences. He lives in New York City.